Volume 2

Ema Toyama

**Translated and adapted by
Alethea Nibley and Athena Nibley**

Lettered by Paige Pumphrey

Missions of Love
Ema Toyama

Mission 5
I Order You to Act Like My Boyfriend!

Mission 6
I Order You to Call Me By My First Name!

Mission 7
I Order You to Do Whatever You Want!

Mission 8
I Order You to Confess Your Love to Me!

Extra Mission
Operation: Make Yukina a Princess

Missions of Love: Character Talk

Character

Shigure Kitami

The ever-popular, yet black-hearted, student body president. He made a game of charming all the girls and making them confess their love to him, then writing it all down in his student notebook, but Yukina discovered his secret!

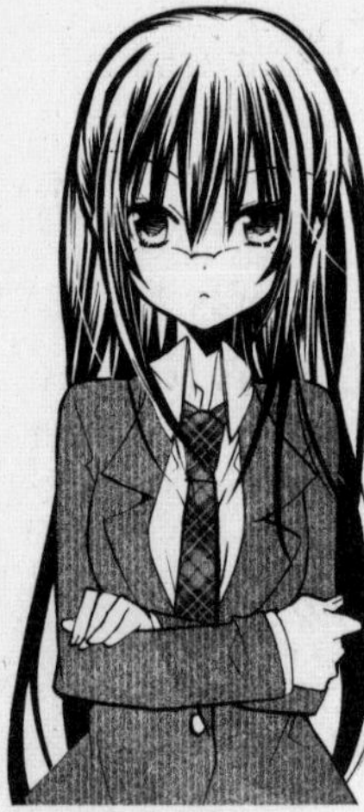

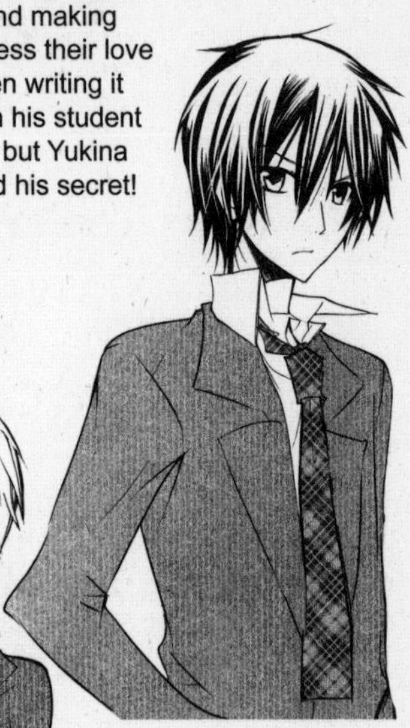

Yukina Himuro

A third-year junior high student who strikes terror in the hearts of all around her with her piercing gaze, feared as the “Absolute Zero Snow Woman.” Only Akira knows that she is also the popular cell phone novelist Yupina.

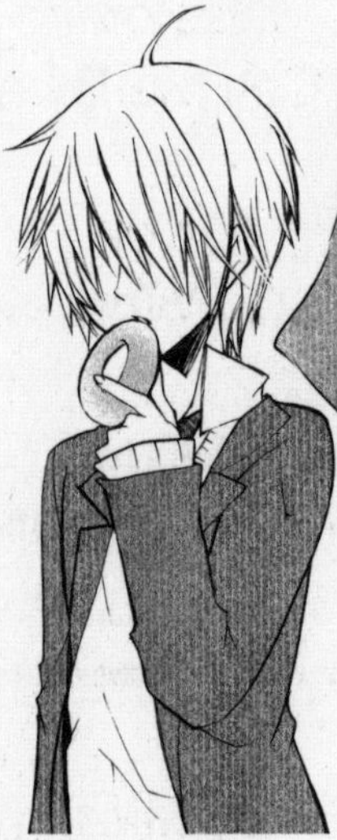

Akira Shimotsuki

Yukina's cousin and fellow student. He loves to eat. As Yukina's confidant, he can always be found nearby, watching over her. Is there a good-looking face hiding behind that hair?

Story

Yukina, who is secretly a cell phone author, has one major concern: her utter lack of romantic experience makes it impossible for her to write love stories. But she happens upon a certain student notebook, which allows her to blackmail Shigure. She decides to learn about love by forcing Shigure into romantic situations--holding her hand, putting his arms around her, kissing her, etc. But now he's learned her weakness--that she can't look people in the face without her glasses! Have the tables been turned? To overcome this obstacle, Yukina removes her glasses and stands before Shigure. “I want you...to teach me...what real love is...”

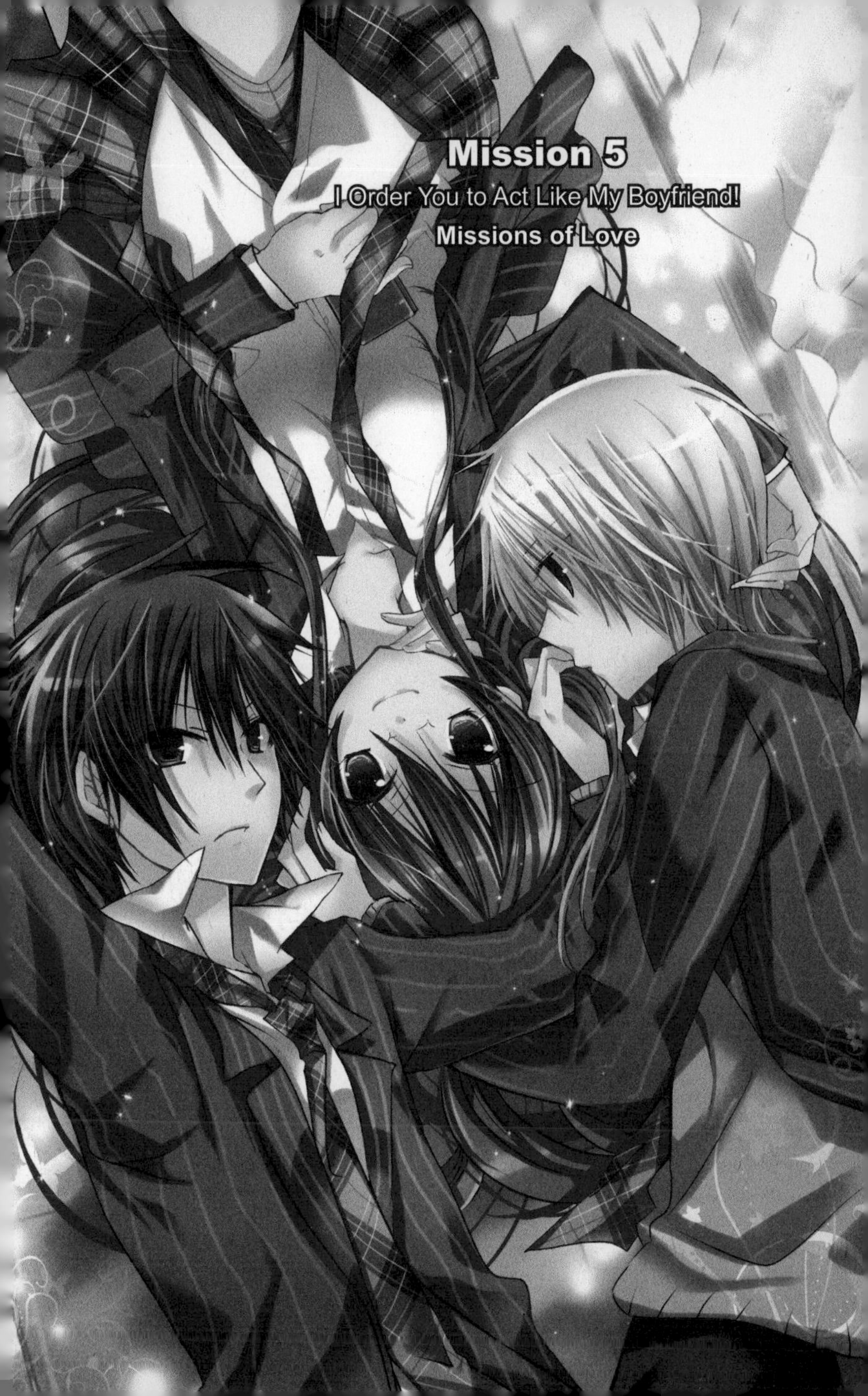
Mission 5
I Order You to Act Like My Boyfriend!
Missions of Love

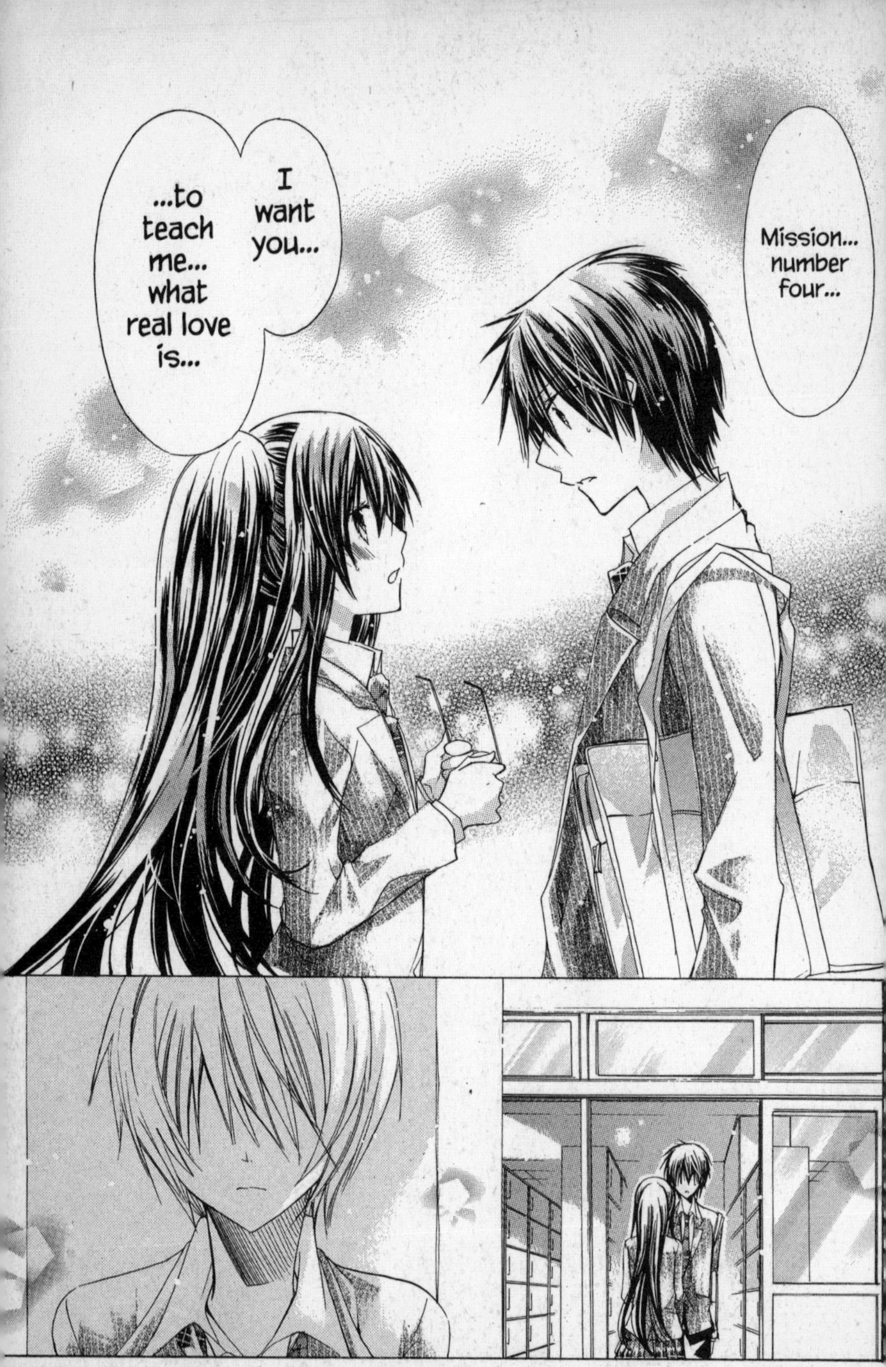
Mission... number four...
I want you...
...to teach me... what real love is...

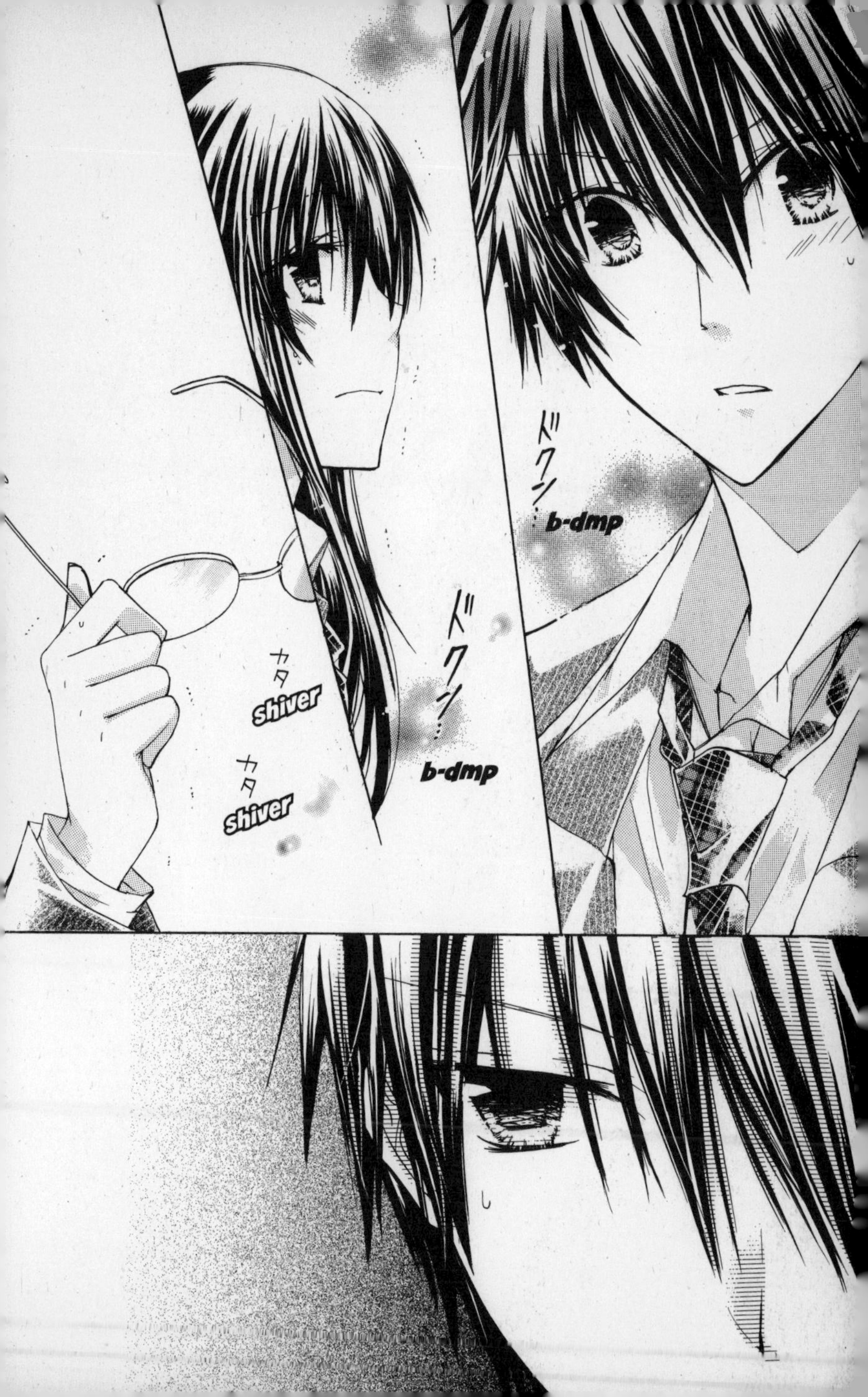
ドクン
b-dmp
ドクン
b-dmp
カタ
shiver
カタ
shiver

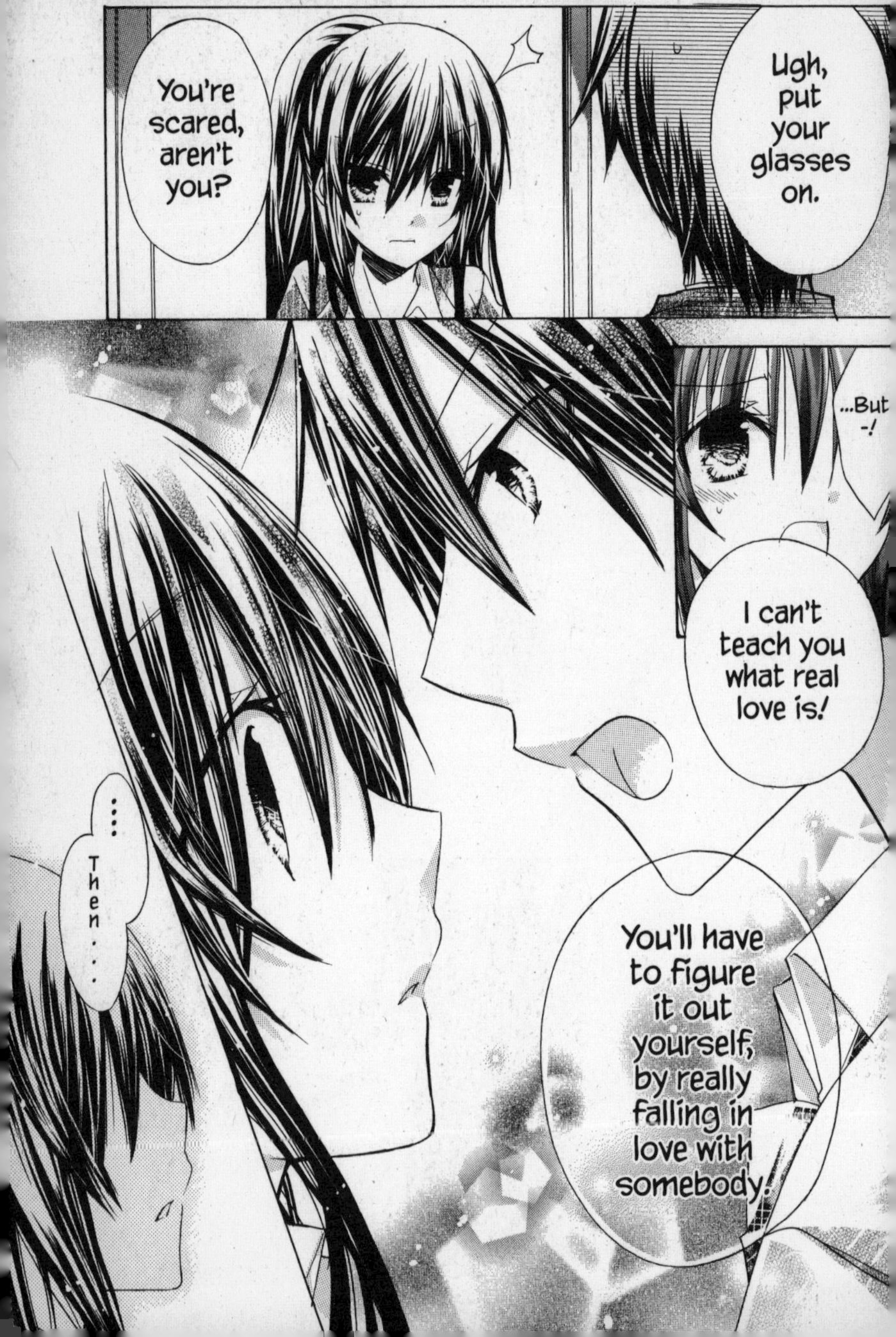
Ugh, put your glasses on.
You're scared, aren't you?
...But -!
I can't teach you what real love is!
You'll have to figure it out yourself, by really falling in love with somebody!
.... Then...

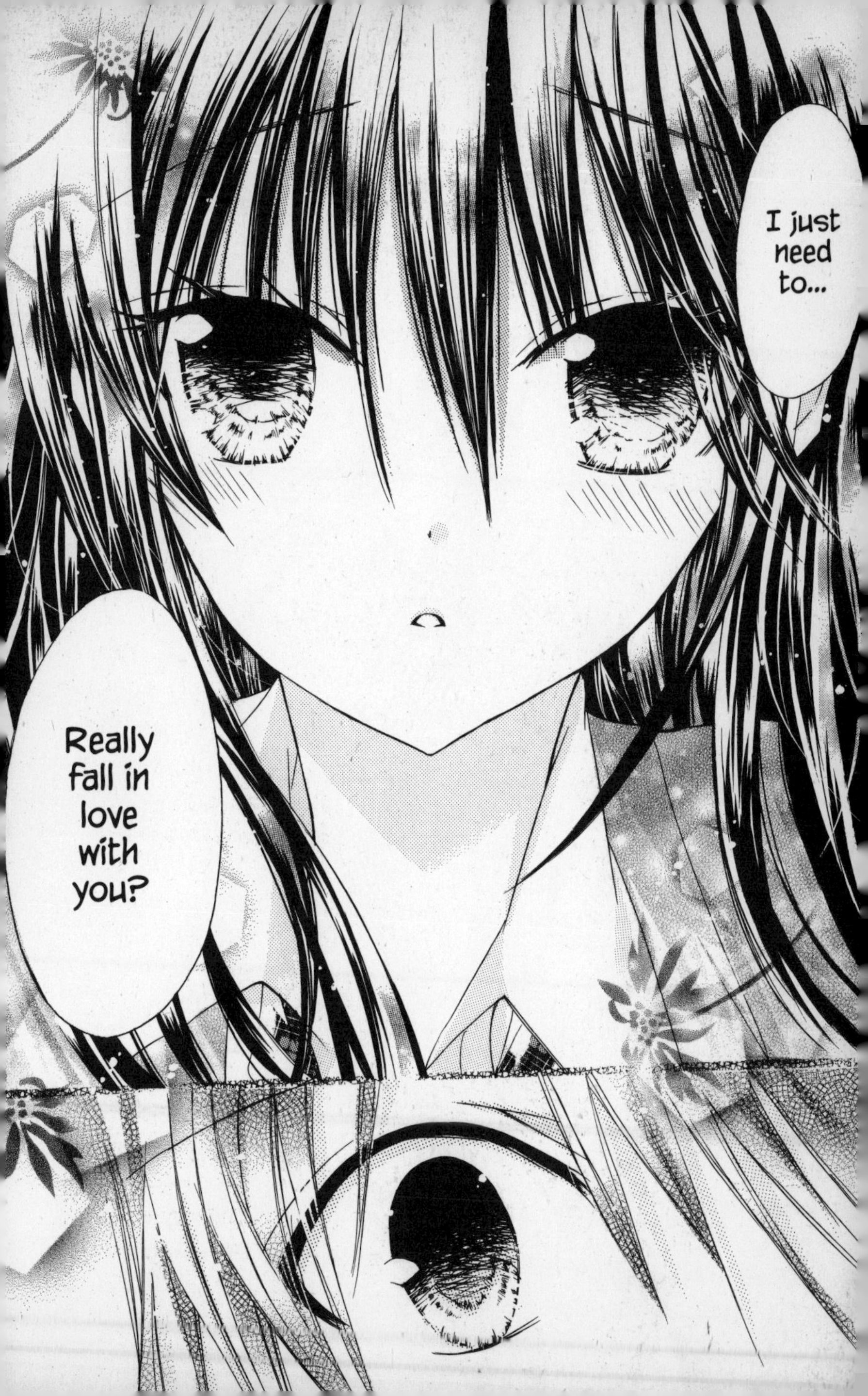
I just need to...
Really fall in love with you?

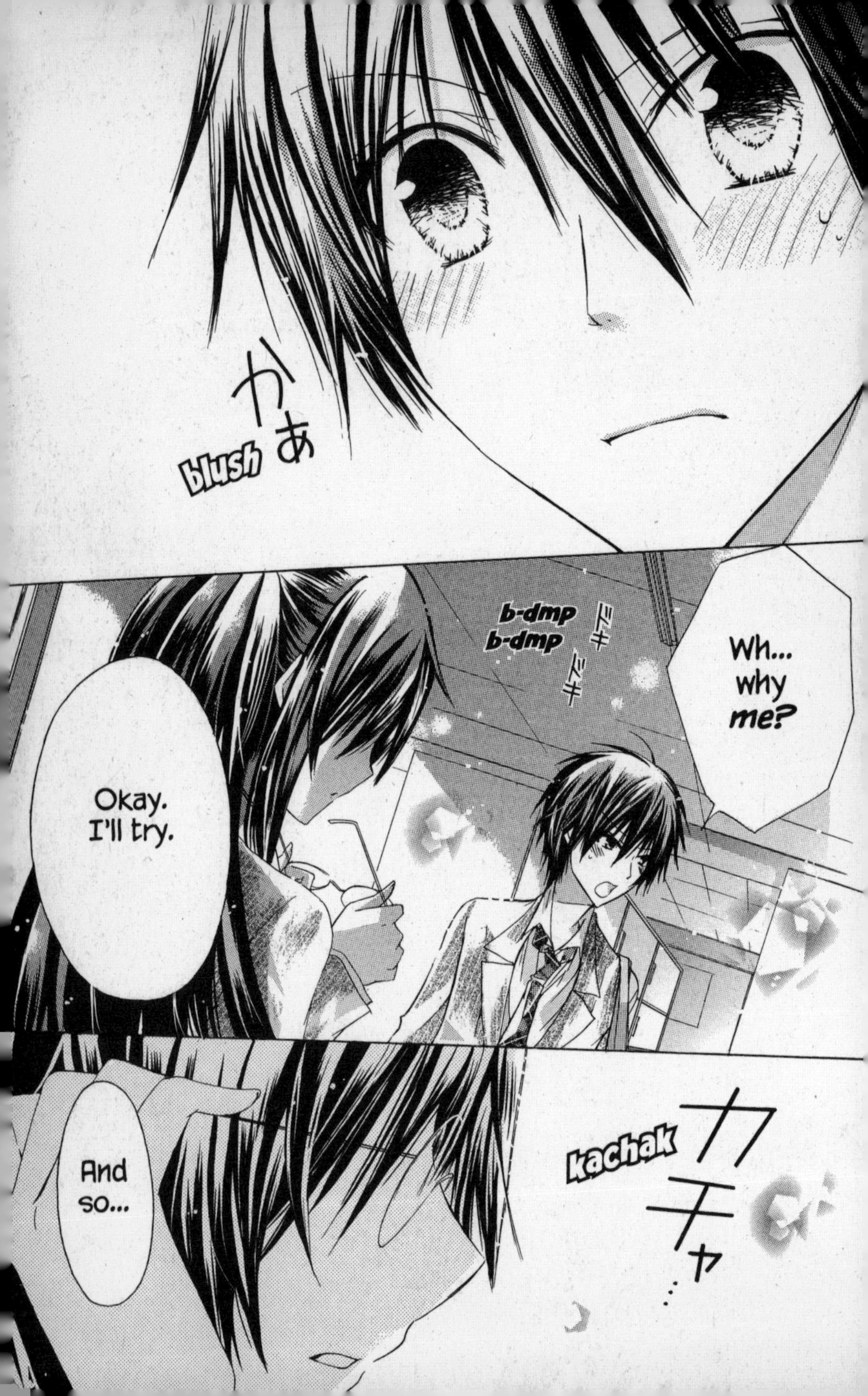かあ
blush
Wh... why me?
b-dmp b-dmp
ドキ ドキ
Okay. I'll try.
カチャ...
kachak
And so...

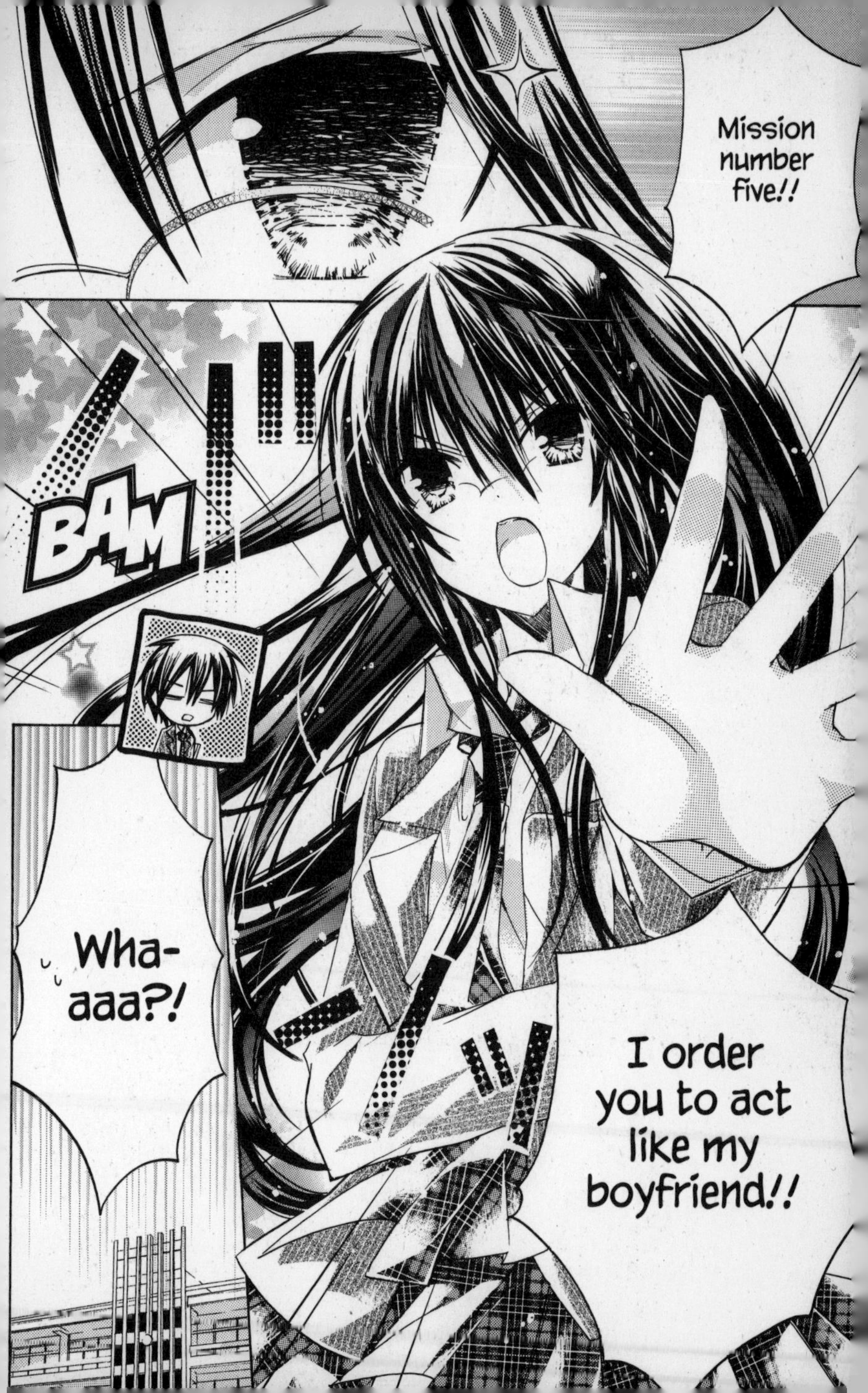
Mission number five!!
BAM
I order you to act like my boyfriend!!
Wha-aaa?!

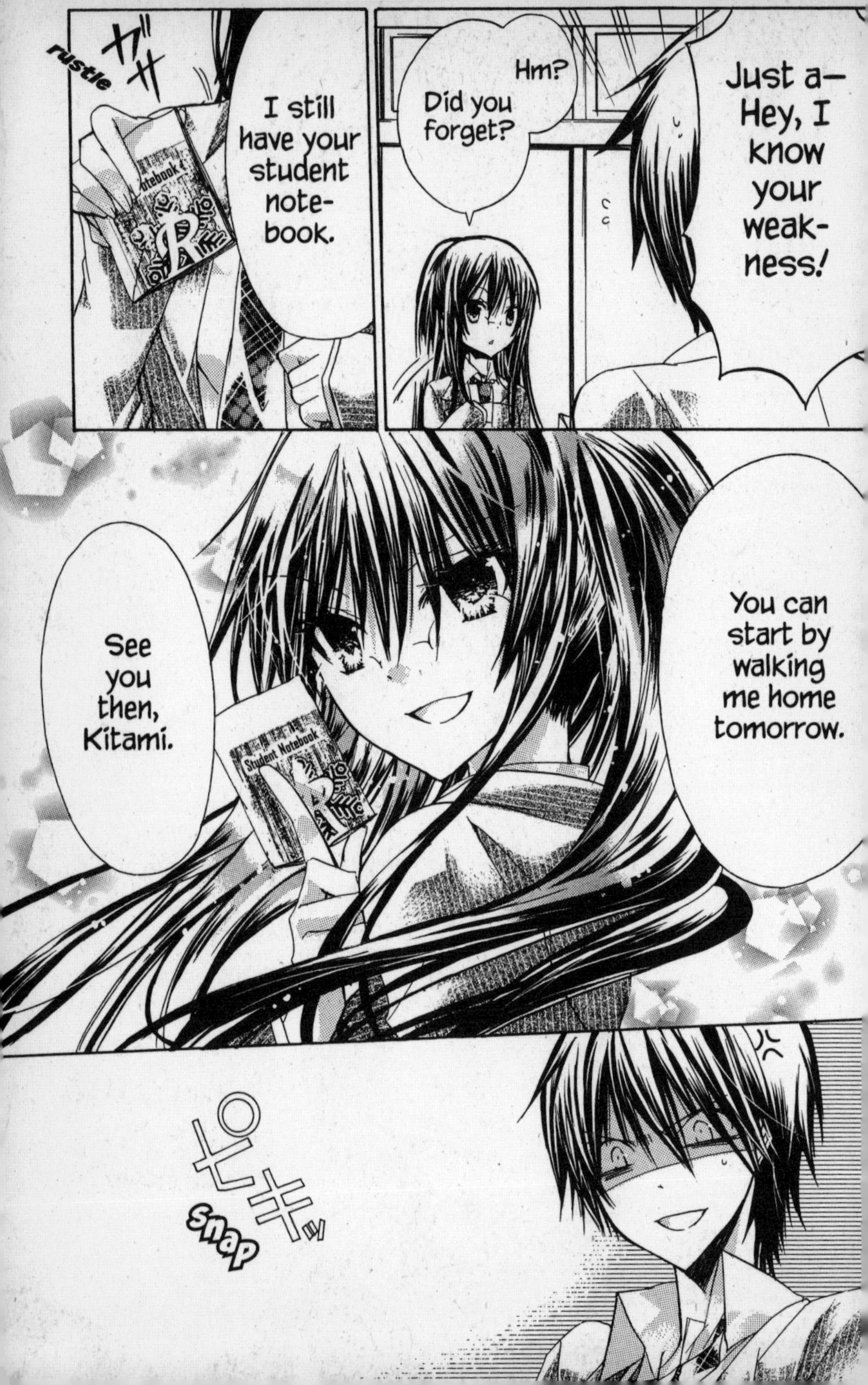
Just a— Hey, I know your weakness!
Hm? Did you forget?
ガサ
rustle
I still have your student notebook.
You can start by walking me home tomorrow.
See you then, Kitami.
Student Notebook
ピキッ
snap

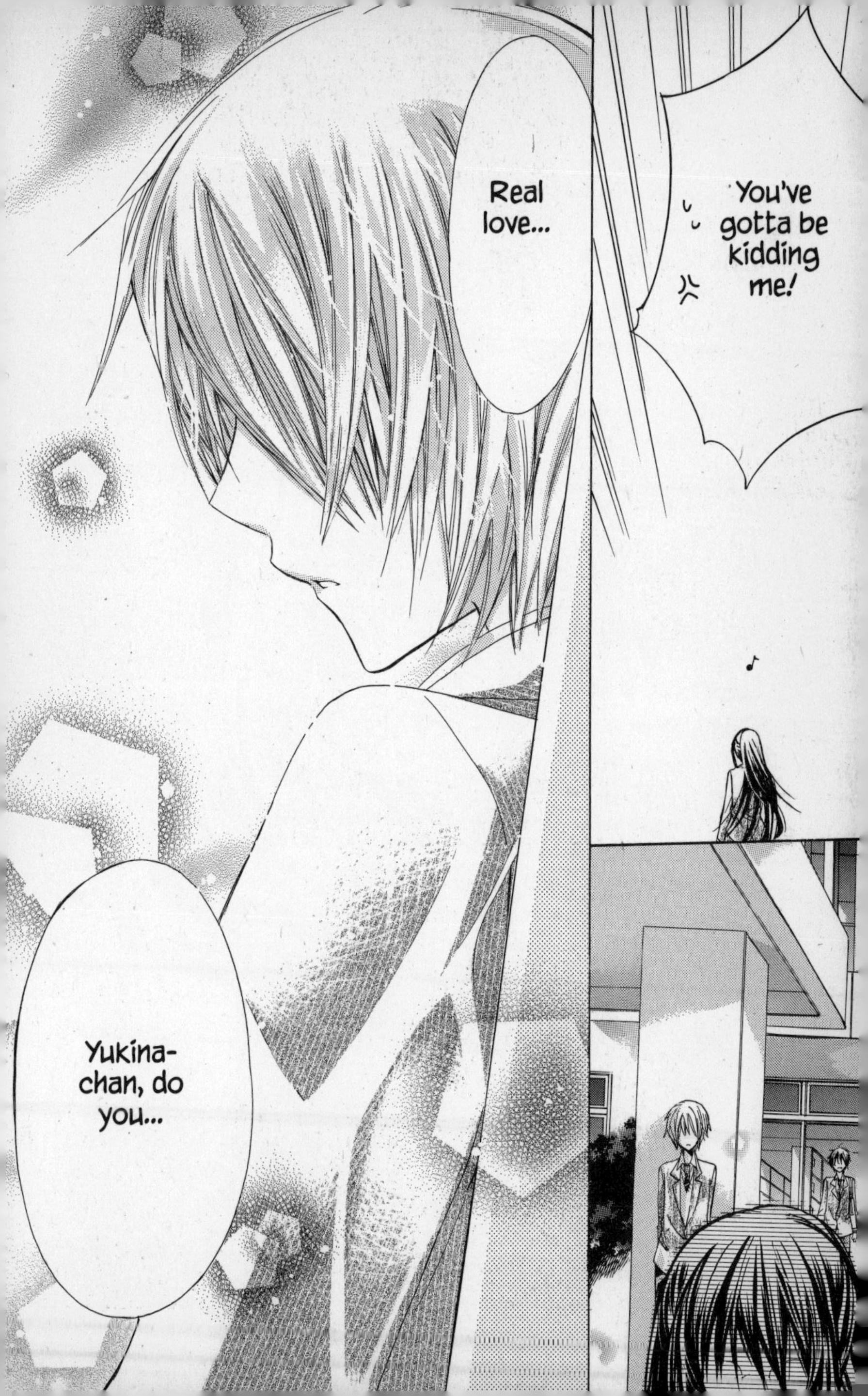
You've gotta be kidding me!
Real love...
Yukina-chan, do you...

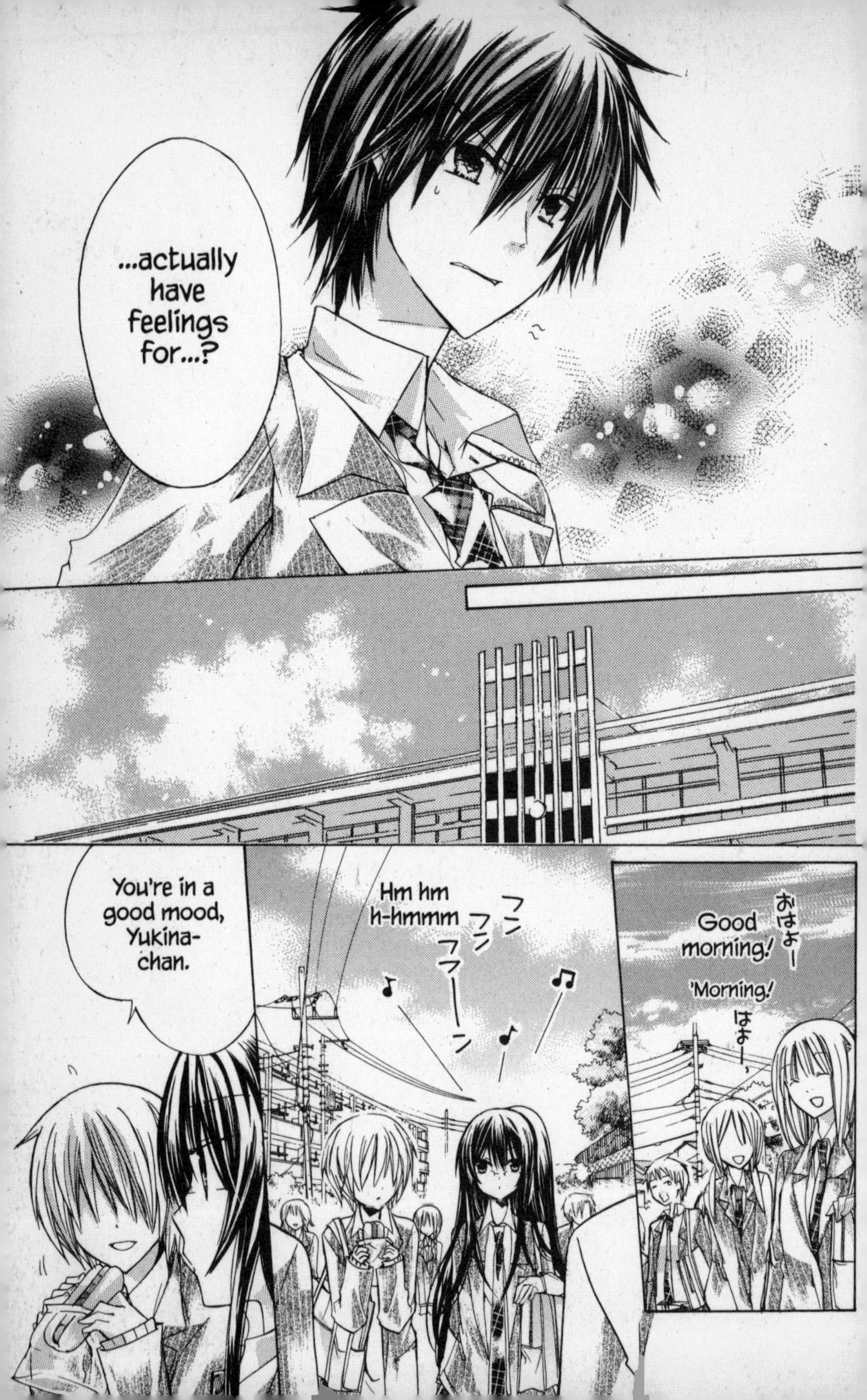
...actually have feelings for...?
Good morning!
おはよー
'Morning!
はよー
Hm hm h-hmmm
フンフンフーン
You're in a good mood, Yukina-chan.

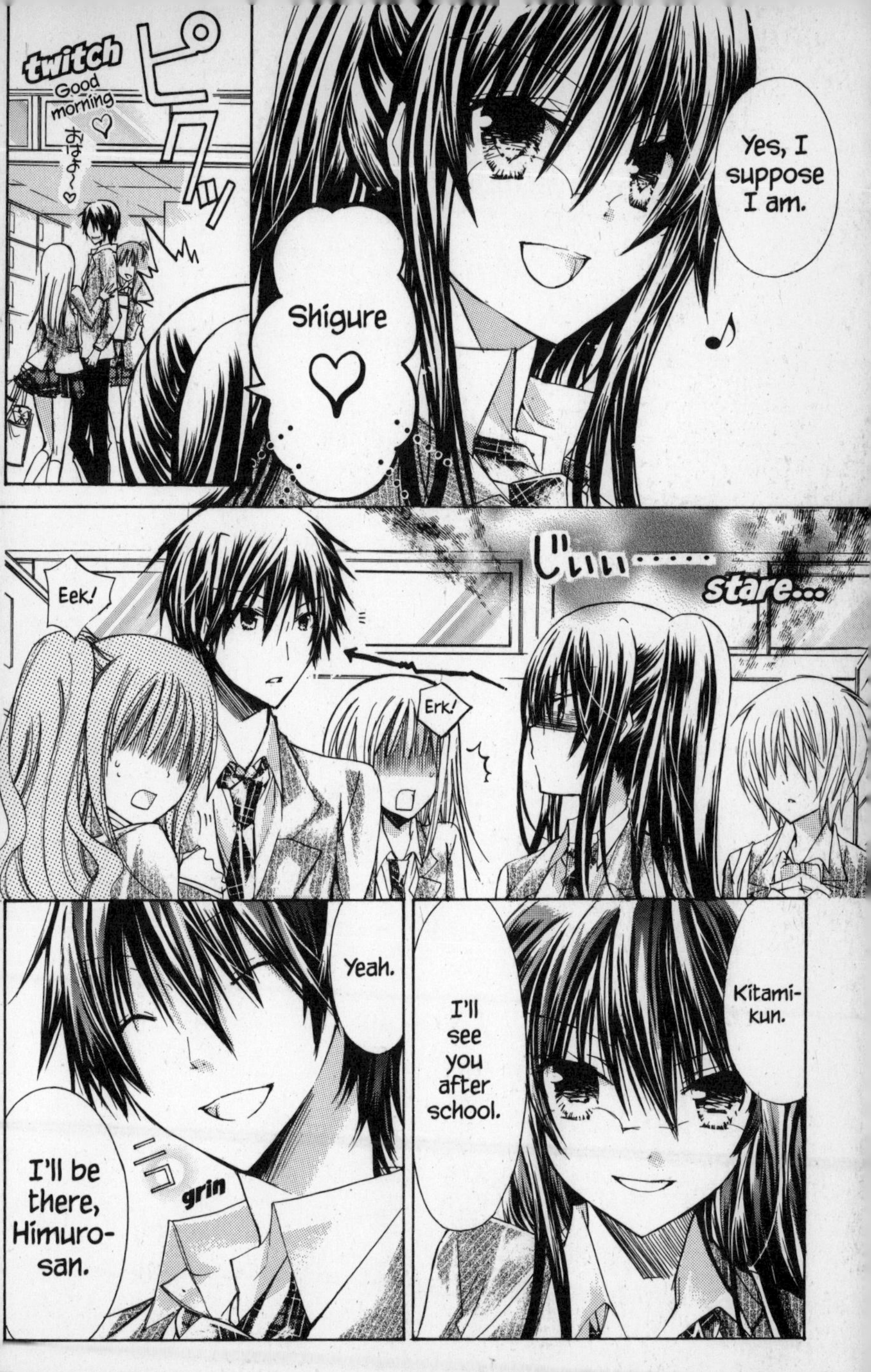
Yes, I suppose I am.
Shigure ♥
twitch
Good morning ♥
おはよ～♡
じぃぃ……
stare...
Erk!
Eek!
Kitami-kun.
I'll see you after school.
Yeah.
I'll be there, Himuro-san.
grin

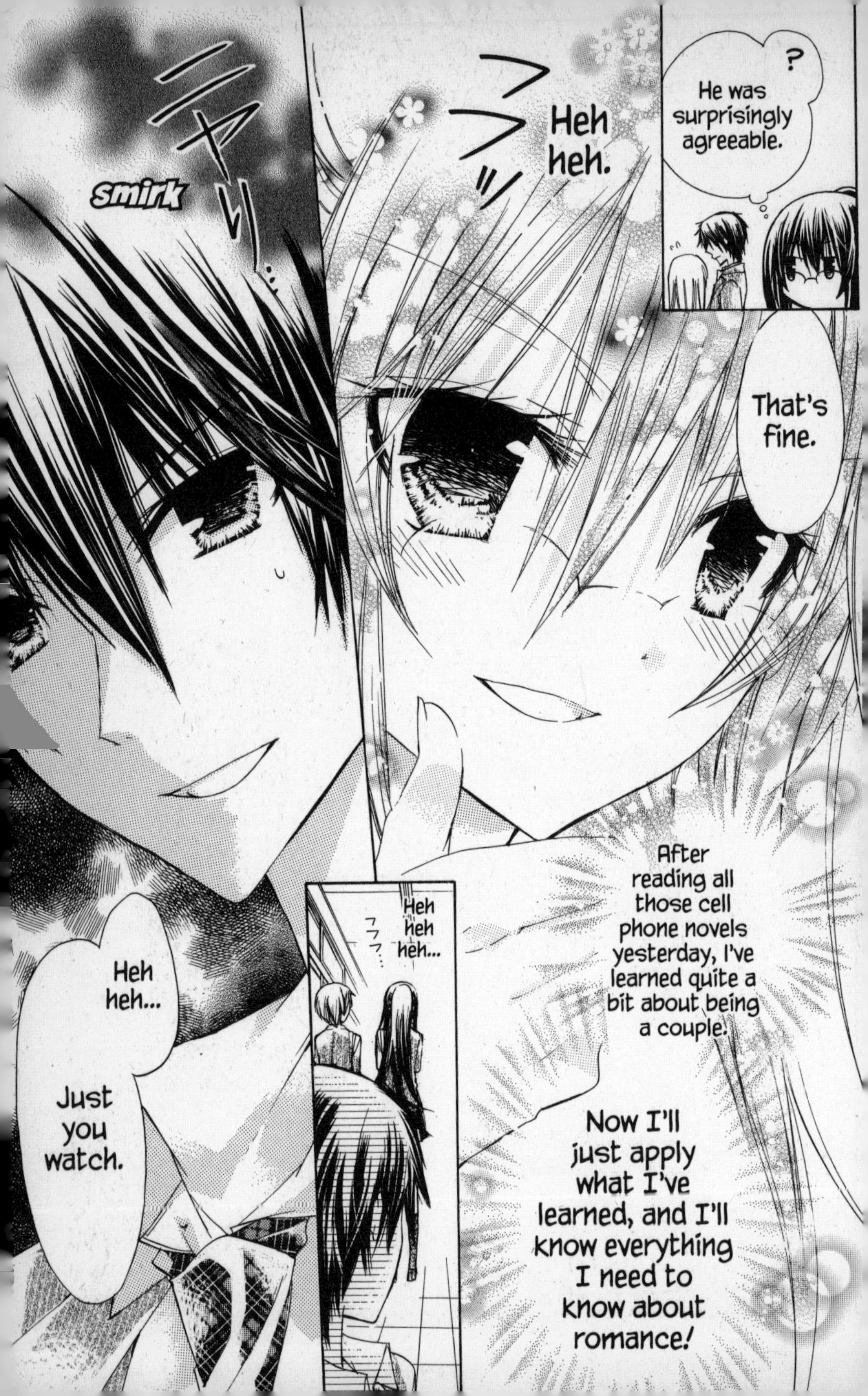
?
He was surprisingly agreeable.
フフッ
Heh heh.
That's fine.
After reading all those cell phone novels yesterday, I've learned quite a bit about being a couple.
Now I'll just apply what I've learned, and I'll know everything I need to know about romance!
フフフ…
Heh heh heh...
ニヤリ…
smirk
Heh heh...
Just you watch.

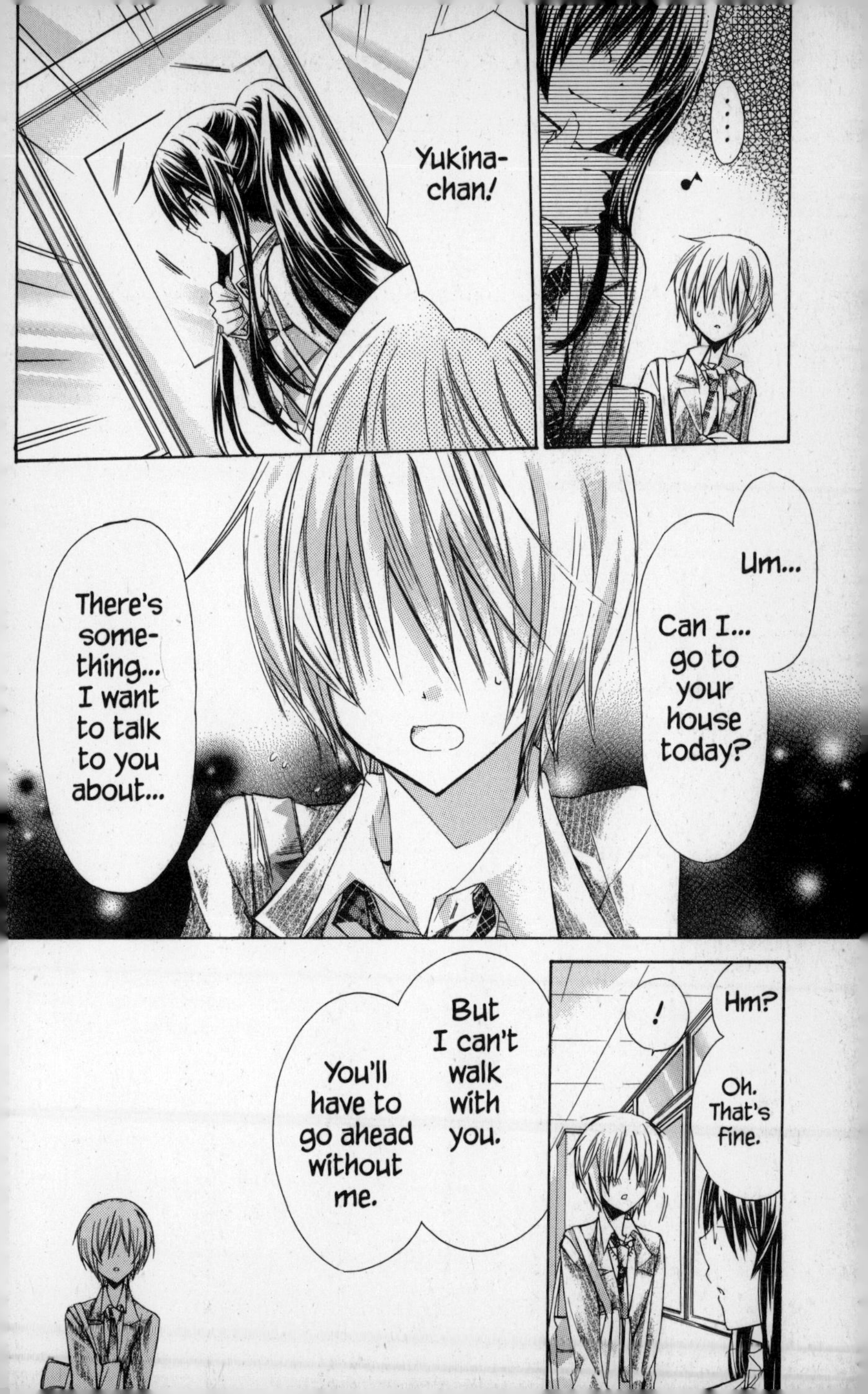
......
Yukina-chan!
Um... Can I... go to your house today?
There's something... I want to talk to you about...
Hm?
!
Oh. That's fine.
But I can't walk with you.
You'll have to go ahead without me.

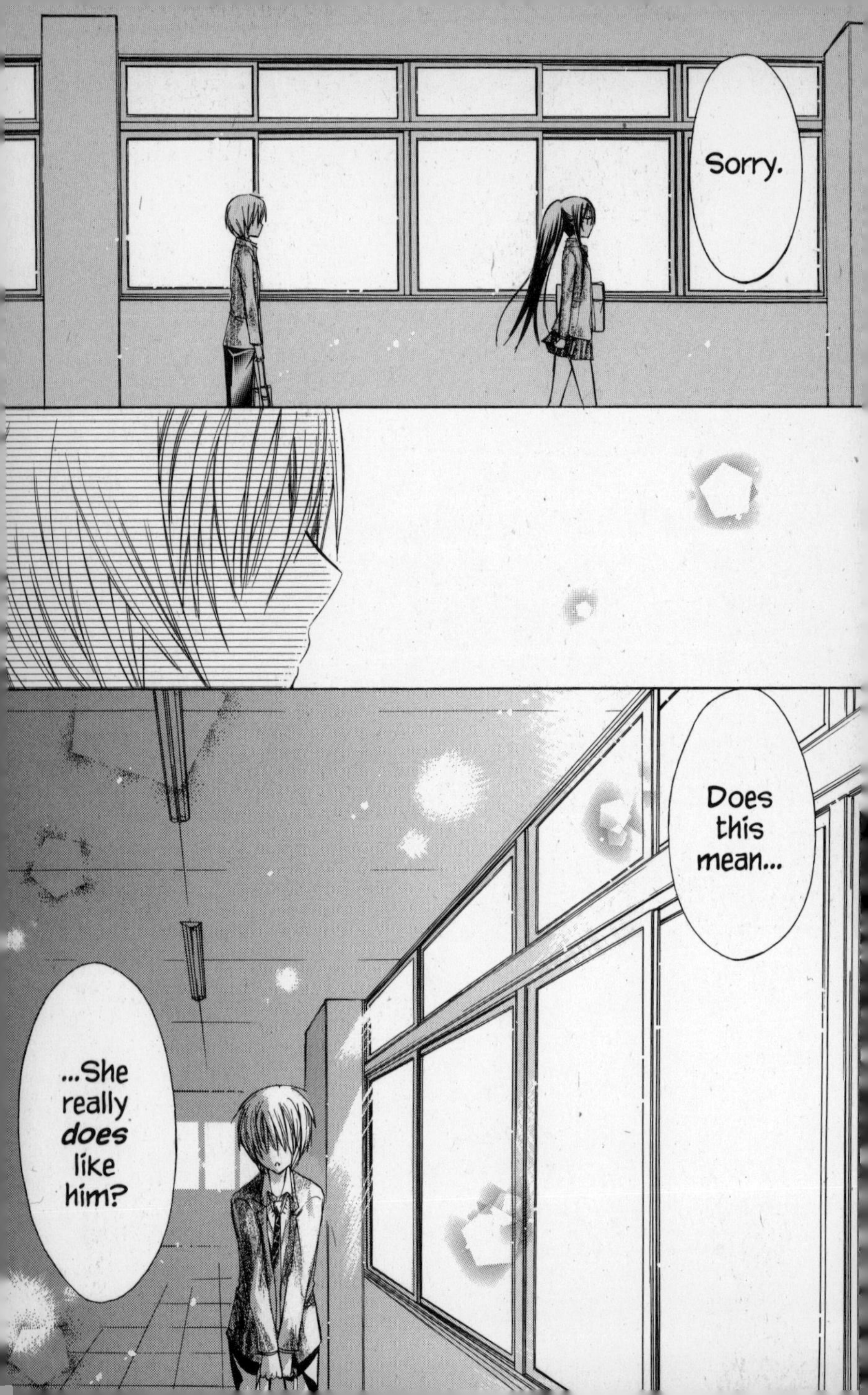
Sorry.
Does this mean...
...She really *does* like him?

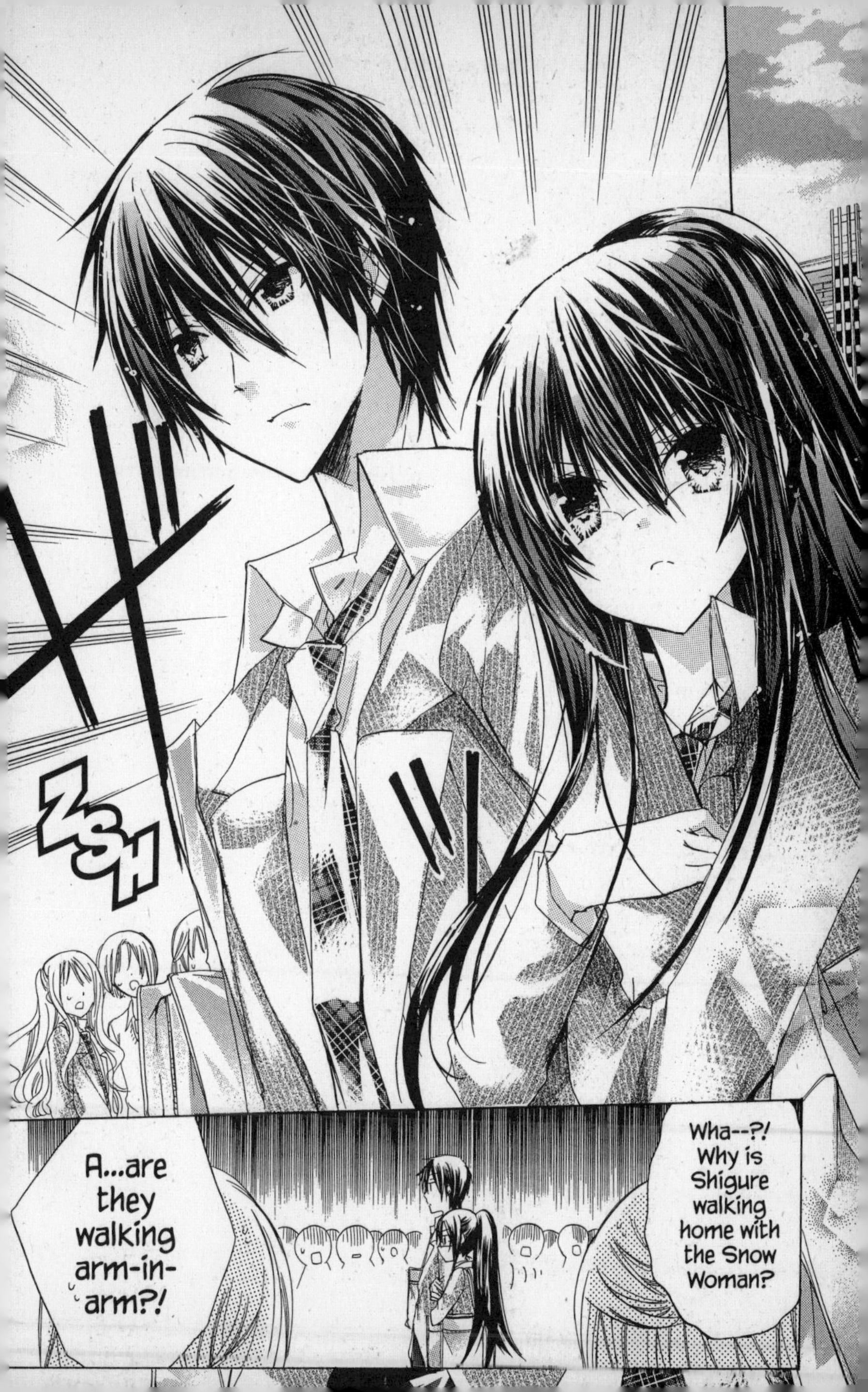
ZSH
Wha--?! Why is Shigure walking home with the Snow Woman?
A...are they walking arm-in-arm?!

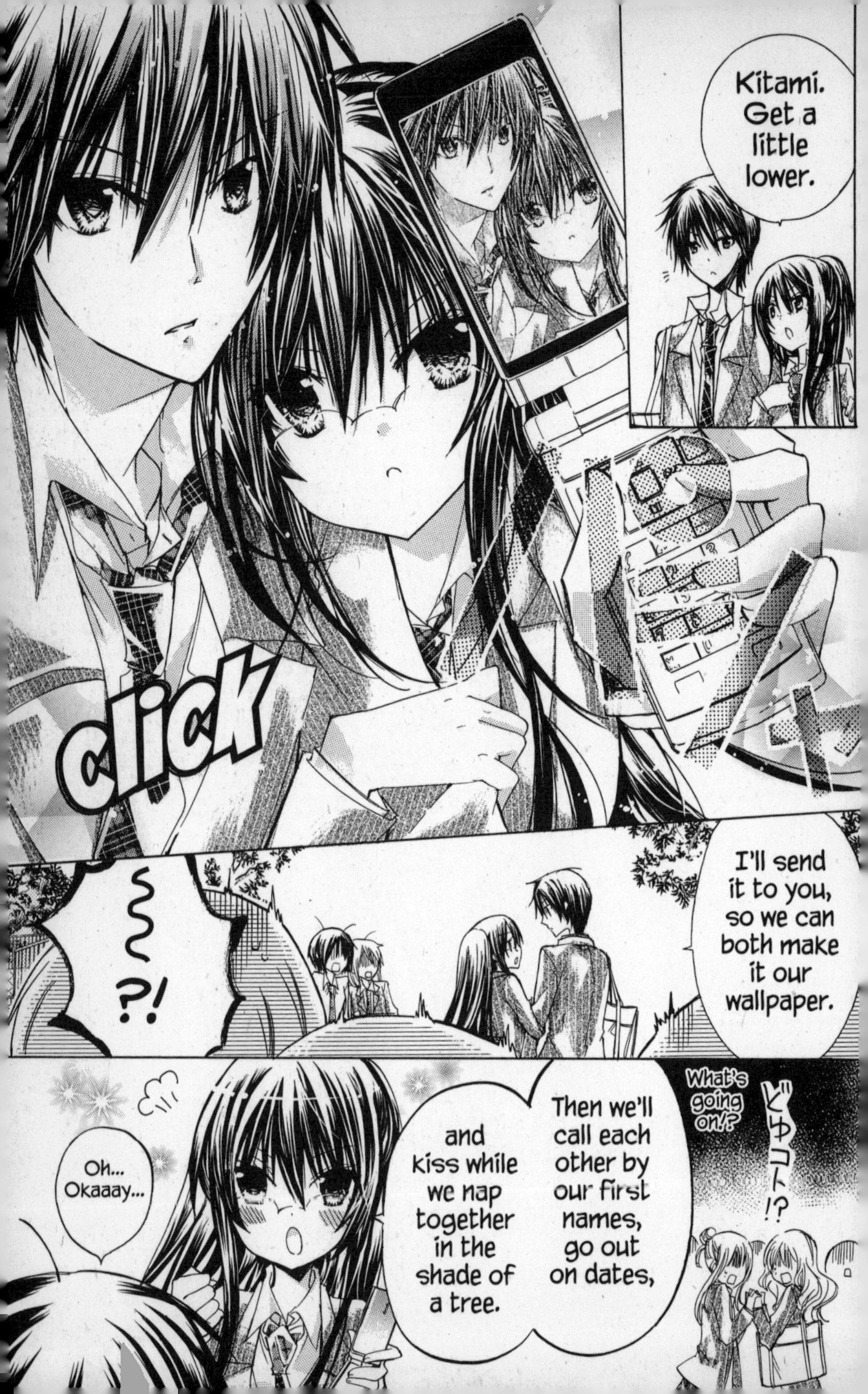
Kitami. Get a little lower.
click
I'll send it to you, so we can both make it our wallpaper.
?!
What's going on!?
どゆコト!?
Then we'll call each other by our first names, go out on dates,
and kiss while we nap together in the shade of a tree.
Oh... Okaaay...

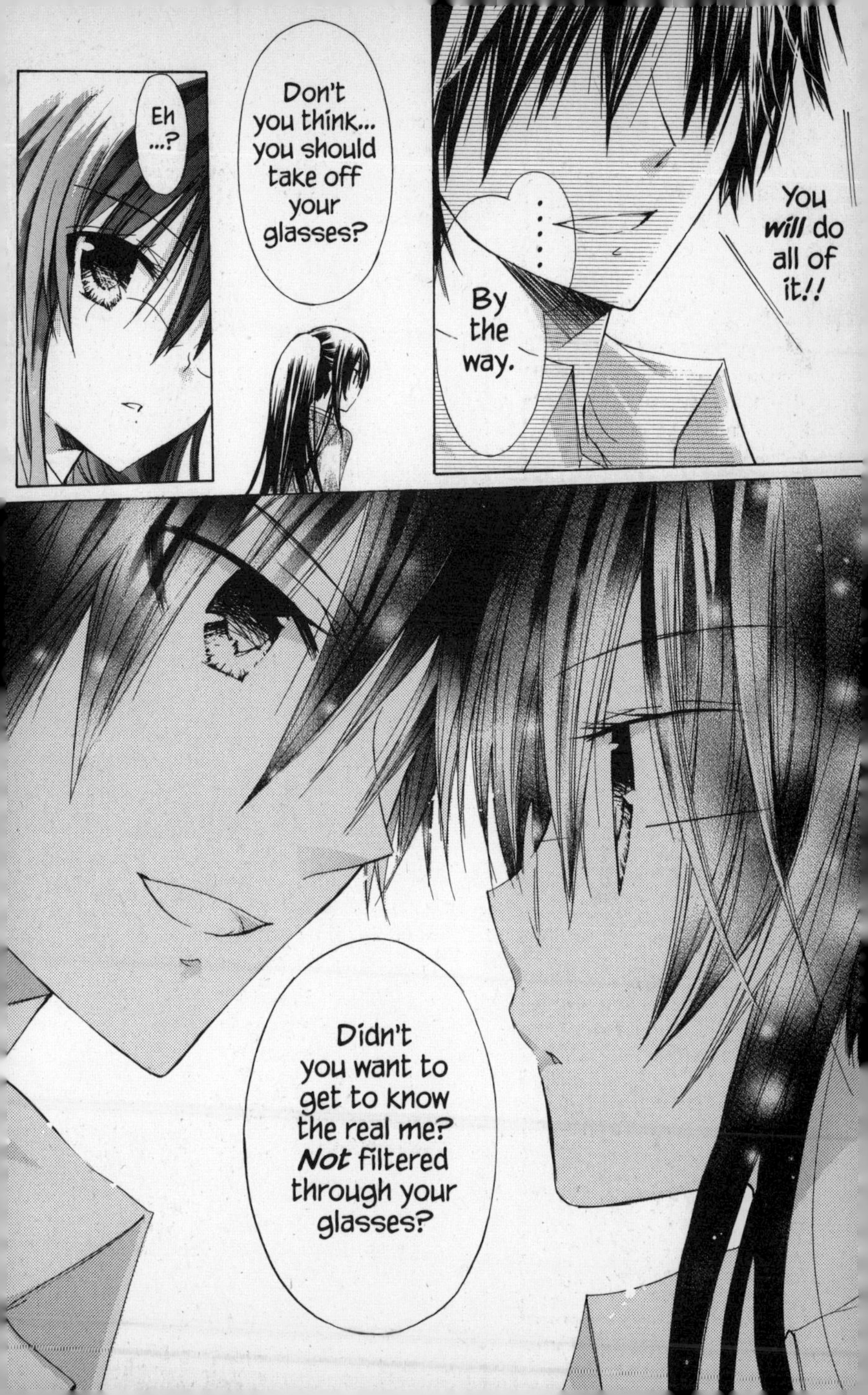
You *will* do all of it!!
....
By the way.
Don't you think... you should take off your glasses?
Eh ...?
Didn't you want to get to know the real me? *Not* filtered through your glasses?

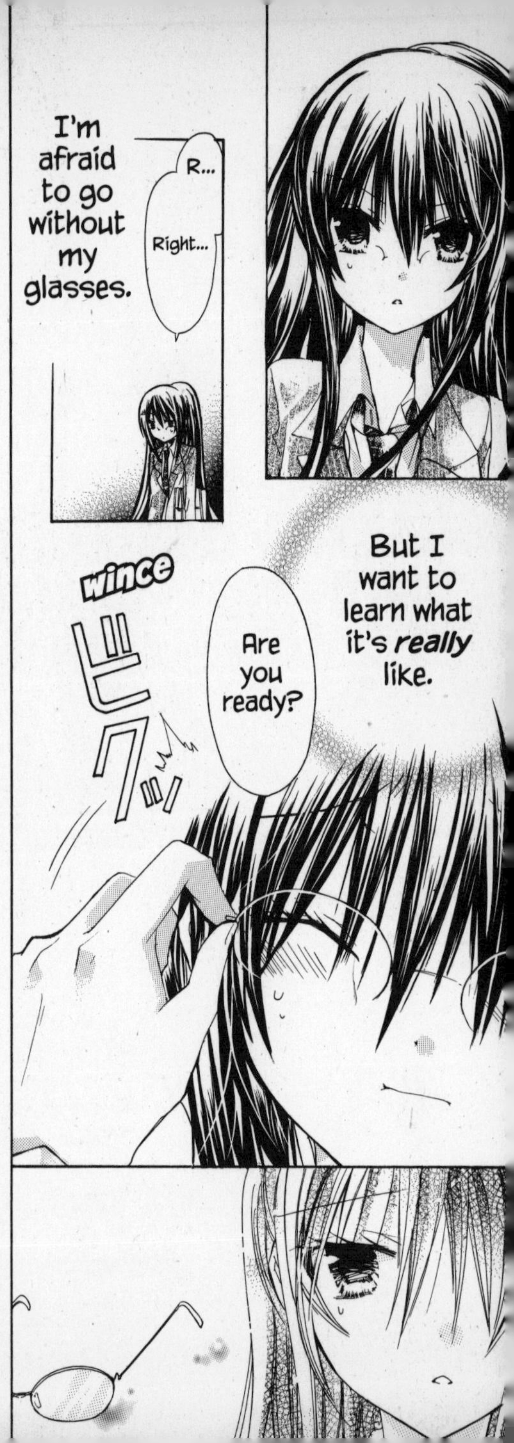
R...
Right...
I'm afraid to go without my glasses.
But I want to learn what it's *really* like.
Are you ready?
wince

Snow Yukina

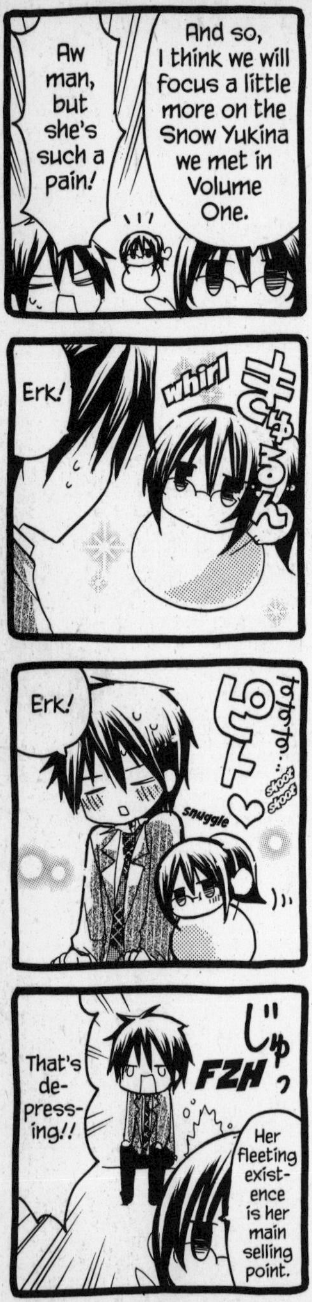
And so, I think we will focus a little more on the Snow Yukina we met in Volume One.
Aw man, but she's such a pain!
Erk!
whirl
Erk!
skoot skoot
snuggle
That's de-press-ing!!
FZH
Her fleeting exist-ence is her main selling point.

She melts when she gets warm.

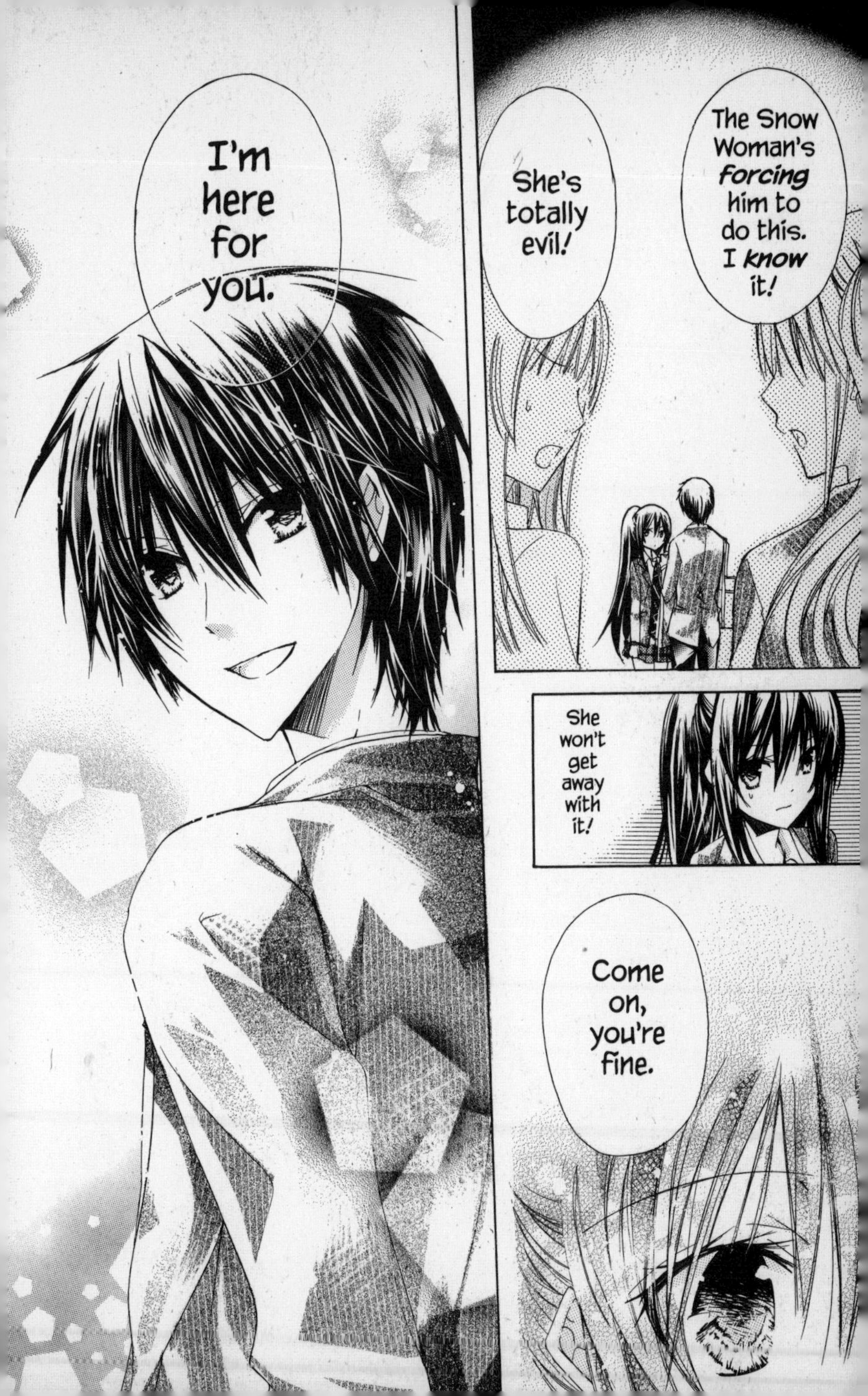

The Snow Woman's *forcing* him to do this. I *know* it!
She's totally evil!
She won't get away with it!
Come on, you're fine.
I'm here for you.

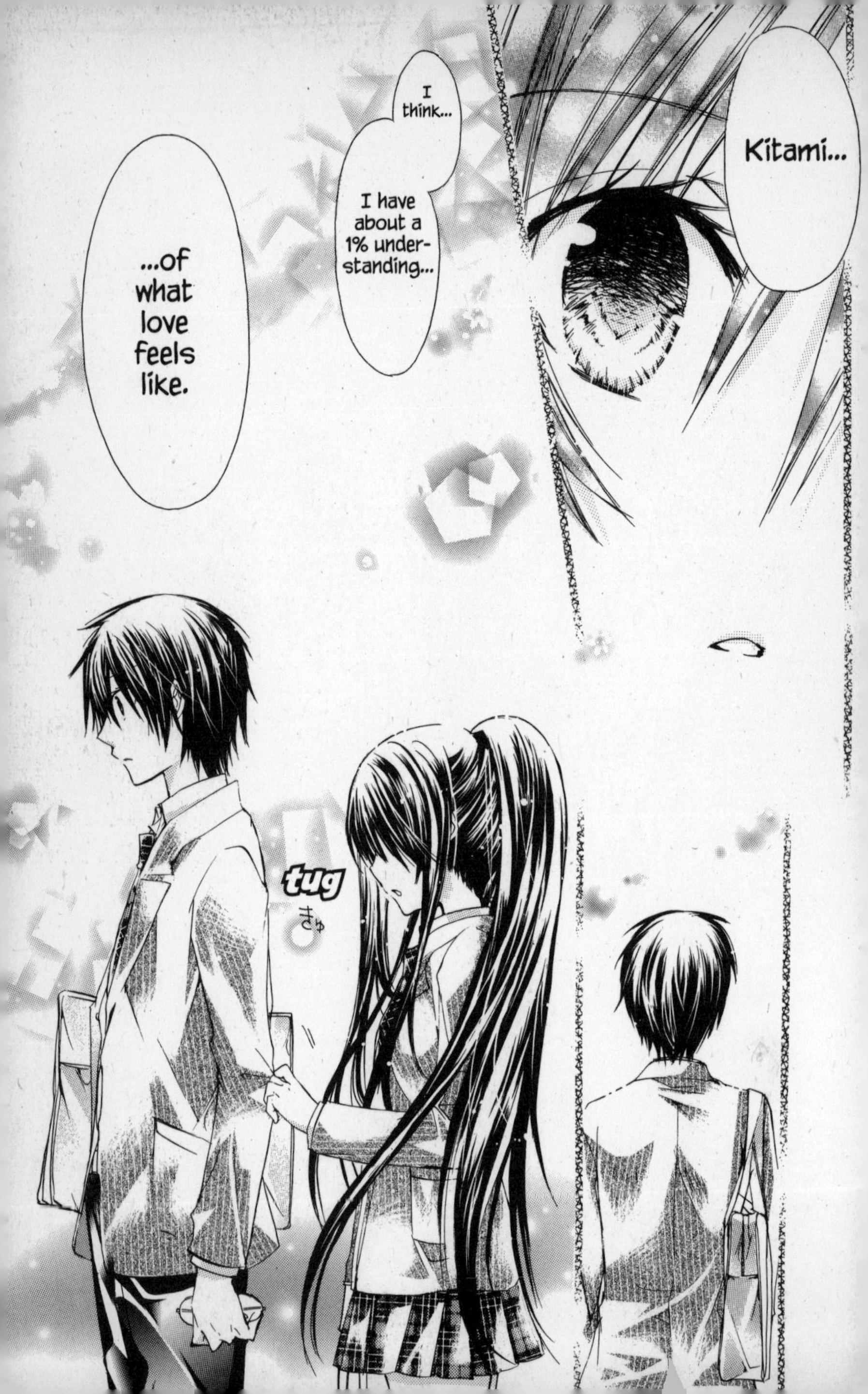
Kitami...
I think...
I have about a 1% under-standing...
...of what love feels like.
tug
きゅ

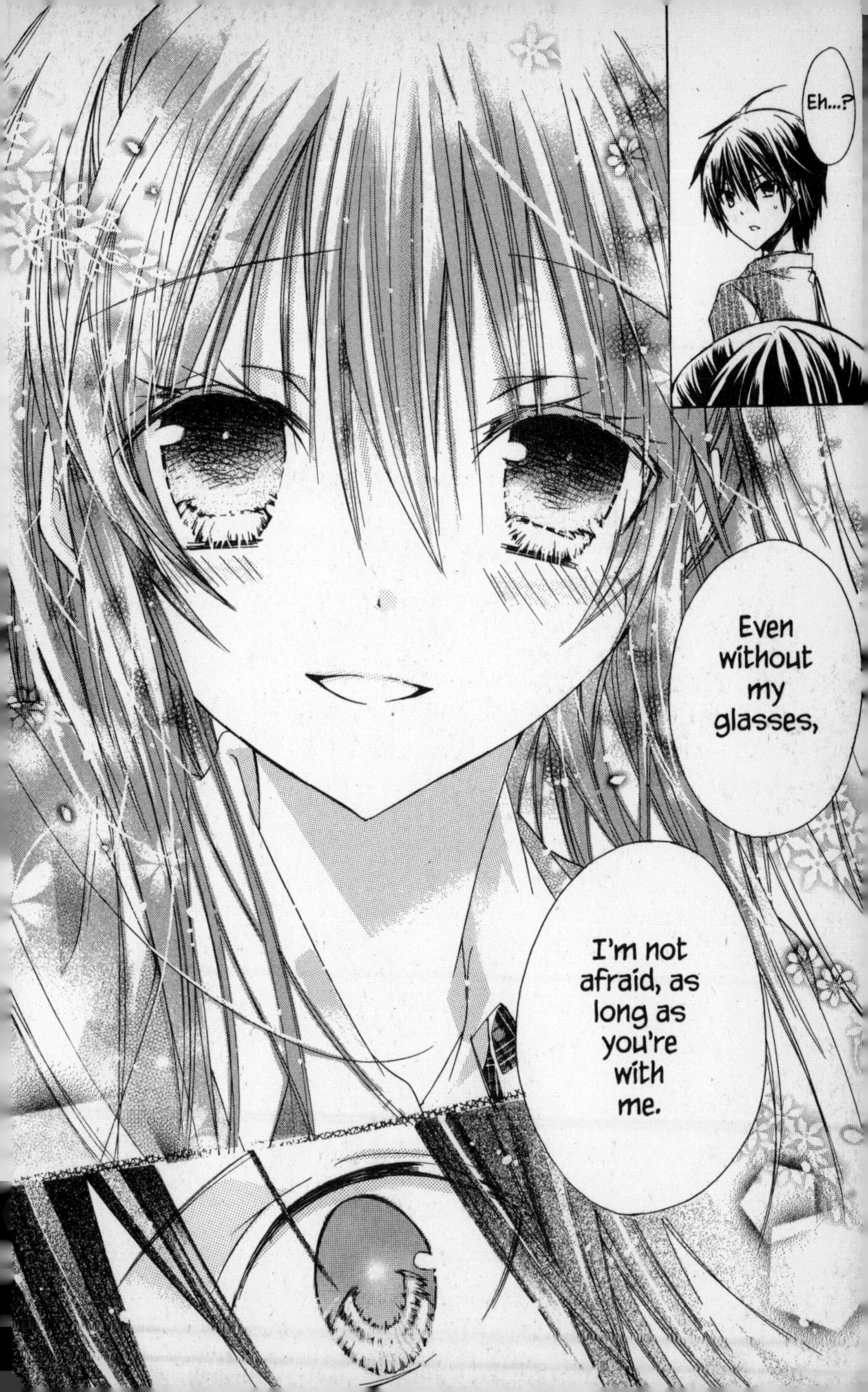
Eh...?
Even without my glasses,
I'm not afraid, as long as you're with me.

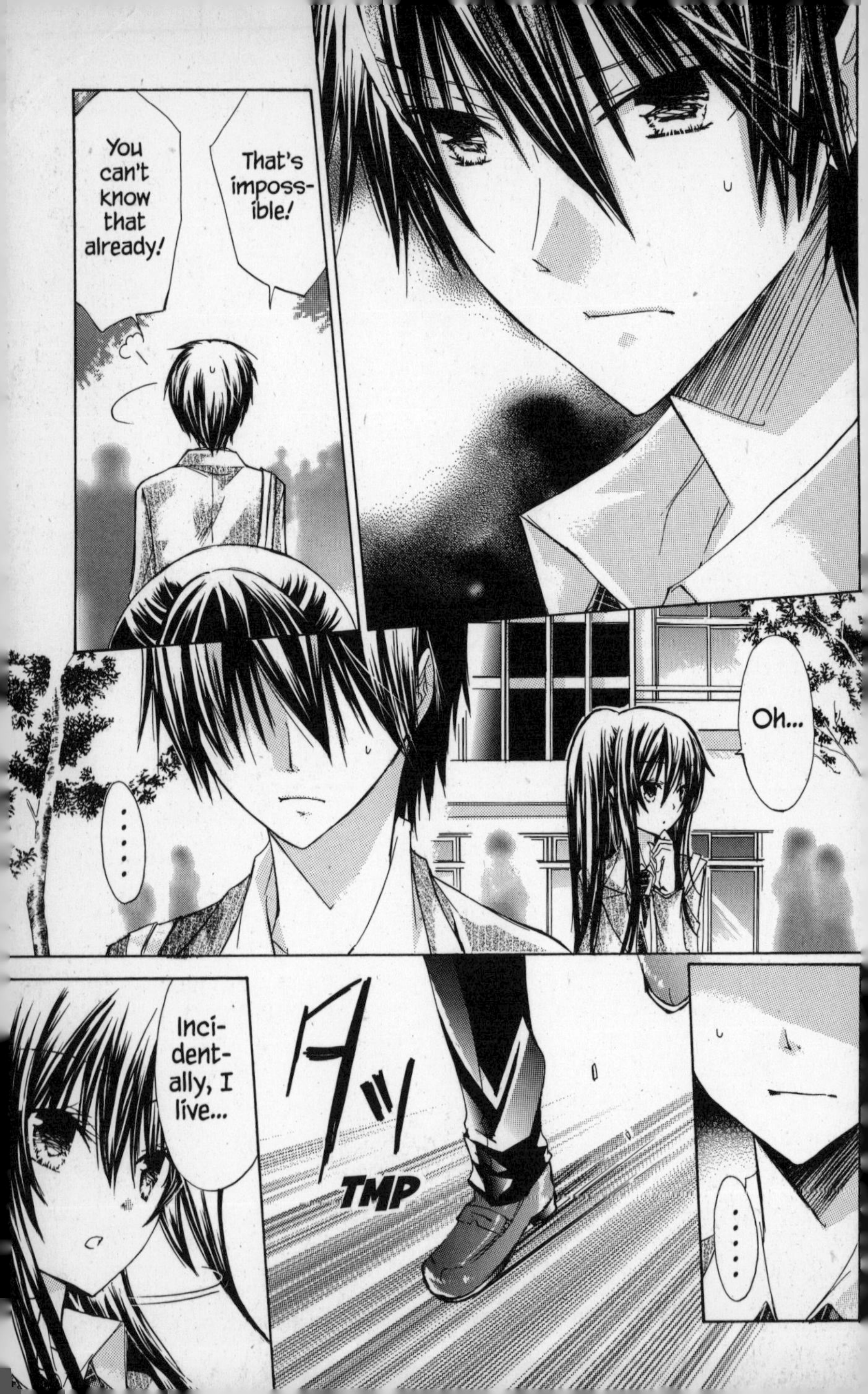
That's impossible!
You can't know that already!
Oh...
......
......
TMP
Incidentally, I live...

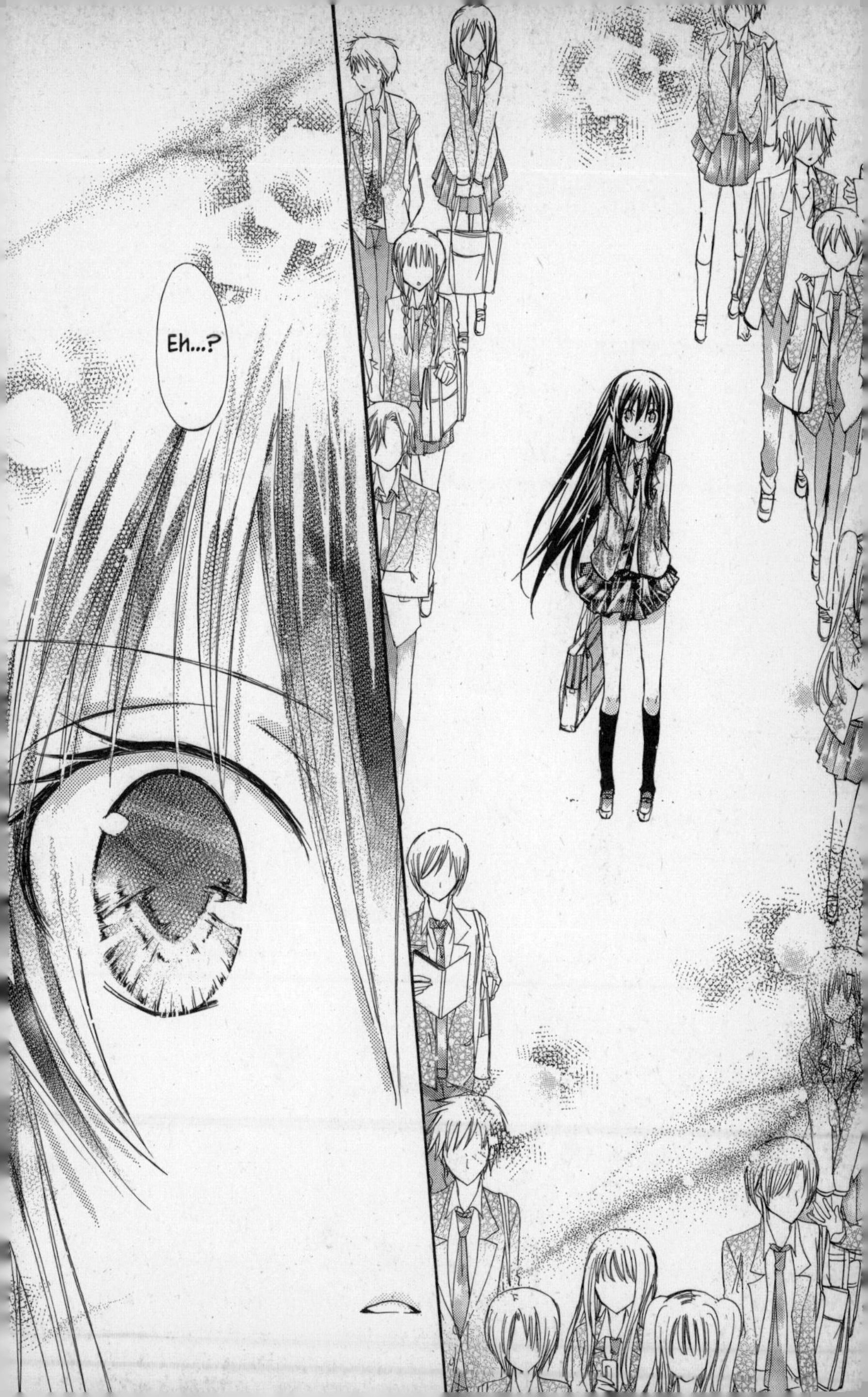
Eh...?

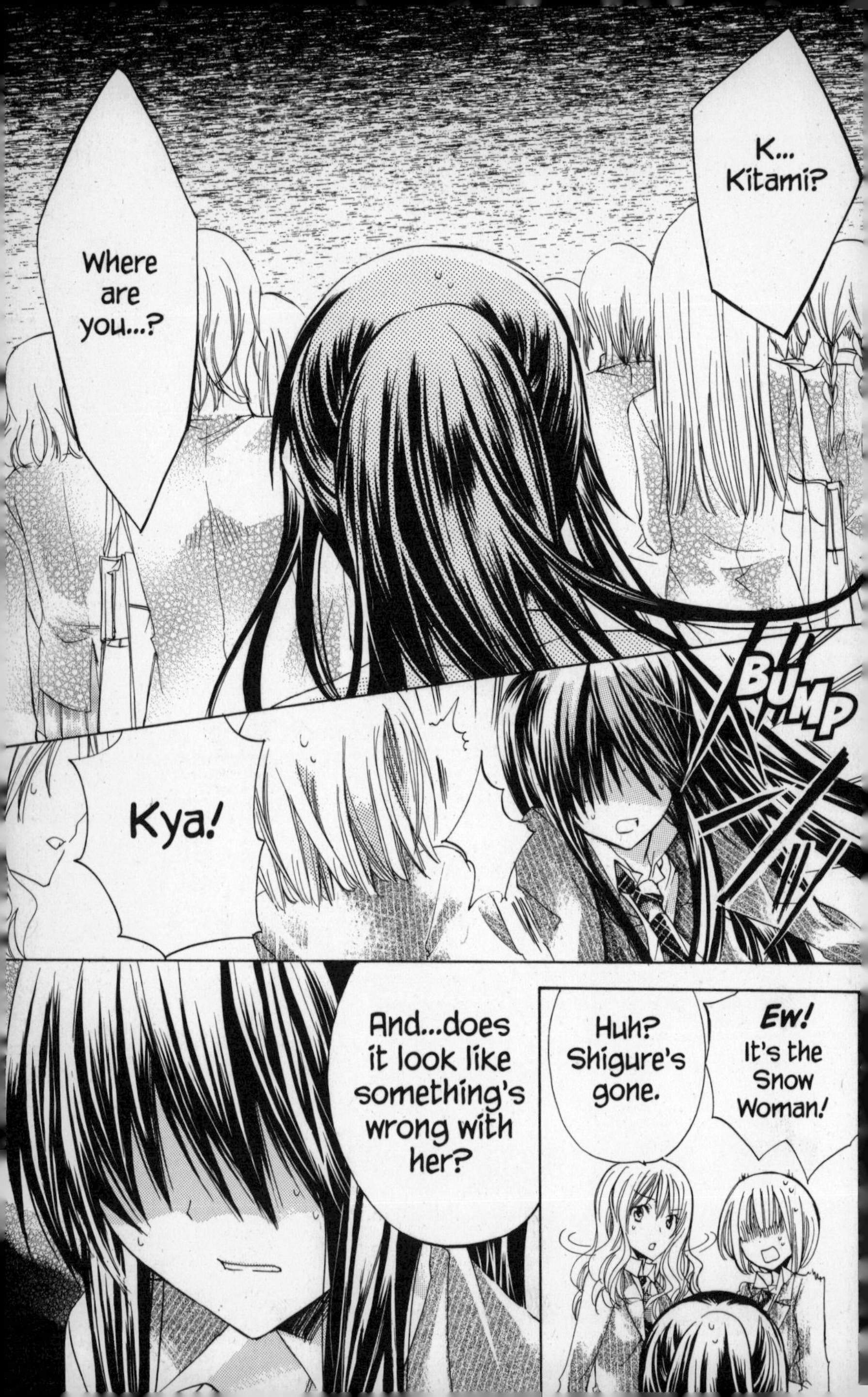
K... Kitami?
Where are you...?
BUMP
Kya!
Ew! It's the Snow Woman!
Huh? Shigure's gone.
And...does it look like something's wrong with her?

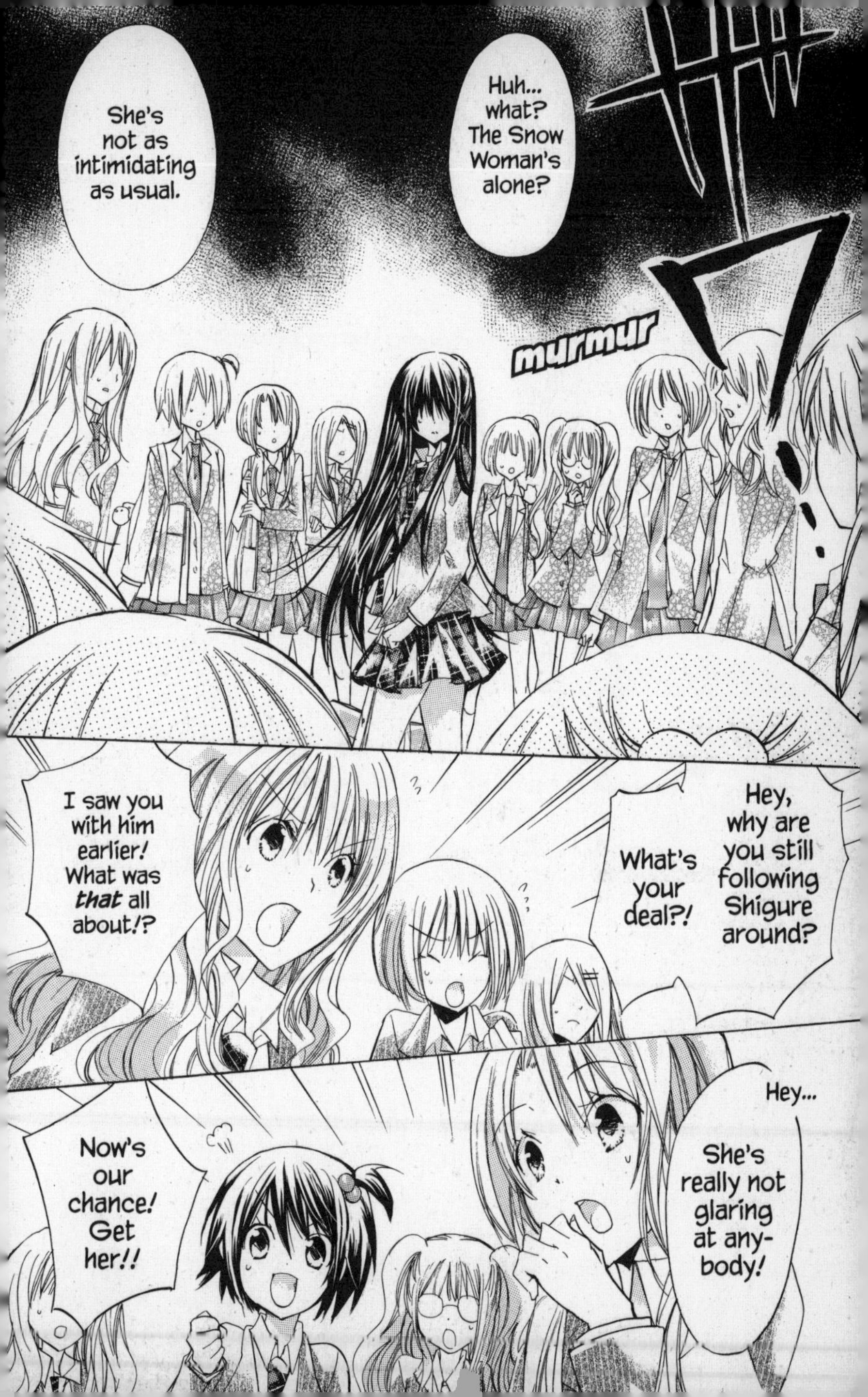
Huh... what? The Snow Woman's alone?
She's not as intimidating as usual.
murmur
Hey, why are you still following Shigure around?
What's your deal?!
I saw you with him earlier! What was *that* all about!?
Hey...
She's really not glaring at any-body!
Now's our chance! Get her!!

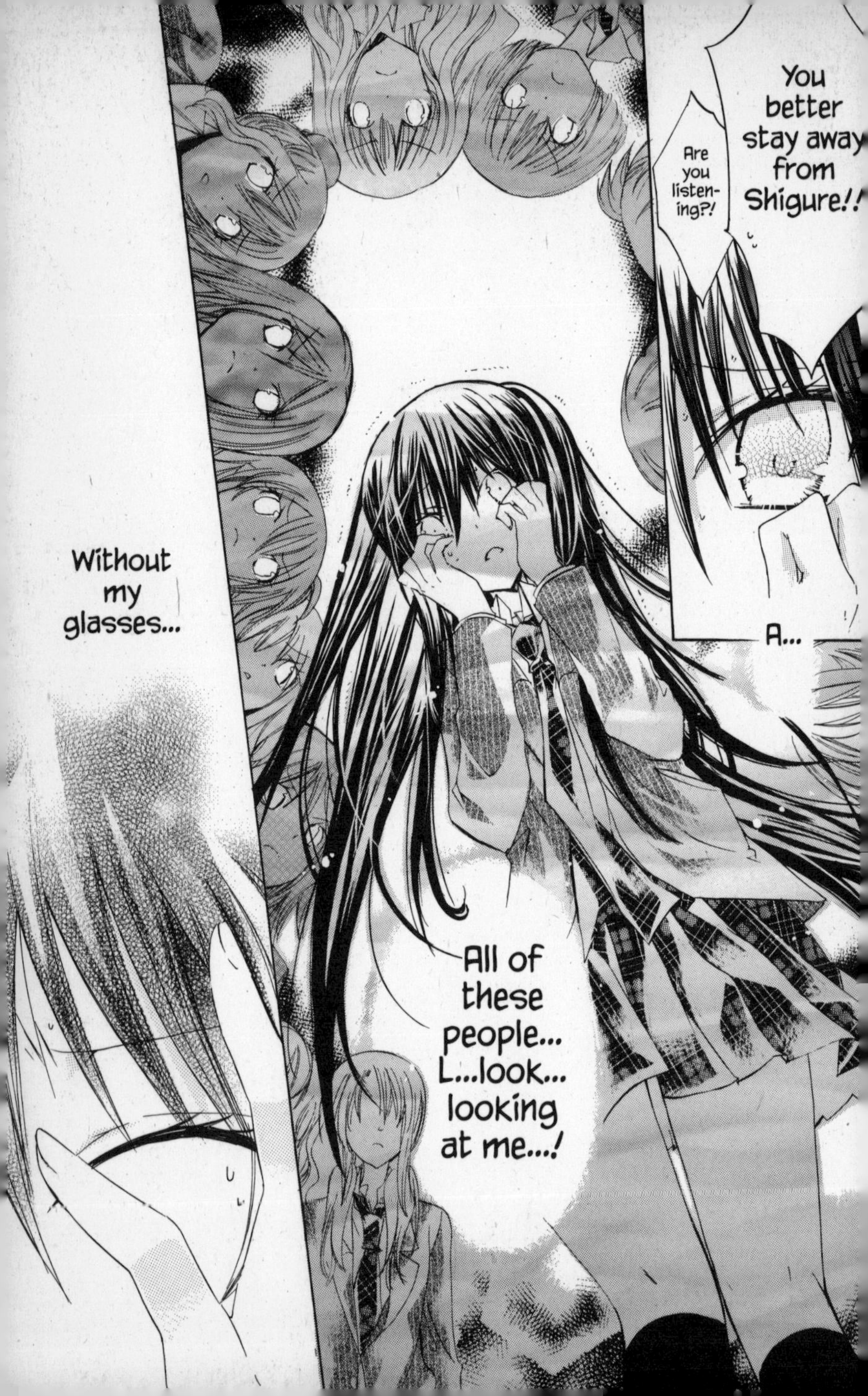
You better stay away from Shigure!!
Are you listening?!
A...
All of these people... L...look... looking at me...!
Without my glasses...

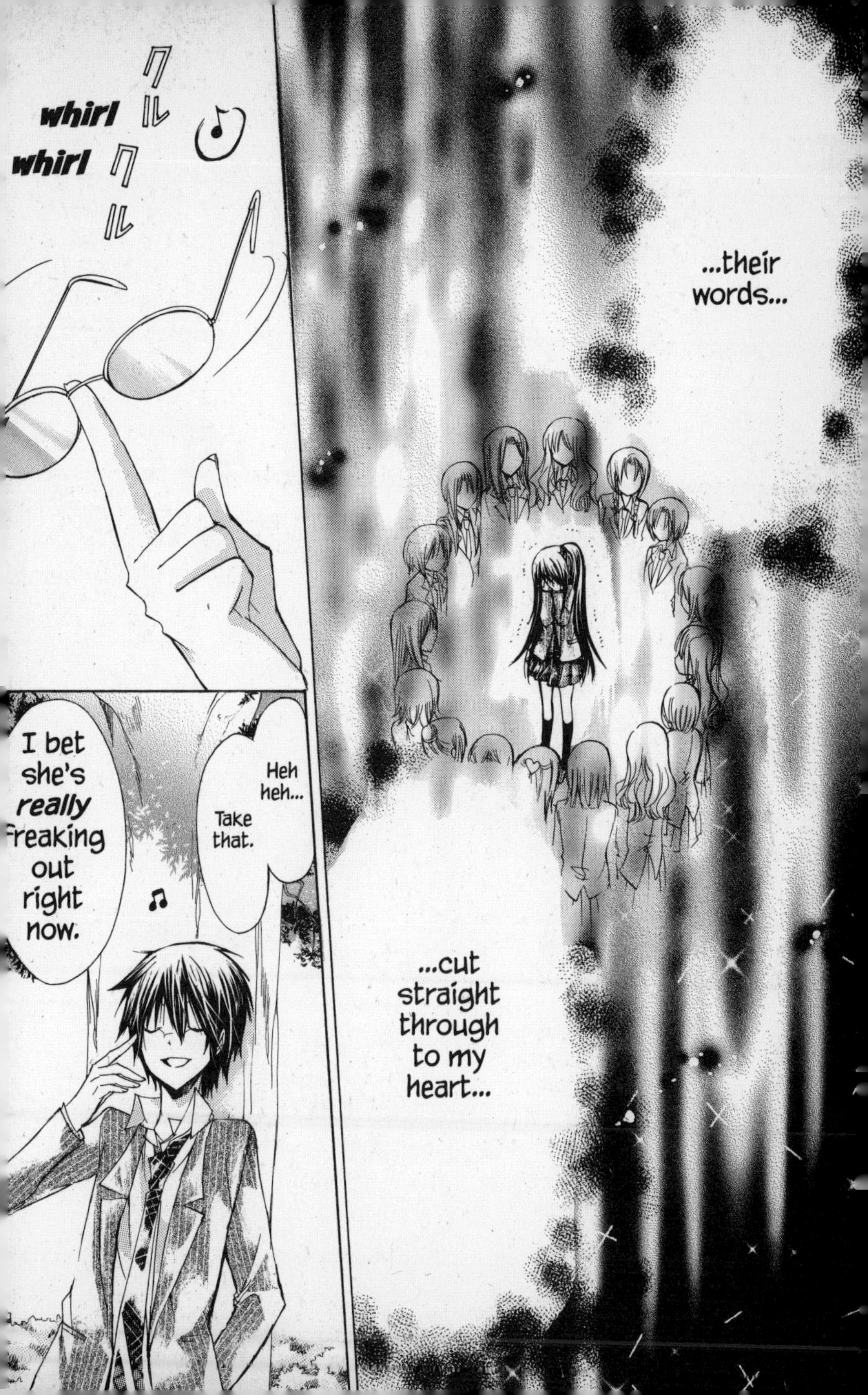
...their words...
...cut straight through to my heart...
クルクル
whirl whirl
Heh heh... Take that.
I bet she's *really* freaking out right now.

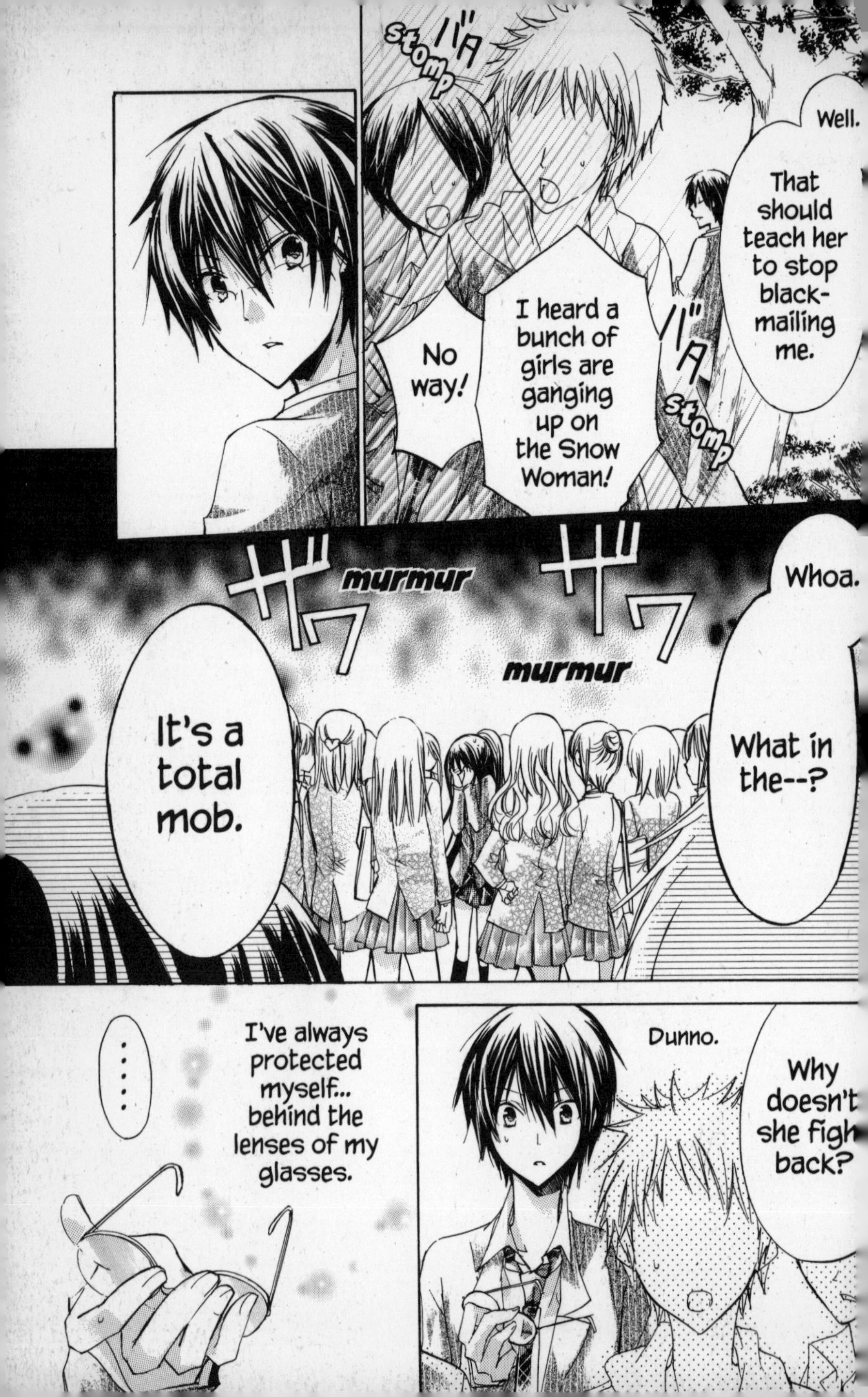
Well.
That should teach her to stop black-mailing me.
バタ
stomp
I heard a bunch of girls are ganging up on the Snow Woman!
No way!
バタ
stomp
Whoa.
What in the--?
ザワ
murmur
ザワ
murmur
It's a total mob.
Why doesn't she figh back?
Dunno.
I've always protected myself... behind the lenses of my glasses.
......

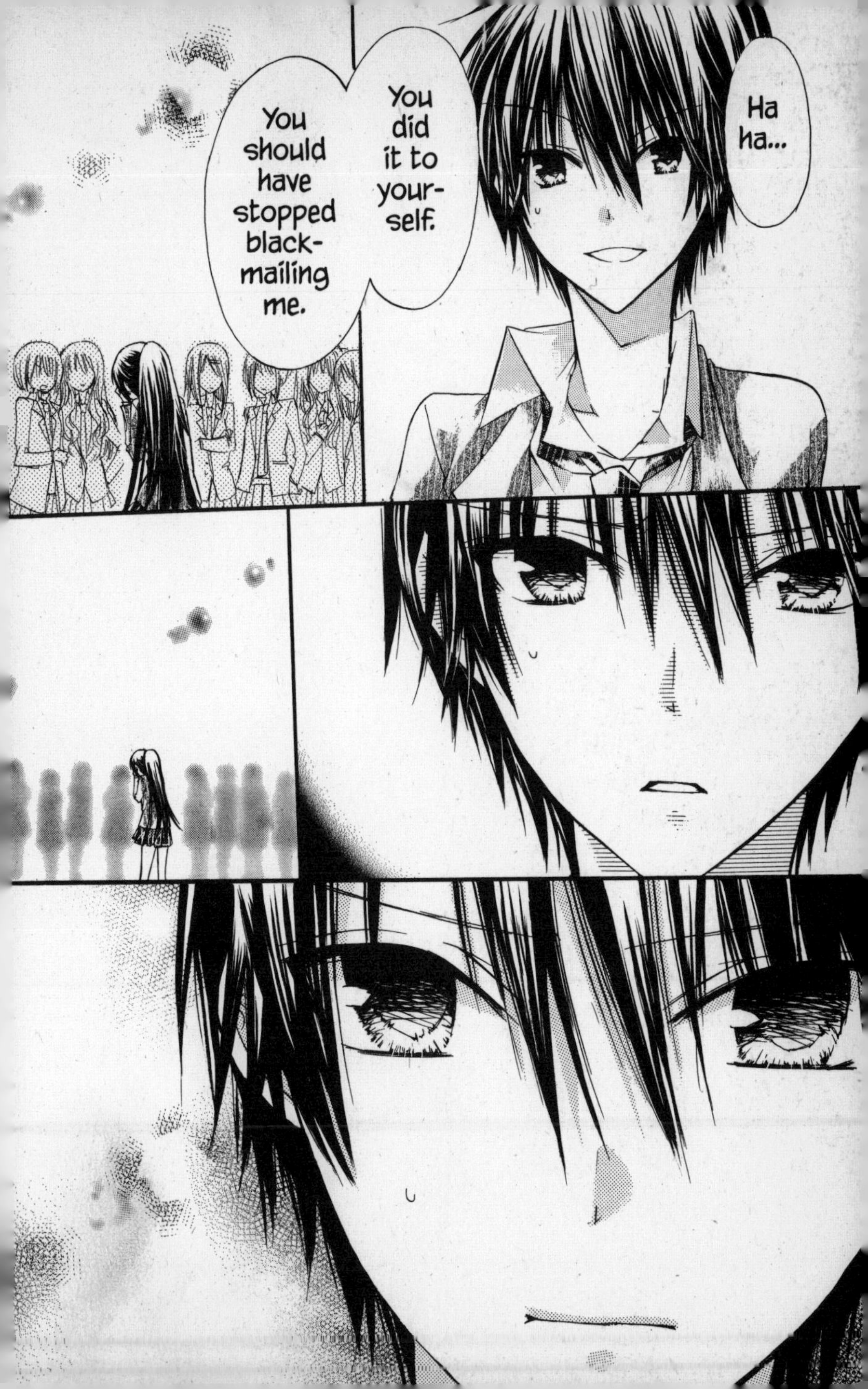
Ha ha...
You did it to your-self.
You should have stopped black-mailing me.

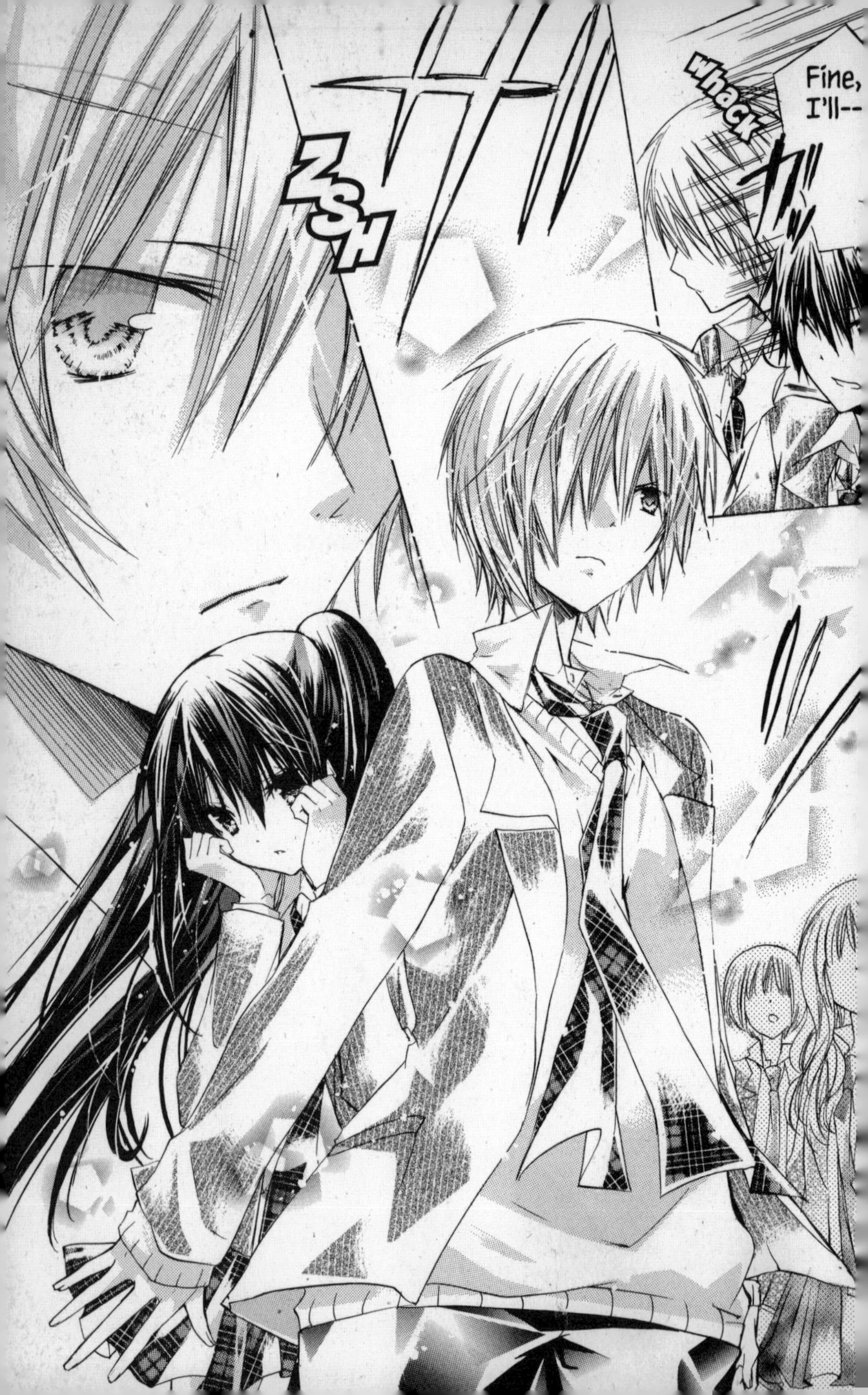
Fine, I'll--
whack
ZSH

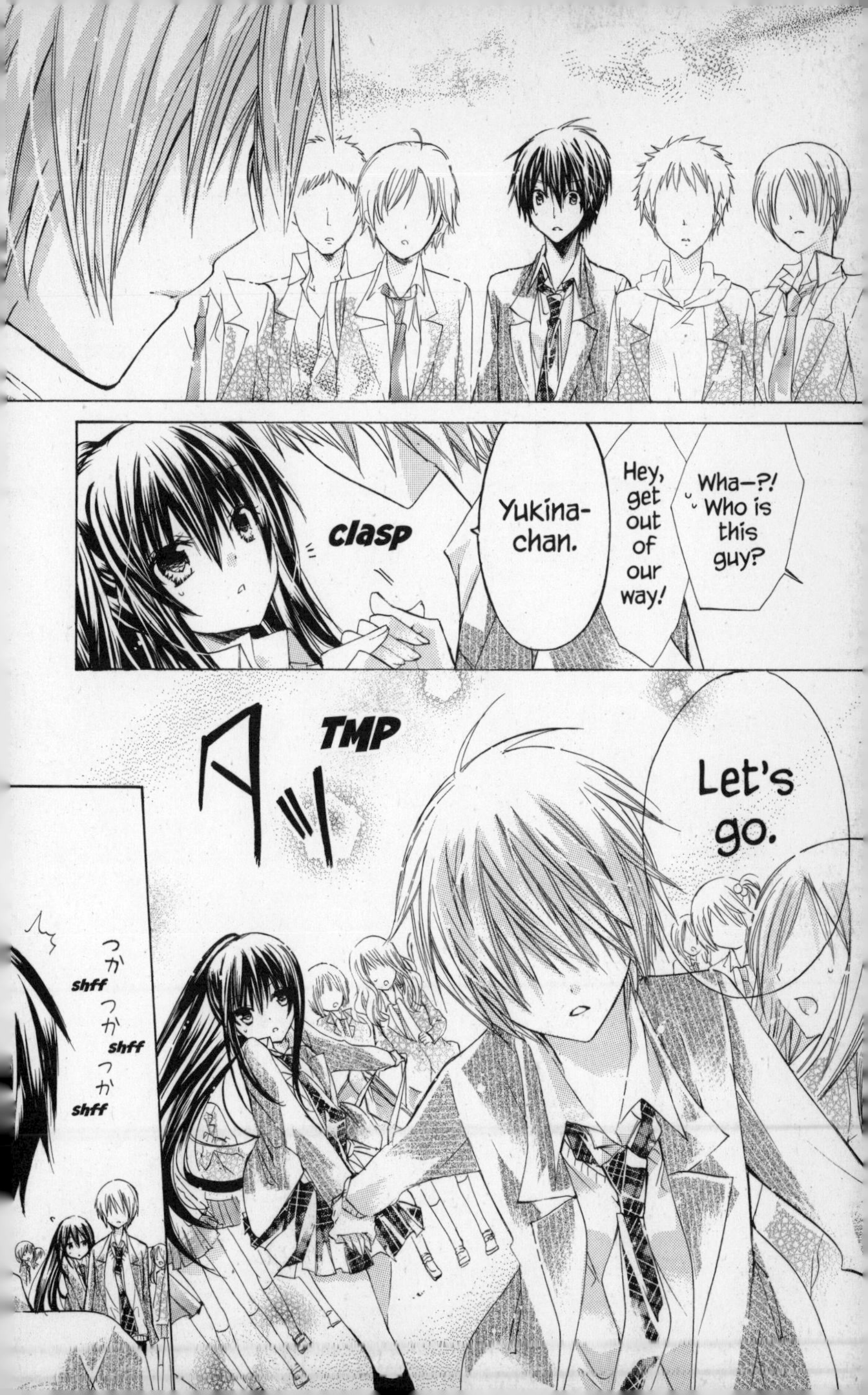
Wha—?! Who is this guy?
Hey, get out of our way!
Yukina-chan.
clasp
Let's go.
TMP
つか shff
つか shff
つか shff

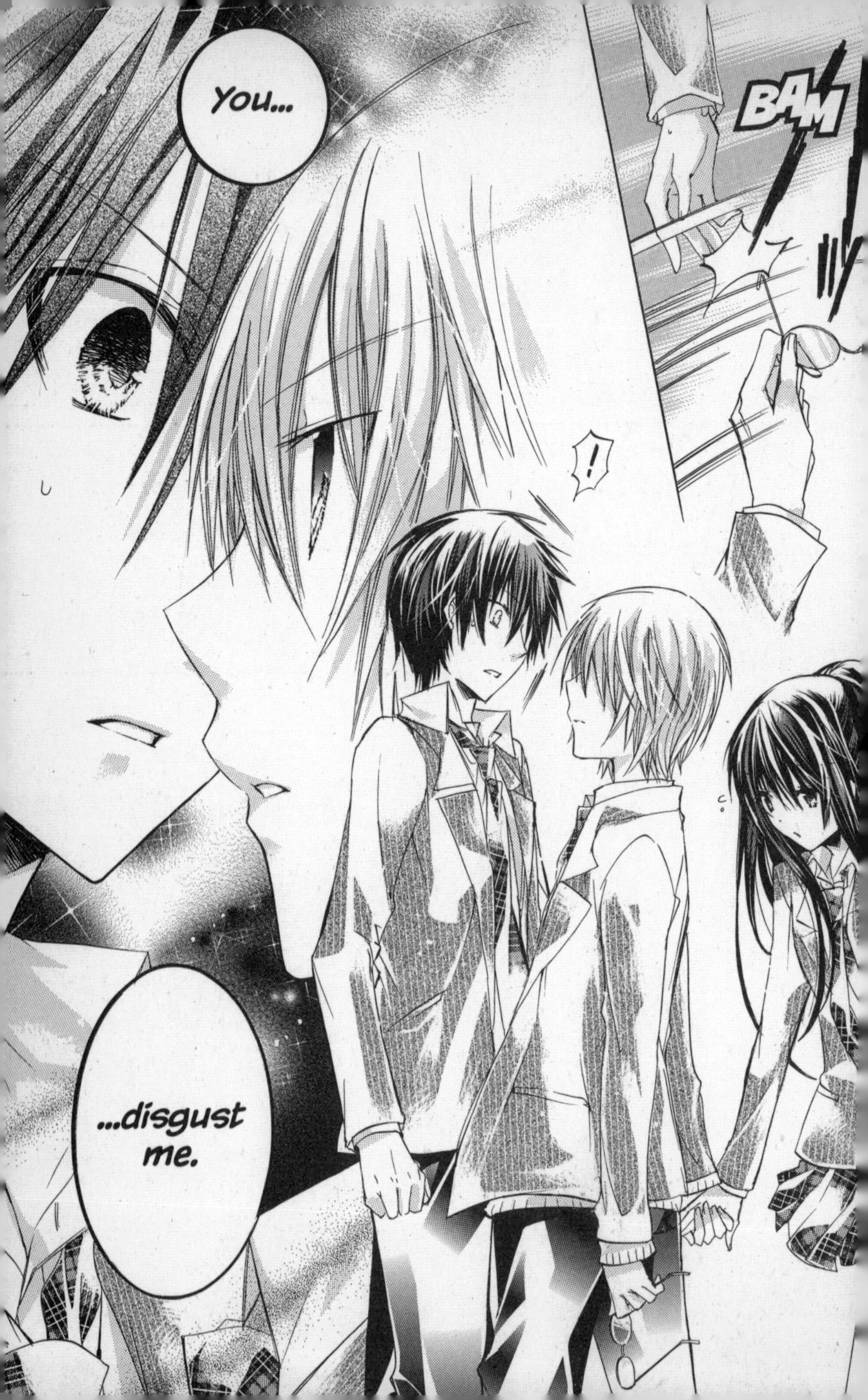
BAM
You...
!
...disgust me.

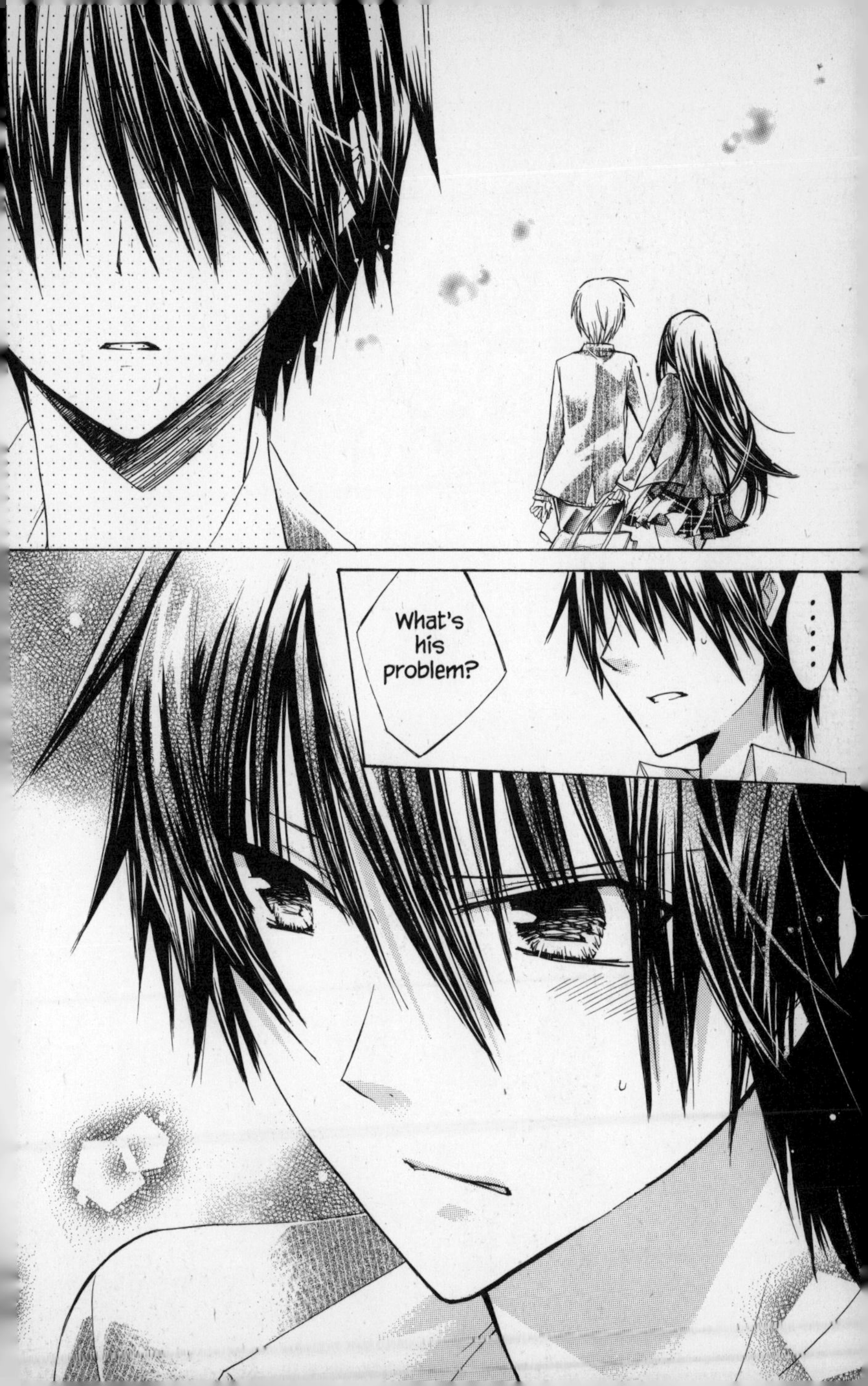
......
What's his problem?

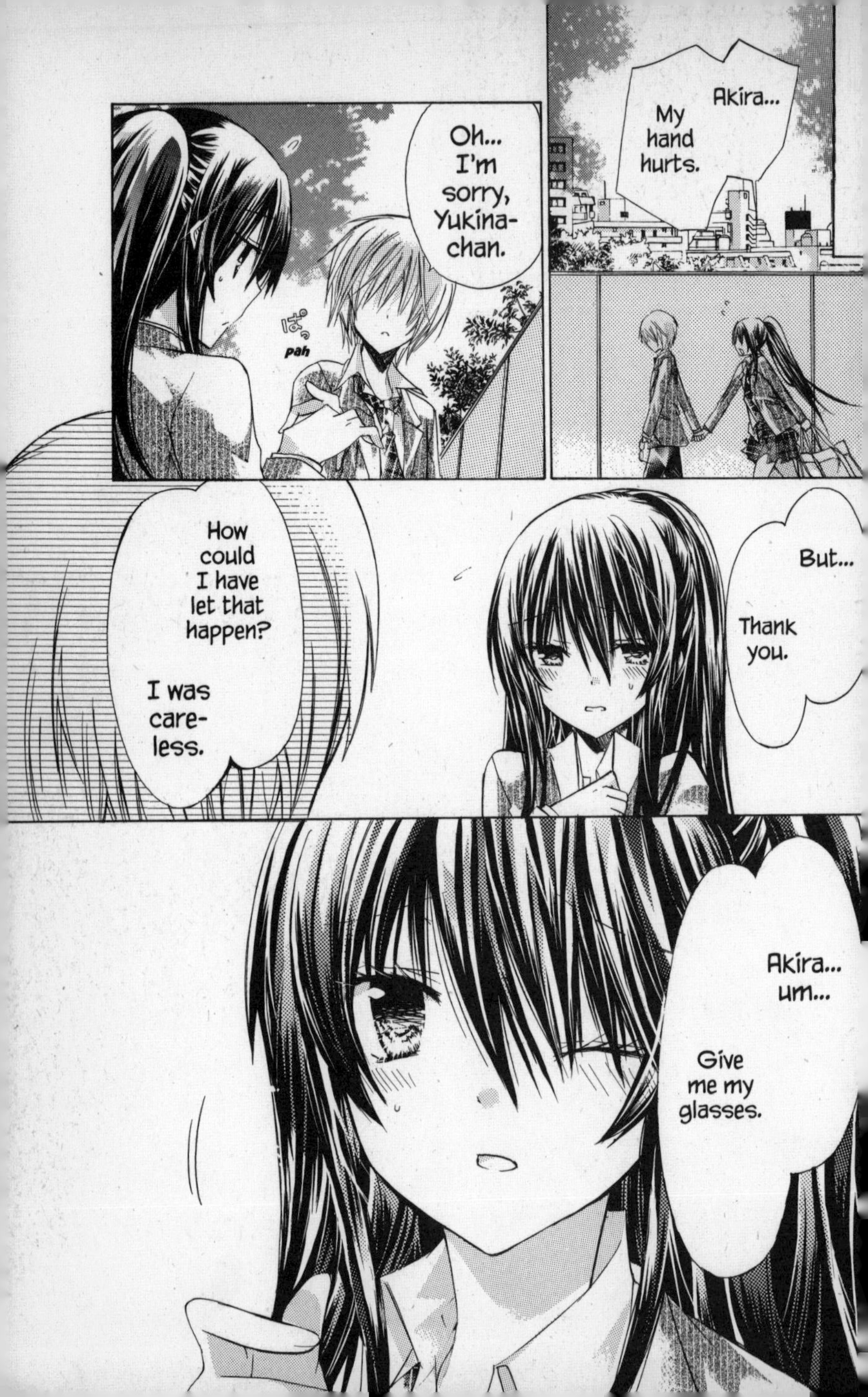
Akira... My hand hurts.
Oh... I'm sorry, Yukina-chan.
ぱっ
pah
But... Thank you.
How could I have let that happen? I was careless.
Akira... um... Give me my glasses.

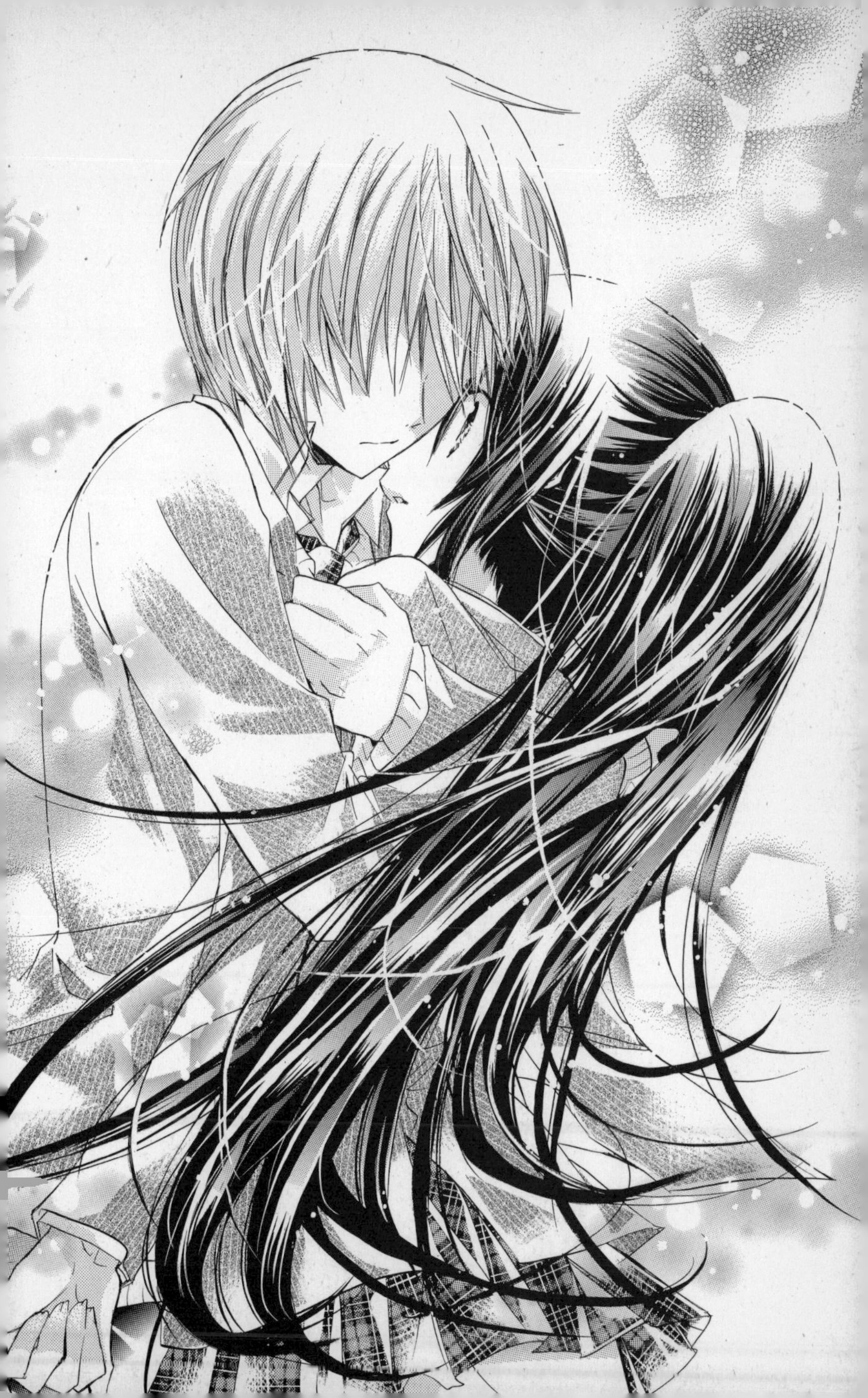

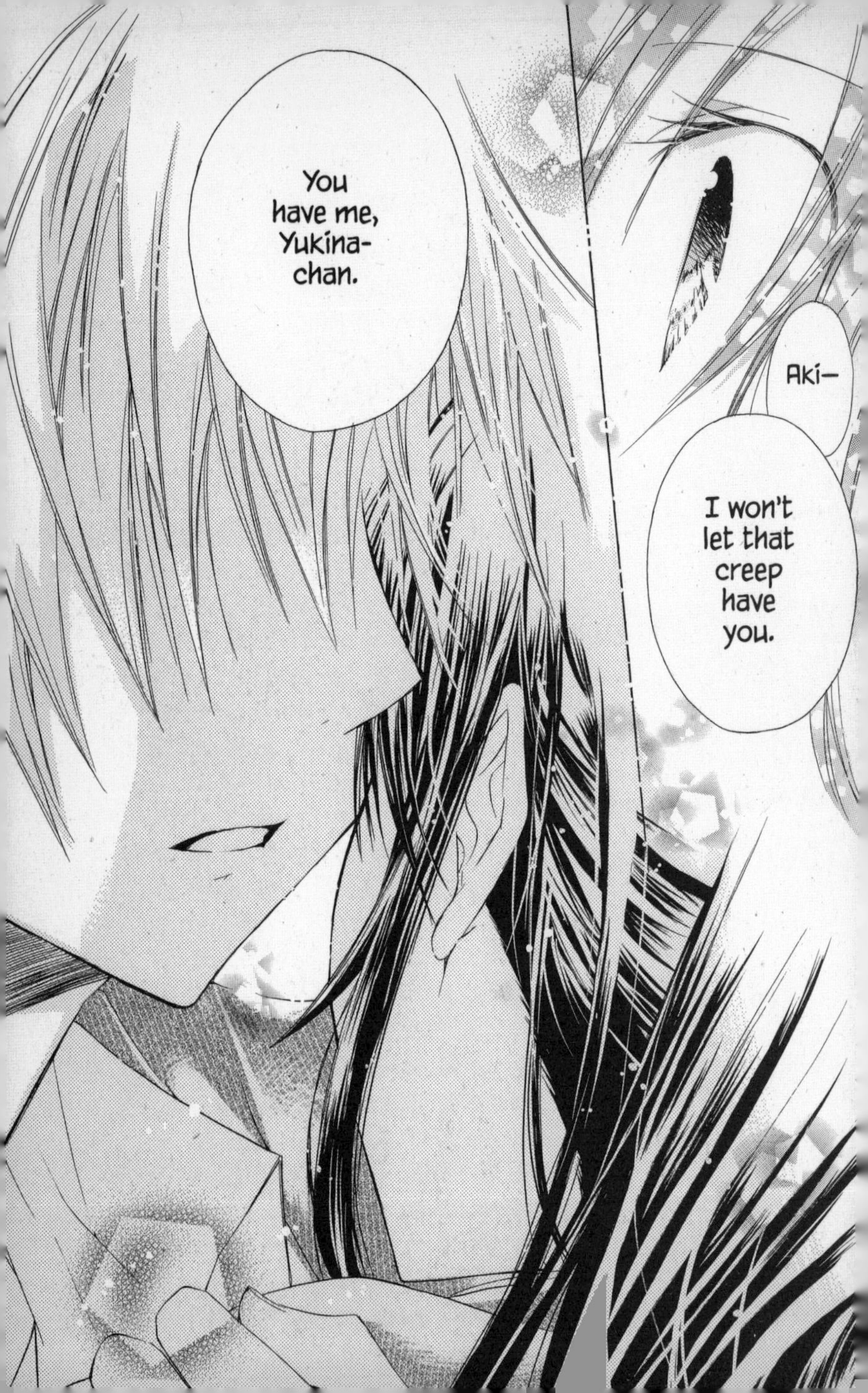
Aki—
I won't let that creep have you.
You have me, Yukina-chan.

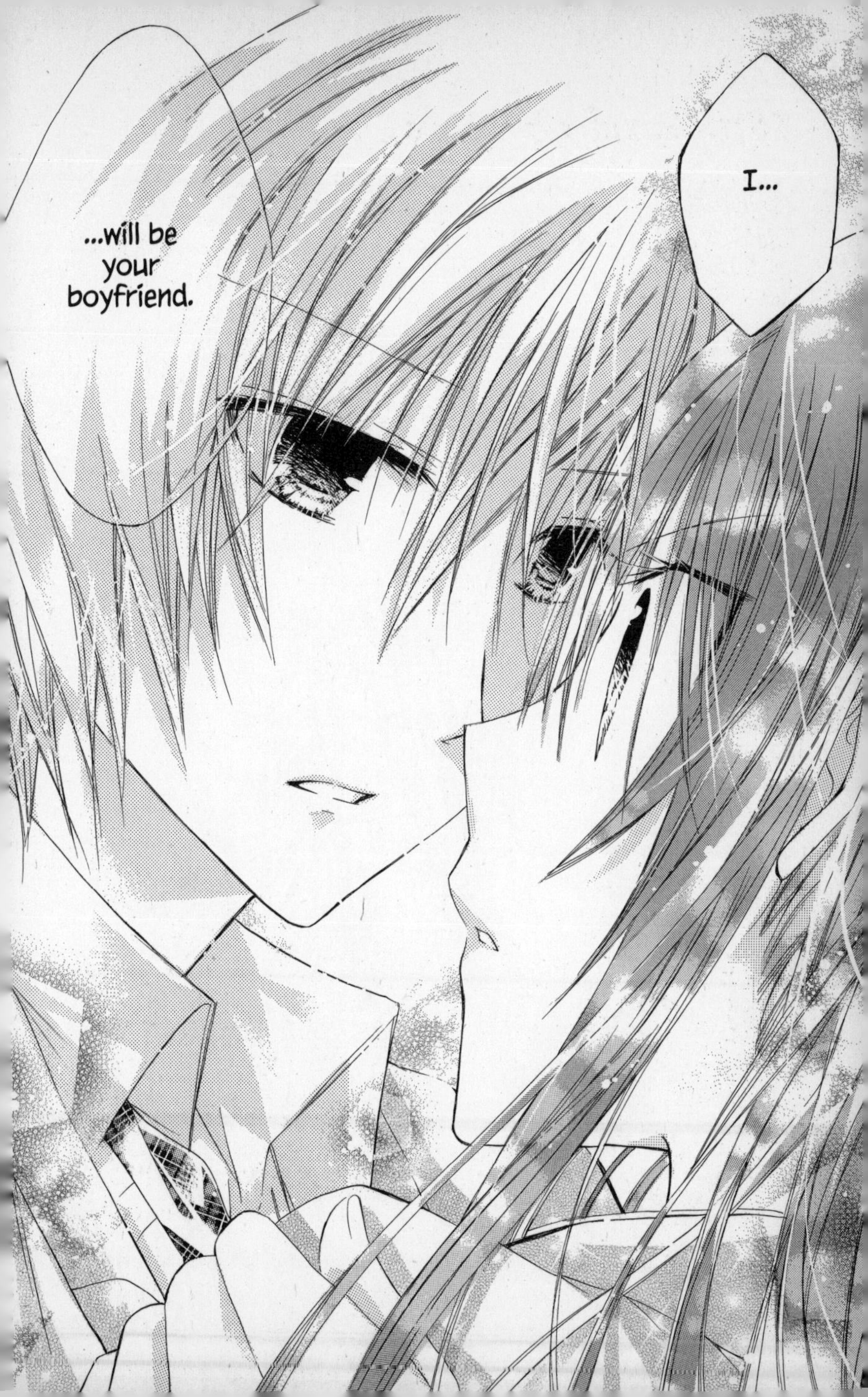
I...
...will be your boyfriend.

Missions of Love

**It is time for love.
Secret cell phone
novelist vs. the most
popular boy in school.
A mission of love for
absolute servitude.**

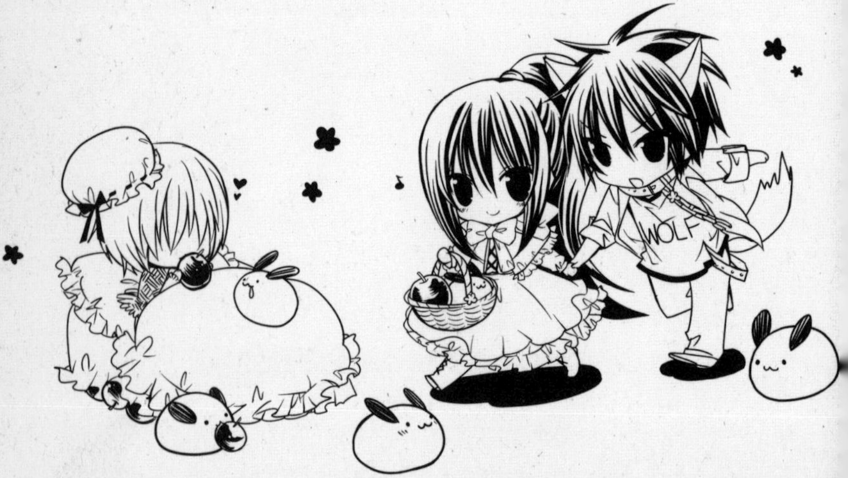
WOLF

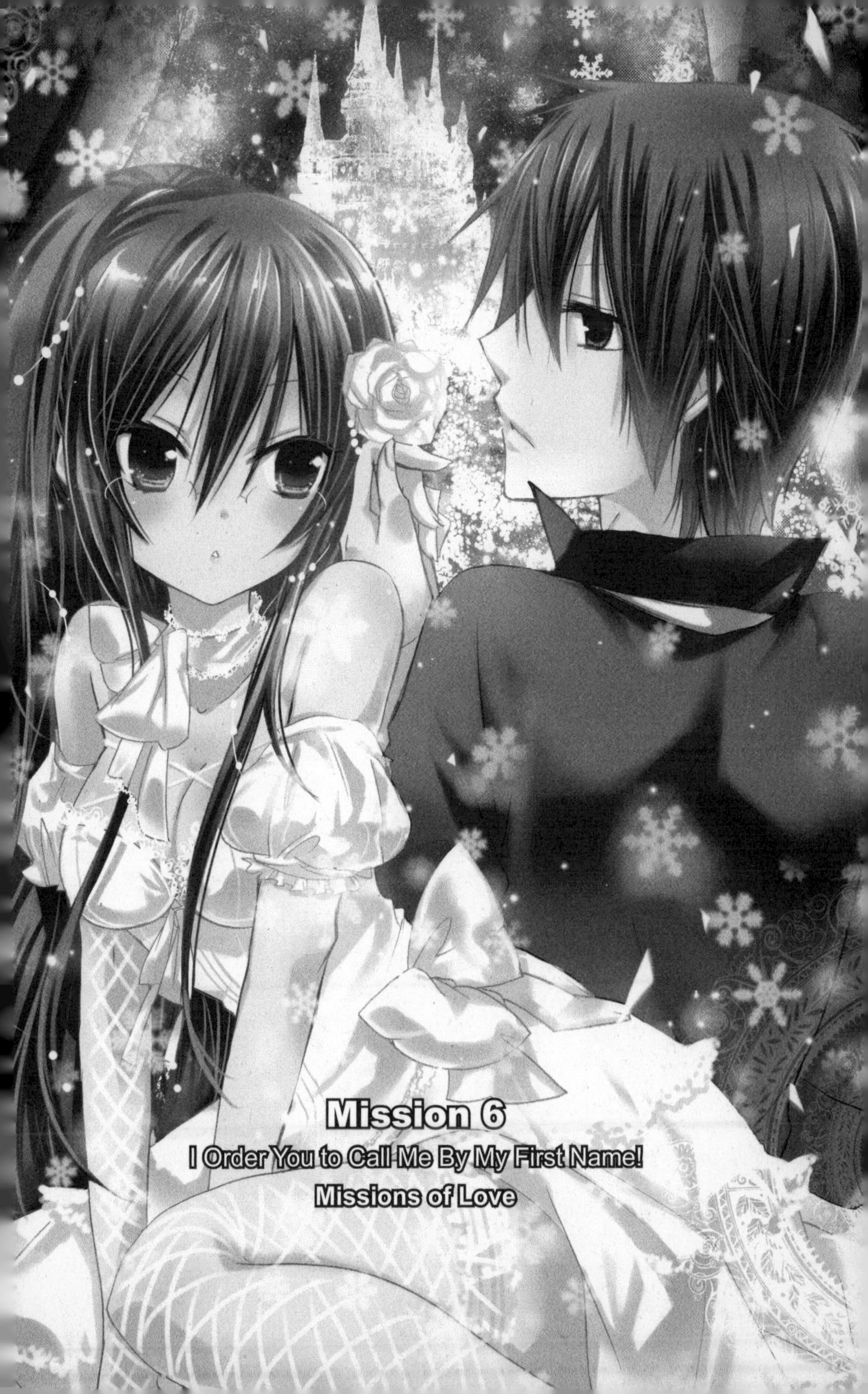
Mission 6
I Order You to Call Me By My First Name!
Missions of Love

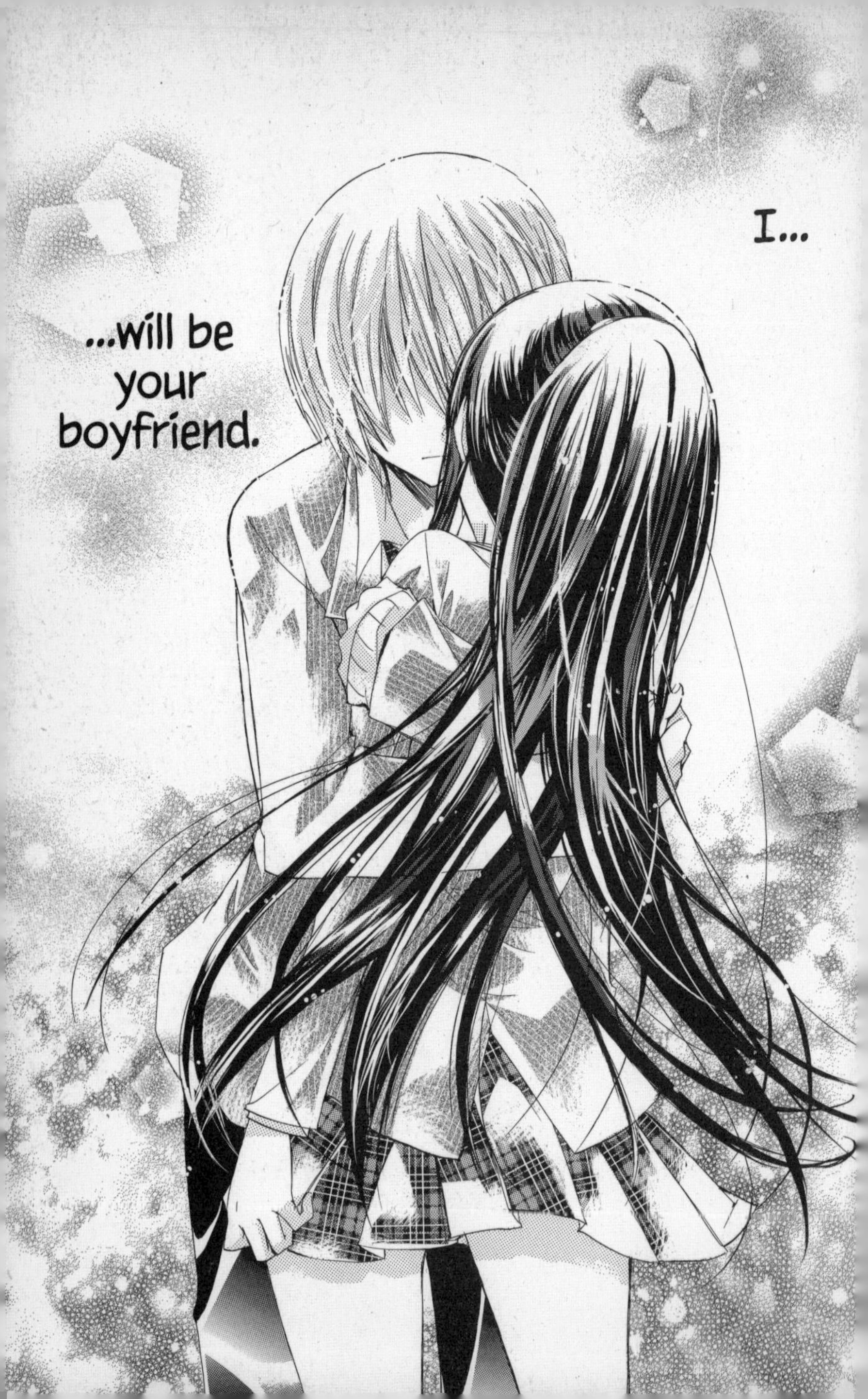
I...
...will be your boyfriend.

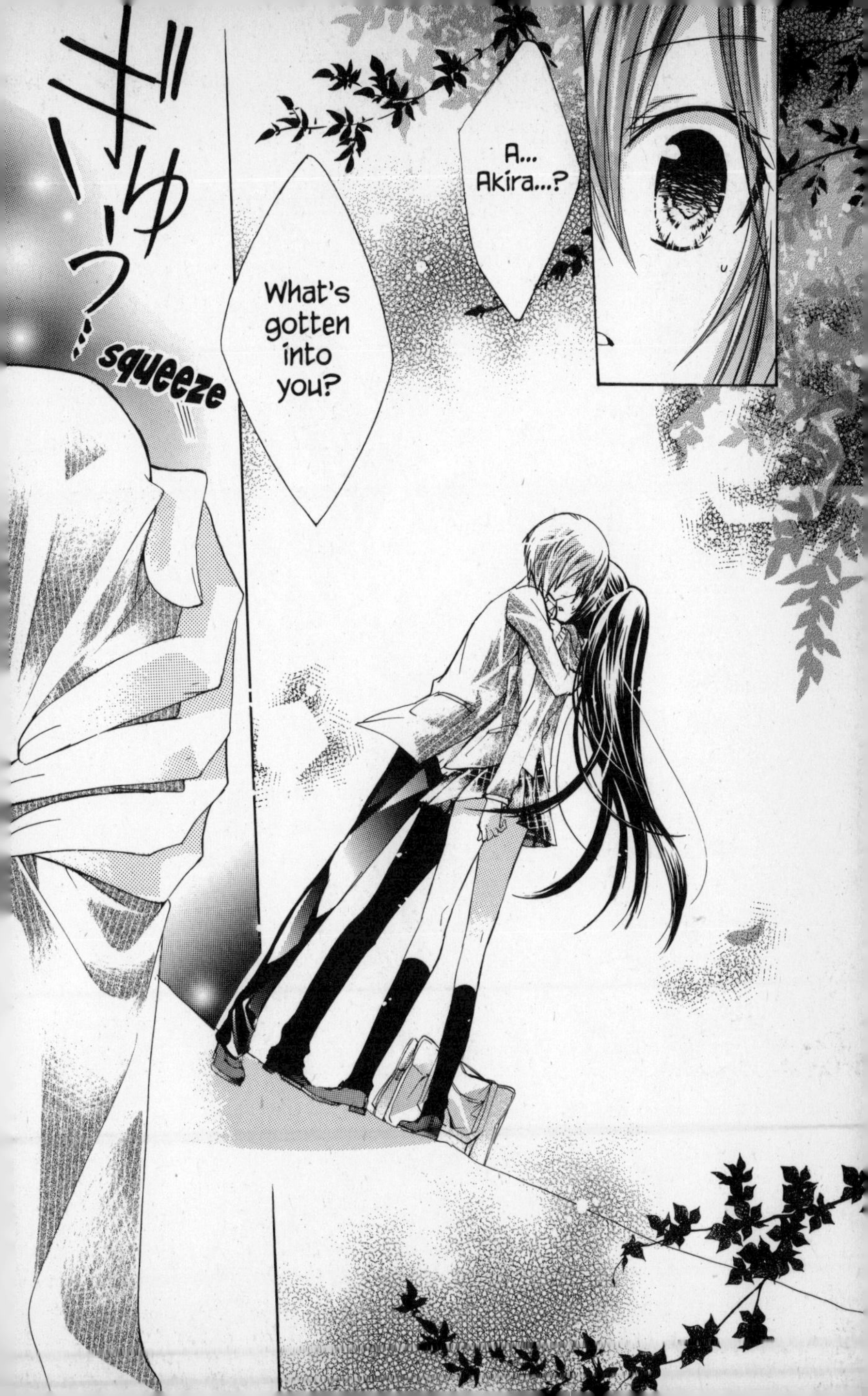
A... Akira...?
What's gotten into you?
ぎゅう…
squeeze

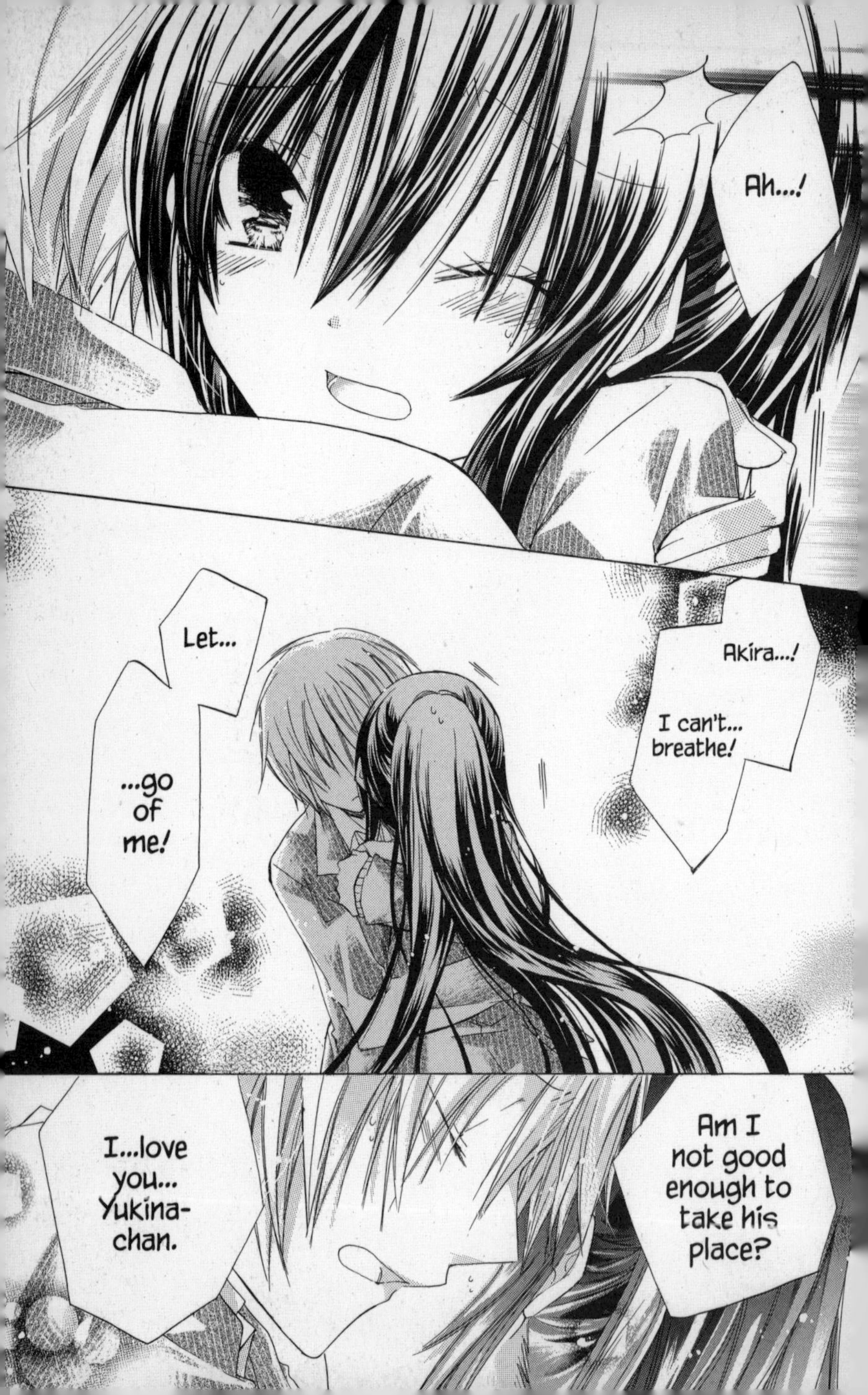
Ah...!
Akira...!
I can't... breathe!
Let...
...go of me!
Am I not good enough to take his place?
I...love you... Yukina-chan.

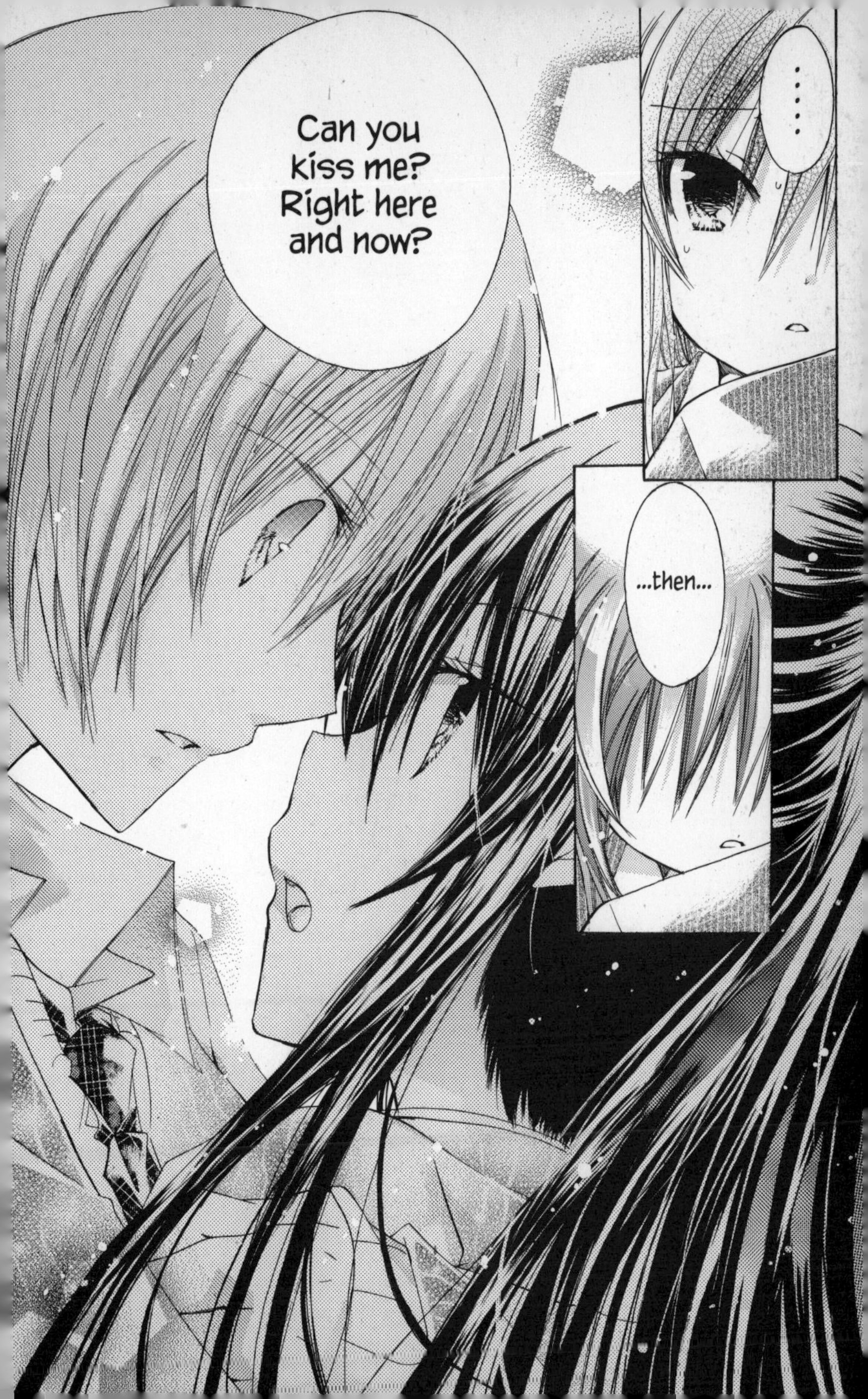
.....
...then...
Can you kiss me? Right here and now?

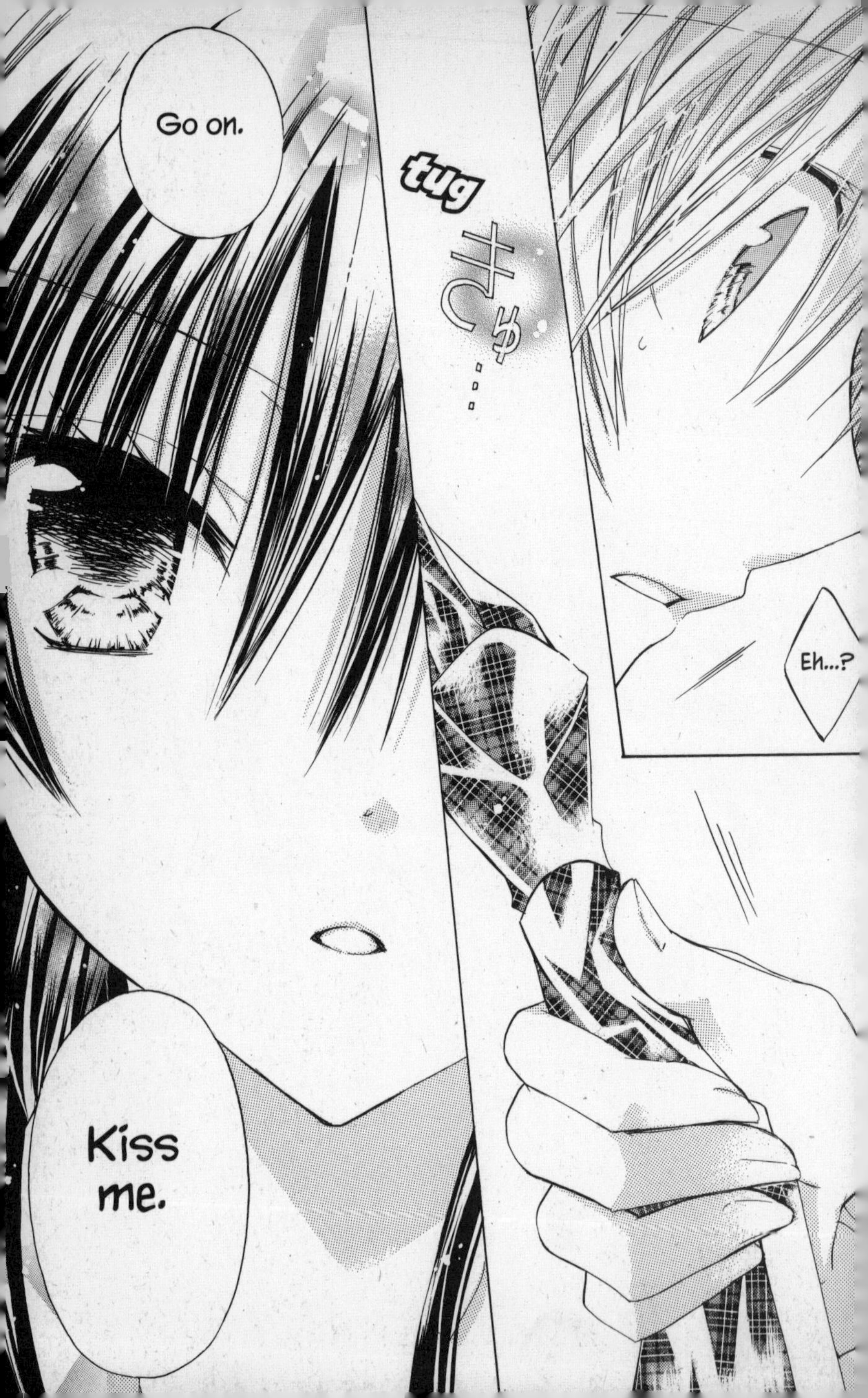

Eh...?
tug
きゅ...
Go on.
Kiss me.

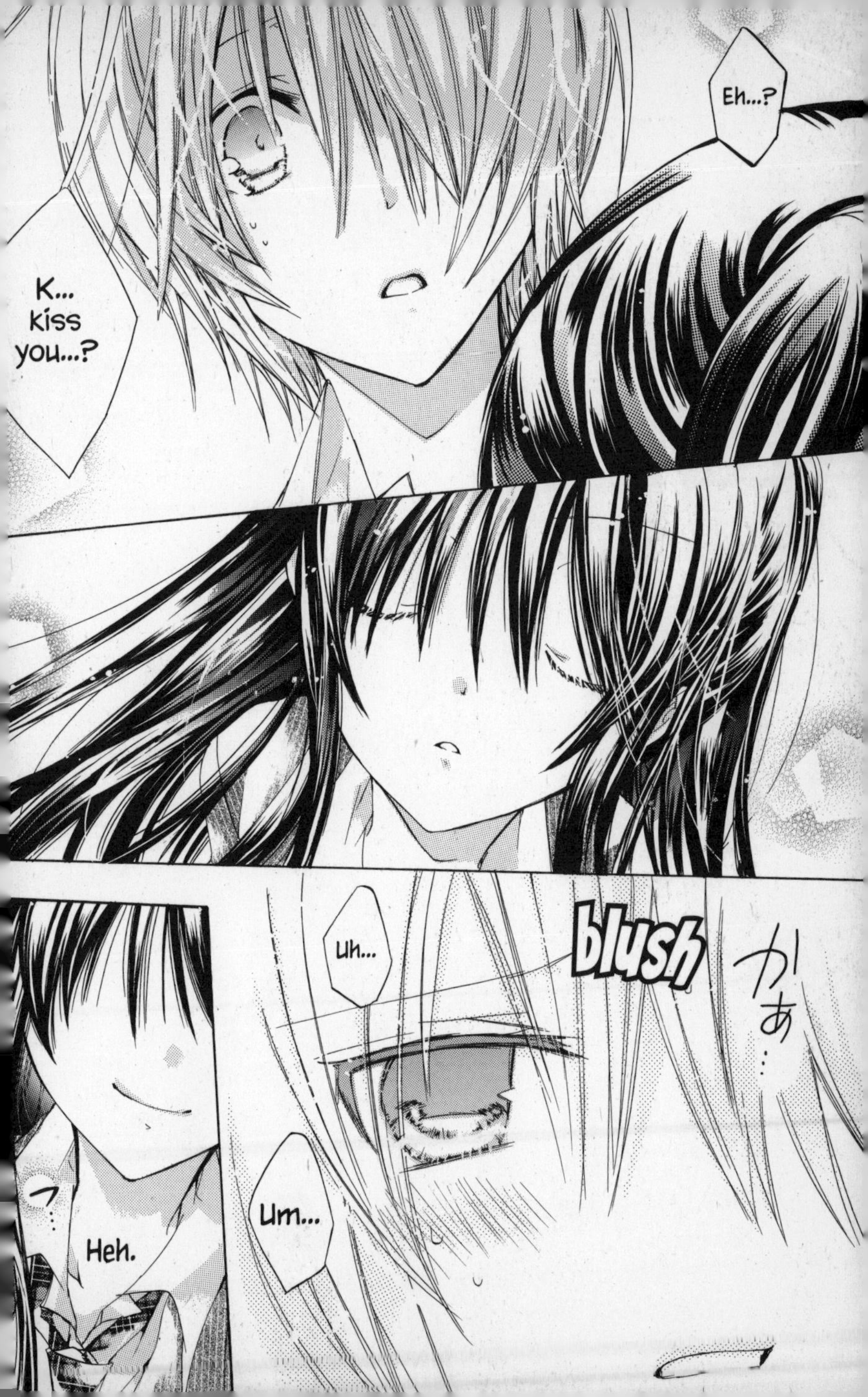
Eh...?
K... kiss you...?
blush
かぁ…
Uh...
Um...
Heh.

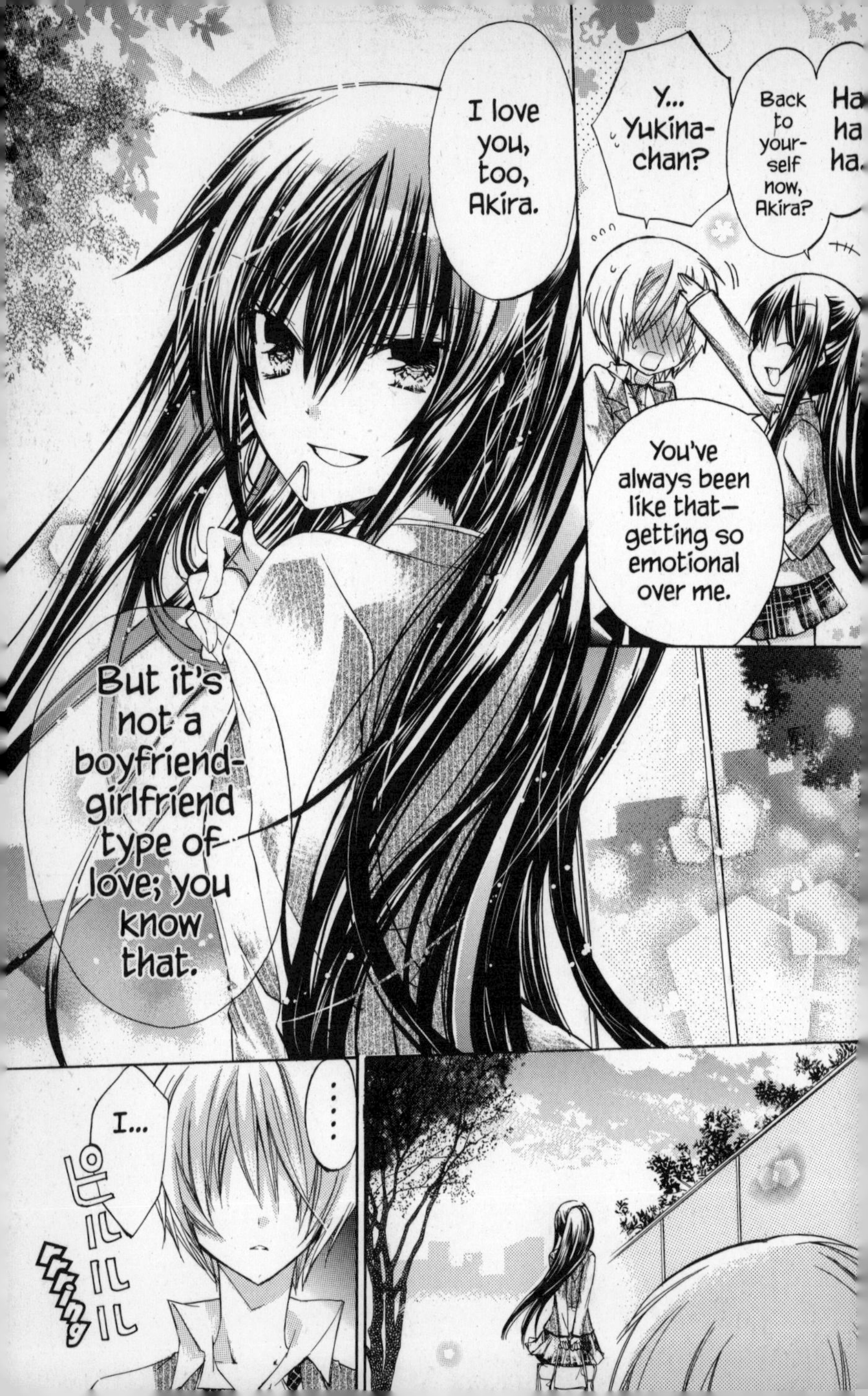
Ha ha ha.
Back to your-self now, Akira?
Y... Yukina-chan?
You've always been like that—getting so emotional over me.
I love you, too, Akira.
But it's not a boyfriend-girlfriend type of love; you know that.
....
I...
rrring

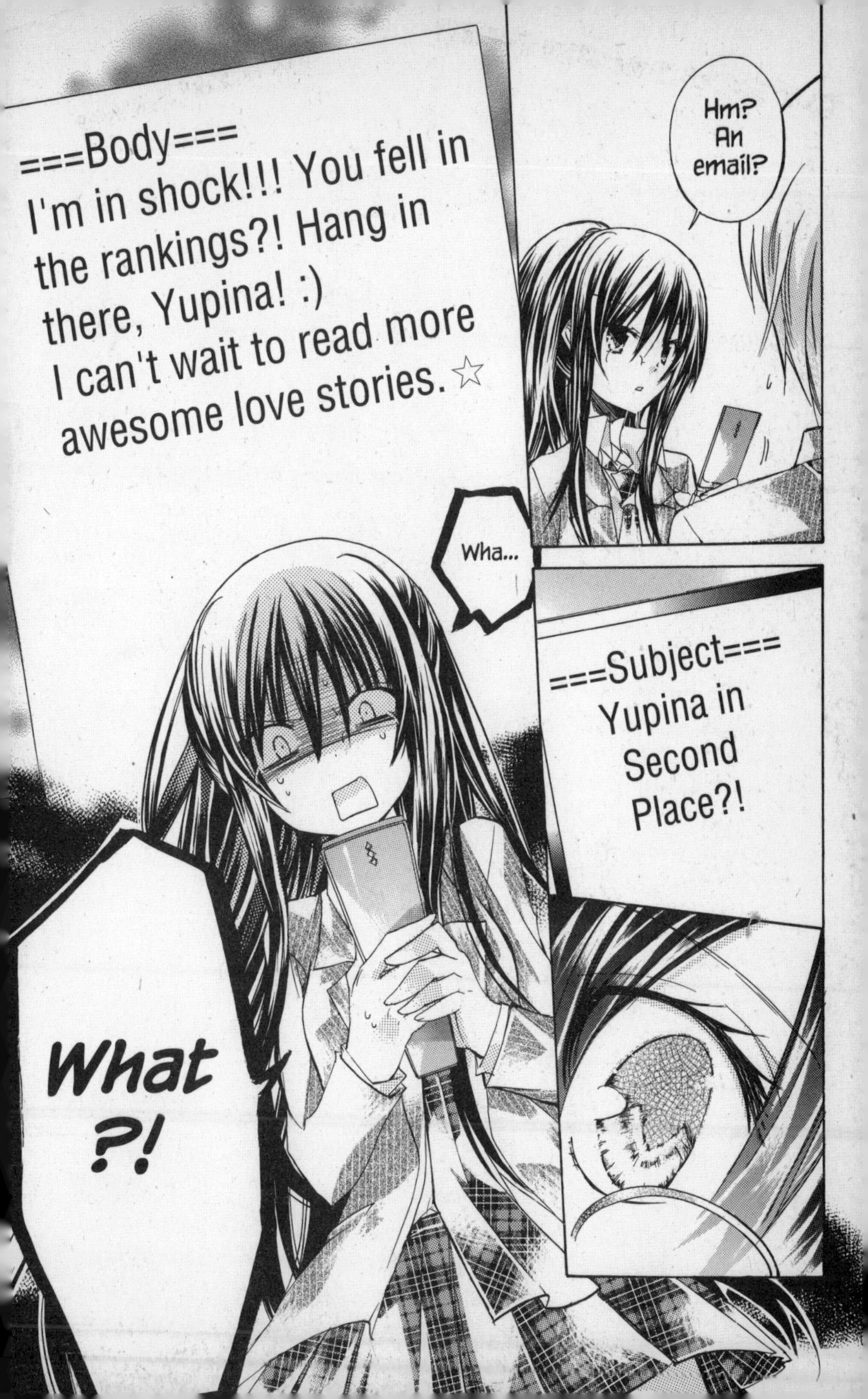
Hm? An email?
===Subject===
Yupina in Second Place?!
===Body===
I'm in shock!!! You fell in the rankings?! Hang in there, Yupina! :)
I can't wait to read more awesome love stories. ☆
Wha...
What?!

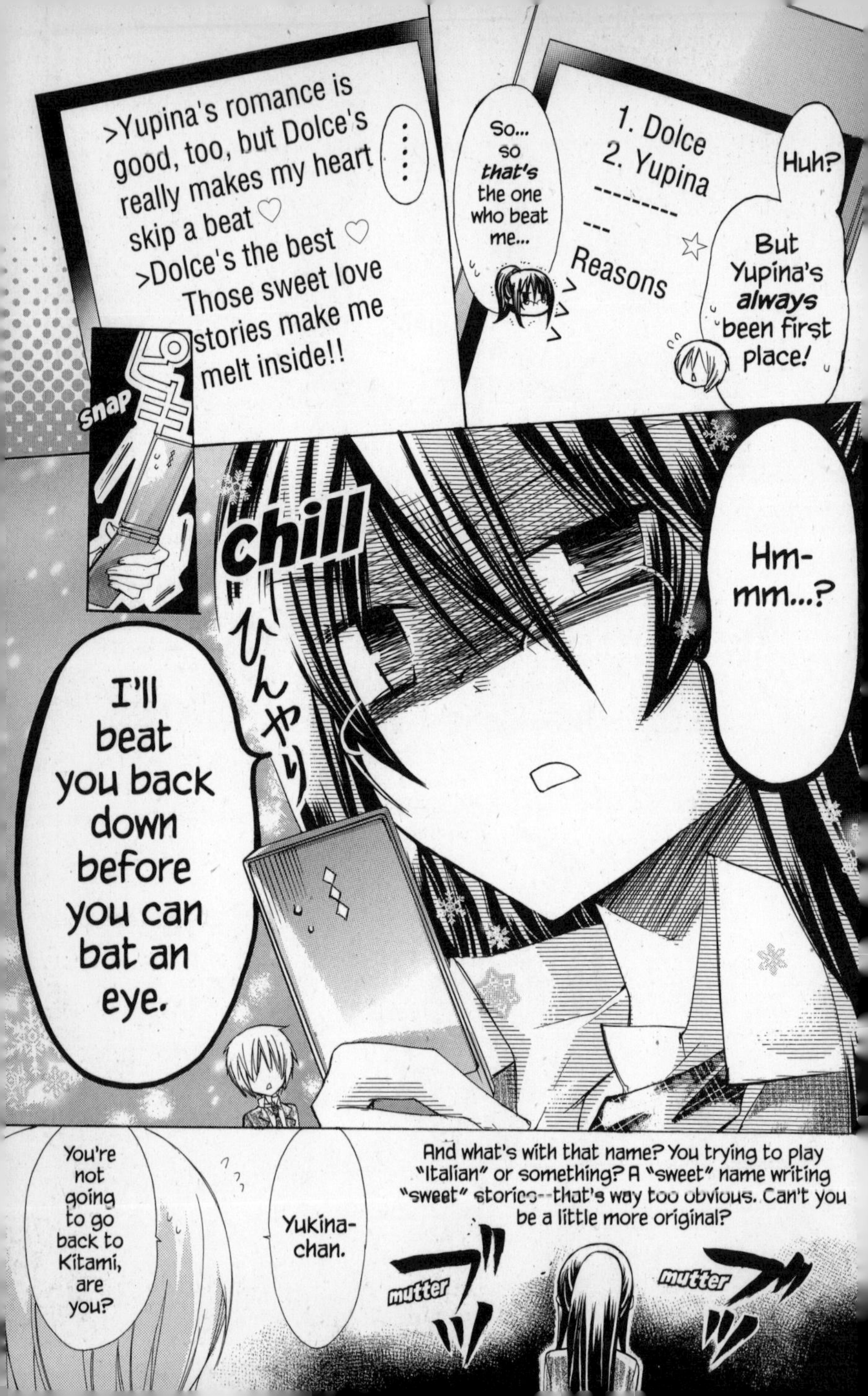
Huh?
1. Dolce
2. Yupina

Reasons
But Yupina's *always* been first place!
So... so *that's* the one who beat me...
......
>Yupina's romance is good, too, but Dolce's really makes my heart skip a beat ♡
>Dolce's the best ♡ Those sweet love stories make me melt inside!!
Snap
Hm-mm...?
chill
ひんやり
I'll beat you back down before you can bat an eye.
And what's with that name? You trying to play "Italian" or something? A "sweet" name writing "sweet" stories--that's way too obvious. Can't you be a little more original?
mutter
mutter
Yukina-chan.
You're not going to go back to Kitami, are you?

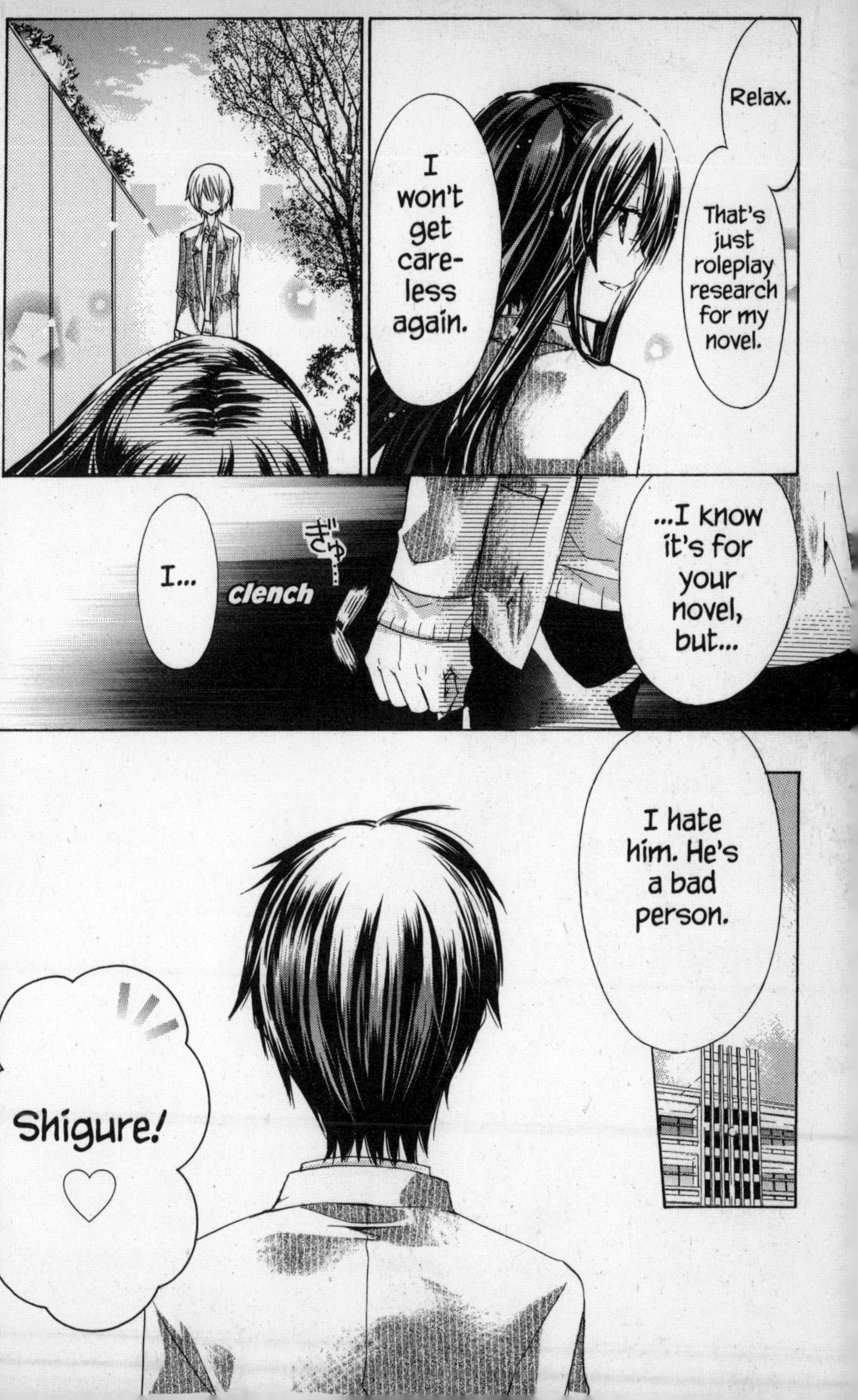
Relax.
That's just roleplay research for my novel.
I won't get care-less again.
...I know it's for your novel, but...
ぎゅ...
clench
I...
I hate him. He's a bad person.
Shigure! ♡

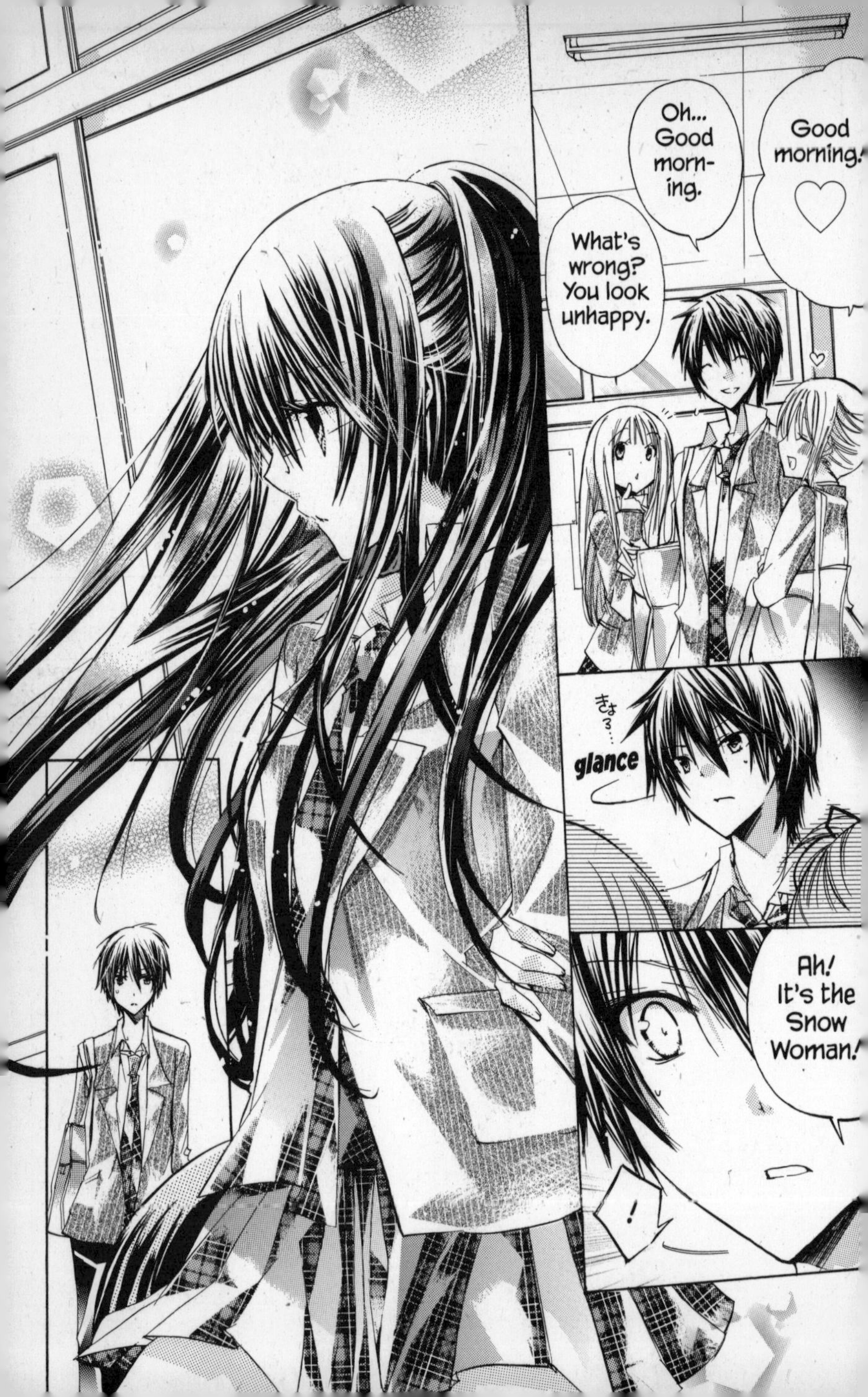
Good morning! ♡
Oh... Good morn-ing.
What's wrong? You look unhappy.
きょろ...
glance
Ah! It's the Snow Woman!
!

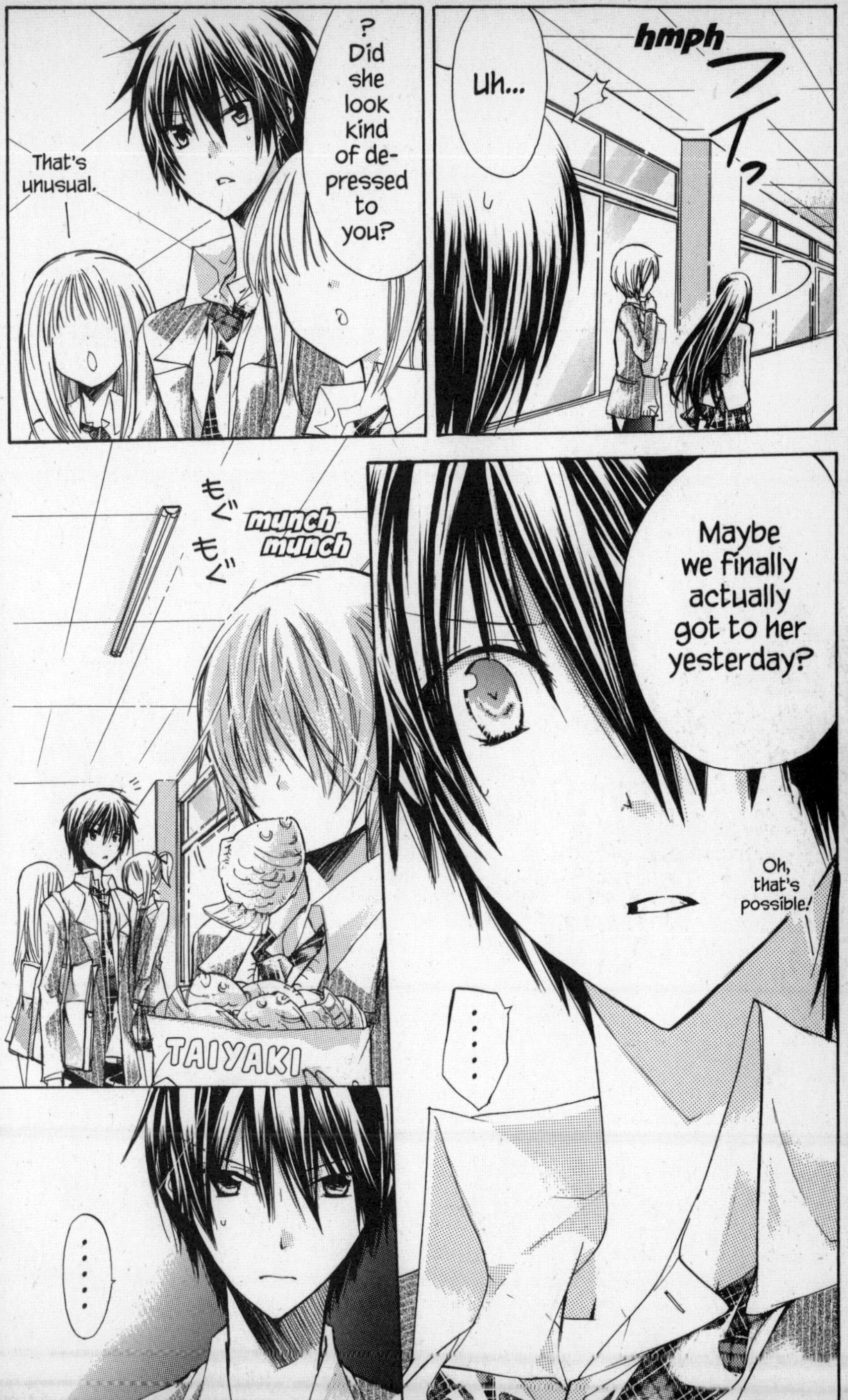
hmph
フイッ
Uh...
? Did she look kind of de-pressed to you?
That's unusual.
Maybe we finally actually got to her yesterday?
Oh, that's possible!
.....
もぐもぐ
munch munch
TAIYAKI
.....

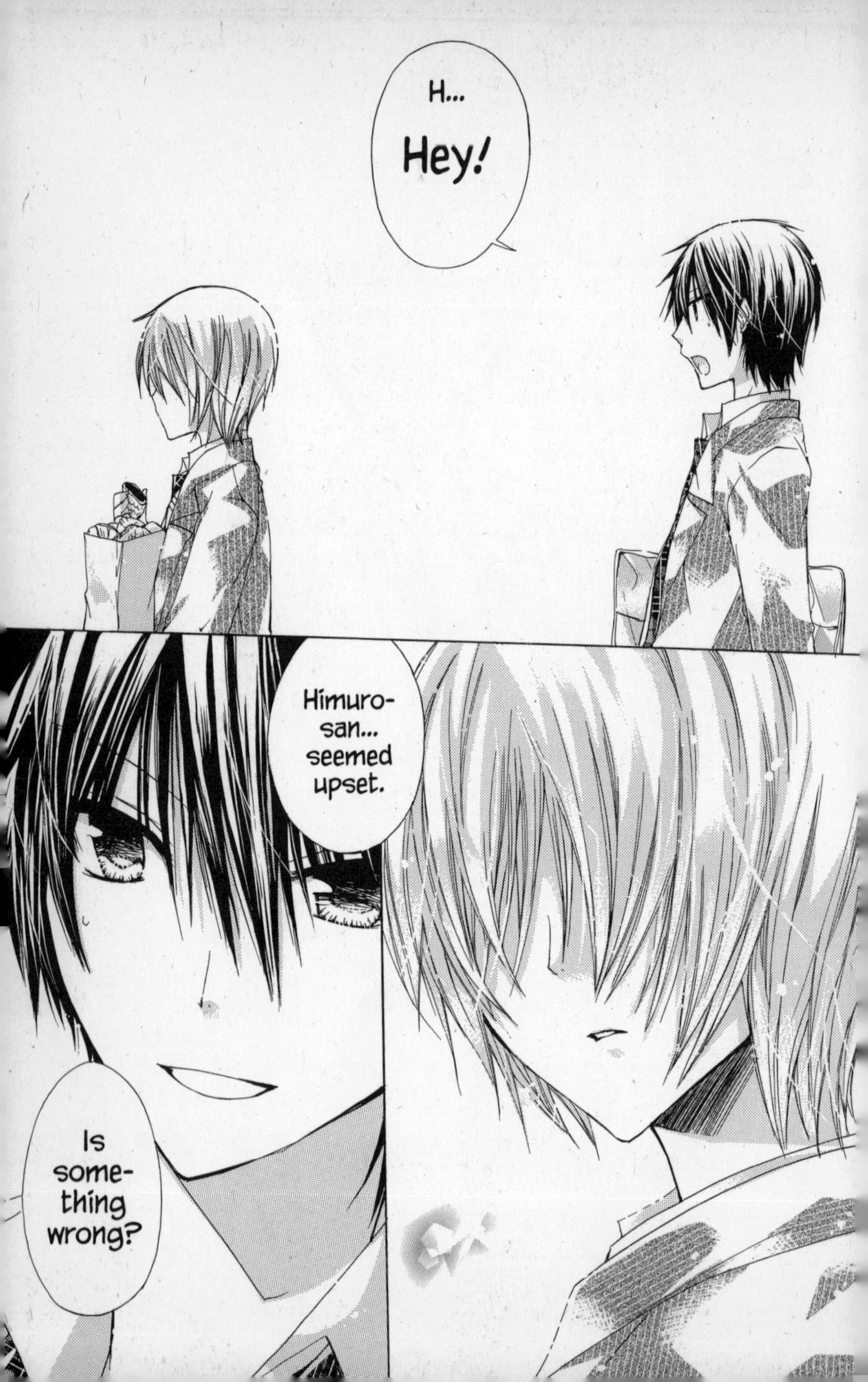
H... Hey!
Himuro-san... seemed upset.
Is something wrong?

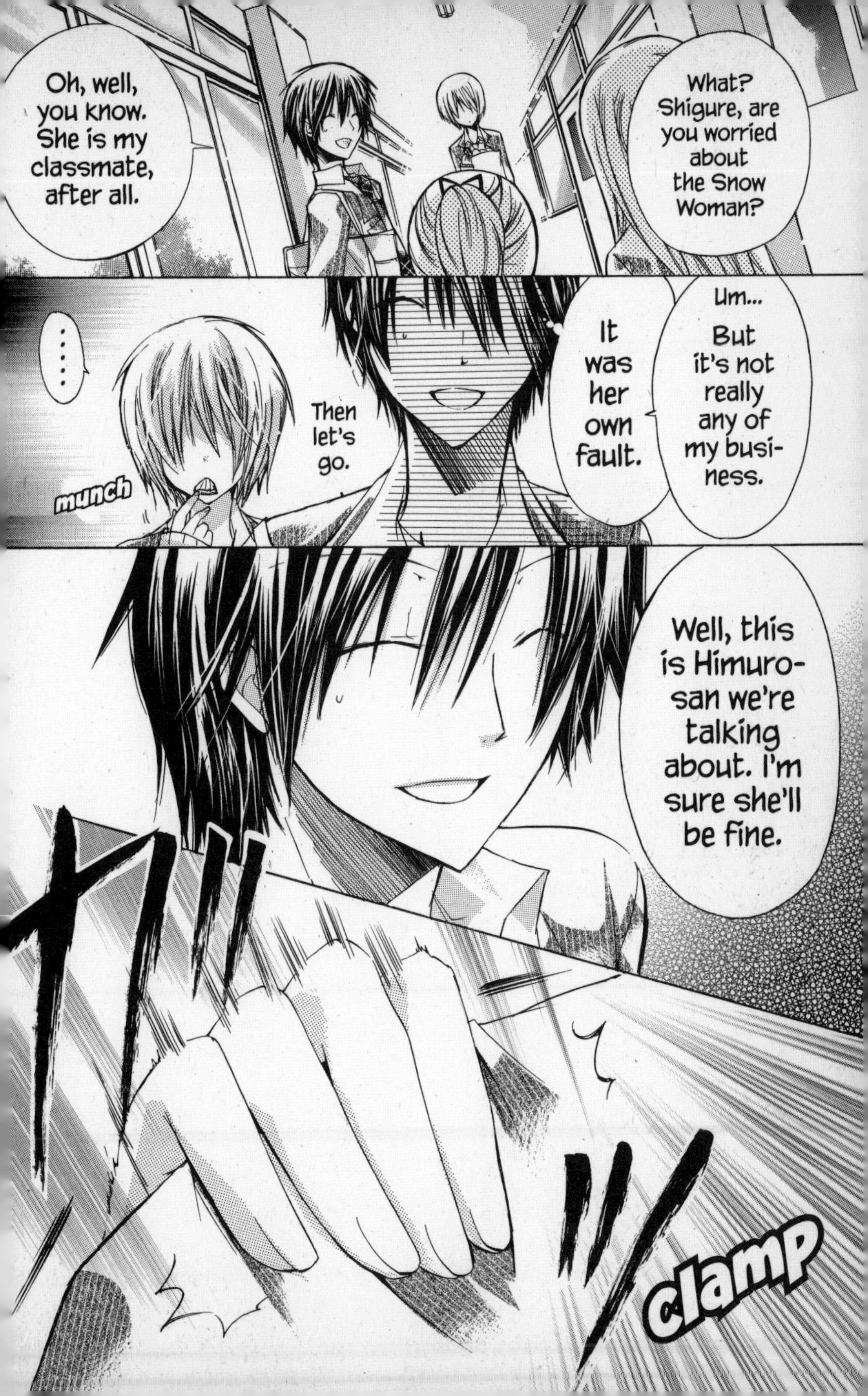
What? Shigure, are you worried about the Snow Woman?
Oh, well, you know. She is my classmate, after all.
Um... But it's not really any of my business.
It was her own fault.
Then let's go.
......
munch
Well, this is Himuro-san we're talking about. I'm sure she'll be fine.
clamp

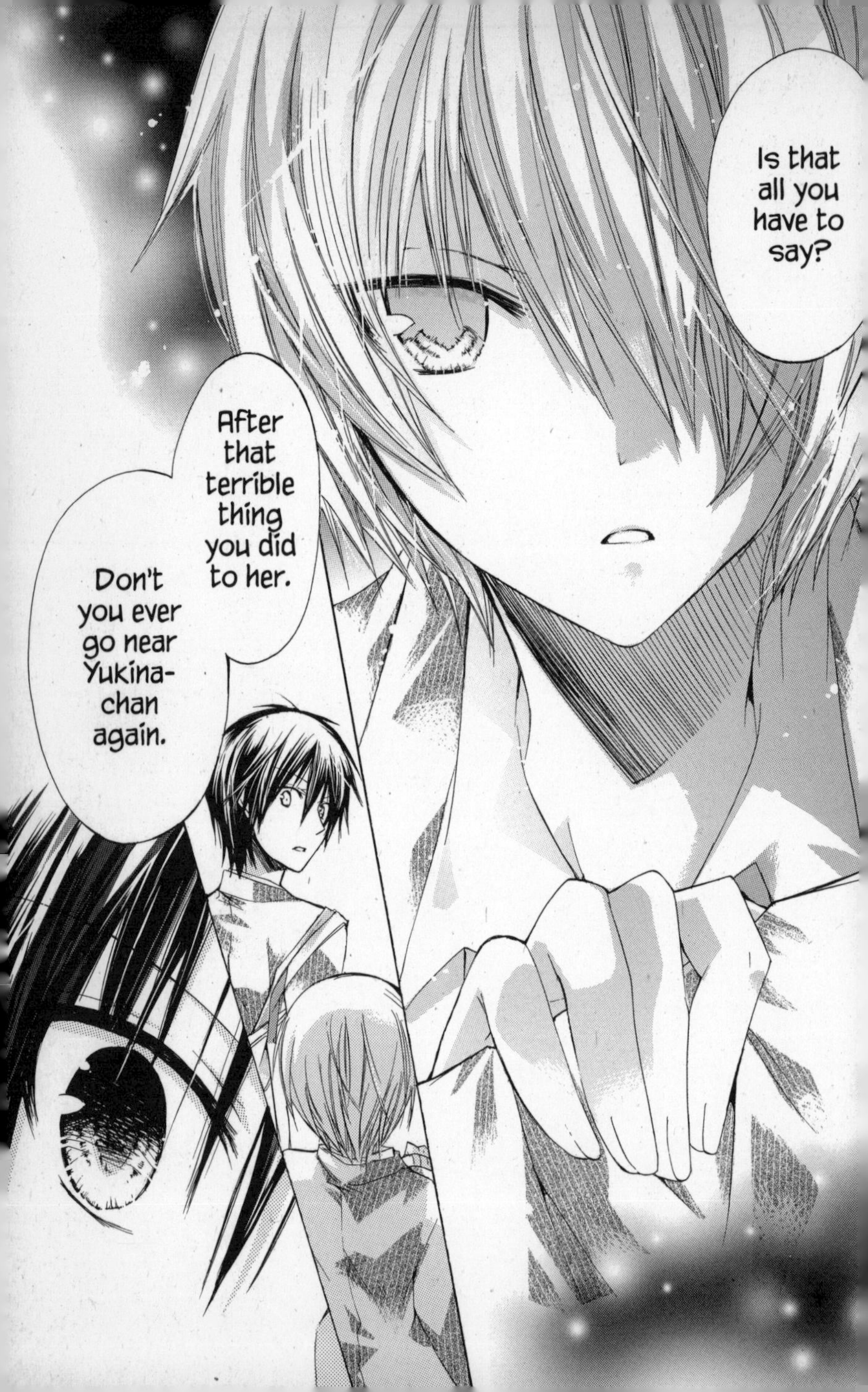
Is that all you have to say?
After that terrible thing you did to her.
Don't you ever go near Yukina-chan again.

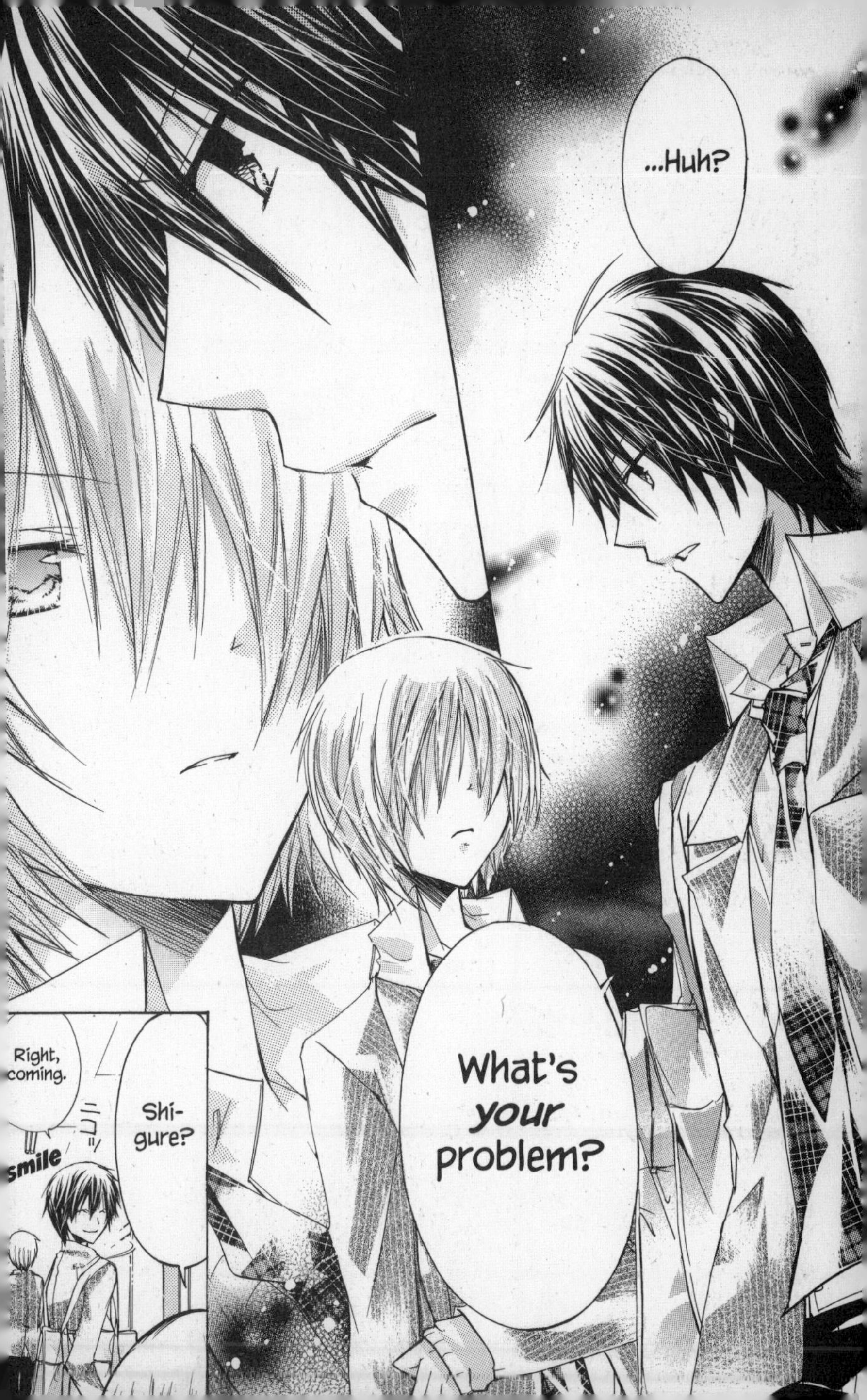
...Huh?
What's *your* problem?
Shi-gure?
Right, coming.
ニコッ
smile

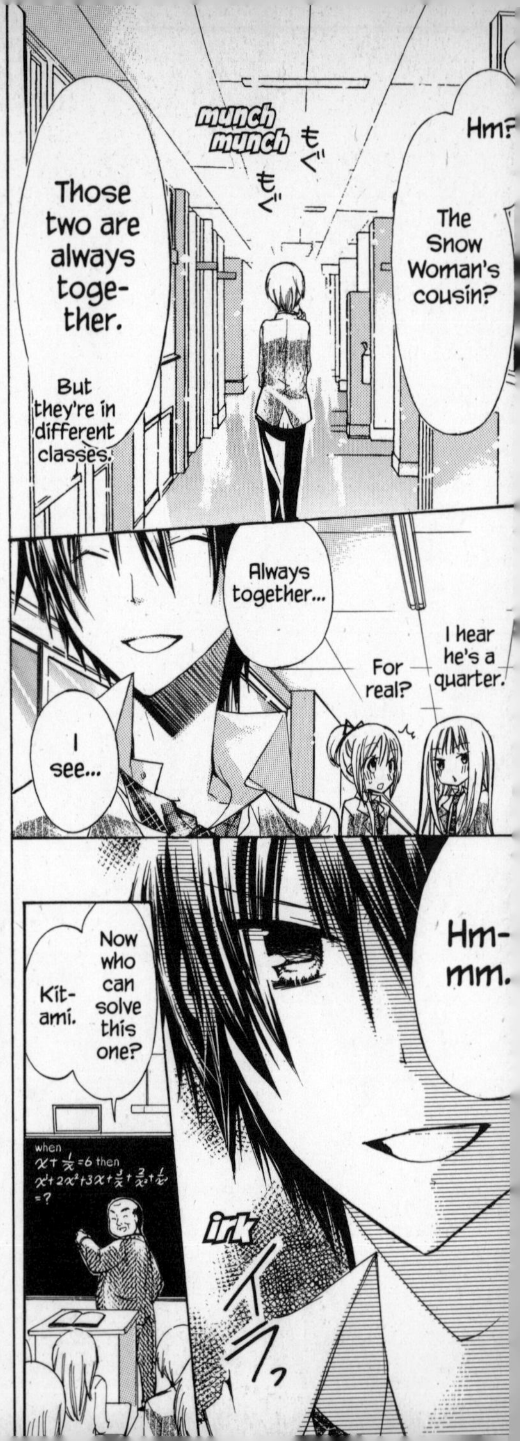
Hm?
The Snow Woman's cousin?
munch munch
もぐもぐ
Those two are always toge-ther.
But they're in different classes.
I hear he's a quarter.
For real?
Always together...
I see...
Hm-mm.
Now who can solve this one?
Kit-ami.
when
$x+\frac{1}{x}=6$ then
$x^3+2x^2+3x+\frac{3}{x}+\frac{2}{x^2}+\frac{1}{x^3}$
$=?$
irk

Snow Yukina (2)

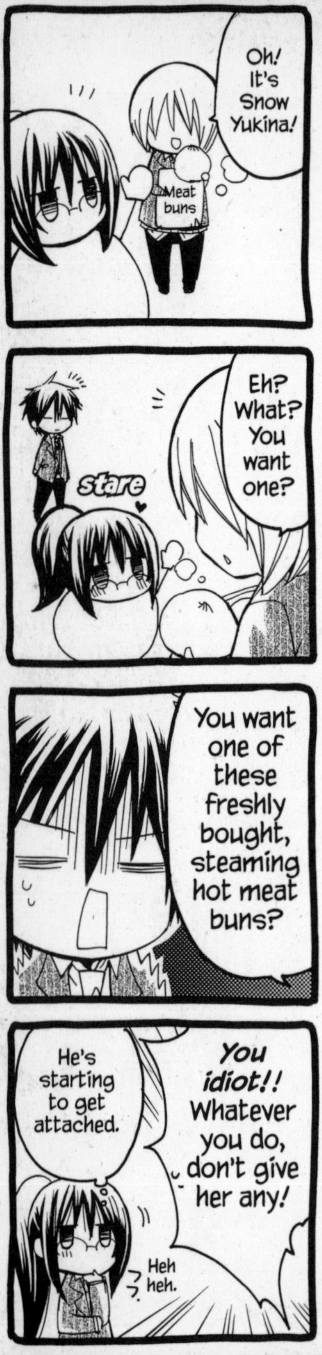
Oh! It's Snow Yukina!
Meat buns
Eh? What? You want one?
stare
You want one of these freshly bought, steaming hot meat buns?
You idiot!! Whatever you do, don't give her any!
He's starting to get attached.
Heh heh.

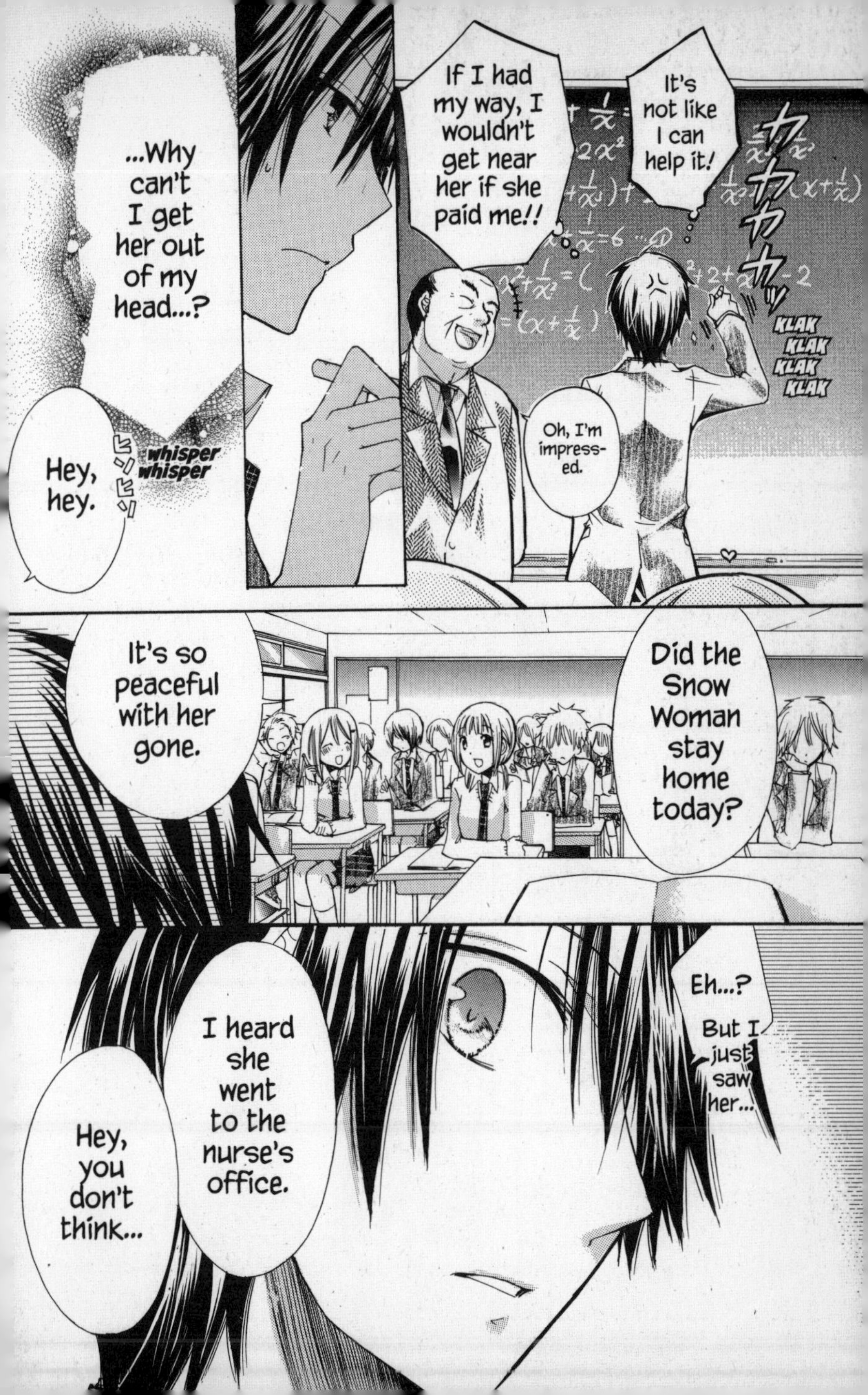

It's not like I can help it!
If I had my way, I wouldn't get near her if she paid me!!
KLAK KLAK KLAK KLAK
Oh, I'm impressed.
...Why can't I get her out of my head...?
whisper whisper
Hey, hey.
Did the Snow Woman stay home today?
It's so peaceful with her gone.
Eh...?
But I just saw her...
I heard she went to the nurse's office.
Hey, you don't think...

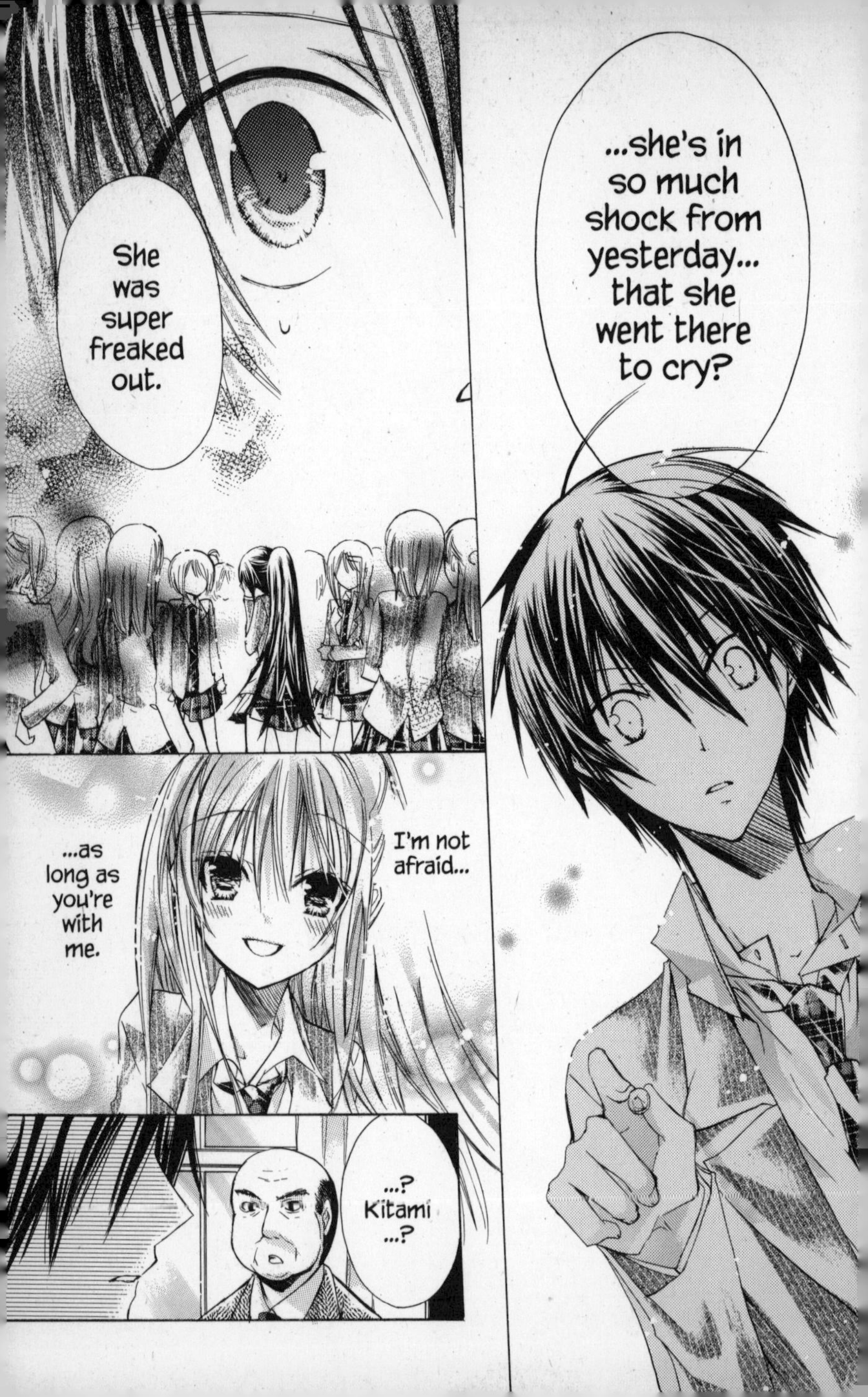
...she's in so much shock from yesterday... that she went there to cry?
She was super freaked out.
I'm not afraid...
...as long as you're with me.
...? Kitami ...?

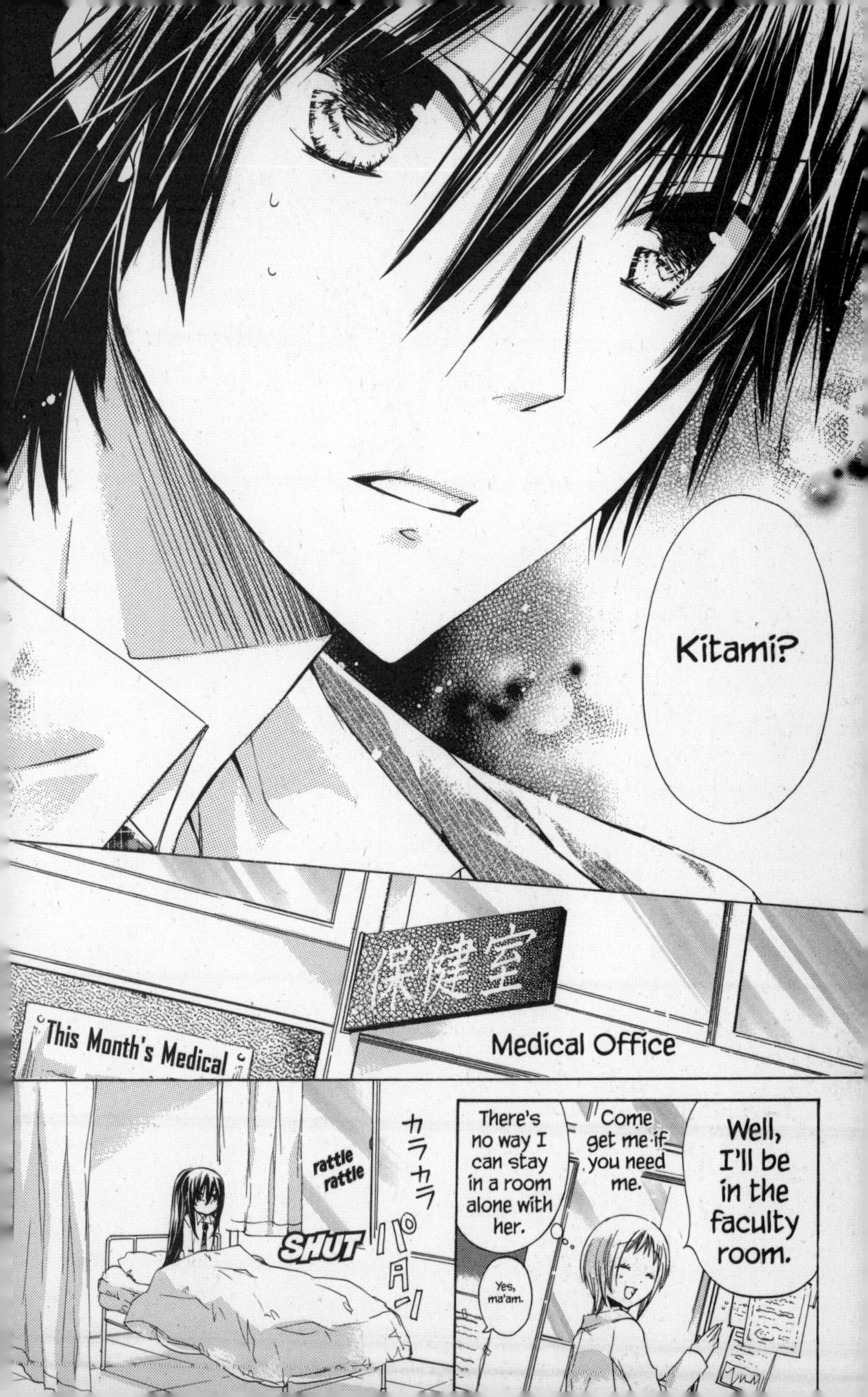
Kitami?
保健室
Medical Office
This Month's Medical
Well, I'll be in the faculty room.
Come get me if you need me.
Yes, ma'am.
There's no way I can stay in a room alone with her.
カラカラ
rattle rattle
パターン
SHUT

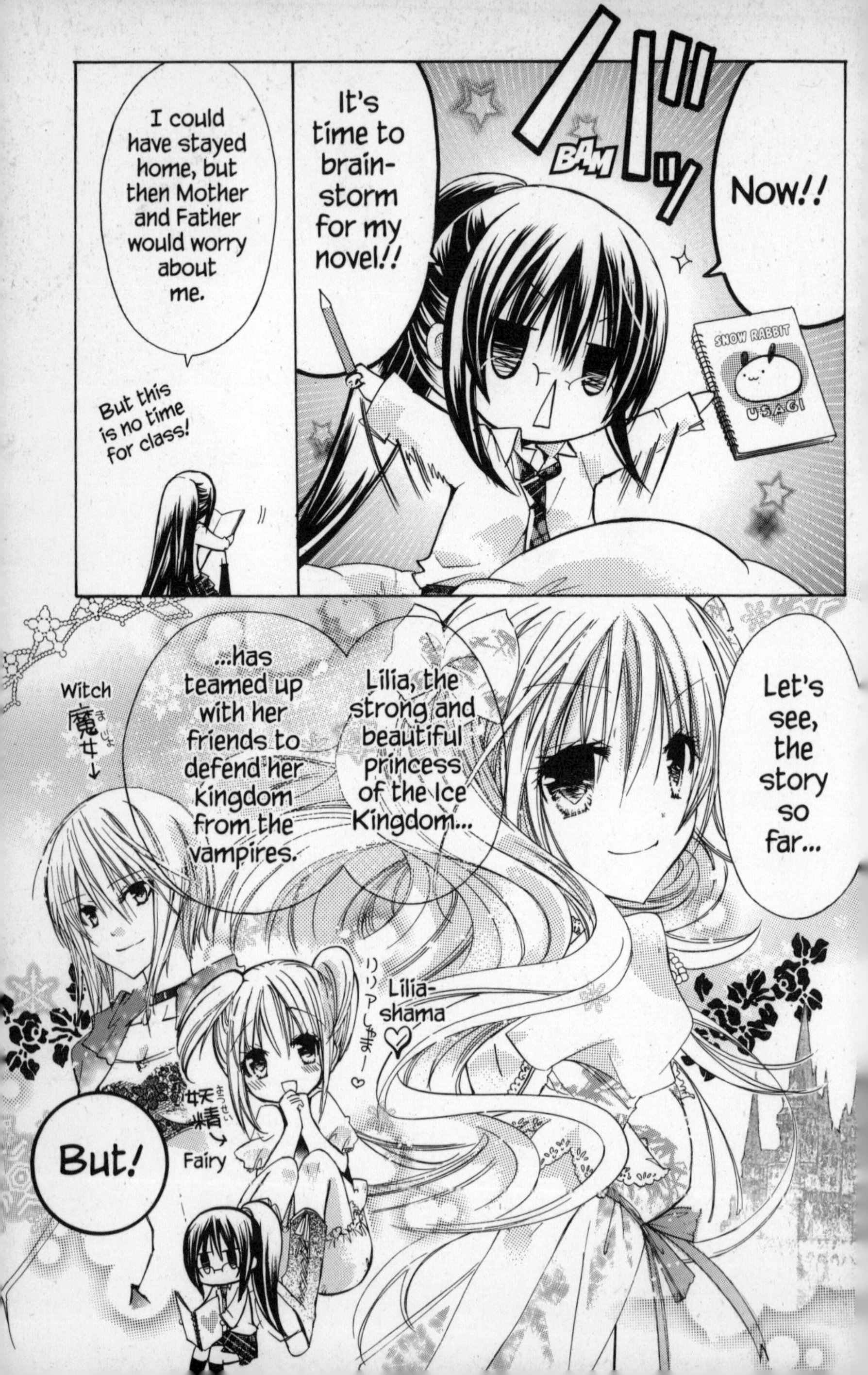

Now!!
BAM
It's time to brainstorm for my novel!!
SNOW RABBIT
USAGI
I could have stayed home, but then Mother and Father would worry about me.
But this is no time for class!
Let's see, the story so far...
Lilia, the strong and beautiful princess of the Ice Kingdom...
...has teamed up with her friends to defend her kingdom from the vampires.
Witch
魔女
リリアしゃまー♡
Lilia-shama ♡
妖精
Fairy
But!

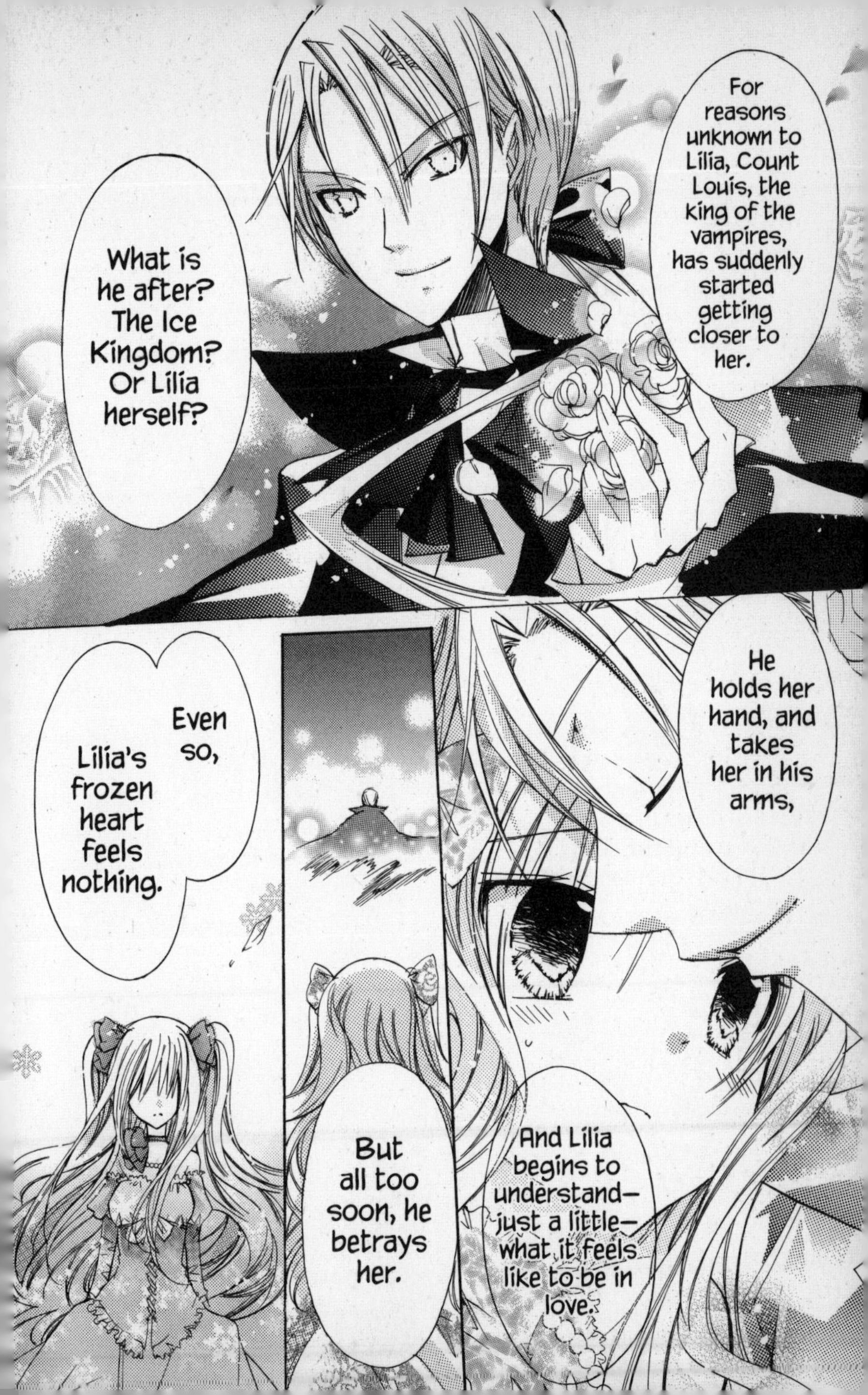
For reasons unknown to Lilia, Count Louis, the king of the vampires, has suddenly started getting closer to her.
What is he after? The Ice Kingdom? Or Lilia herself?
He holds her hand, and takes her in his arms,
And Lilia begins to understand—just a little—what it feels like to be in love.
But all too soon, he betrays her.
Even so, Lilia's frozen heart feels nothing.

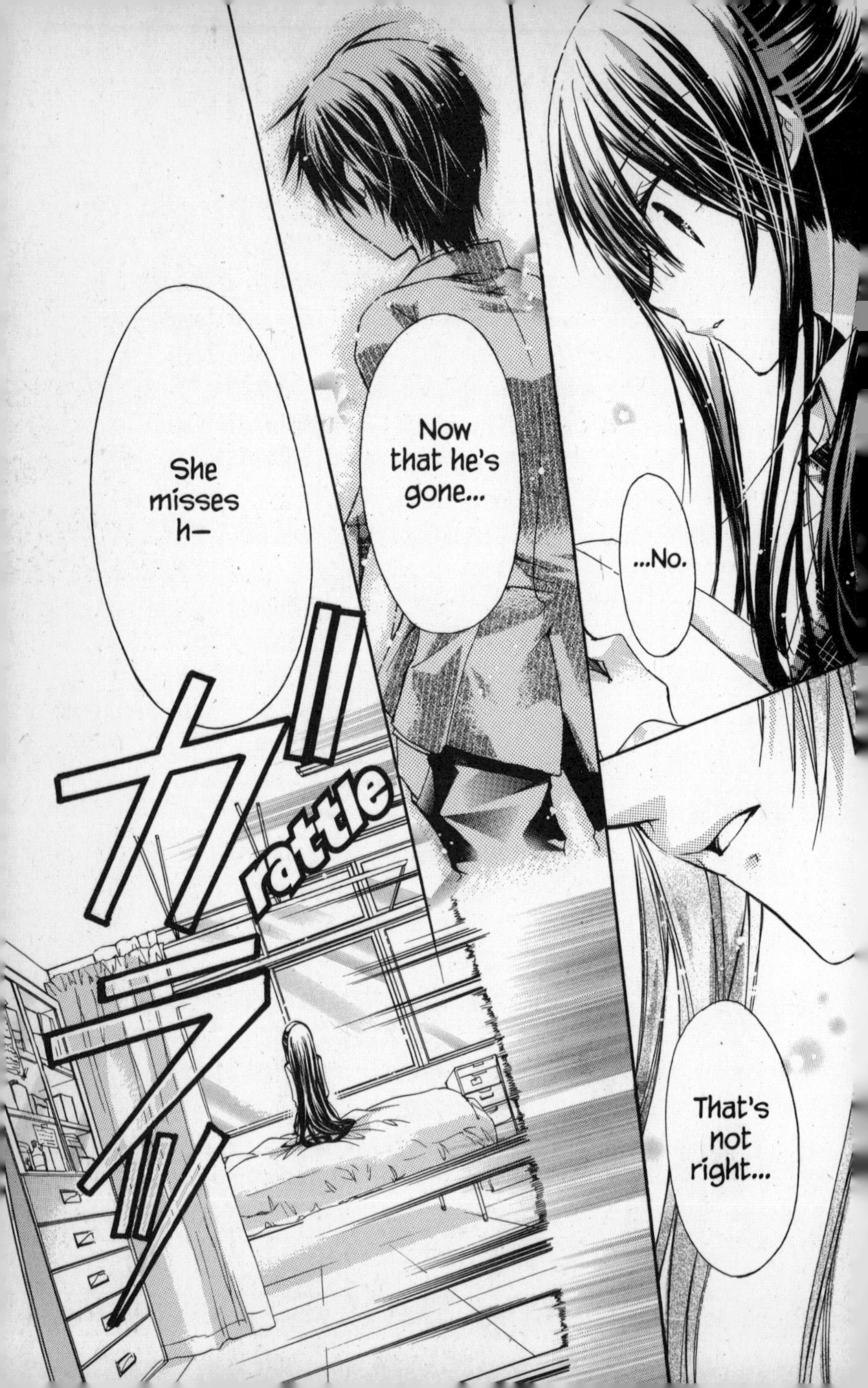
...No.
That's not right...
Now that he's gone...
She misses h–
rattle

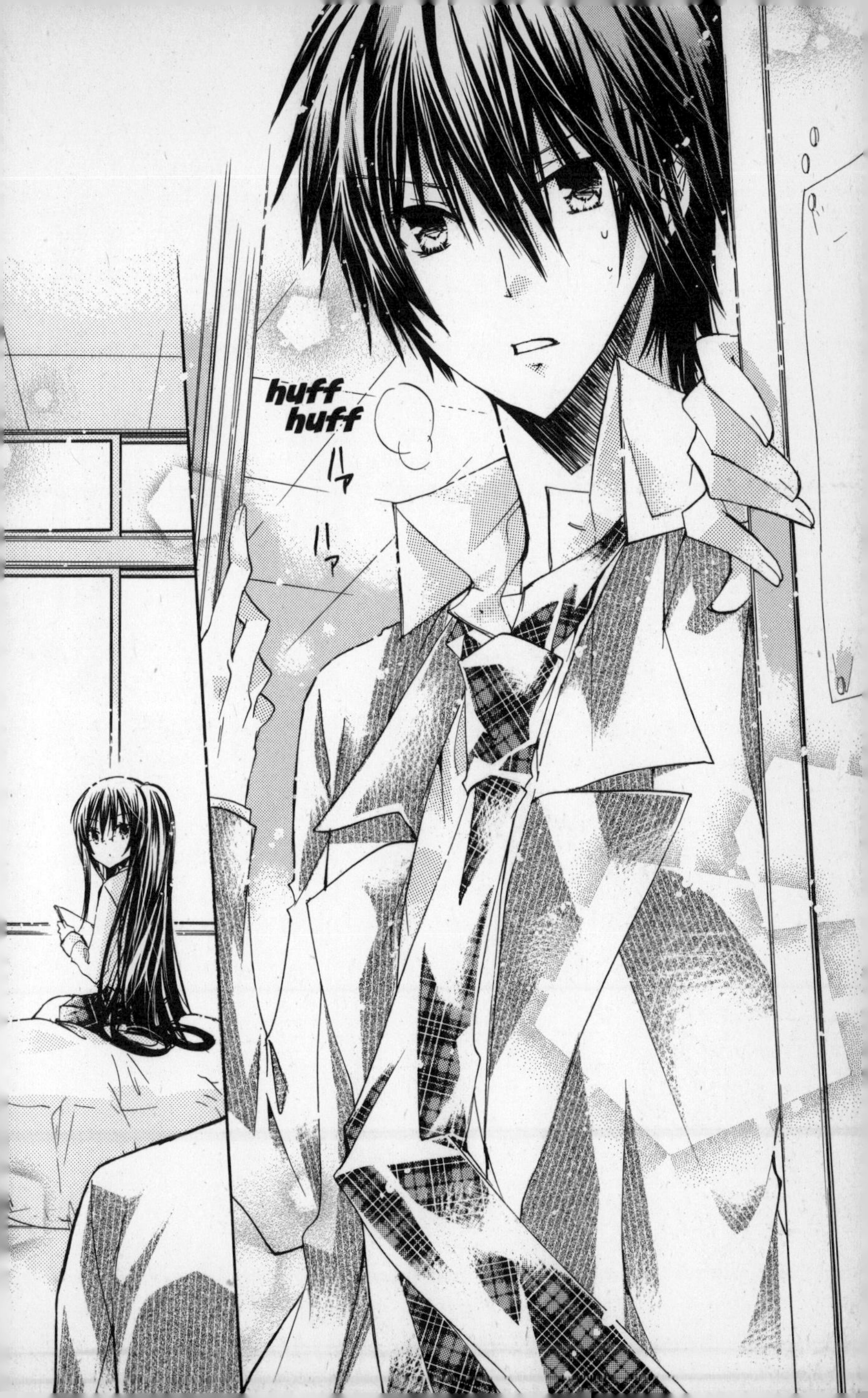
huff huff
ハァ
ハァ

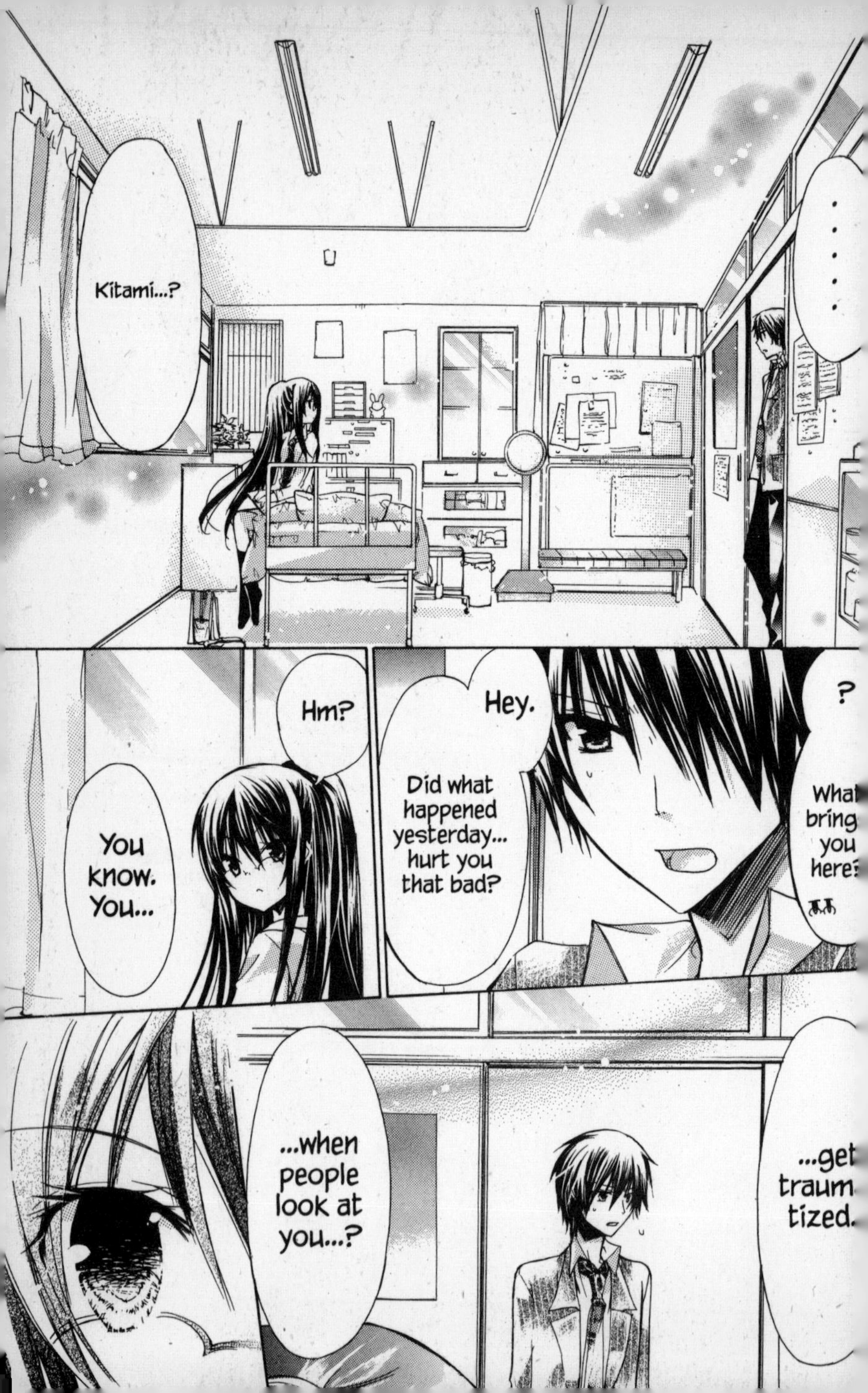
· · · · ·
Kitami...?
?
What bring you here?
Hey.
Did what happened yesterday... hurt you that bad?
Hm?
You know. You...
...get traum tized.
...when people look at you...?

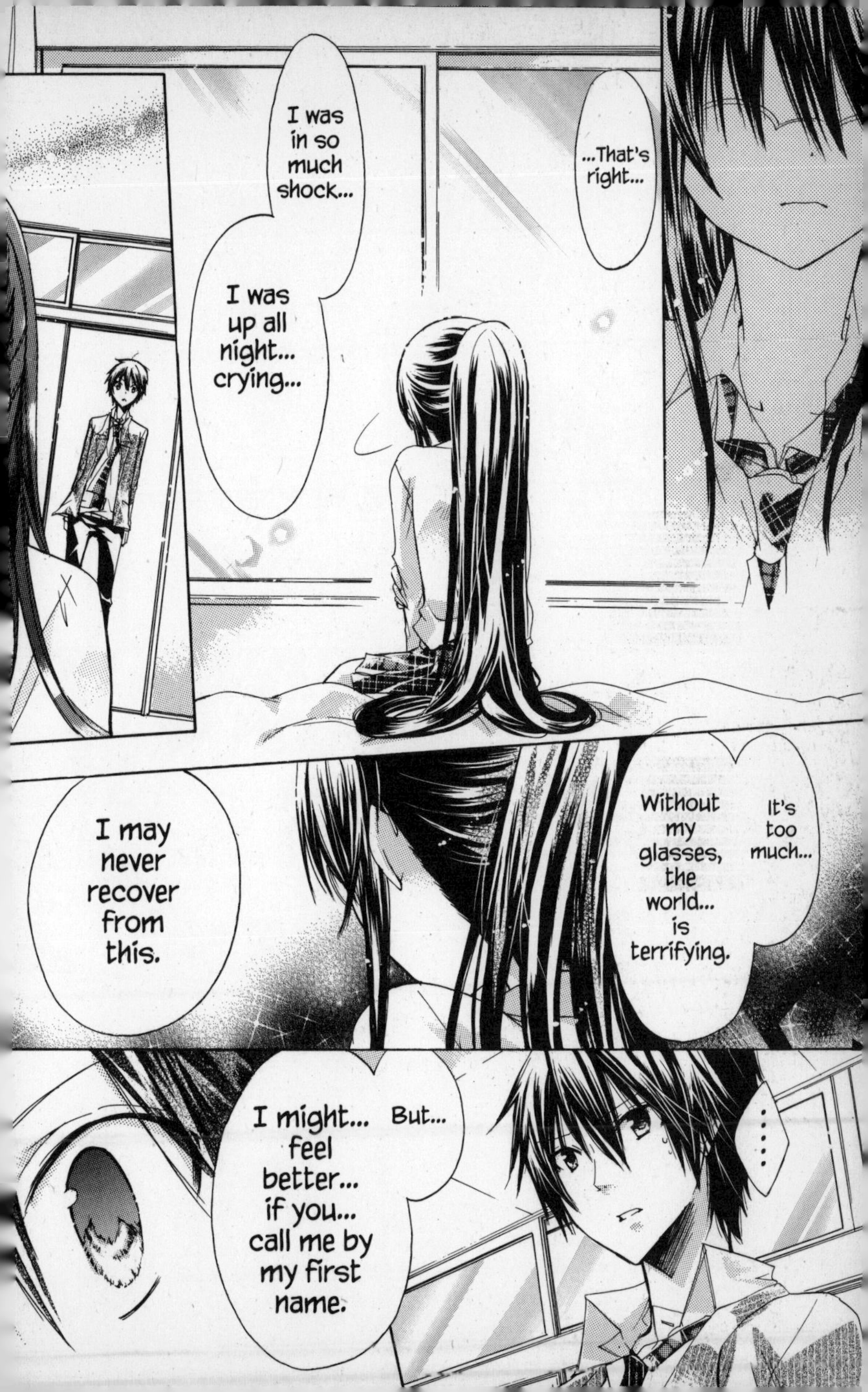
...That's right...
I was in so much shock...
I was up all night... crying...
It's too much...
Without my glasses, the world... is terrifying.
I may never recover from this.
......
But...
I might... feel better... if you... call me by my first name.

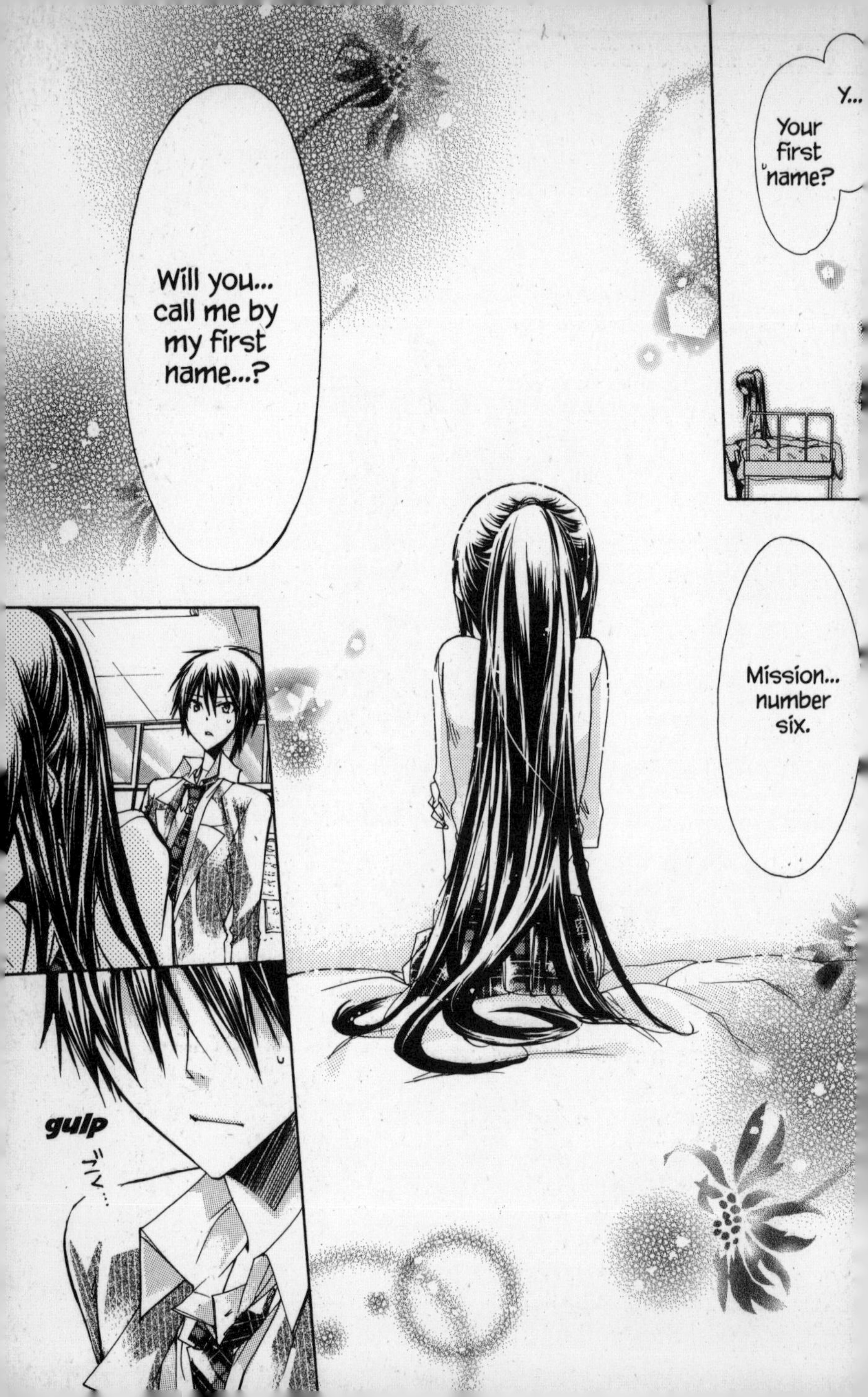
Y... Your first name?
Will you... call me by my first name...?
Mission... number six.
gulp

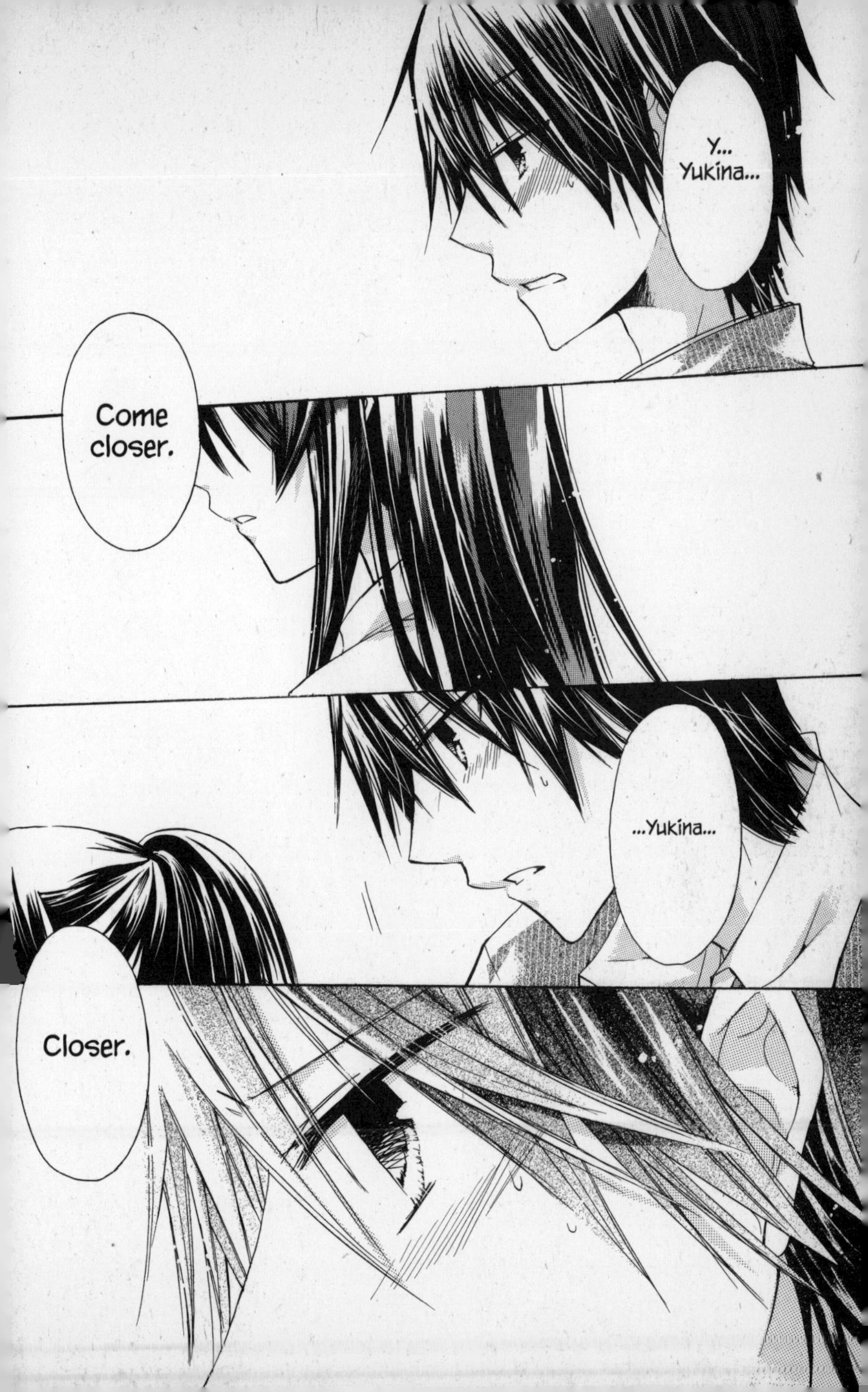
Y... Yukina...
Come closer.
...Yukina...
Closer.

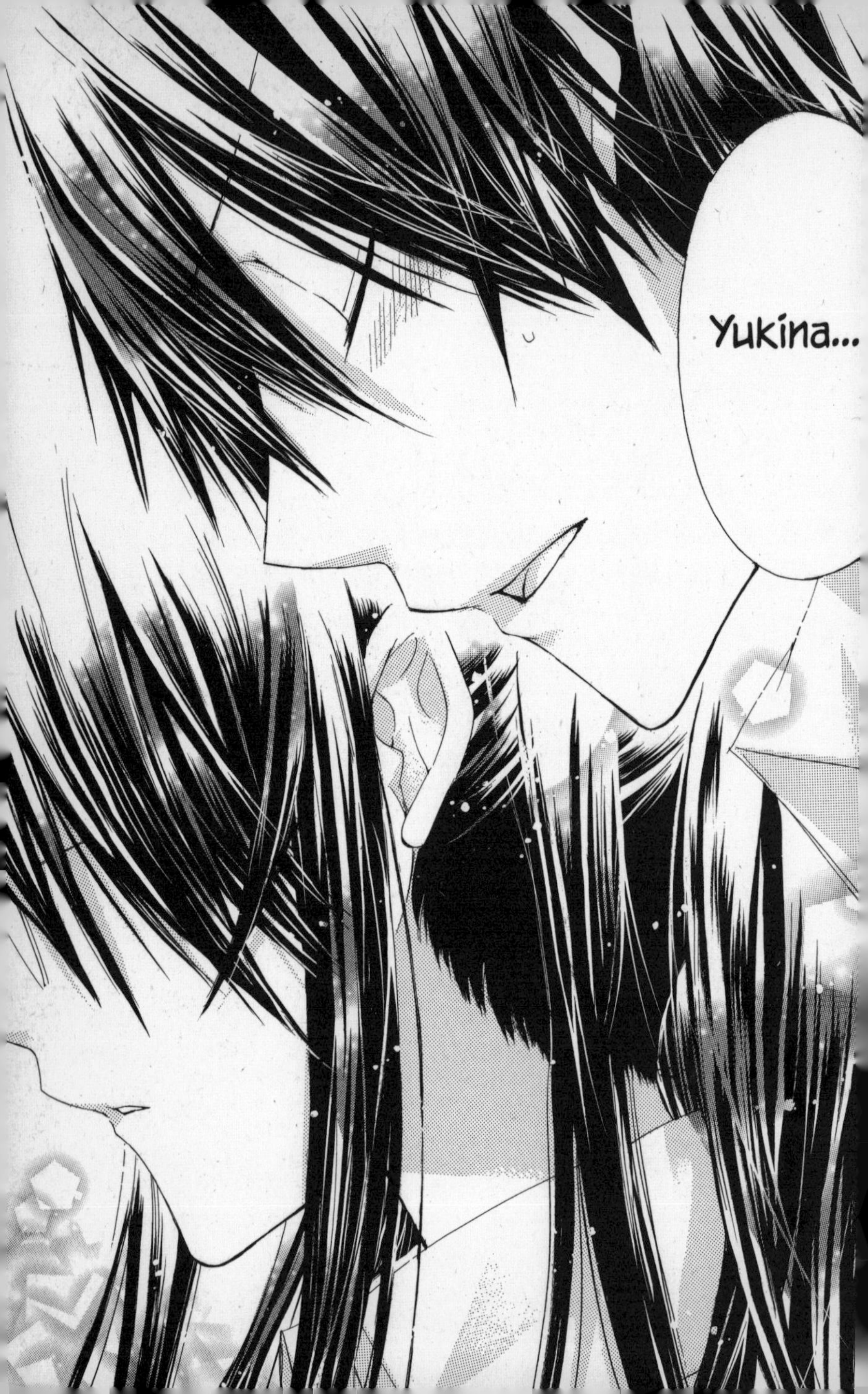
Yukina...

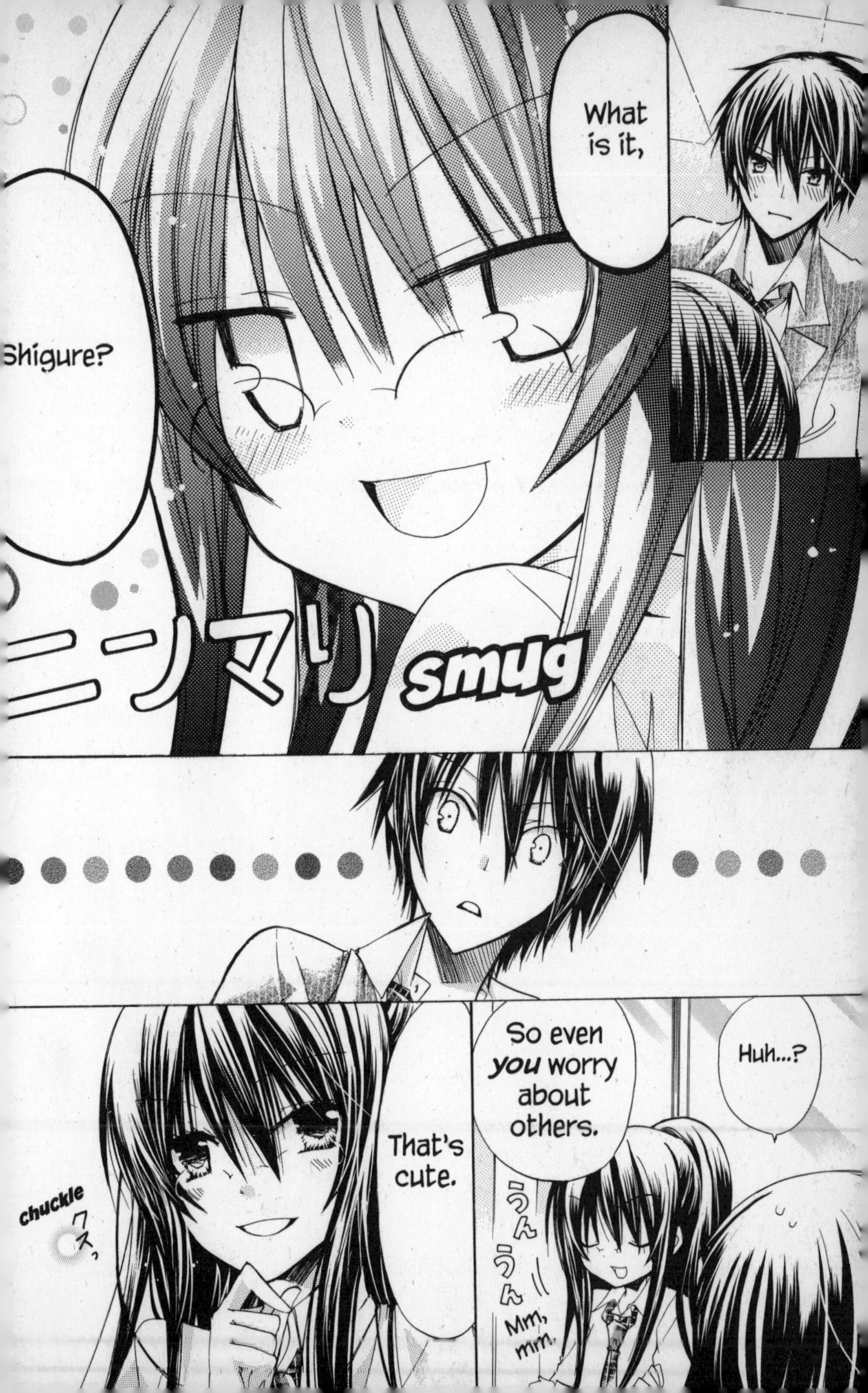

What is it,
Shigure?
smug
Huh...?
So even *you* worry about others.
うんうん
Mm, mm.
That's cute.
chuckle
クスッ

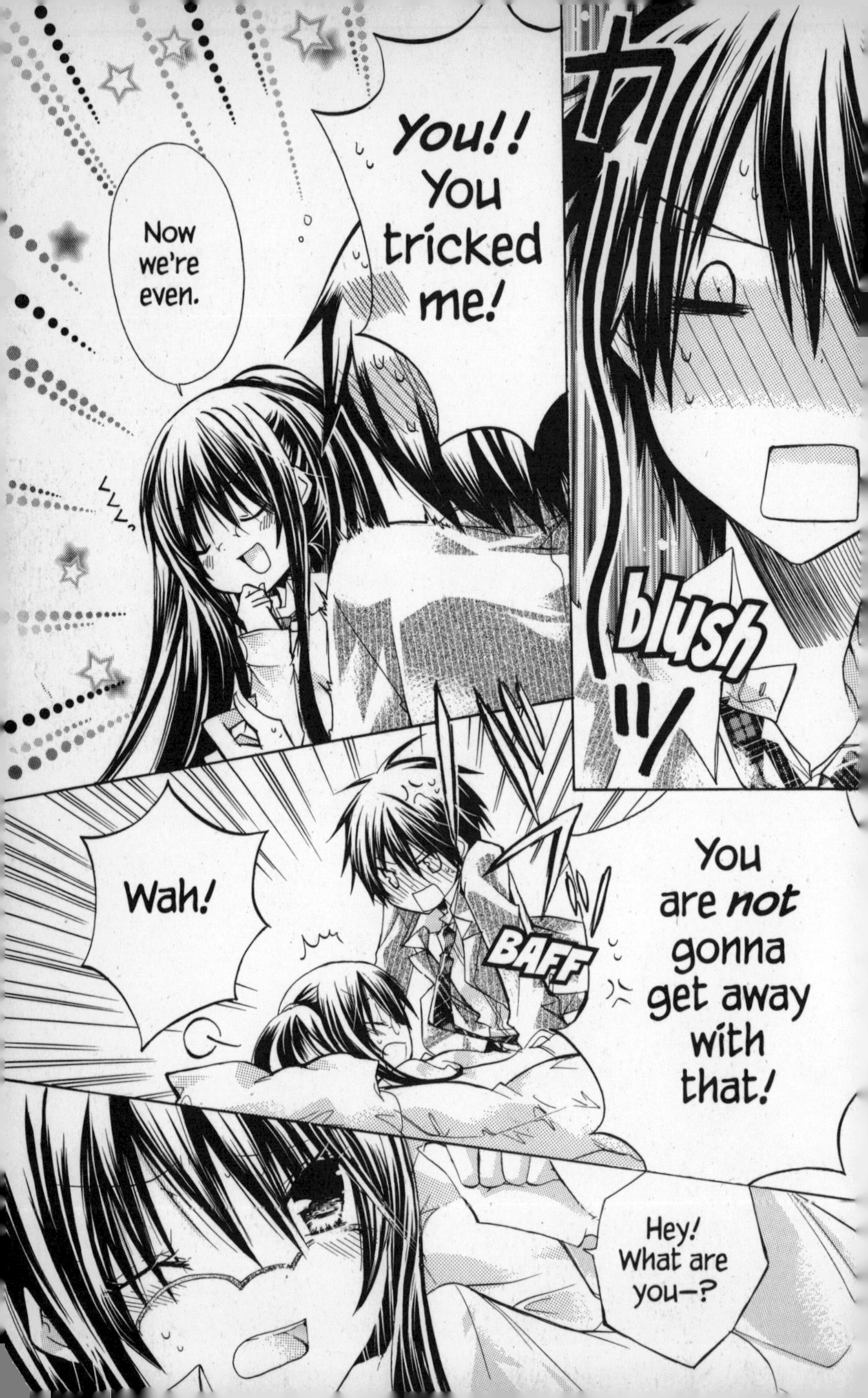
blush
You!! You tricked me!
Now we're even.
You are ***not*** gonna get away with that!
BAFF
Wah!
Hey! What are you—?

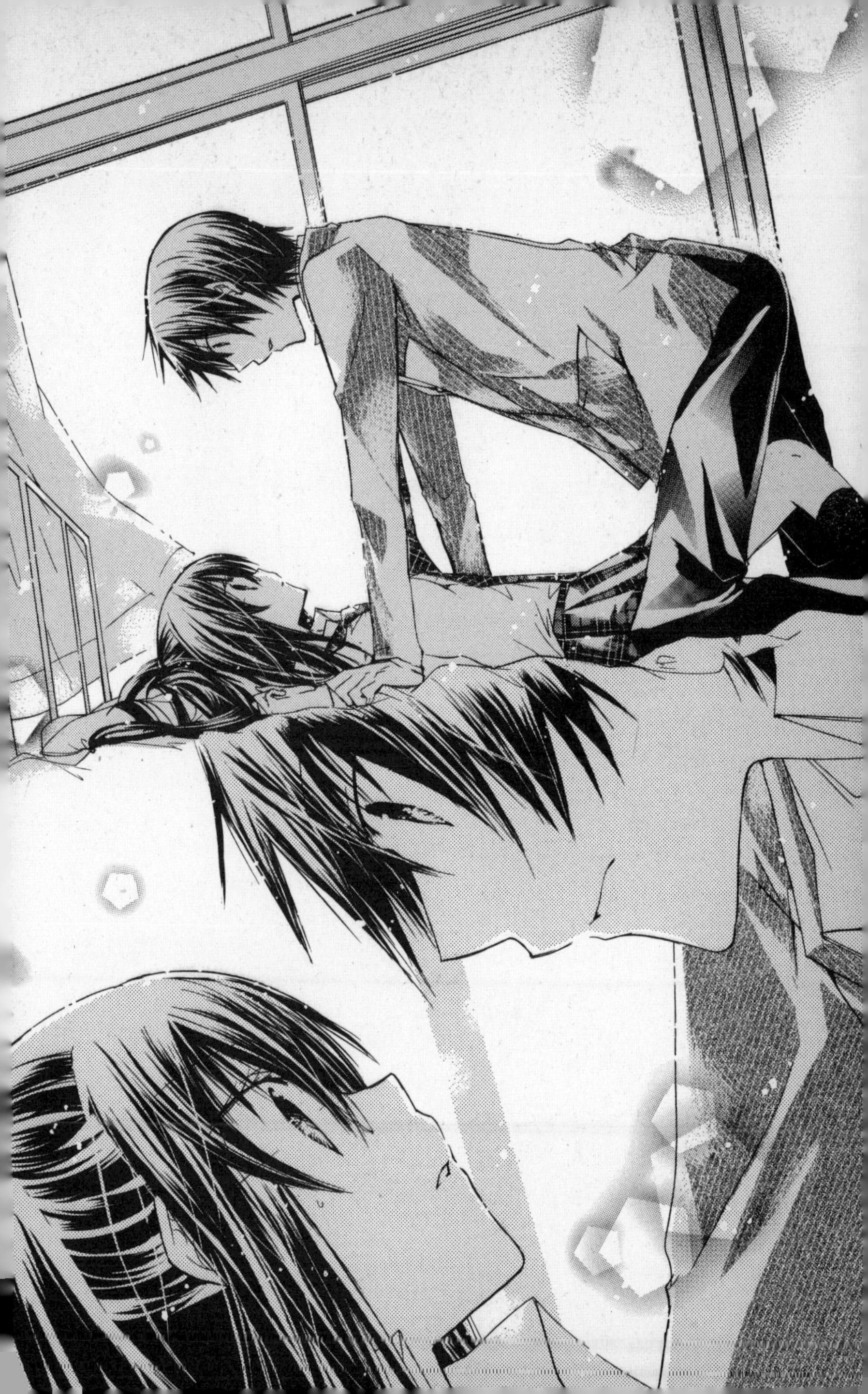

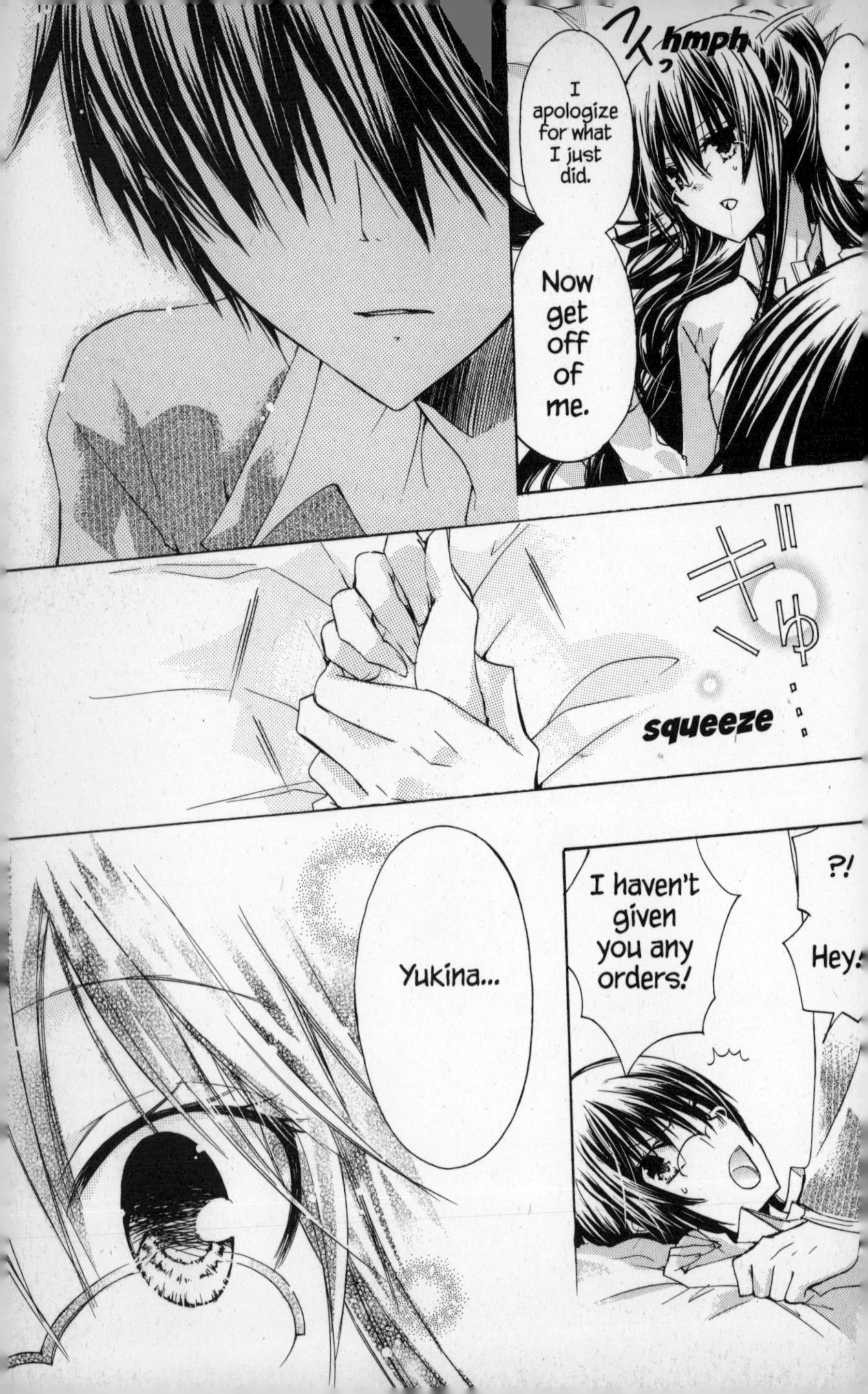
...
hmph
I apologize for what I just did.
Now get off of me.
squeeze
?!
Hey!
I haven't given you any orders!
Yukina...

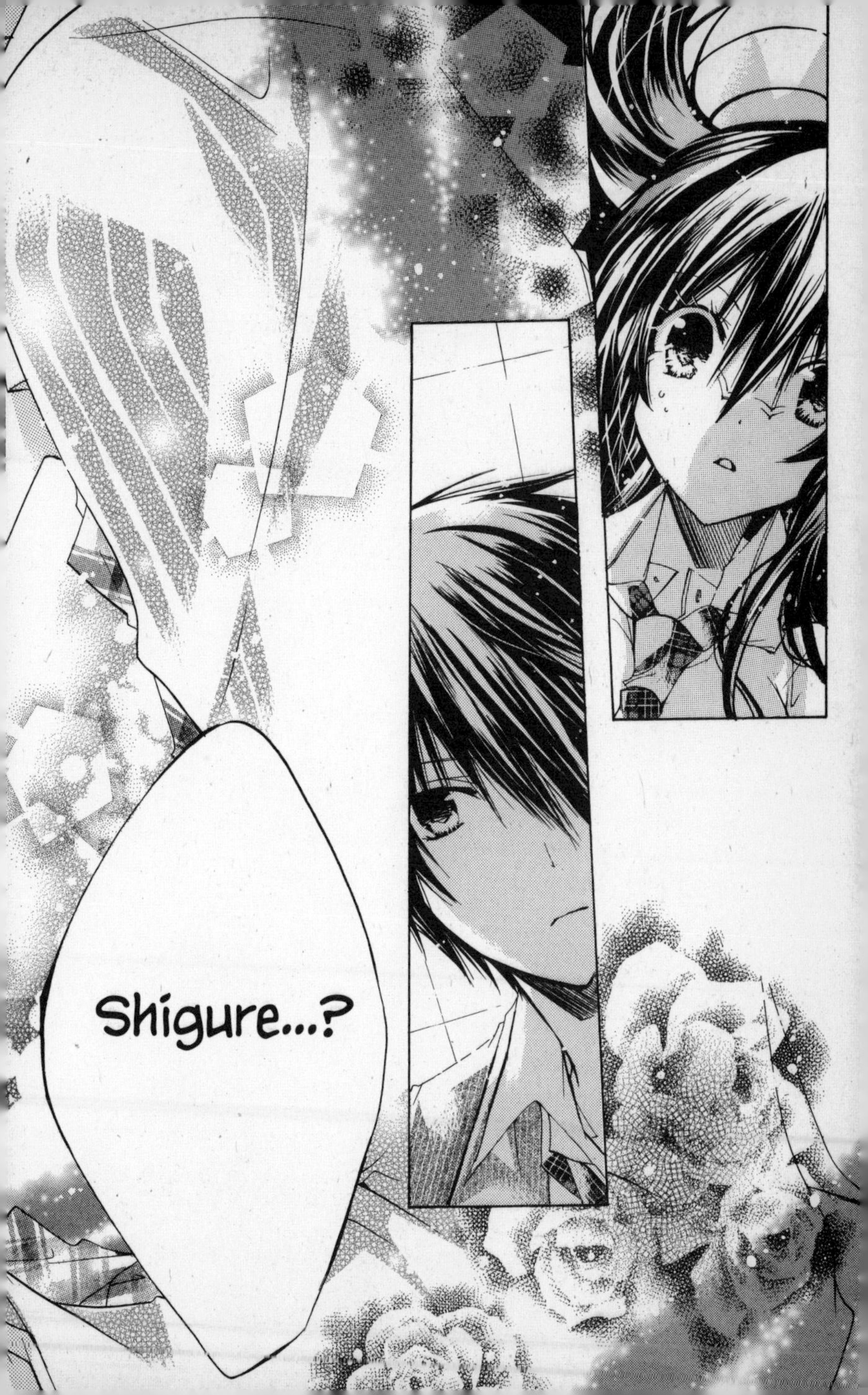
Shigure...?

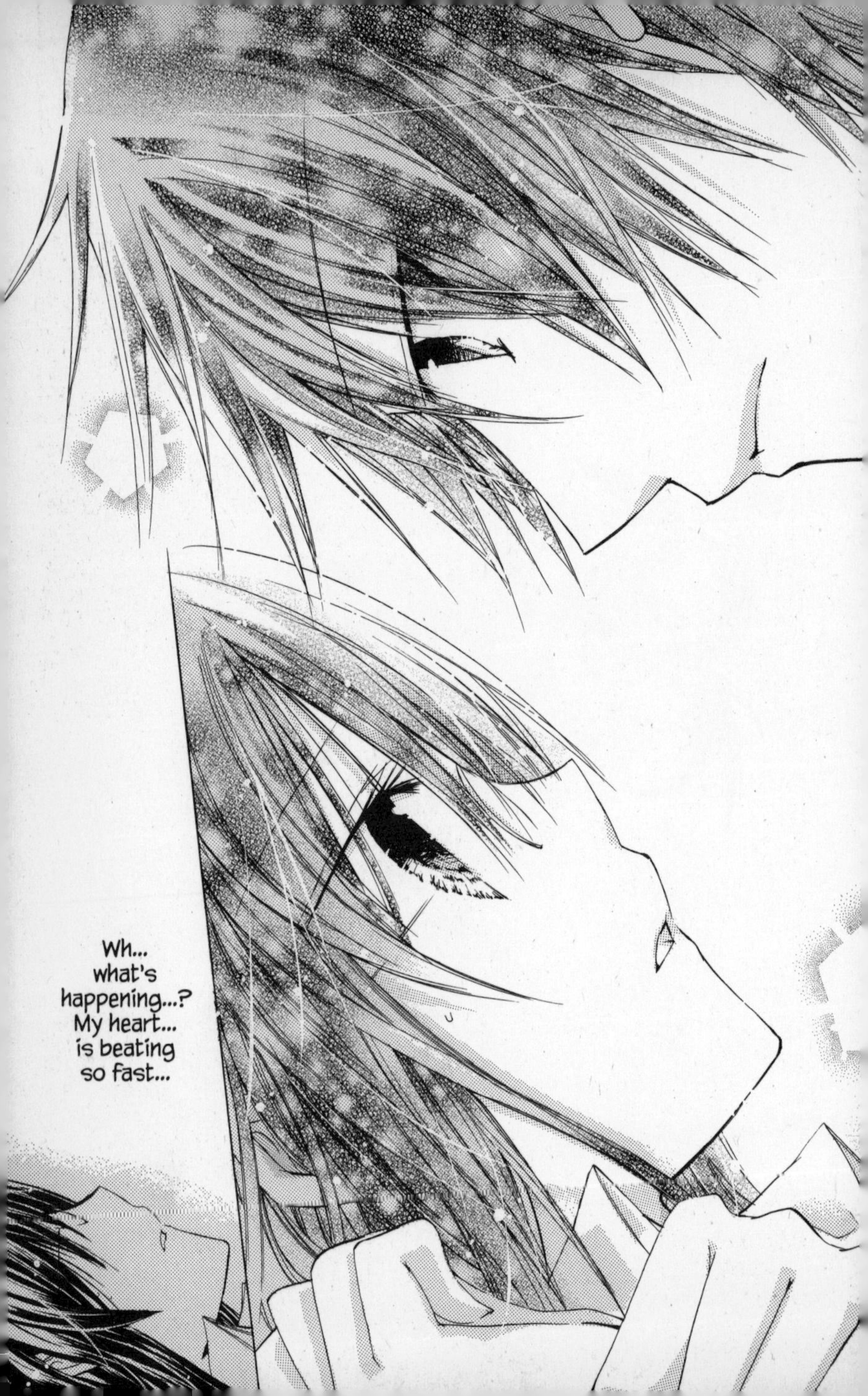
Wh... what's happening...? My heart... is beating so fast...

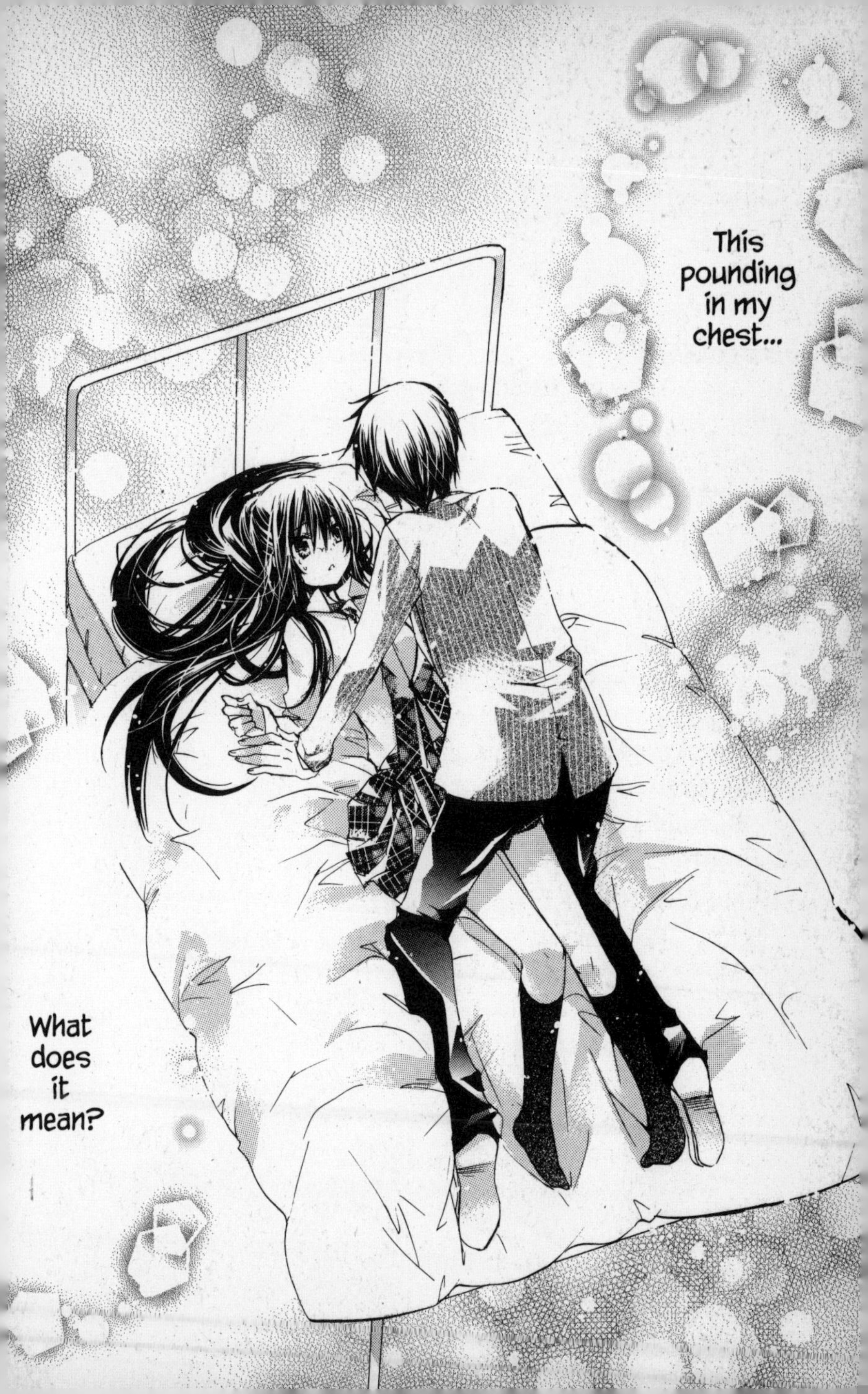
This pounding in my chest...
What does it mean?

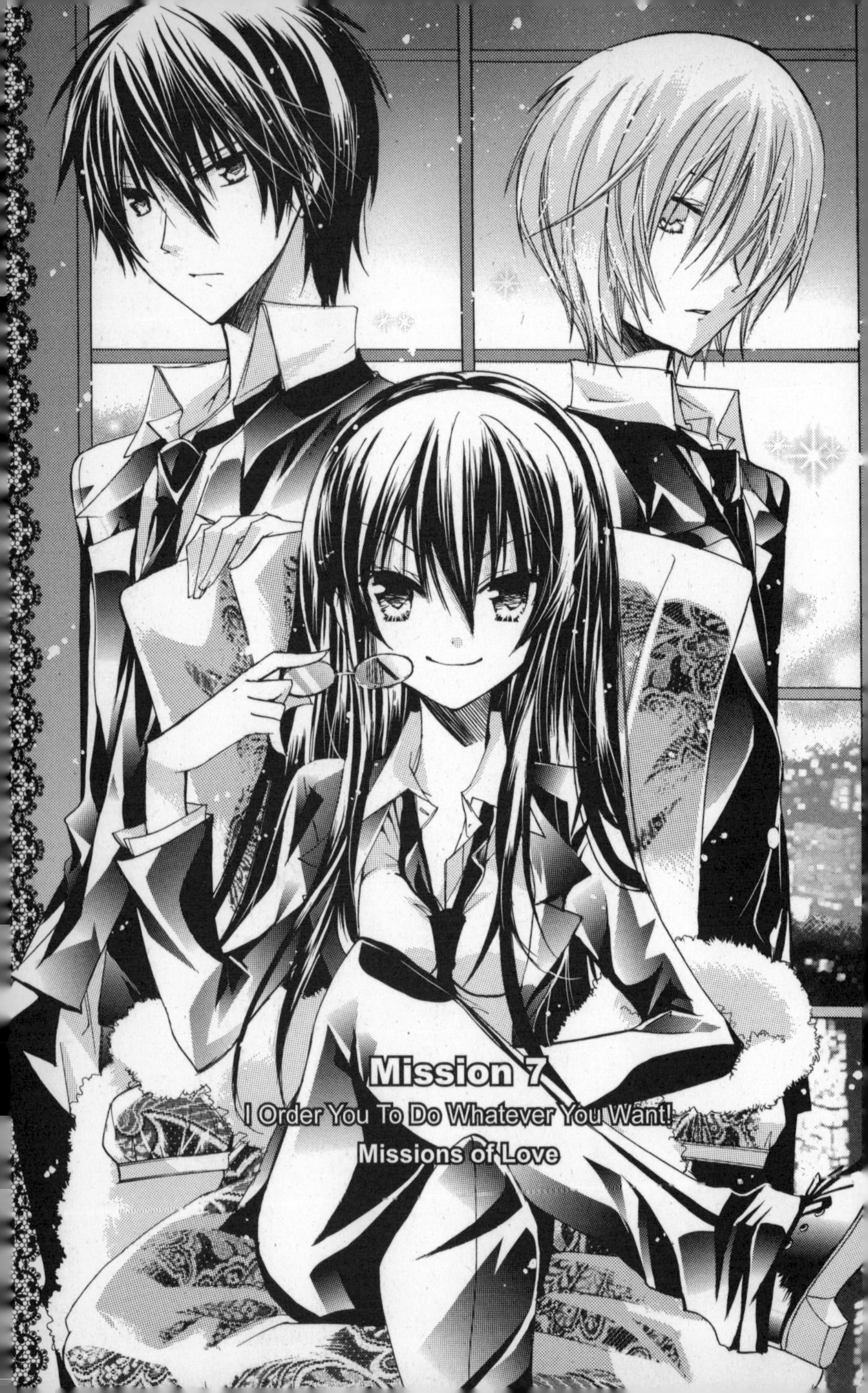
Mission 7
I Order You To Do Whatever You Want!
Missions of Love

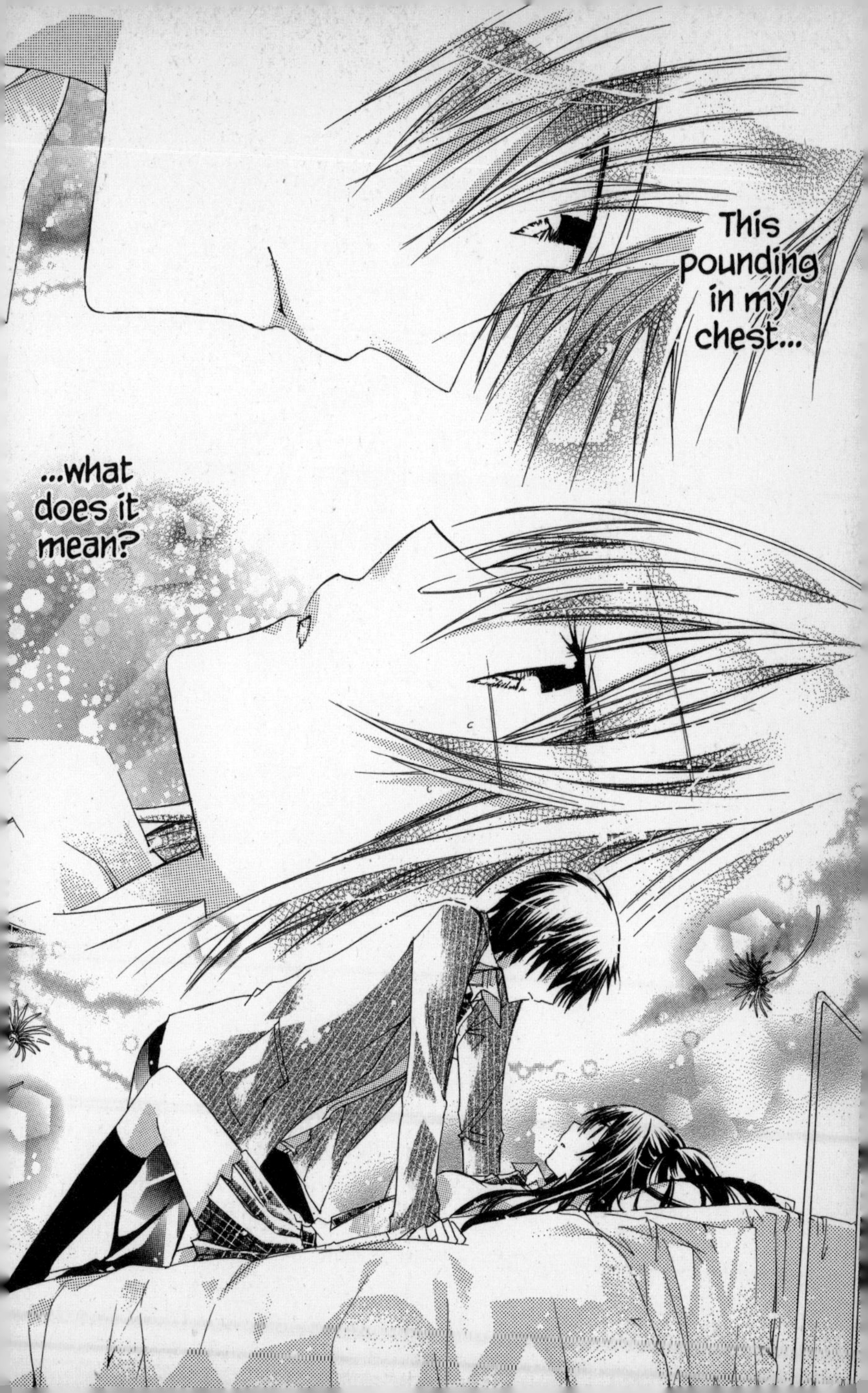
This pounding in my chest...
...what does it mean?

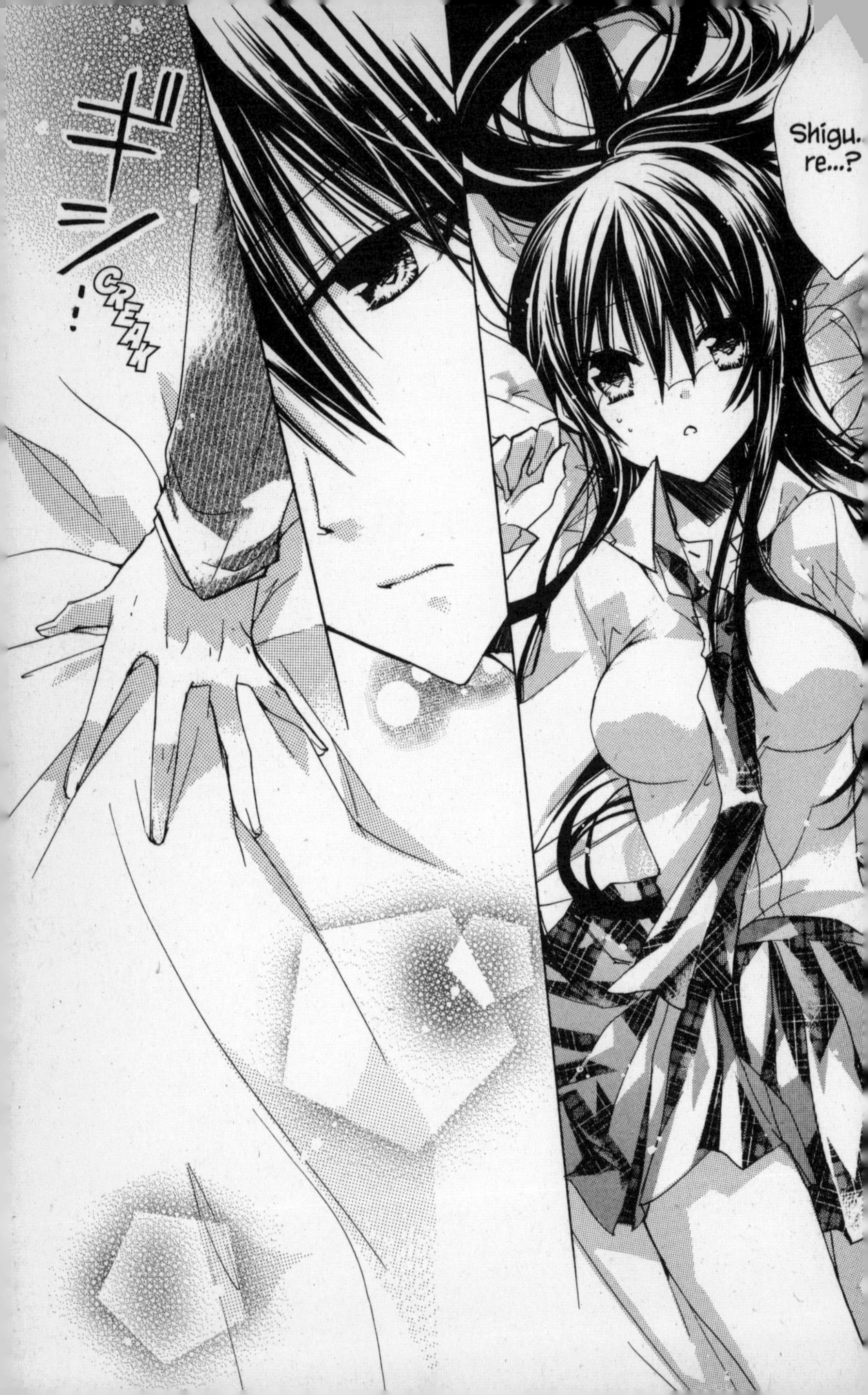
Shigu. re...?
ギシ
CREAK

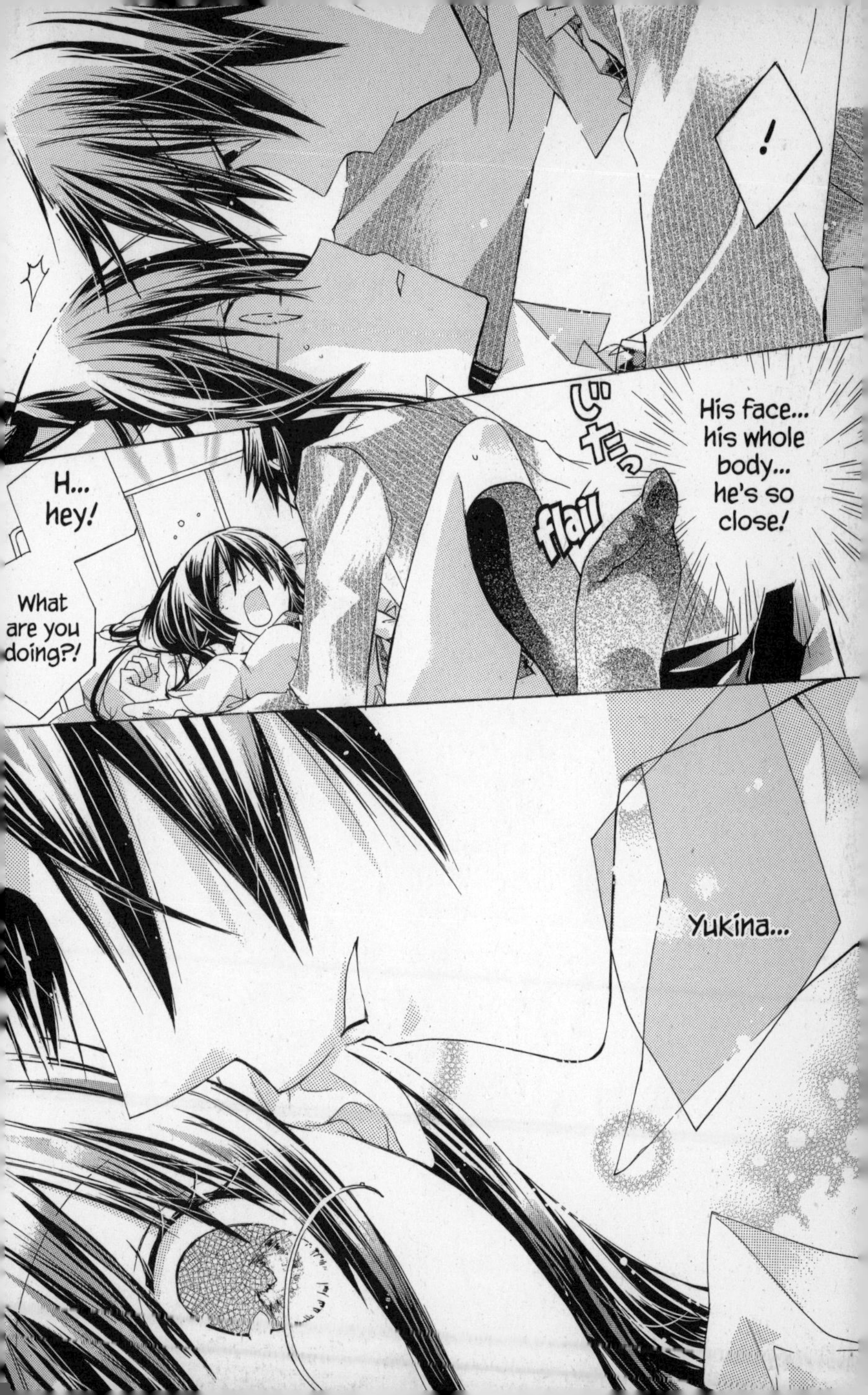
!
His face... his whole body... he's so close!
じたっ
flail
H... hey!
What are you doing?!
Yukina...

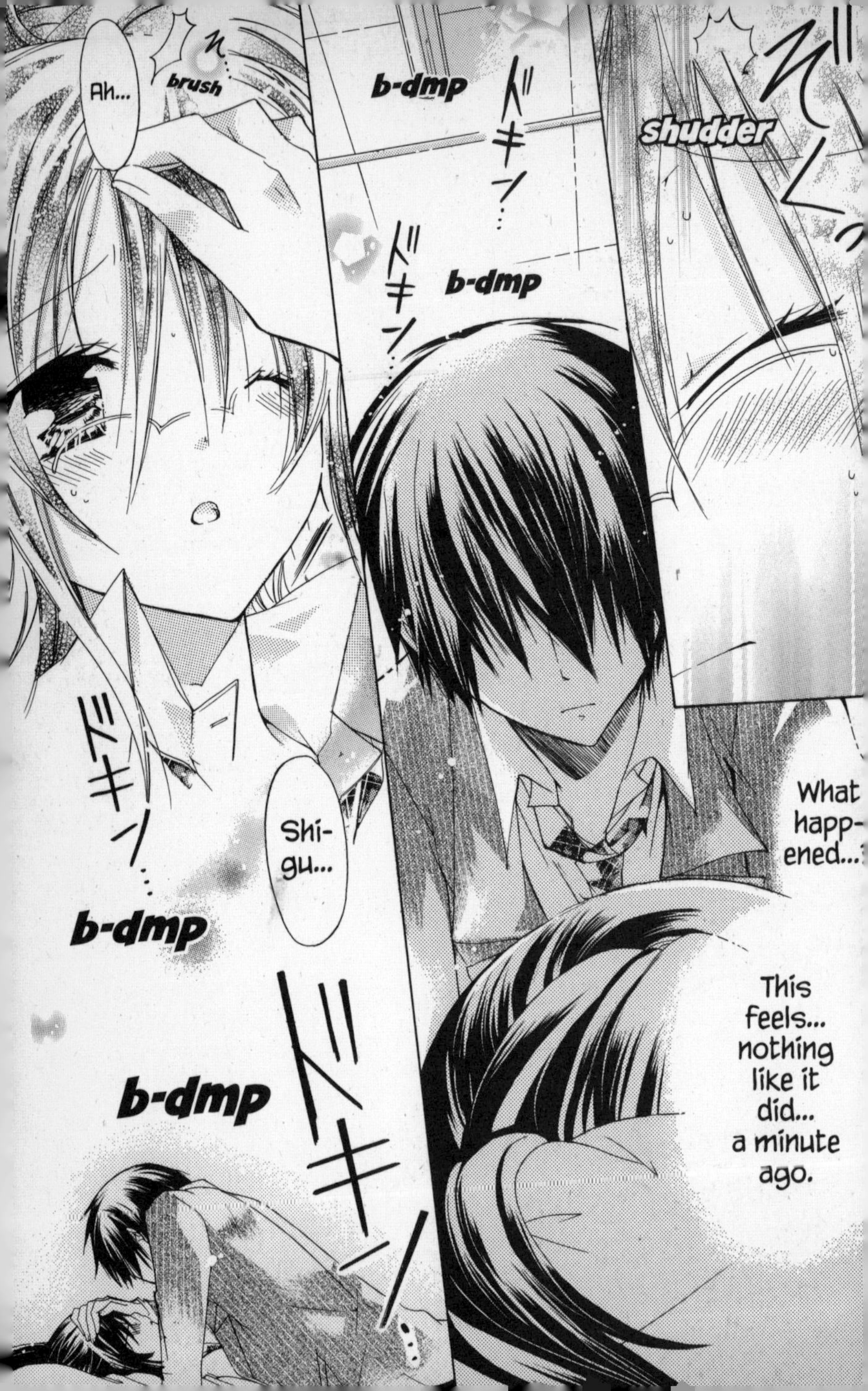
Shudder
b-dmp
b-dmp
What happ-ened...?
This feels... nothing like it did... a minute ago.
Ah...
brush
Shi-gu...
b-dmp
b-dmp

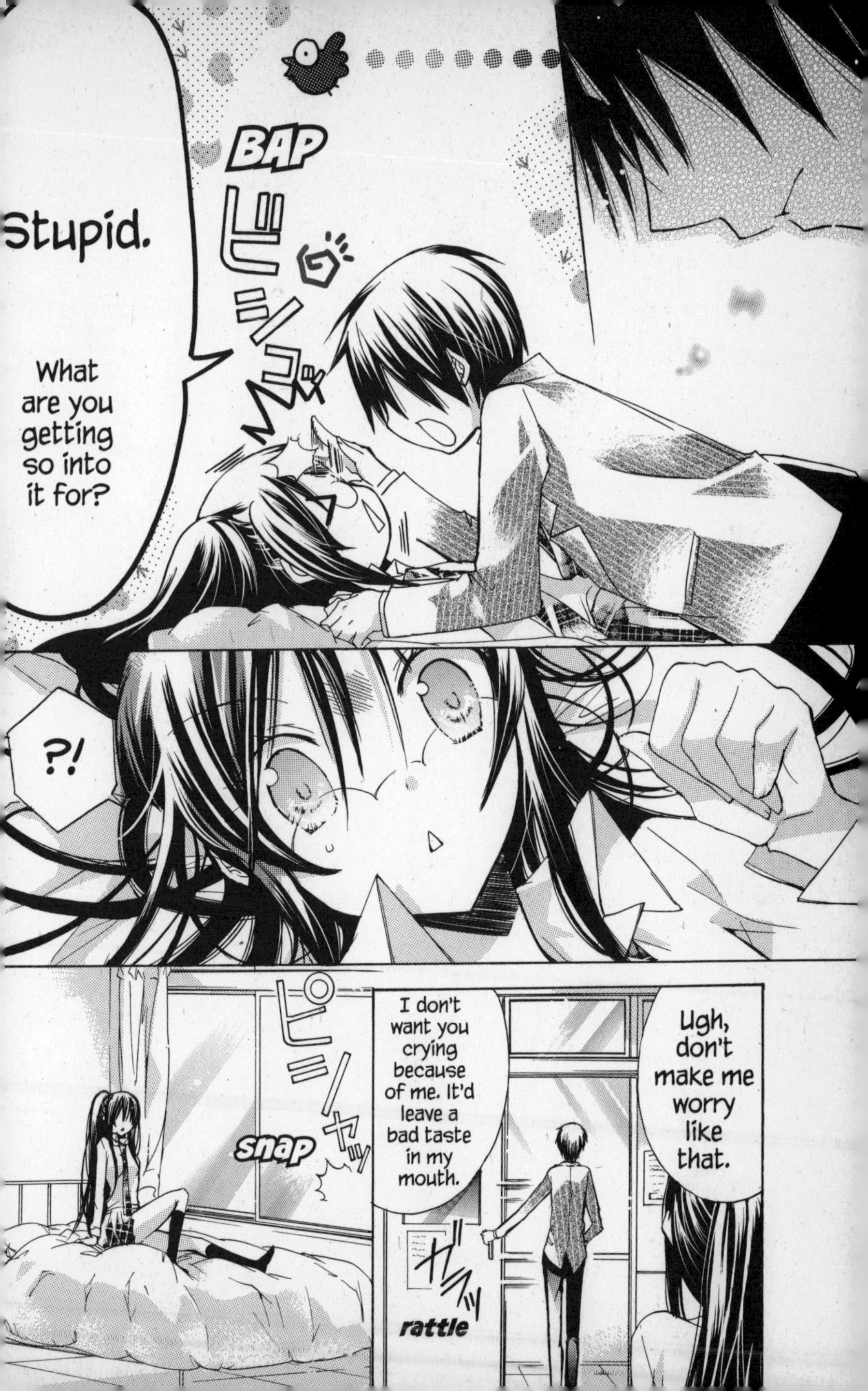
BAP
Stupid.
What are you getting so into it for?
?!
Ugh, don't make me worry like that.
I don't want you crying because of me. It'd leave a bad taste in my mouth.
rattle
snap

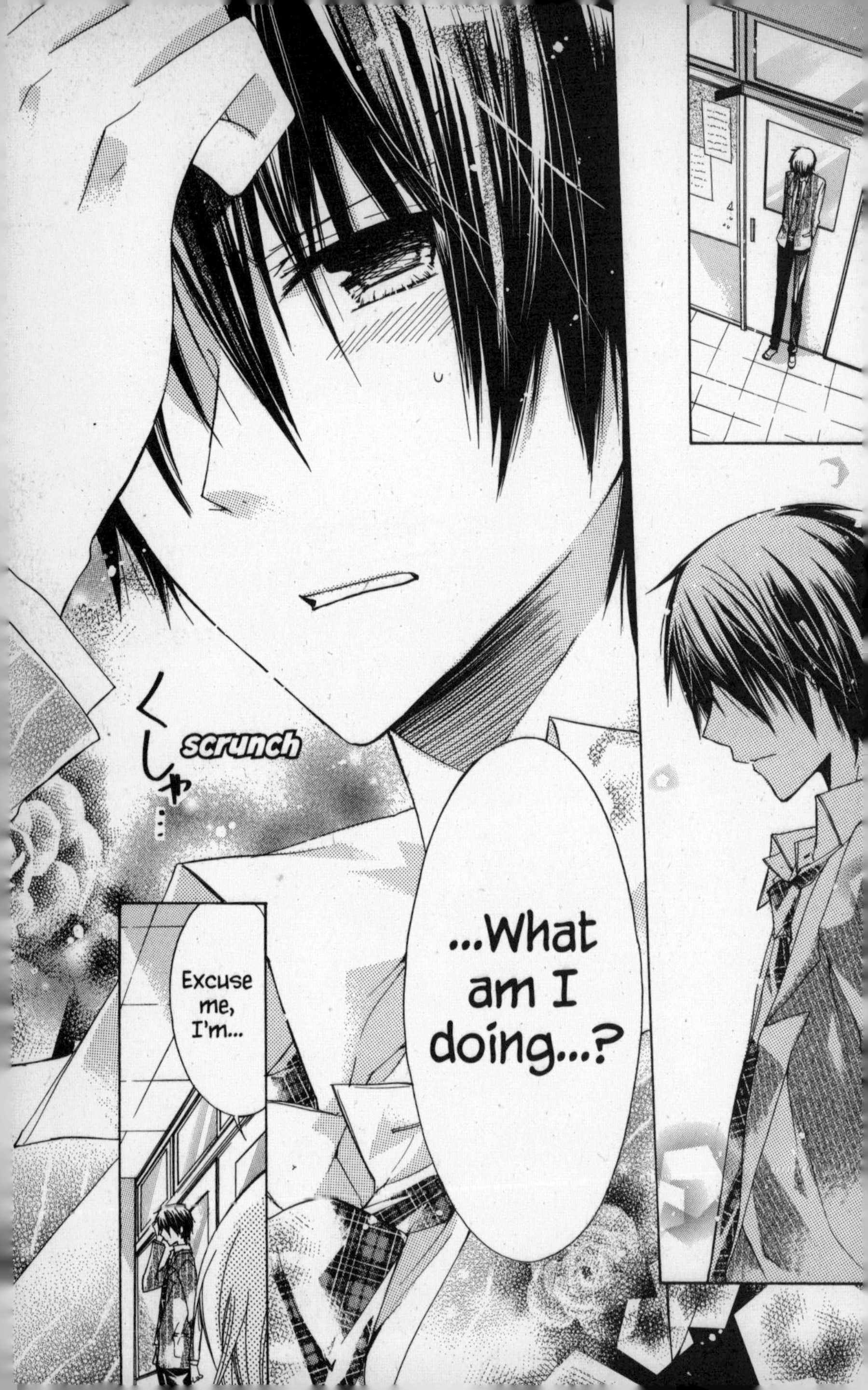
くしゃ…
scrunch
...What am I doing...?
Excuse me, I'm...

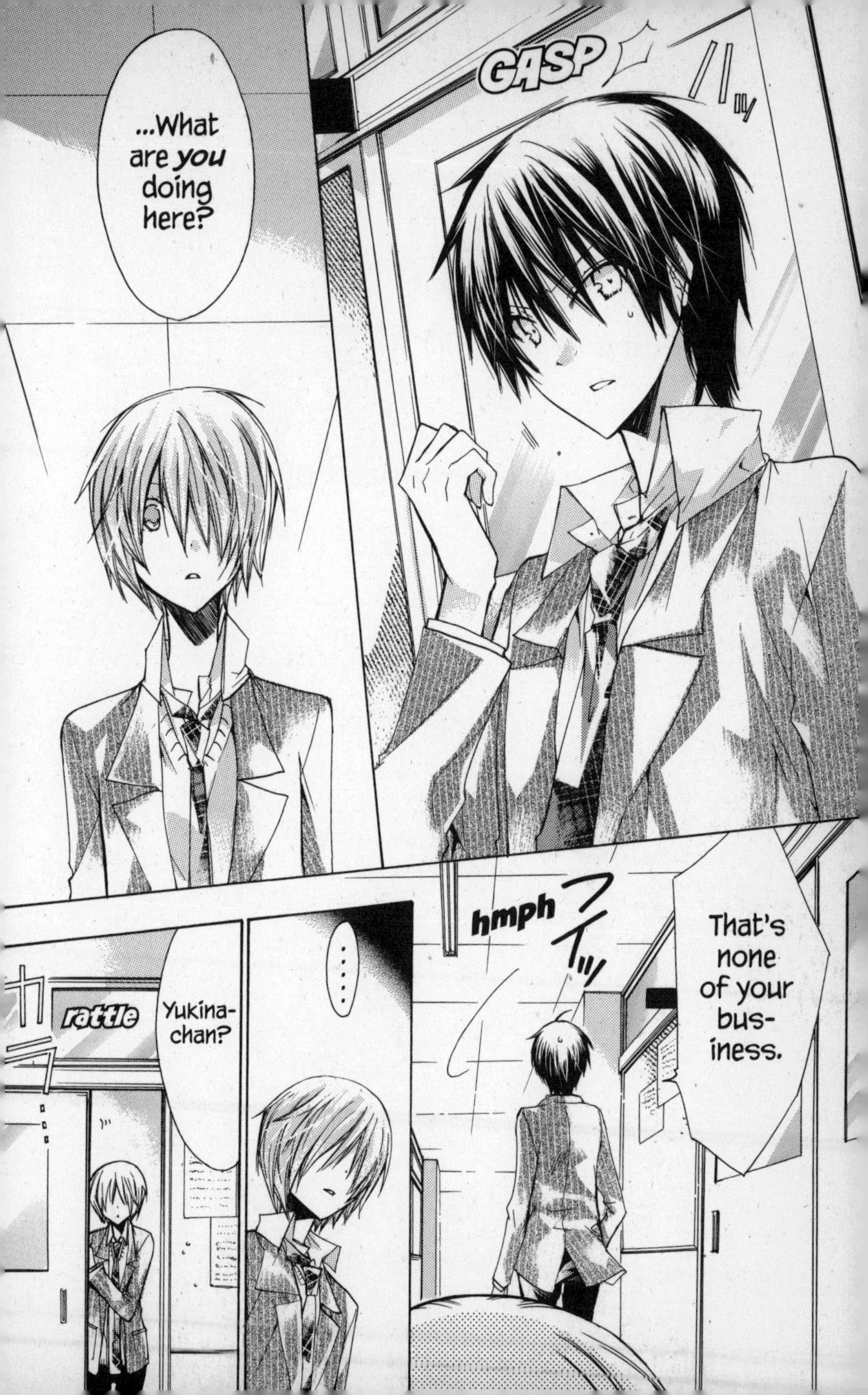
GASP
...What are *you* doing here?
hmph
That's none of your bus-iness.
.....
Yukina-chan?
rattle

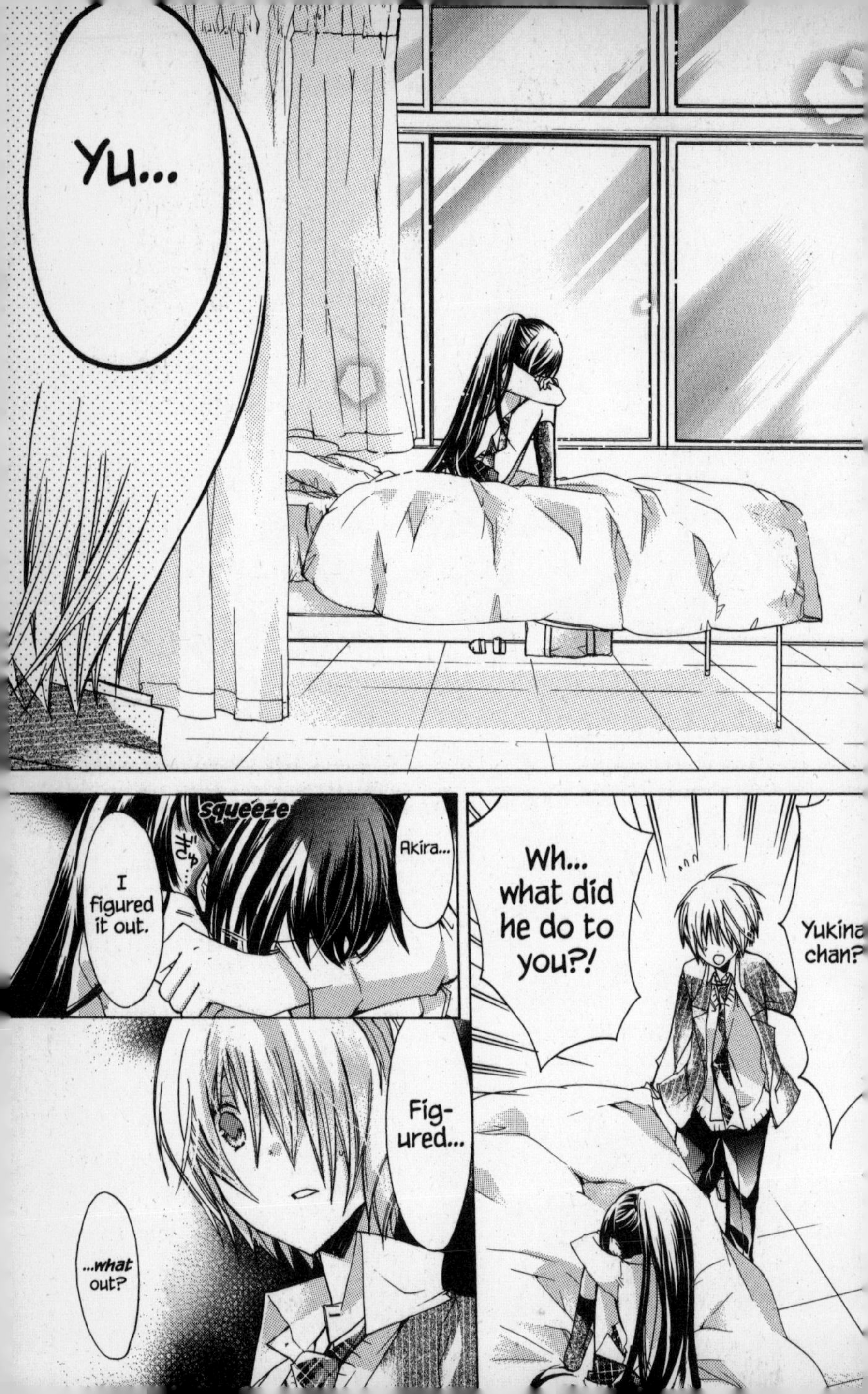
Yu...
Yukina chan?
Wh... what did he do to you?!
Akira...
squeeze
I figured it out.
Fig-ured...
...what out?

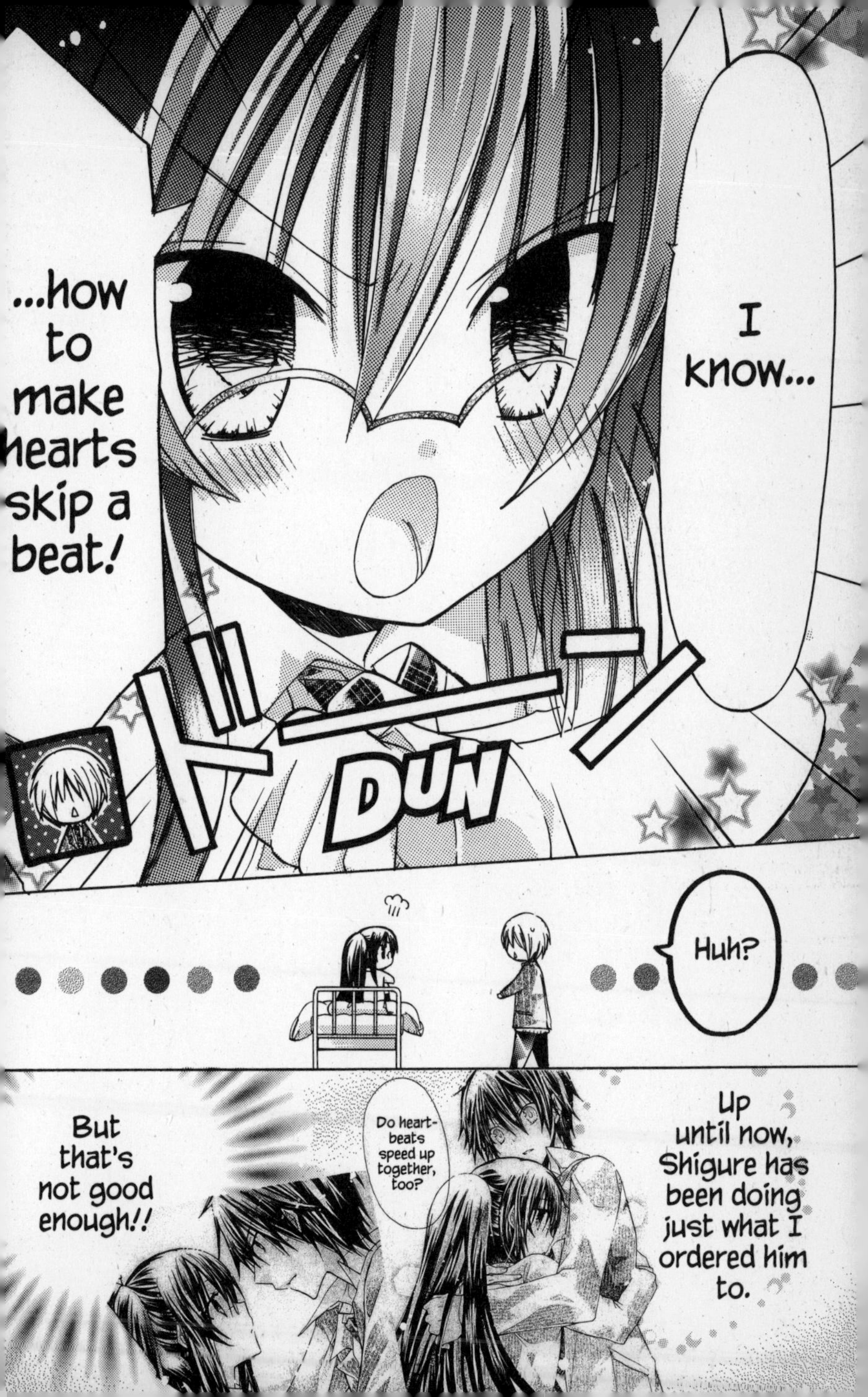
I know...
...how to make hearts skip a beat!
DUN
Huh?
Up until now, Shigure has been doing just what I ordered him to.
Do heart-beats speed up together, too?
But that's not good enough!!

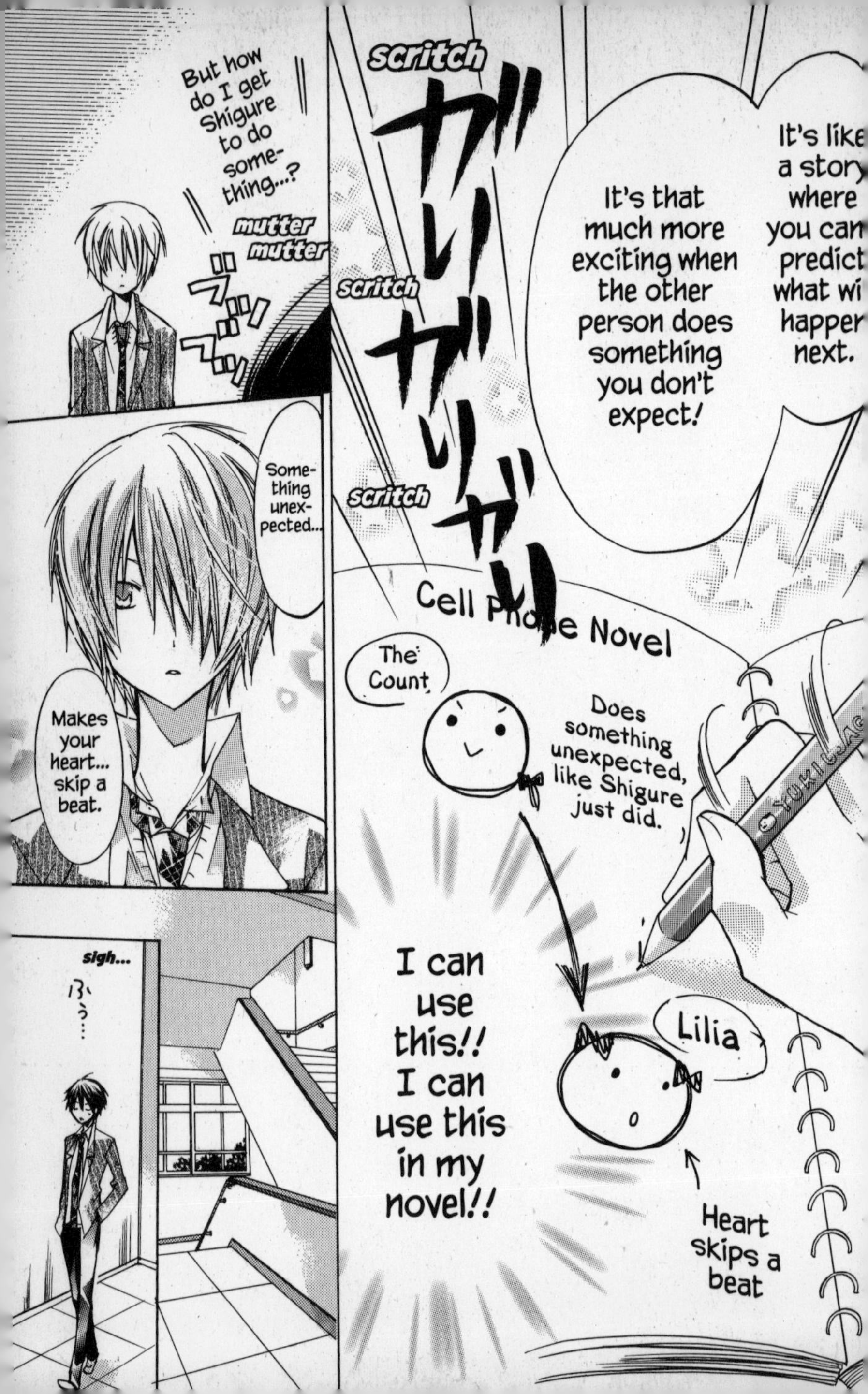
scritch
ガリガリガリ
scritch
scritch
It's like a story where you can predict what wi happen next.
It's that much more exciting when the other person does something you don't expect!
Cell Phone Novel
The Count
Does something unexpected, like Shigure just did.
Lilia
Heart skips a beat
I can use this!! I can use this in my novel!!
But how do I get Shigure to do something...?
mutter mutter
ブツブツ
Something unexpected...
Makes your heart... skip a beat.
sigh...
ふぅ…

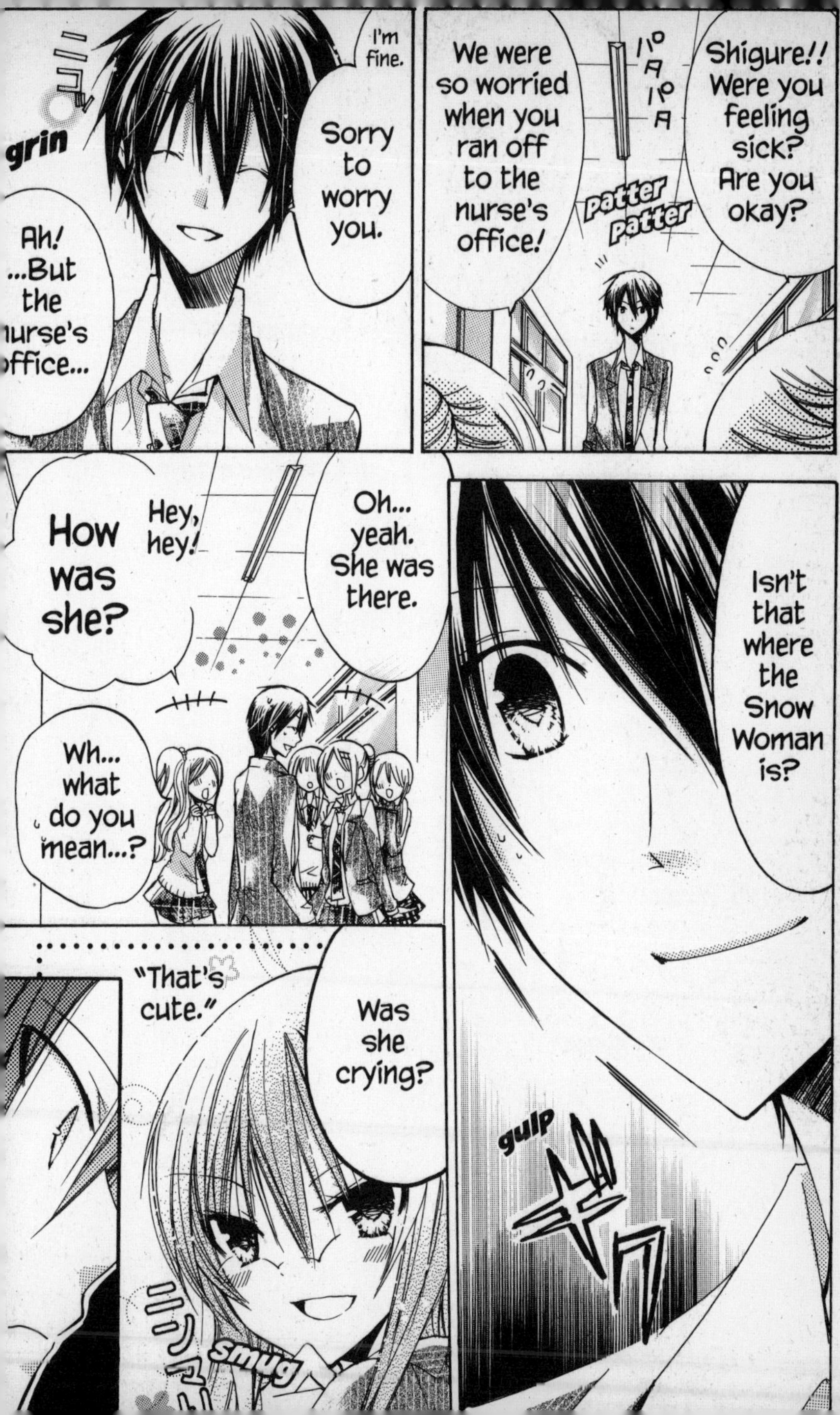
Shigure!! Were you feeling sick? Are you okay?
We were so worried when you ran off to the nurse's office!
パタパタ
Patter patter
I'm fine.
Sorry to worry you.
ニコッ
grin
Ah! ...But the nurse's office...
Isn't that where the Snow Woman is?
ギク
gulp
Oh... yeah. She was there.
Hey, hey!
How was she?
Wh... what do you mean...?
Was she crying?
"That's cute."
......
smug

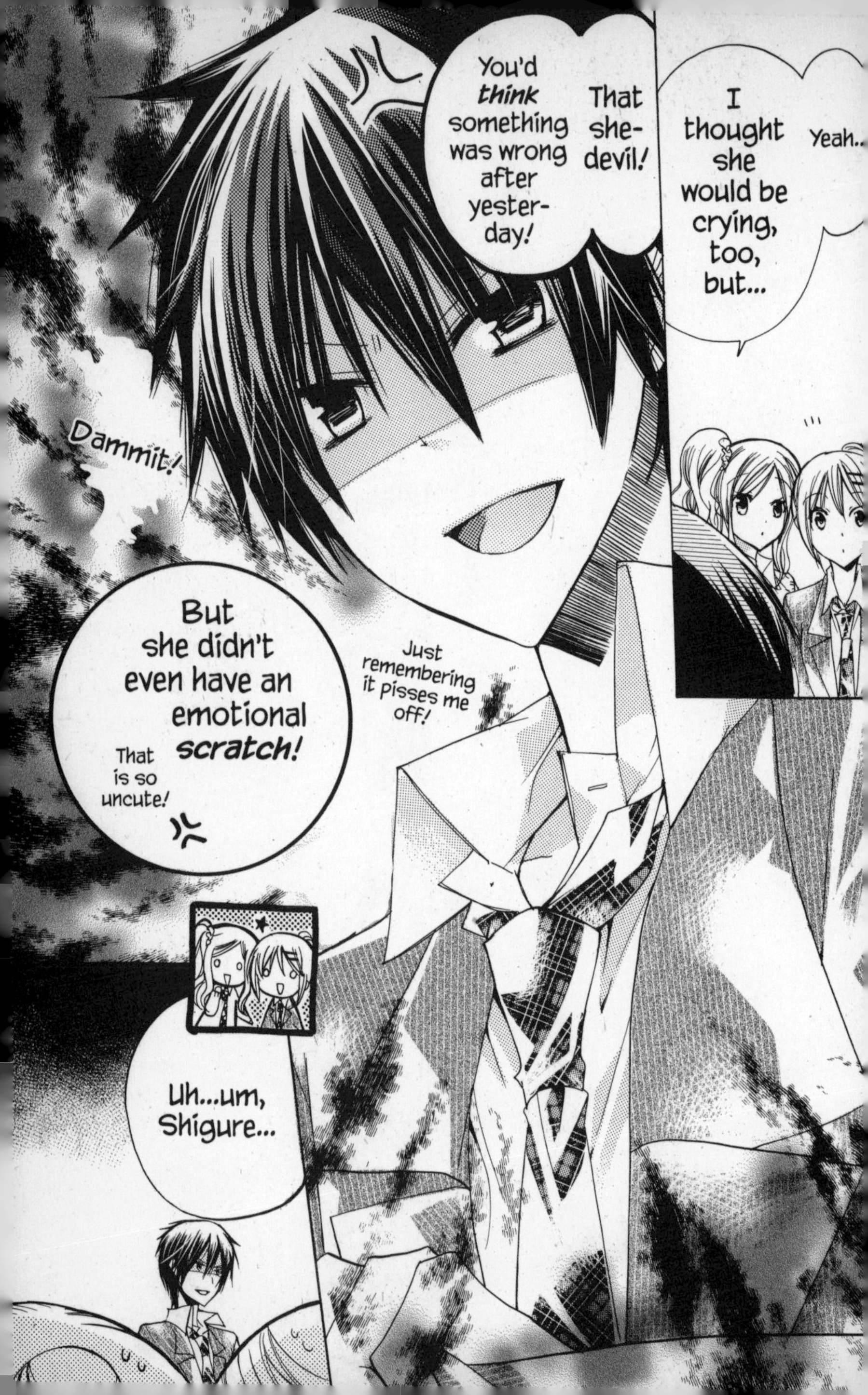
I thought she would be crying, too, but...
Yeah...
You'd think something was wrong after yesterday!
That she-devil!
Dammit!
Just remembering it pisses me off!
But she didn't even have an emotional scratch!
That is so uncute!
Uh...um, Shigure...

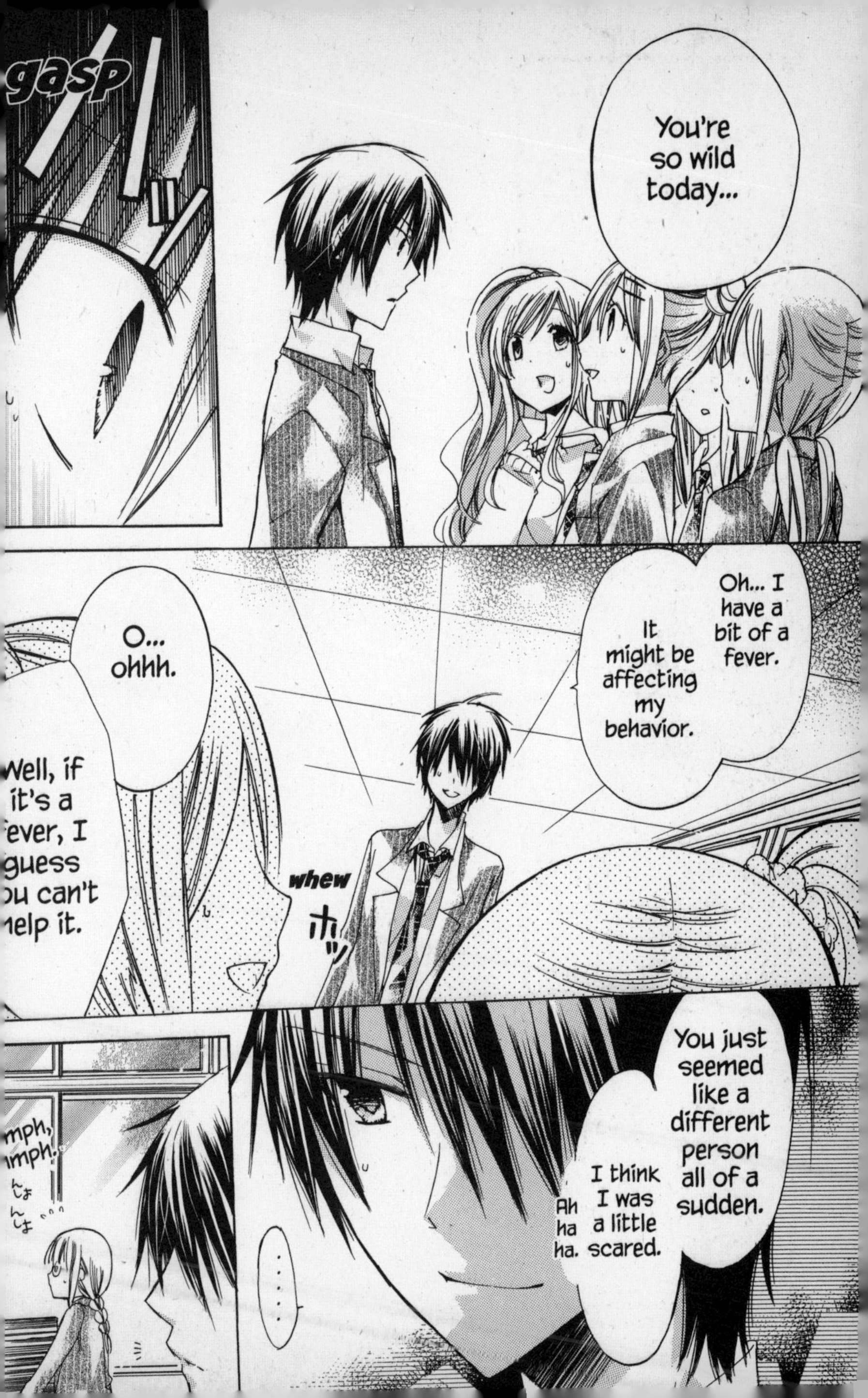

You're so wild today...
gasp
Oh... I have a bit of a fever.
It might be affecting my behavior.
O... ohhh.
Well, if it's a fever, I guess you can't help it.
whew
You just seemed like a different person all of a sudden.
I think I was a little scared.
Ah ha ha.
...
mph, mph.

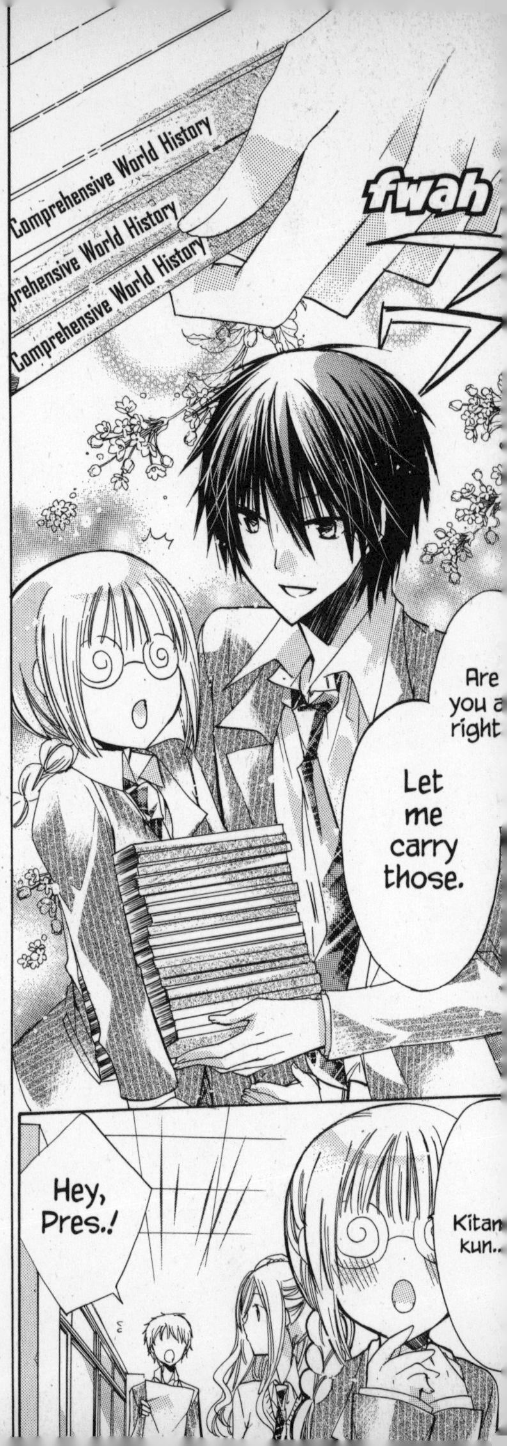
fwah
Comprehensive World History
Comprehensive World History
Comprehensive World History
Are you a right
Let me carry those.
Kitan kun..
Hey, Pres.!

Snow Yukina (3)

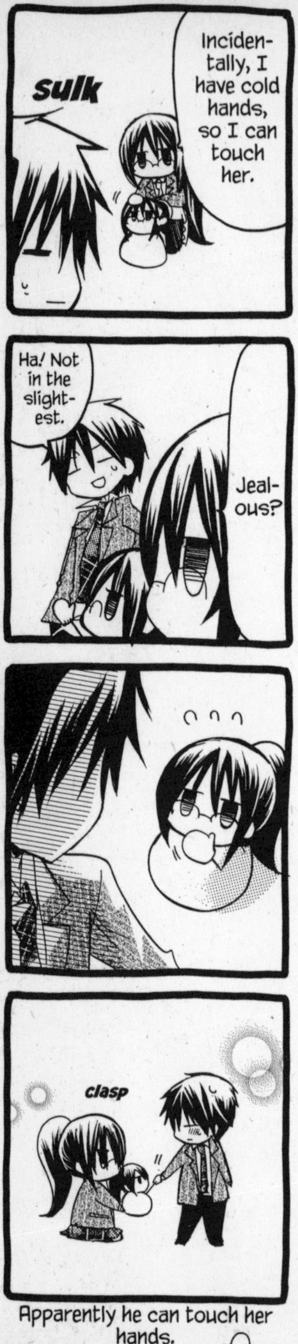
Incidentally, I have cold hands, so I can touch her.
sulk
Jealous?
Ha! Not in the slightest.
clasp

Apparently he can touch her hands.

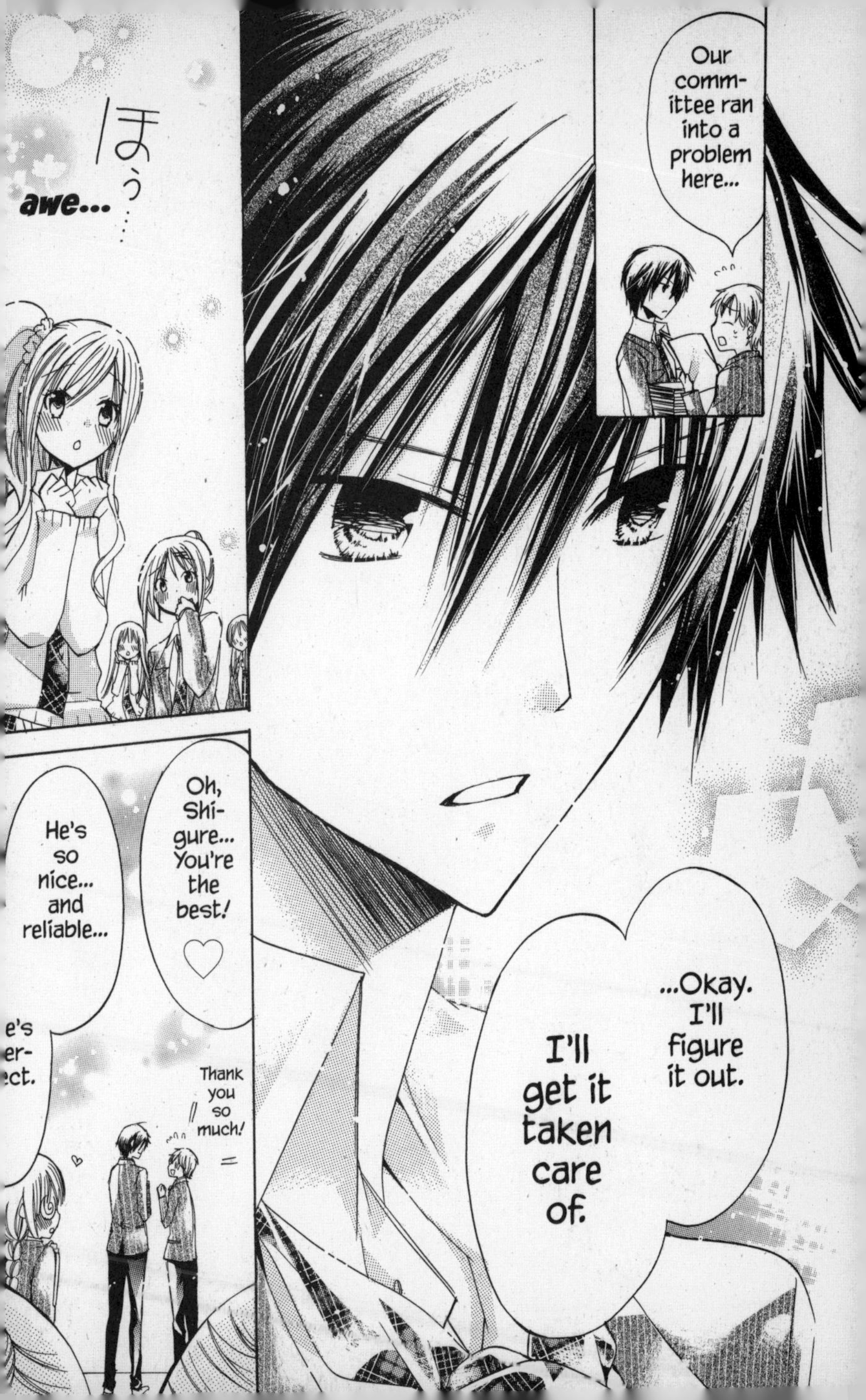
Our committee ran into a problem here...
...Okay. I'll figure it out.
I'll get it taken care of.
ほぅ…
awe...
Oh, Shigure... You're the best!
He's so nice... and reliable...
Thank you so much!

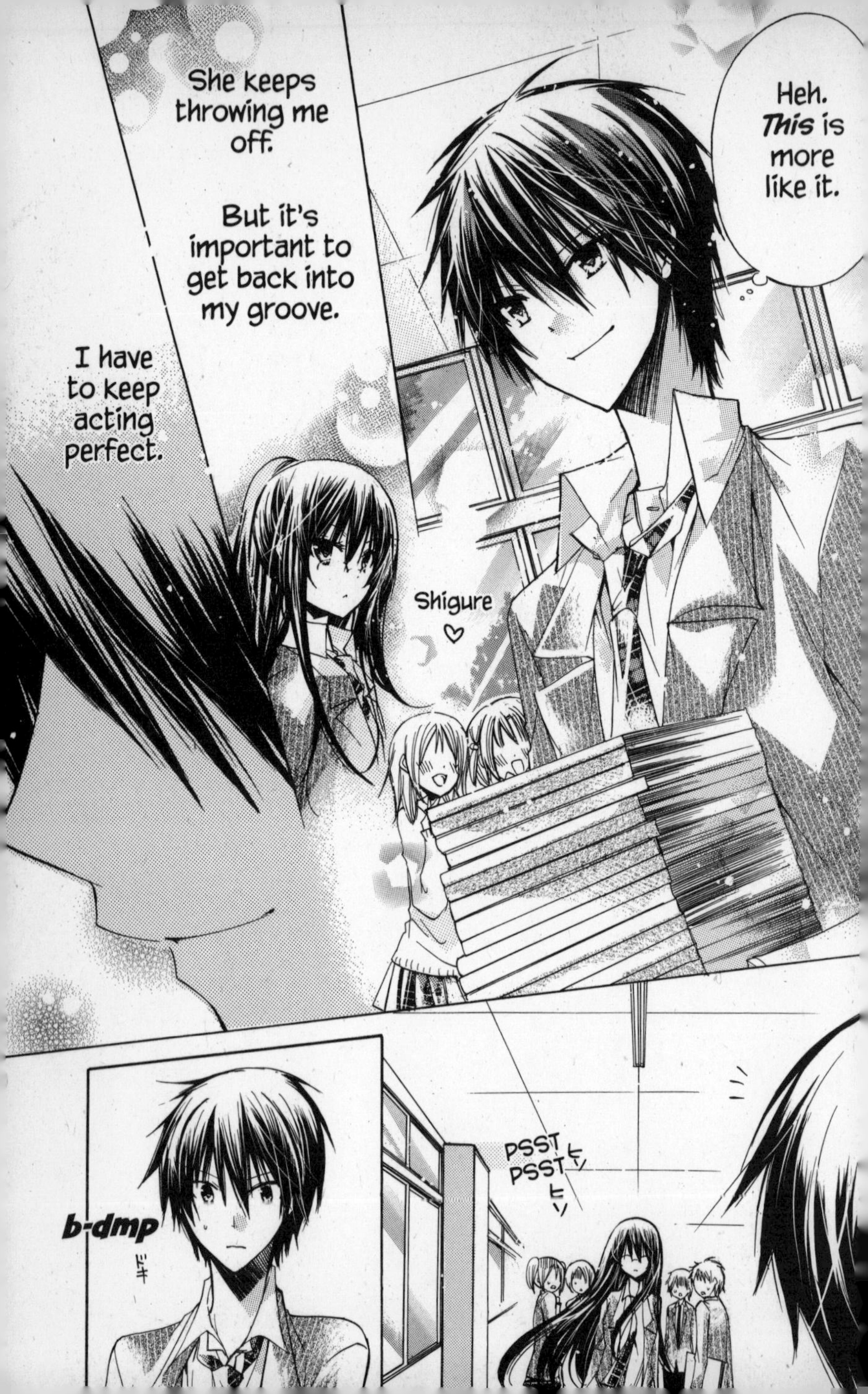
Heh. *This* is more like it.
She keeps throwing me off.
But it's important to get back into my groove.
I have to keep acting perfect.
Shigure ♡
PSST ヒソ
PSST ヒソ
b-dmp
ドキ

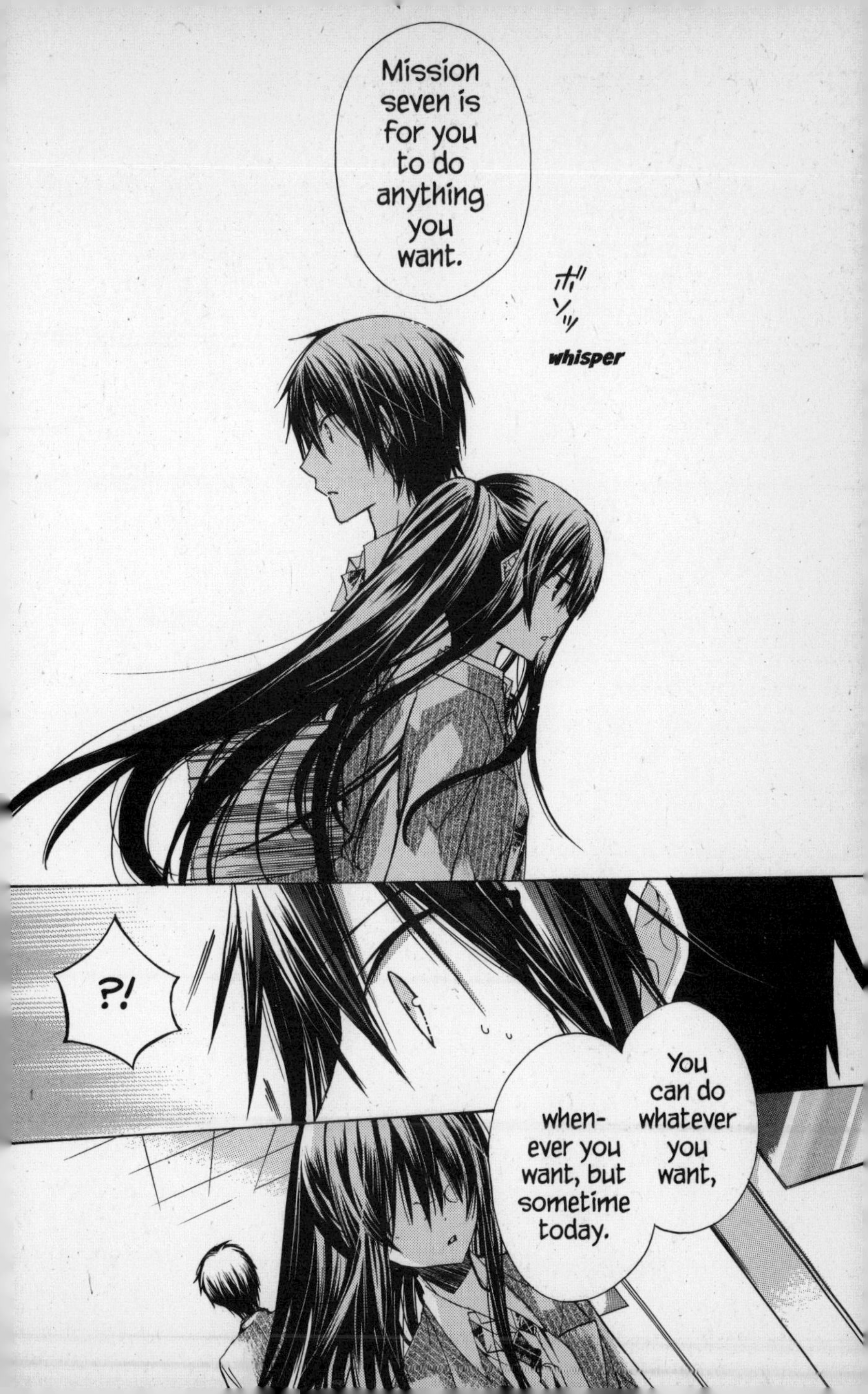
Mission seven is for you to do anything you want.
ボソッ
whisper
?!
You can do whatever you want,
whenever you want, but sometime today.

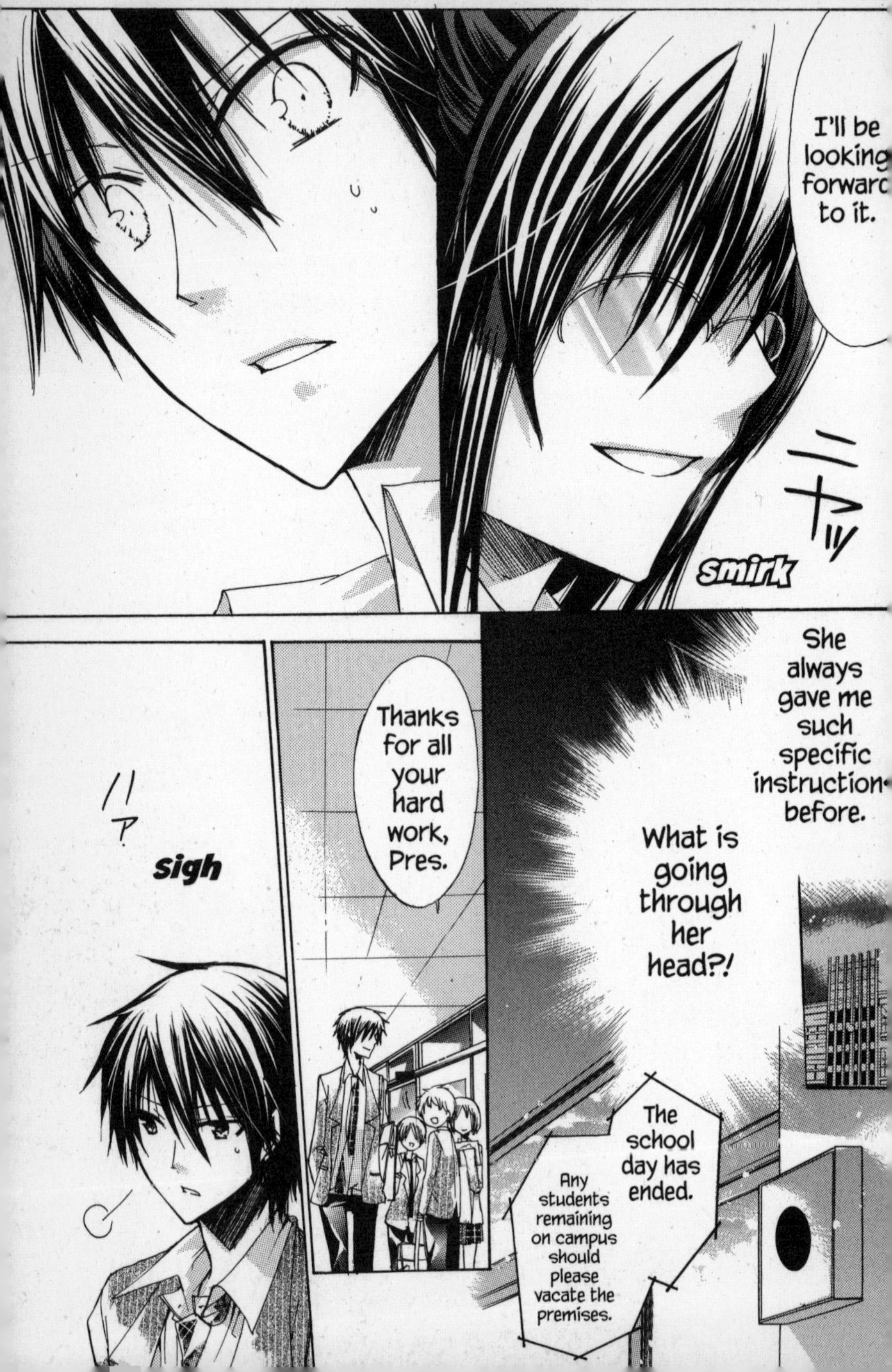

I'll be looking forward to it.
ニヤッ
Smirk
She always gave me such specific instruction before.
What is going through her head?!
The school day has ended.
Any students remaining on campus should please vacate the premises.
Thanks for all your hard work, Pres.
ハァ
Sigh

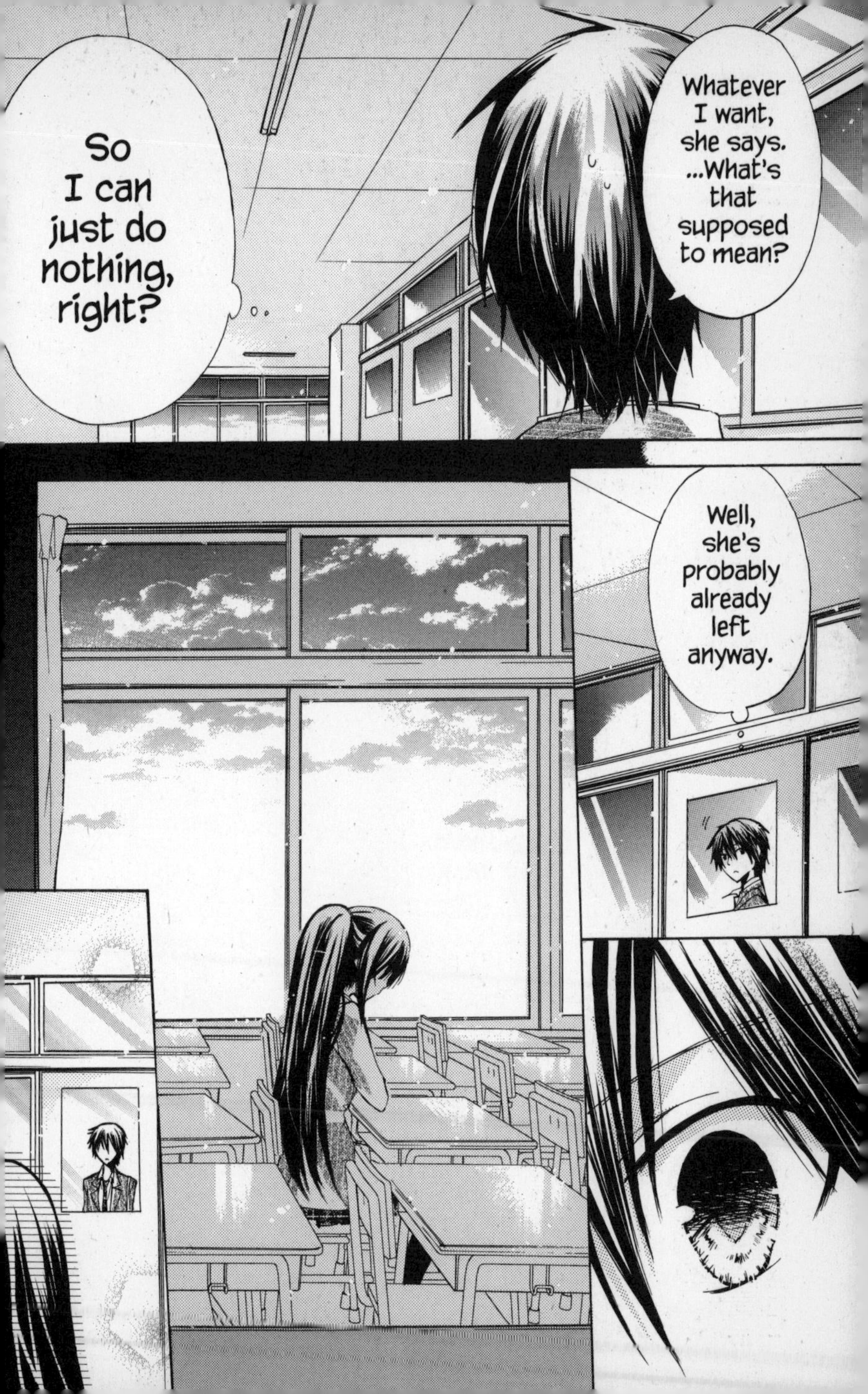
Whatever I want, she says. ...What's that supposed to mean?
So I can just do nothing, right?
Well, she's probably already left anyway.

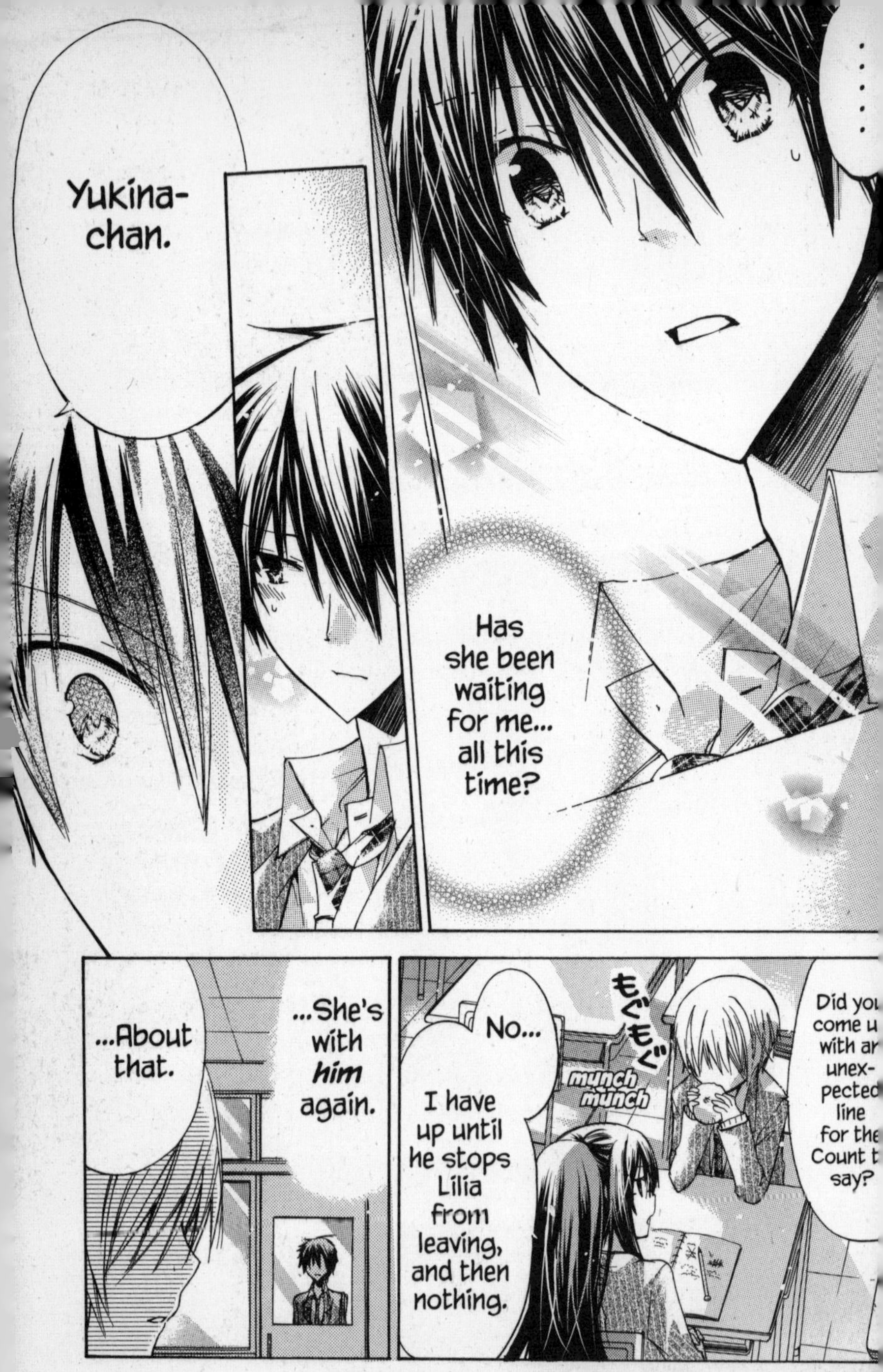
......
Has she been waiting for me... all this time?
Yukina-chan.
Did you come u with ar unex-pected line for the Count t say?
もぐもぐ
munch munch
No...
I have up until he stops Lilia from leaving, and then nothing.
...She's with *him* again.
...About that.

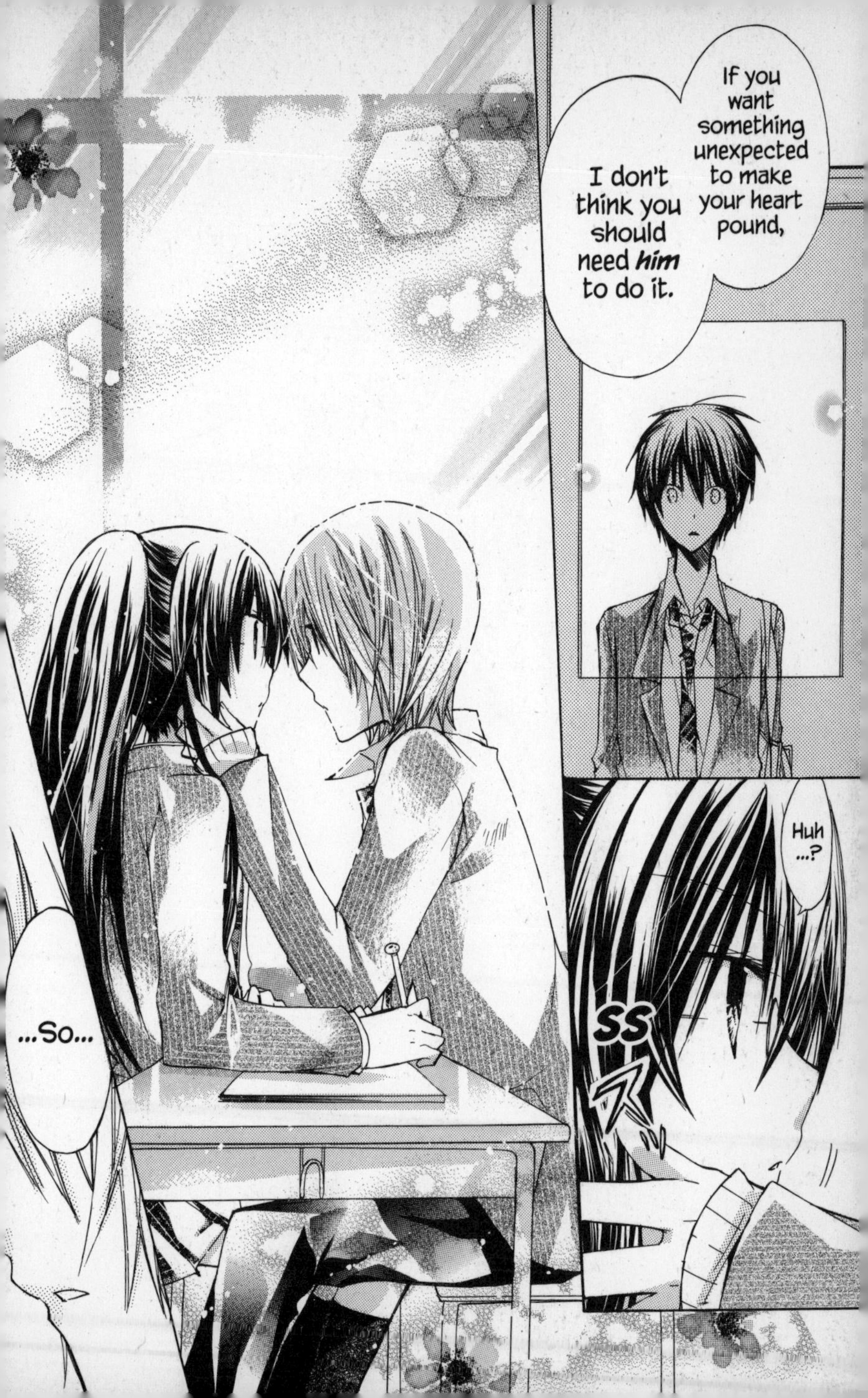
If you want something unexpected to make your heart pound,
I don't think you should need *him* to do it.
Huh ...?
SS
...So...

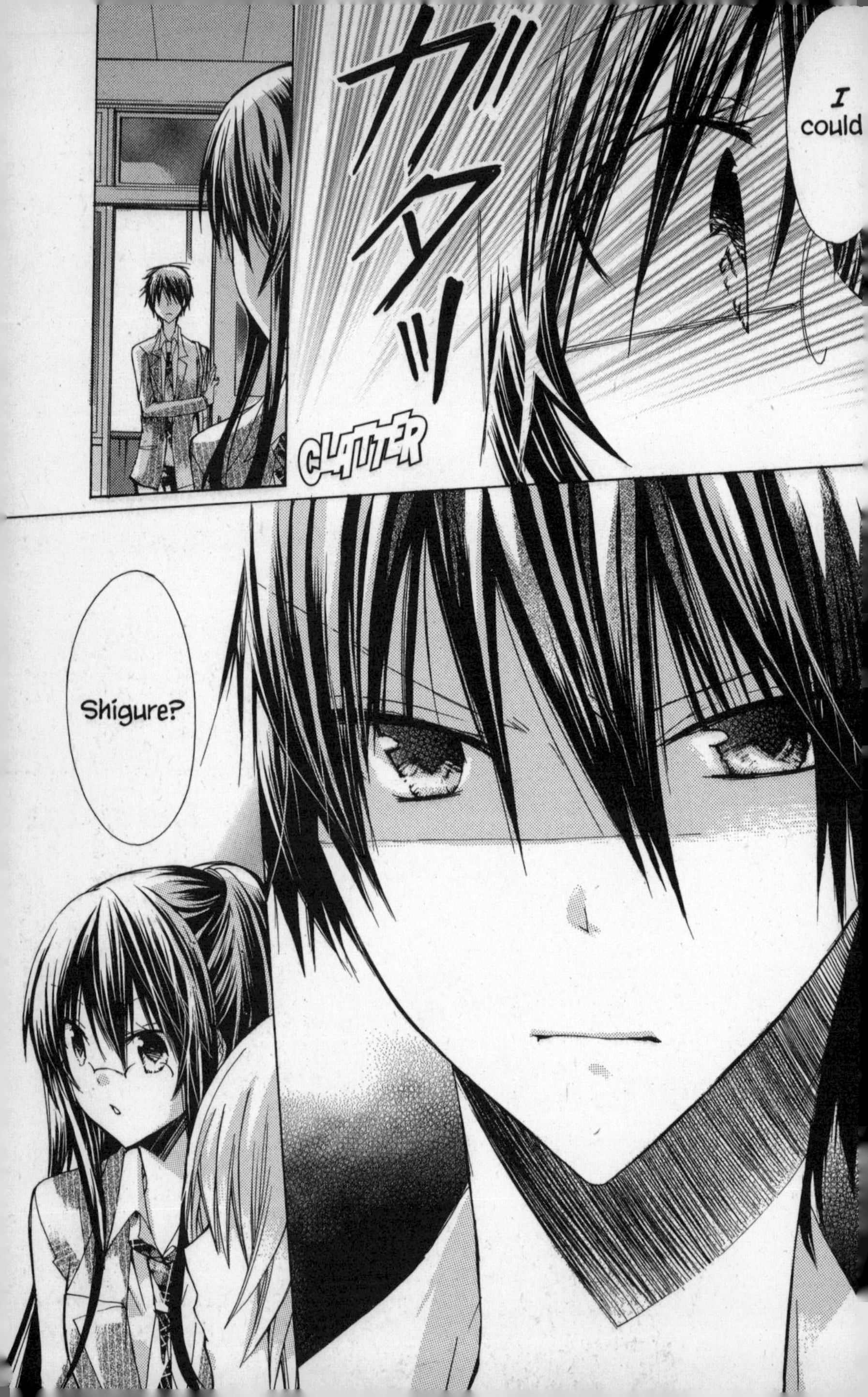
I could
ガタッ
CLATTER
Shigure?

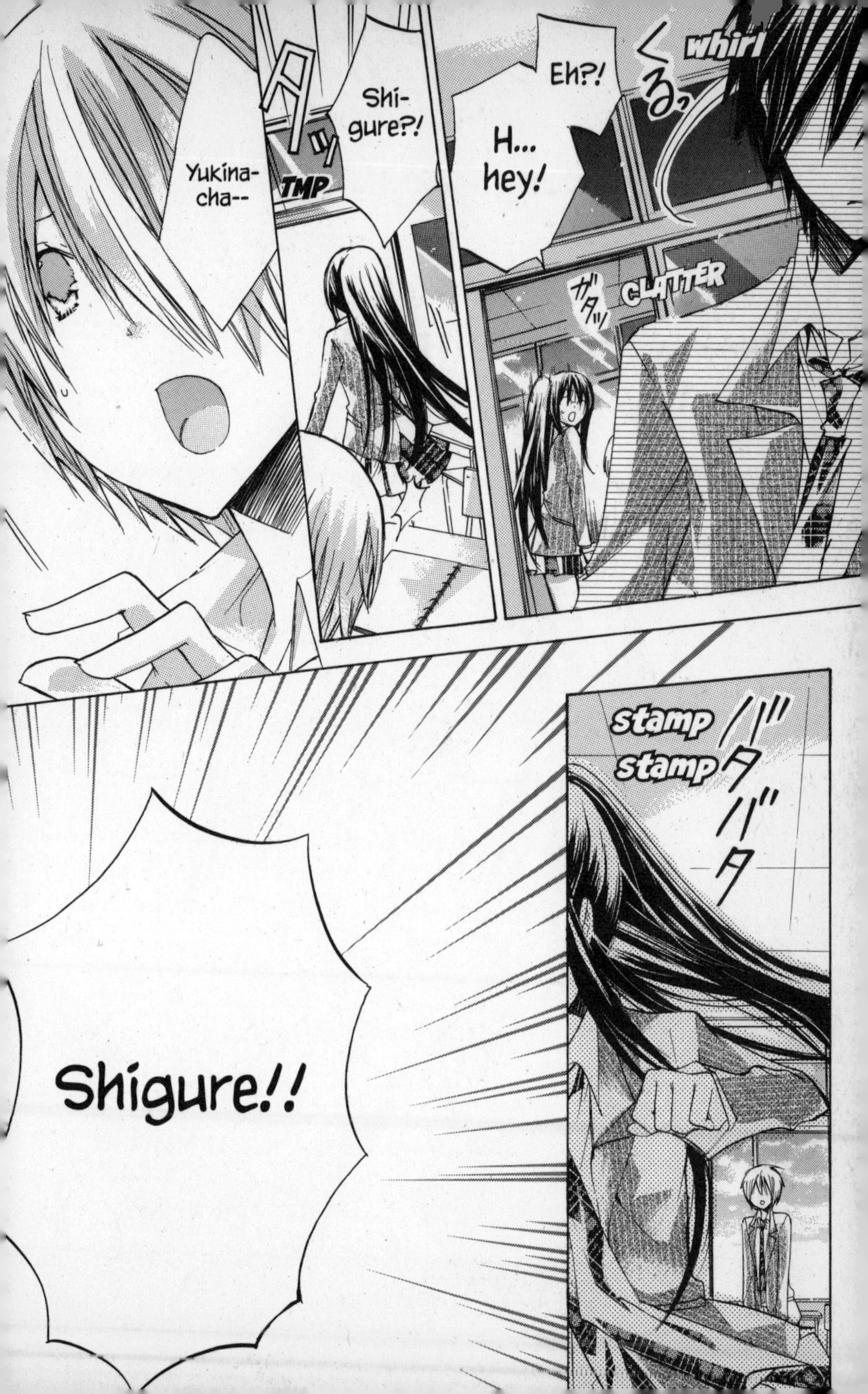
whirl
くるっ
Eh?!
H... hey!
ガタッ
CLATTER
Shi-gure?!
TMP
Yukina-cha--
stamp stamp
バタバタ
Shigure!!

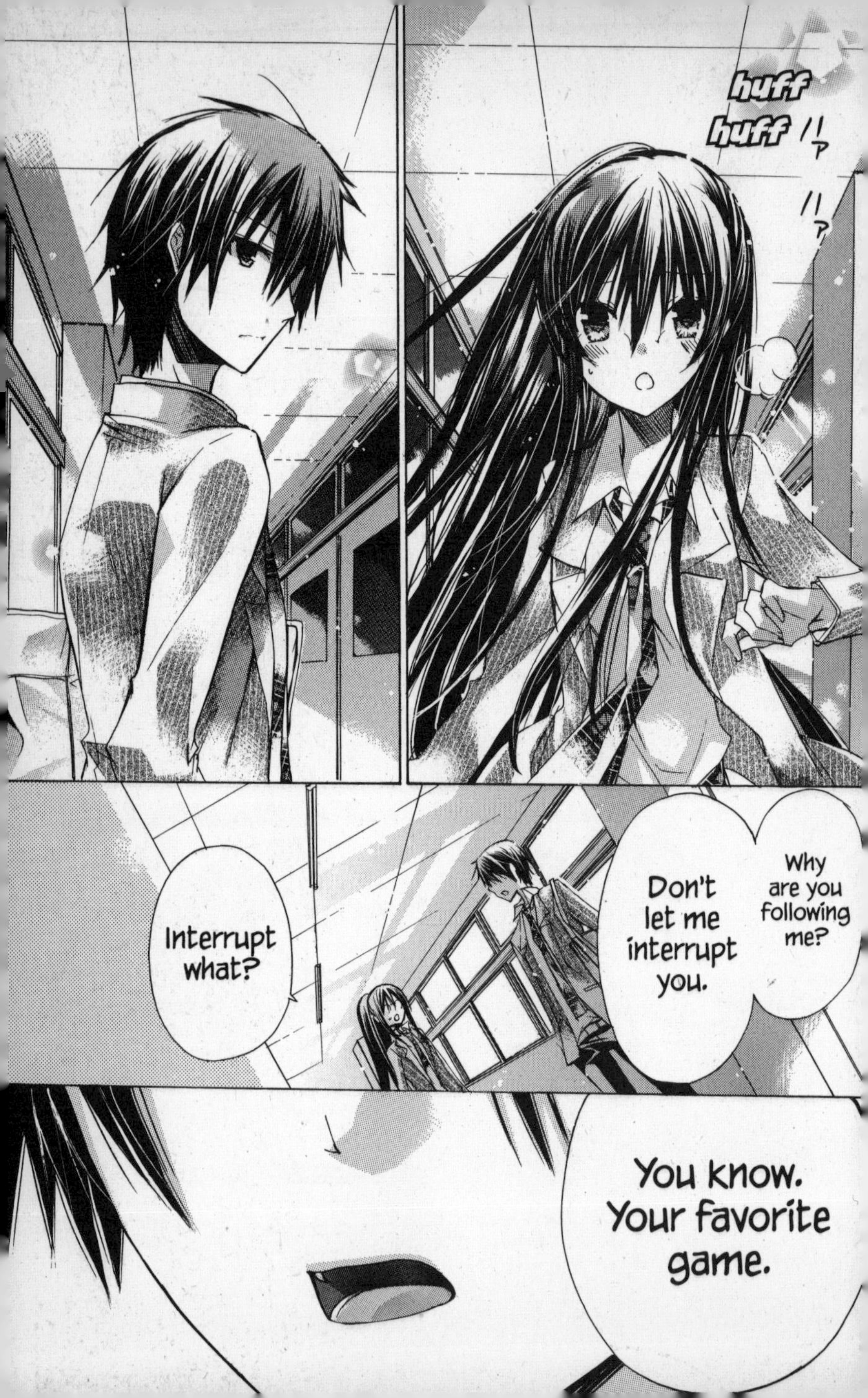
huff
huff
ハァ
ハァ
Why are you following me?
Don't let me interrupt you.
Interrupt what?
You know. Your favorite game.

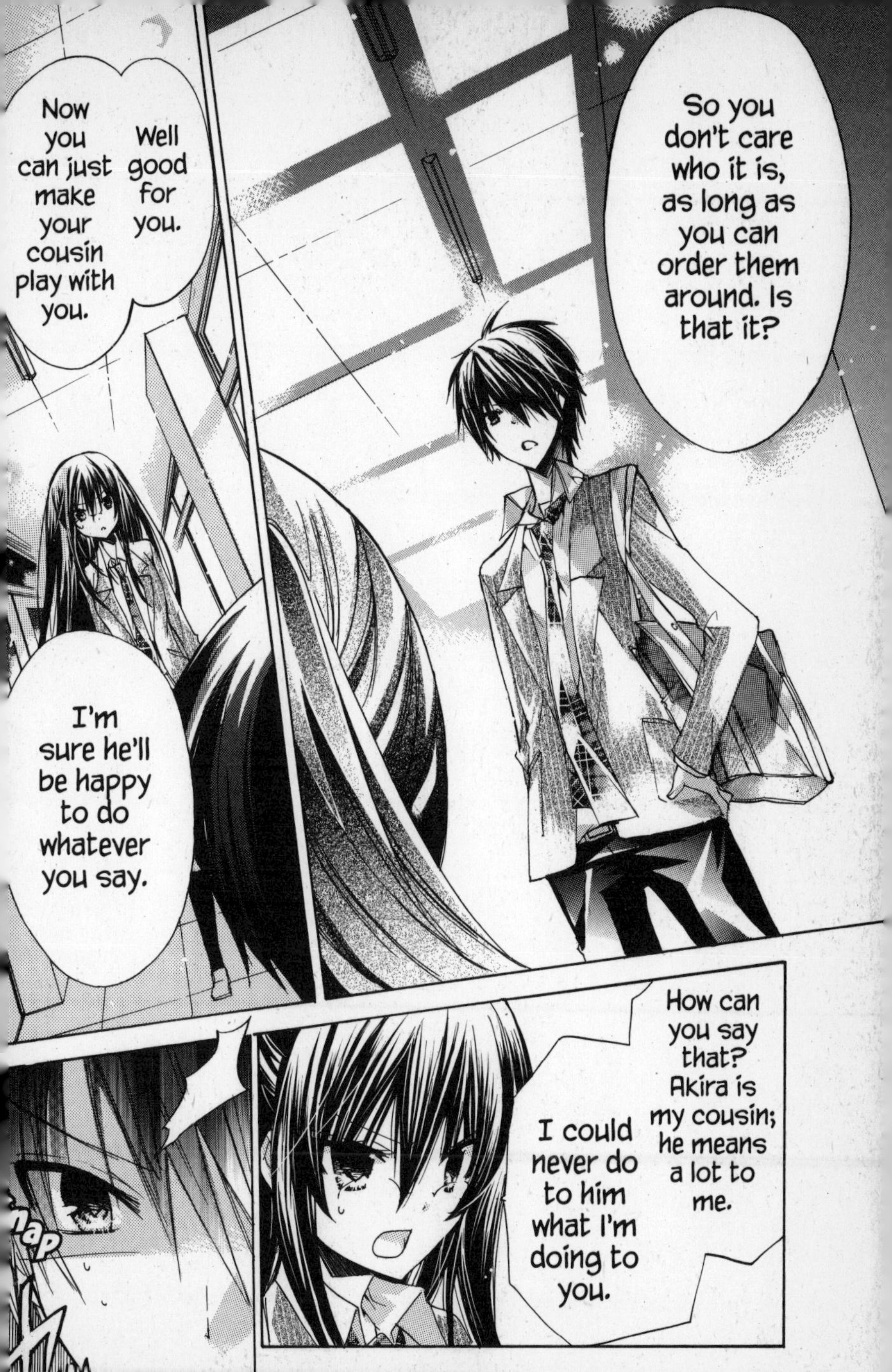
So you don't care who it is, as long as you can order them around. Is that it?
Well good for you.
Now you can just make your cousin play with you.
I'm sure he'll be happy to do whatever you say.
How can you say that? Akira is my cousin; he means a lot to me.
I could never do to him what I'm doing to you.

So you can't use him, but you can use me?!
Of course I can use *you*!!
grrr
hmph
H...
Hey!
tug

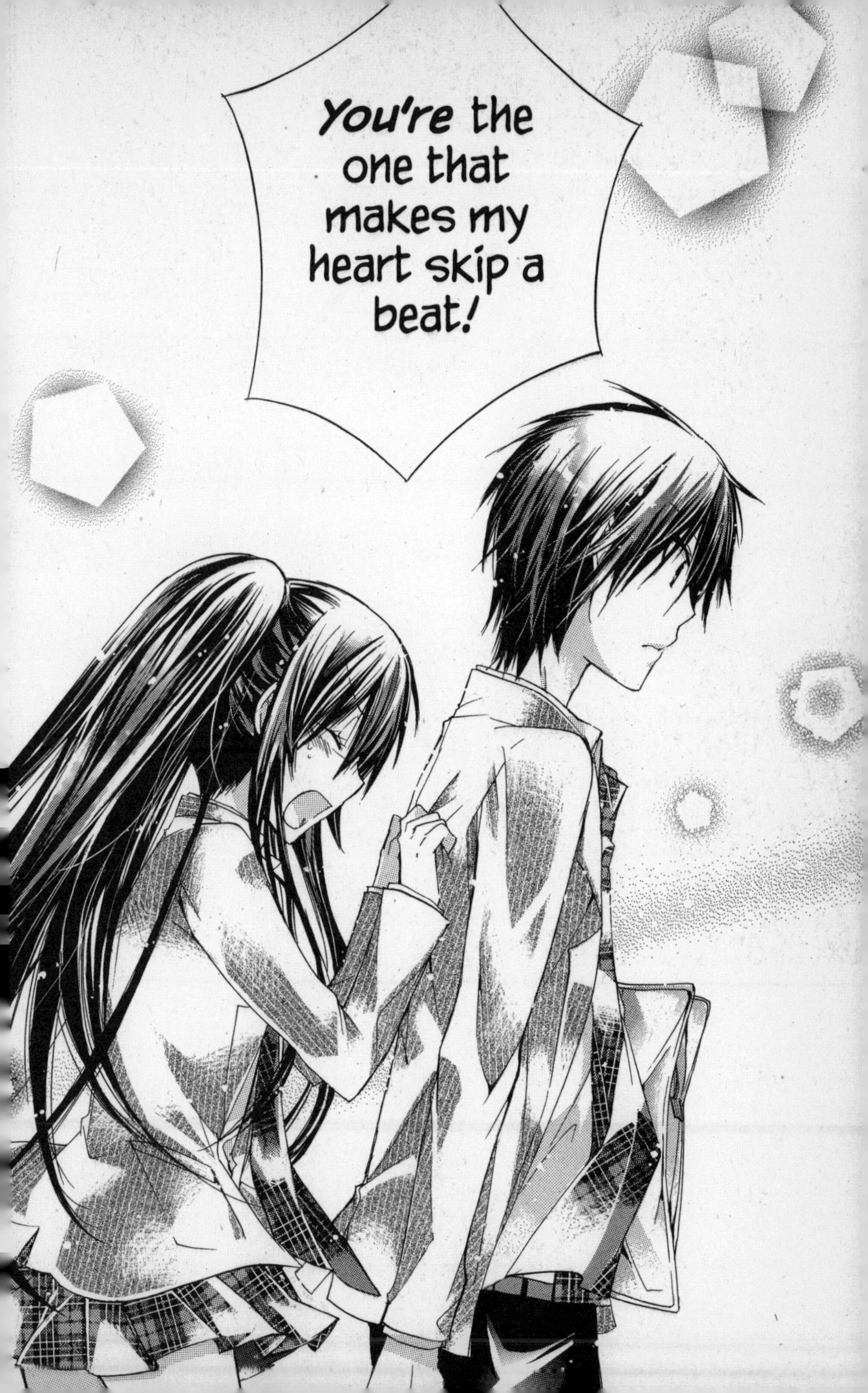
You're the one that makes my heart skip a beat!

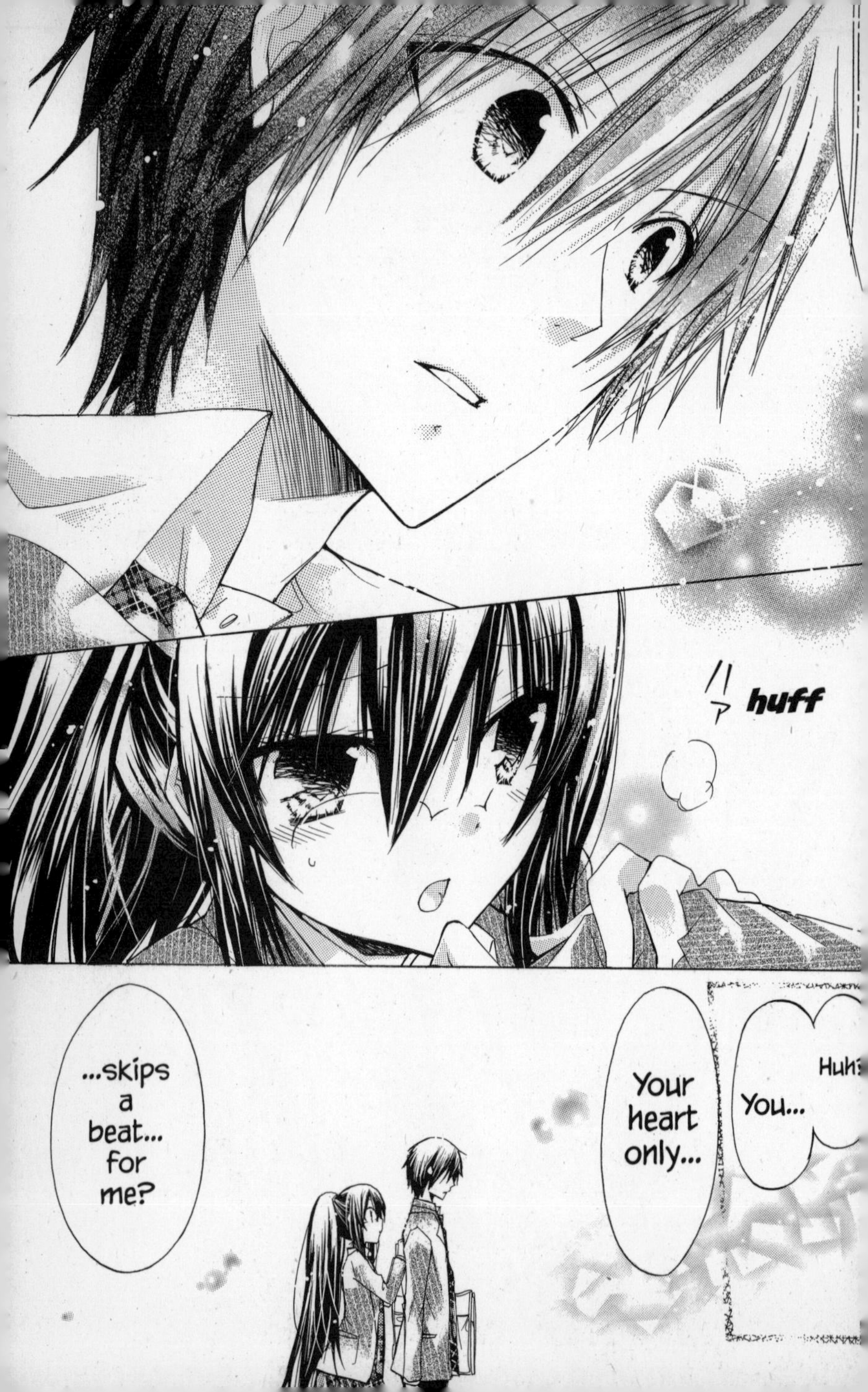
ハァ huff
Huh?
You...
Your heart only...
...skips a beat... for me?

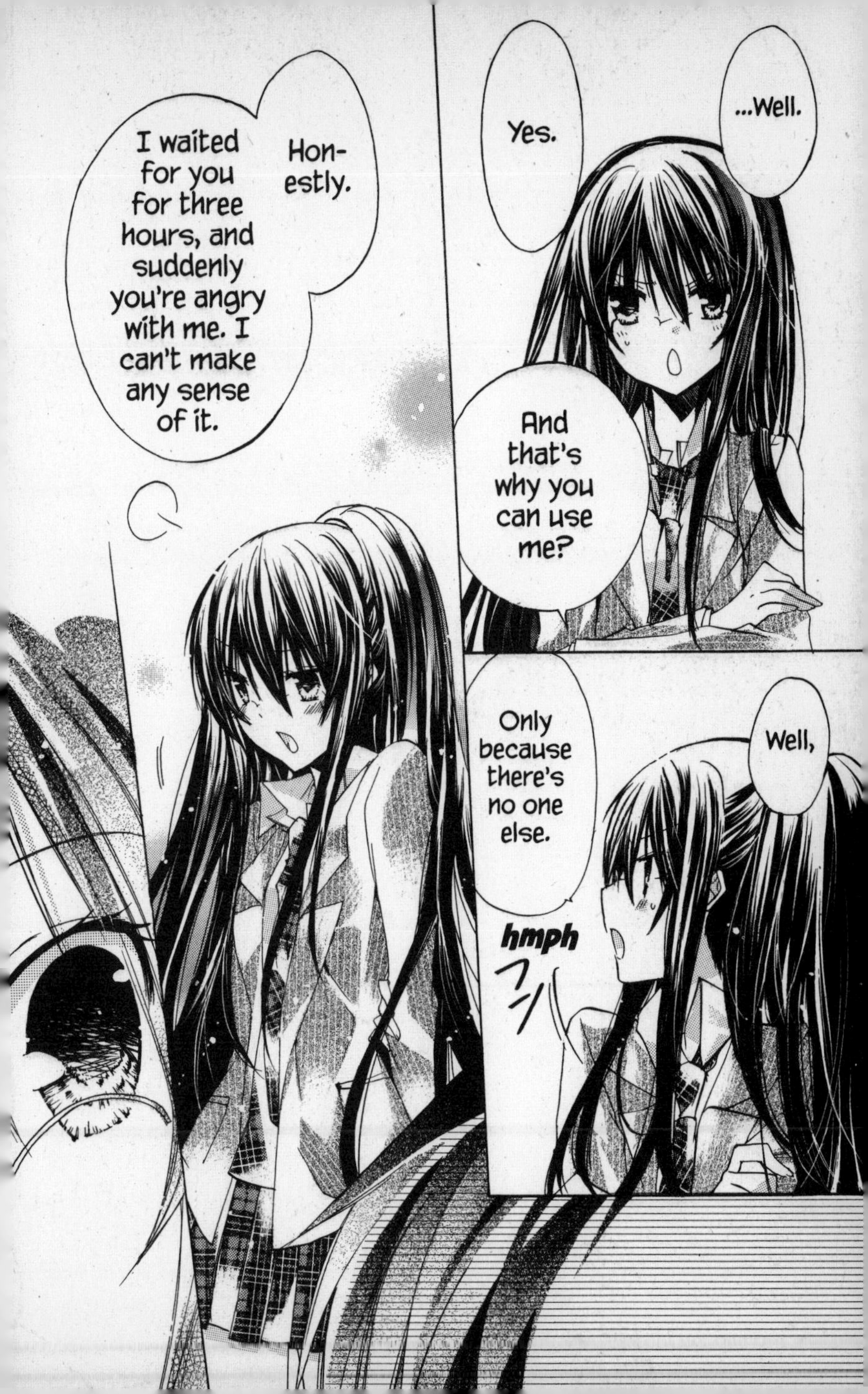
...Well.
Yes.
And that's why you can use me?
Well,
Only because there's no one else.
hmph
Hon-estly.
I waited for you for three hours, and suddenly you're angry with me. I can't make any sense of it.

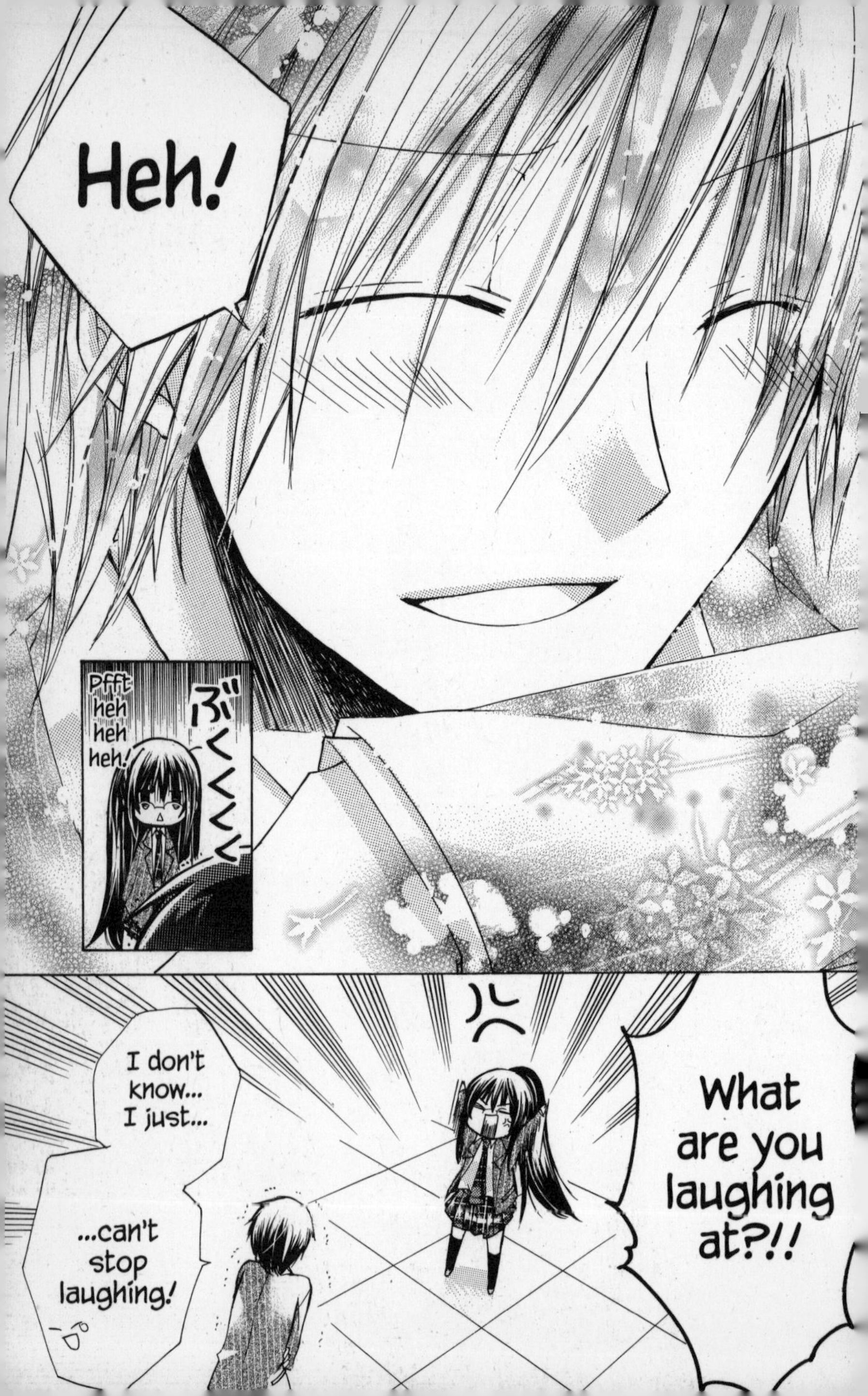
Heh!
ぷくくくく
Pfft heh heh heh!
What are you laughing at?!!
I don't know... I just...
...can't stop laughing!

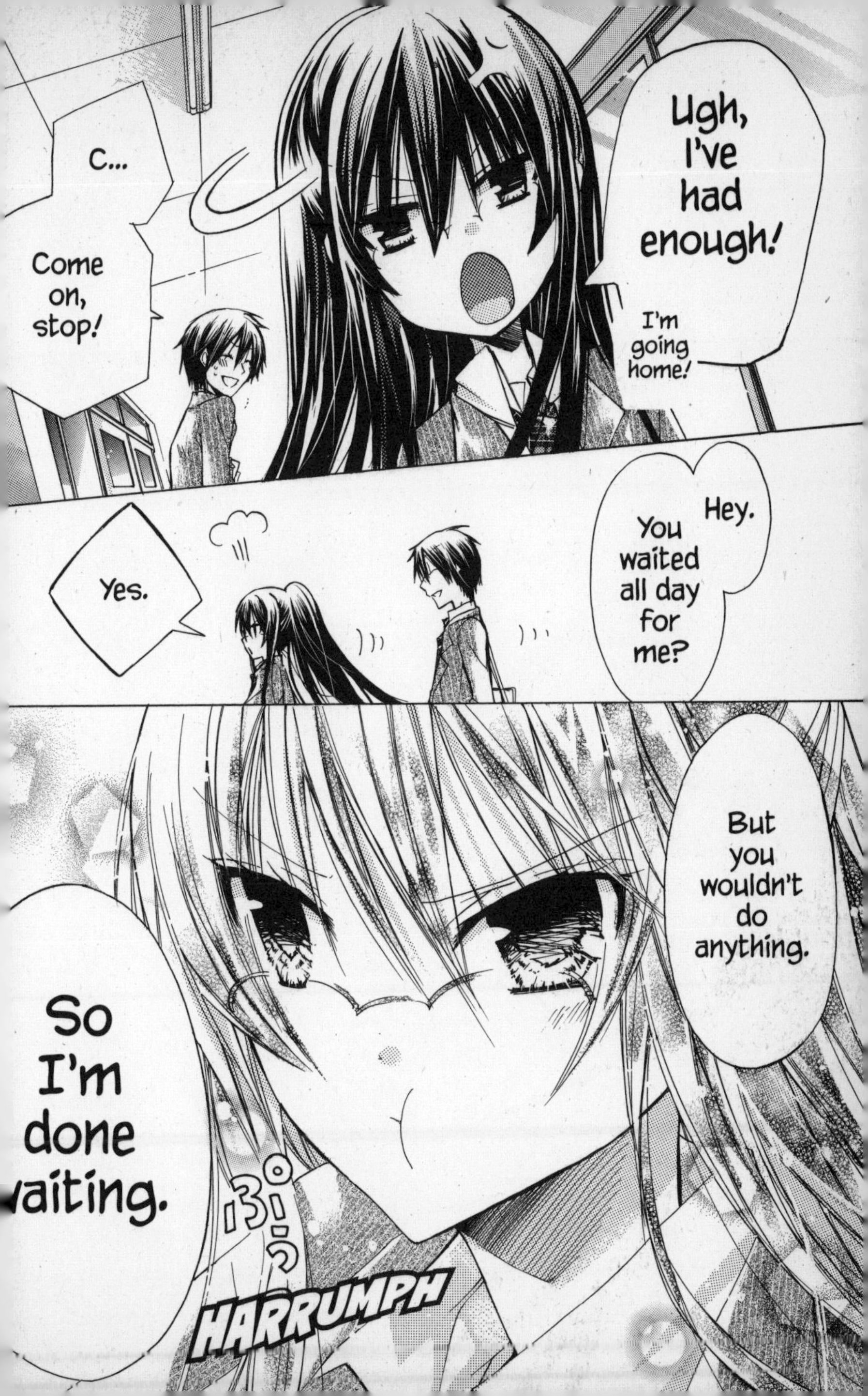
Ugh, I've had enough!
I'm going home!
C...
Come on, stop!
Hey. You waited all day for me?
Yes.
But you wouldn't do anything.
So I'm done waiting.
HARRUMPH

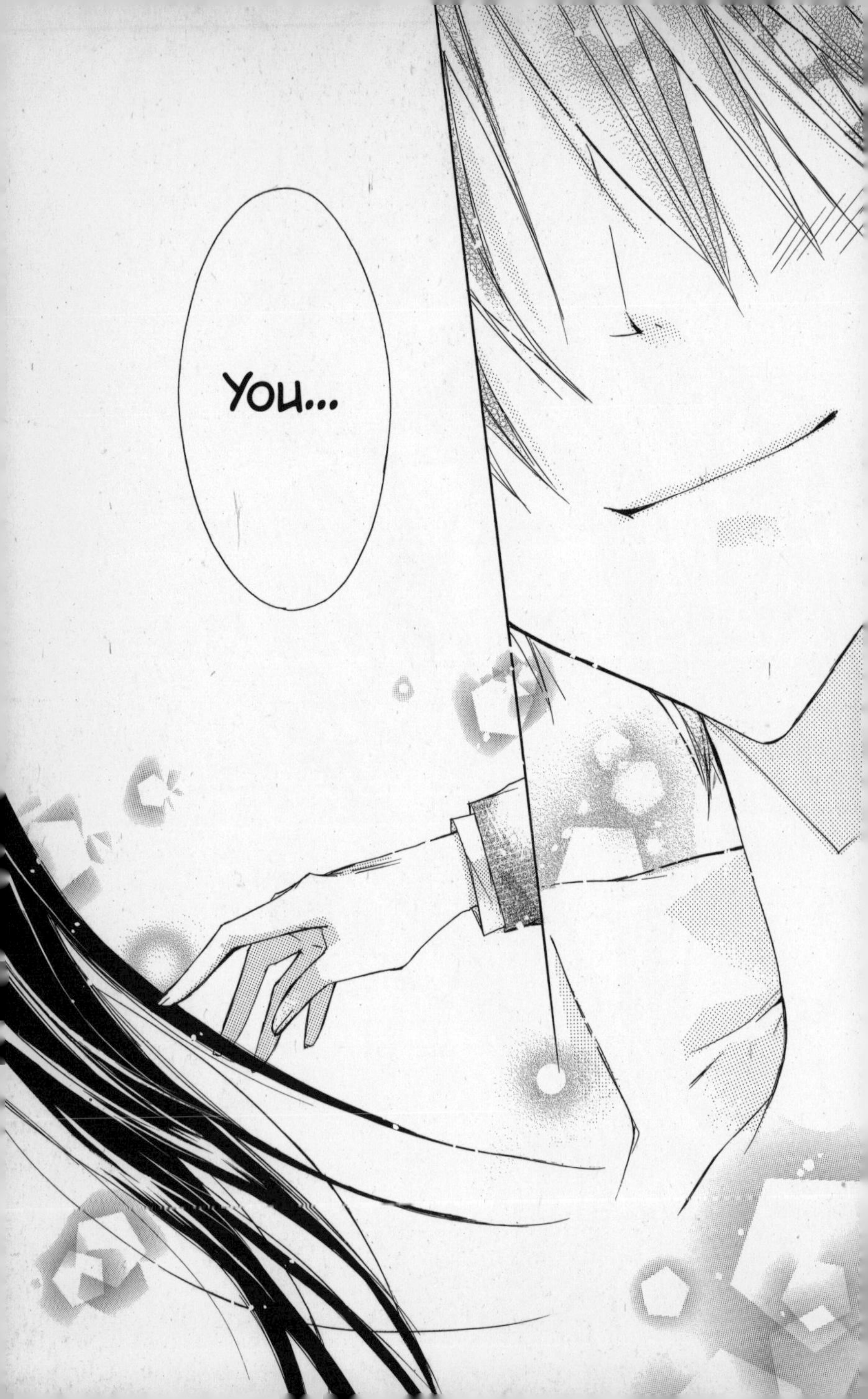
You...

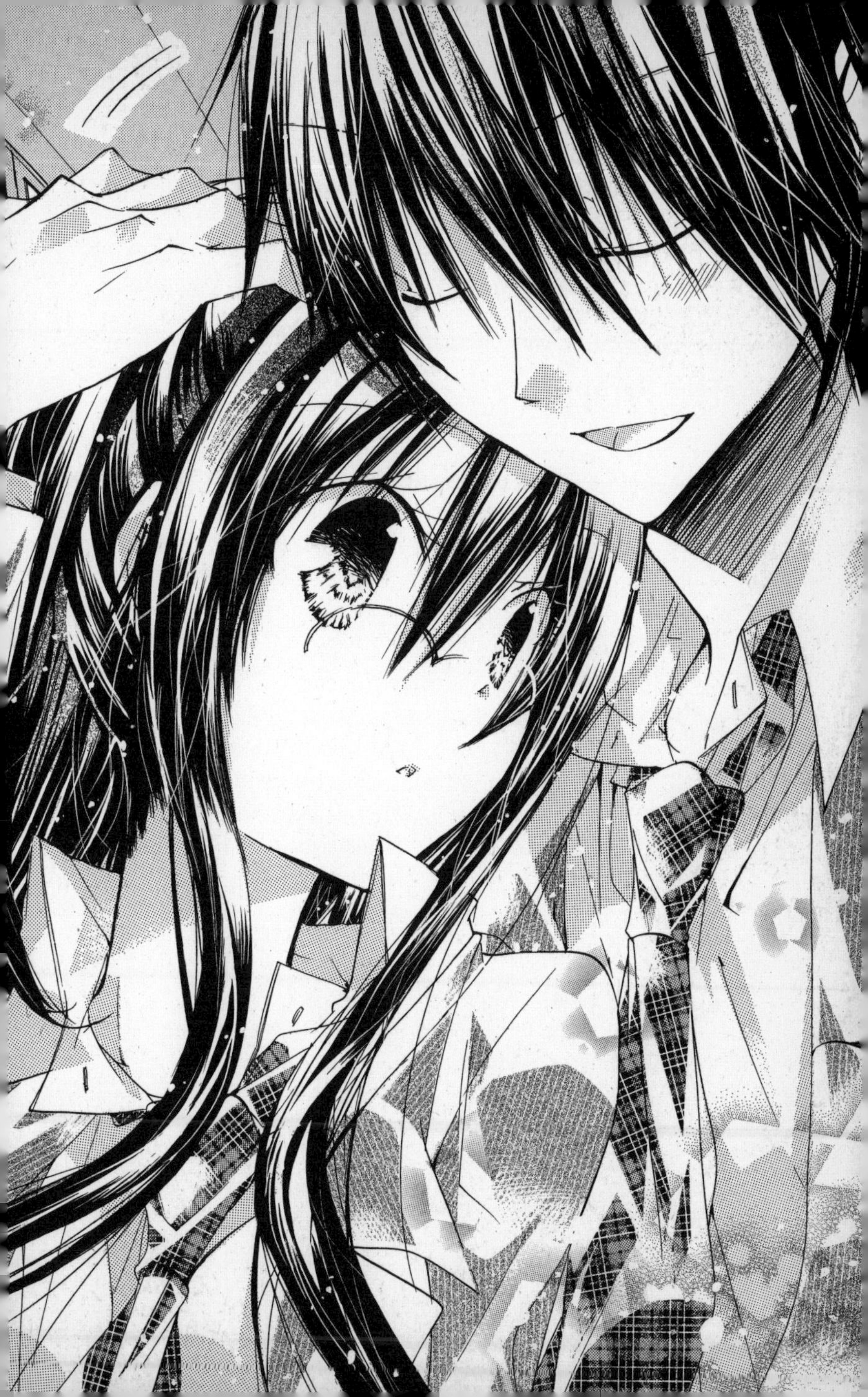

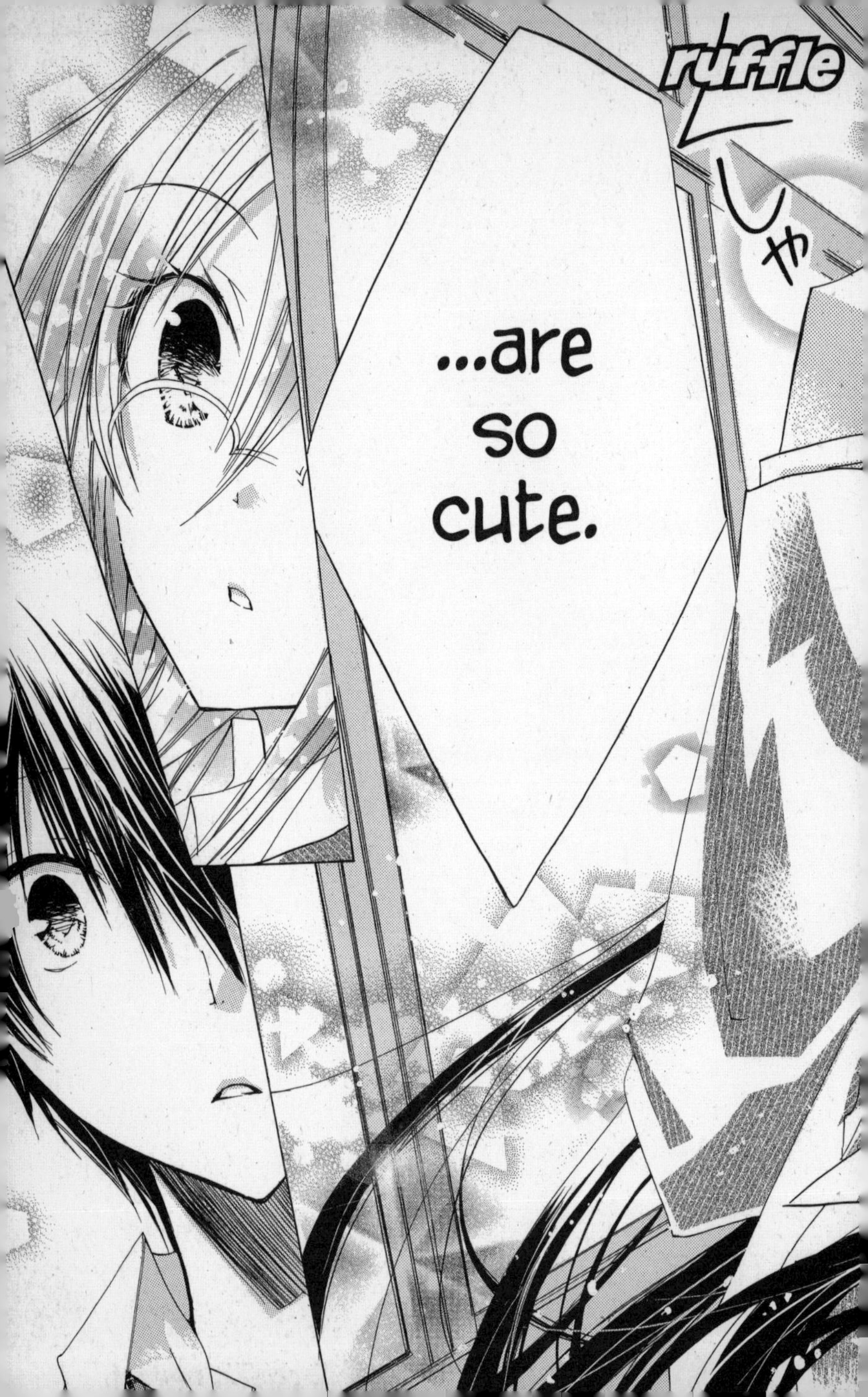
ruffle
しゃ
...are so cute.

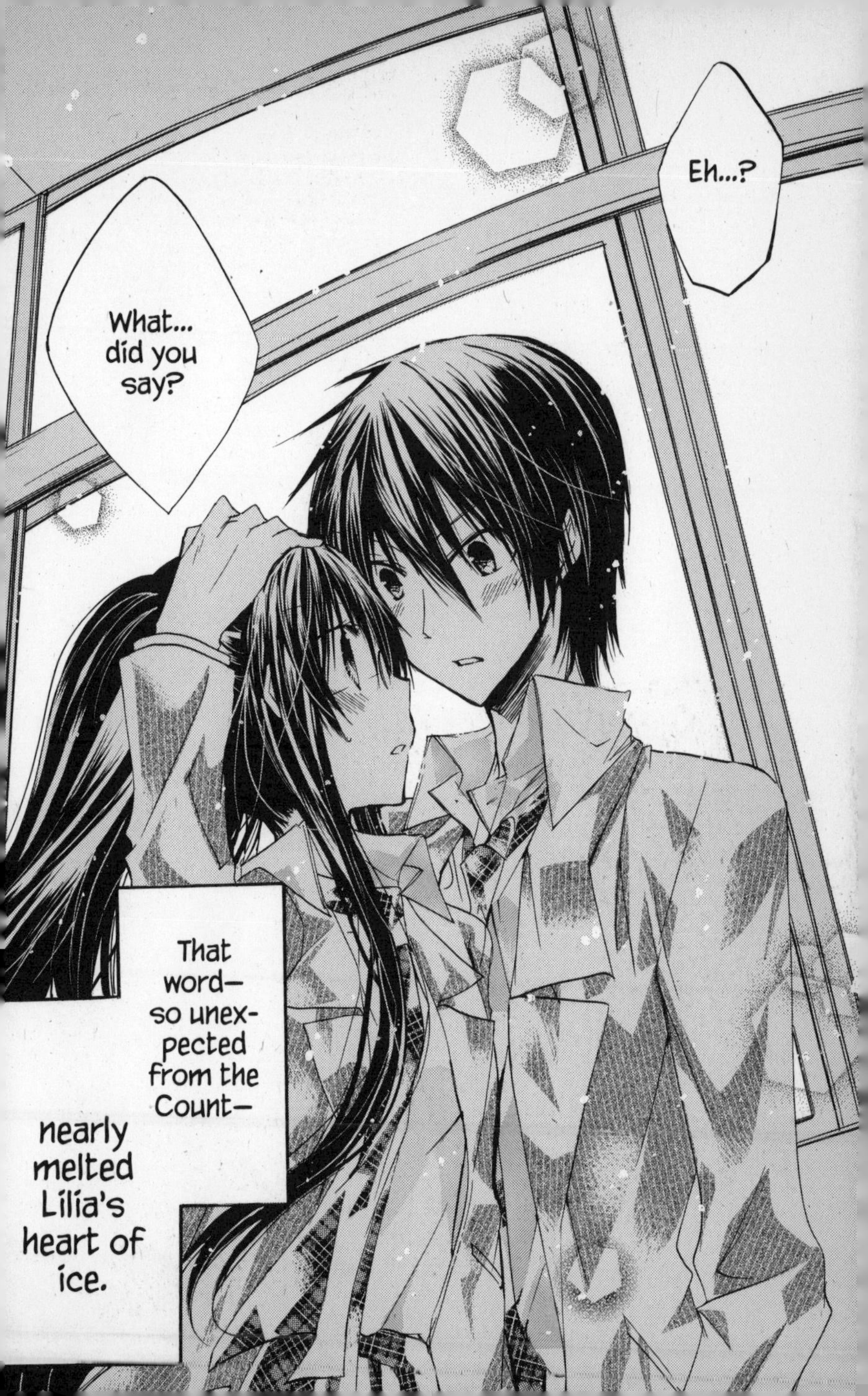
Eh...?
What... did you say?
That word—so unexpected from the Count—nearly melted Lilia's heart of ice.

Missions of Love

**It is time for love.
Secret cell phone
novelist vs. the most
popular boy in school.
A mission of love for
absolute servitude.**

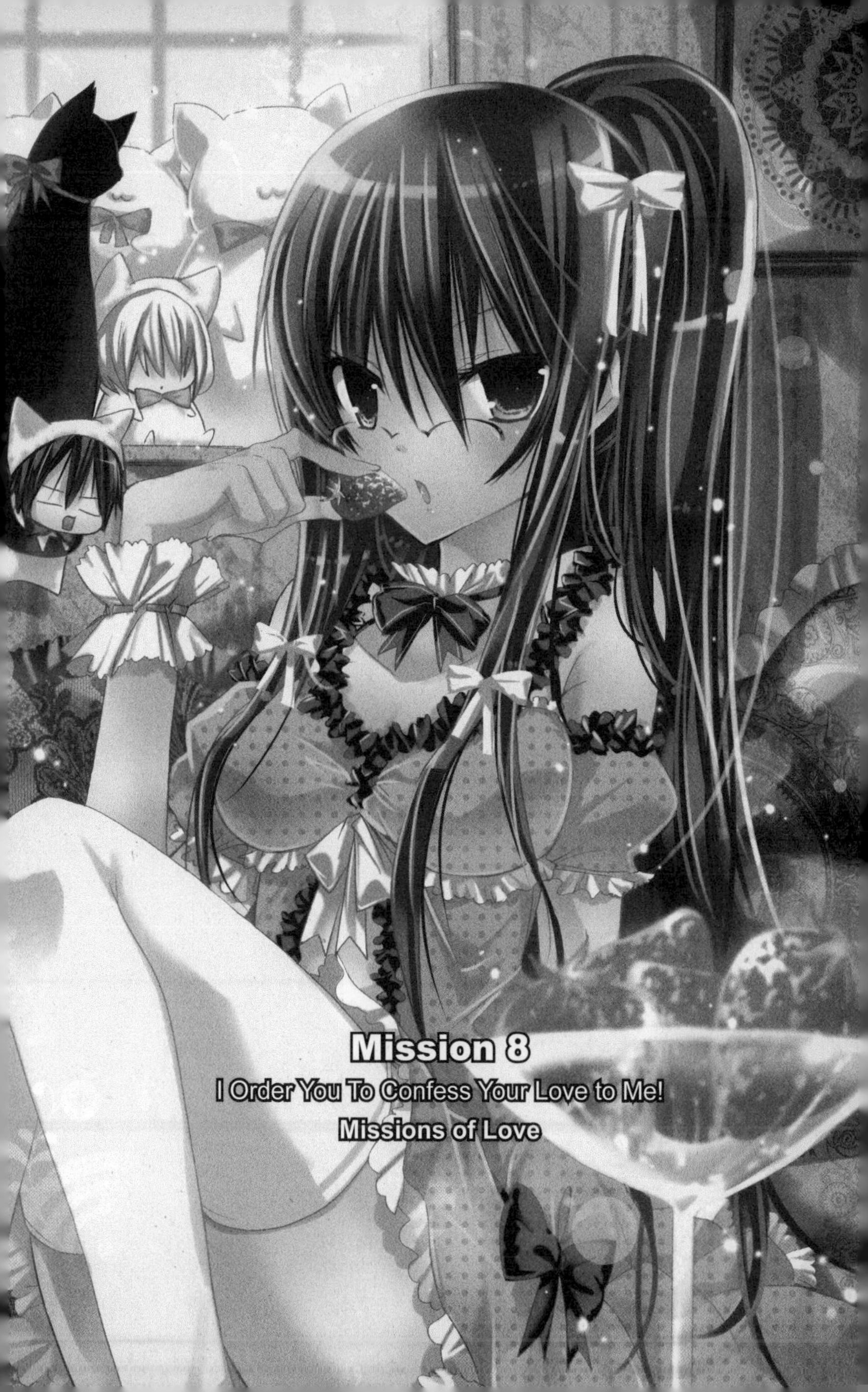
Mission 8
I Order You To Confess Your Love to Me!
Missions of Love

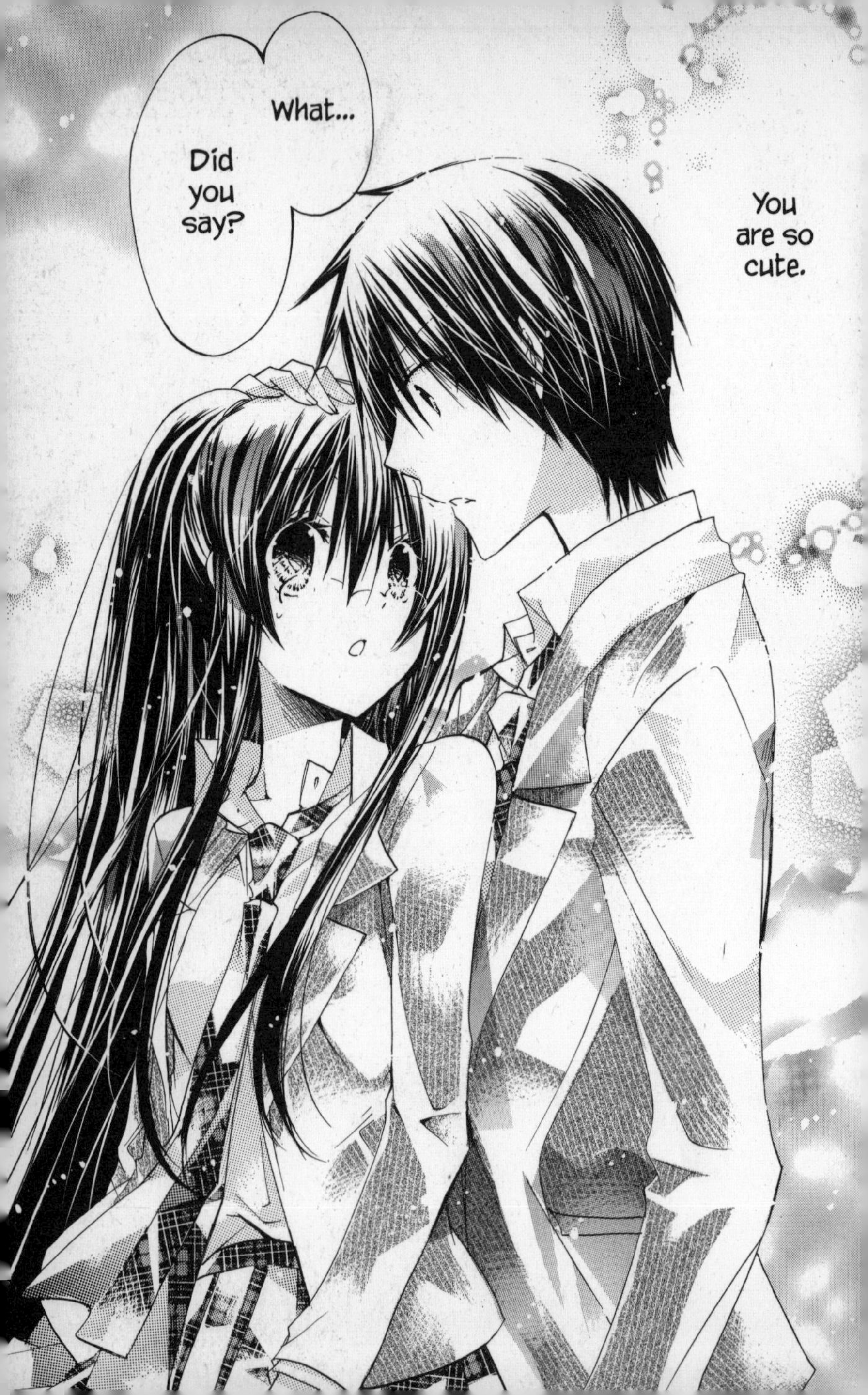
You are so cute.
What... Did you say?

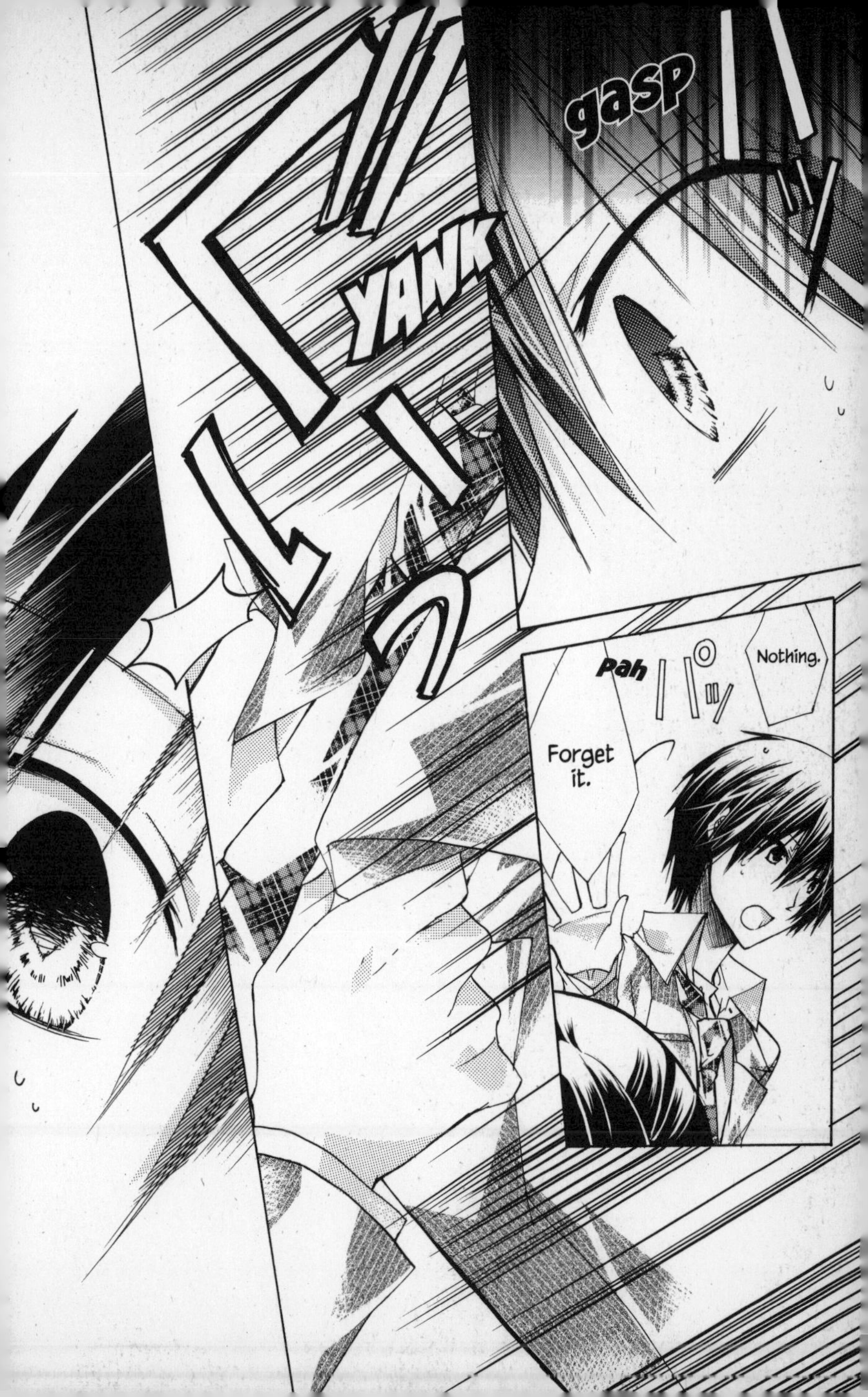
gasp
YANK
Nothing.
Pah
Forget it.

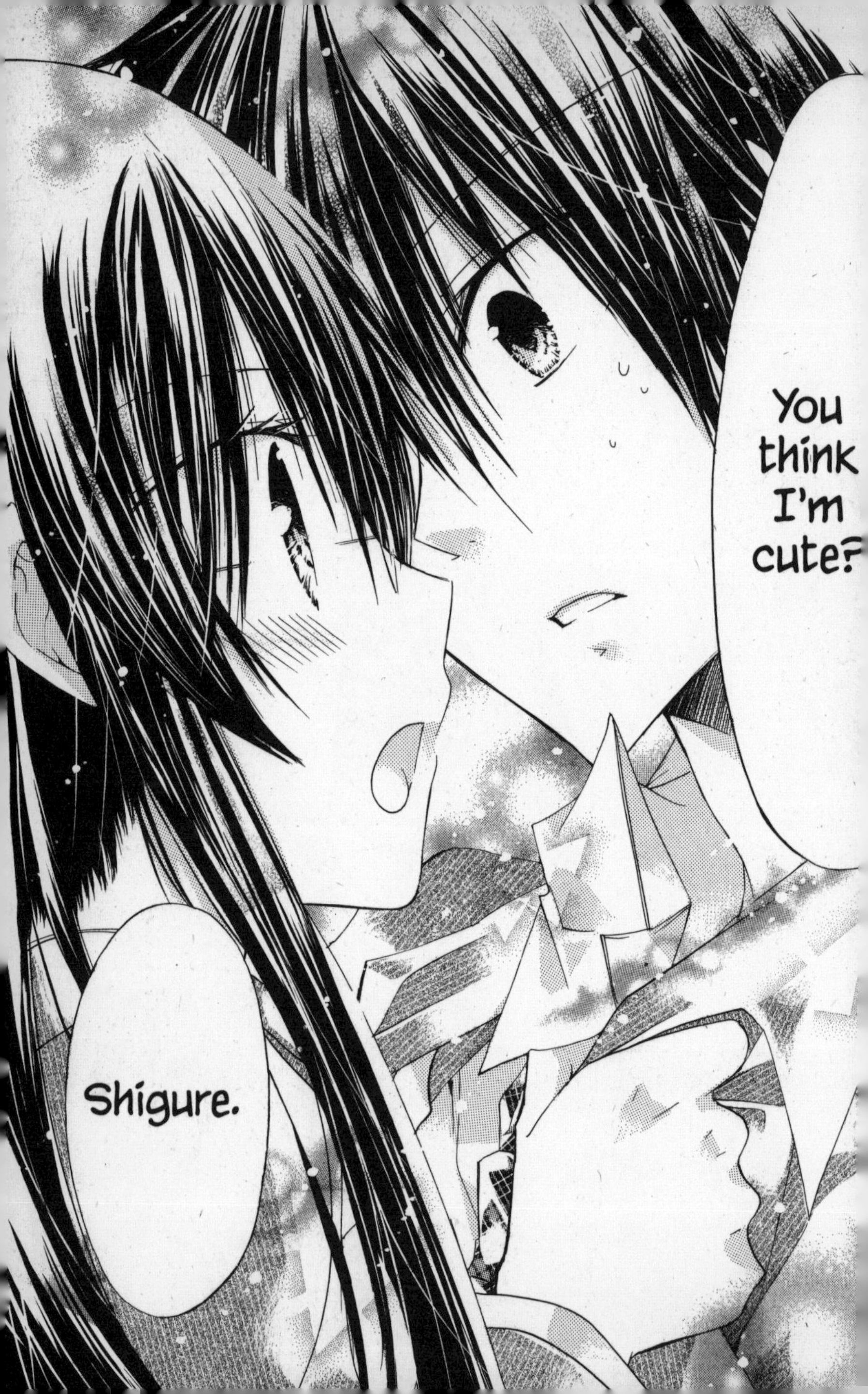
You think I'm cute?
Shigure.

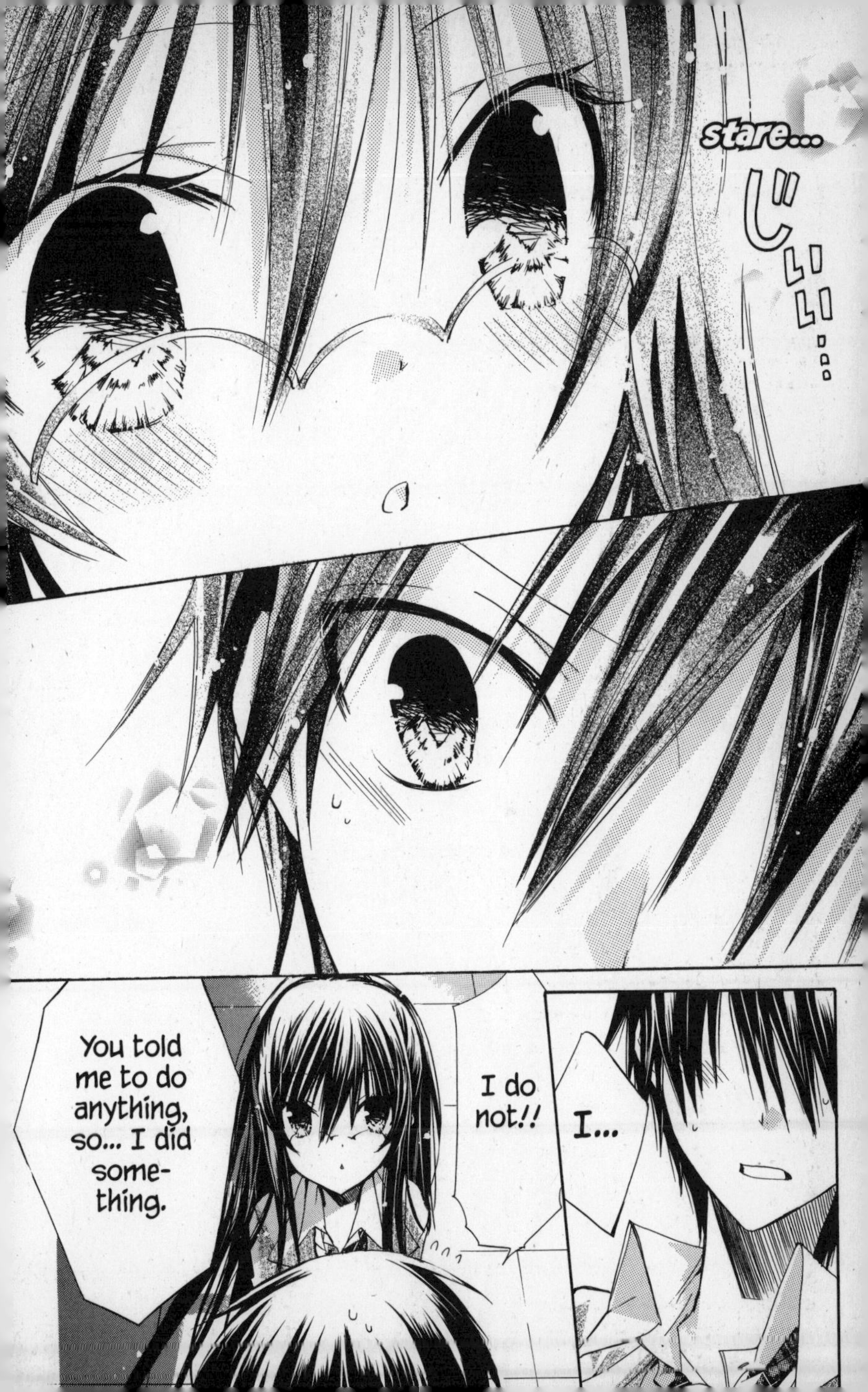
stare...
じぃぃ...
I...
I do not!!
You told me to do anything, so... I did something.

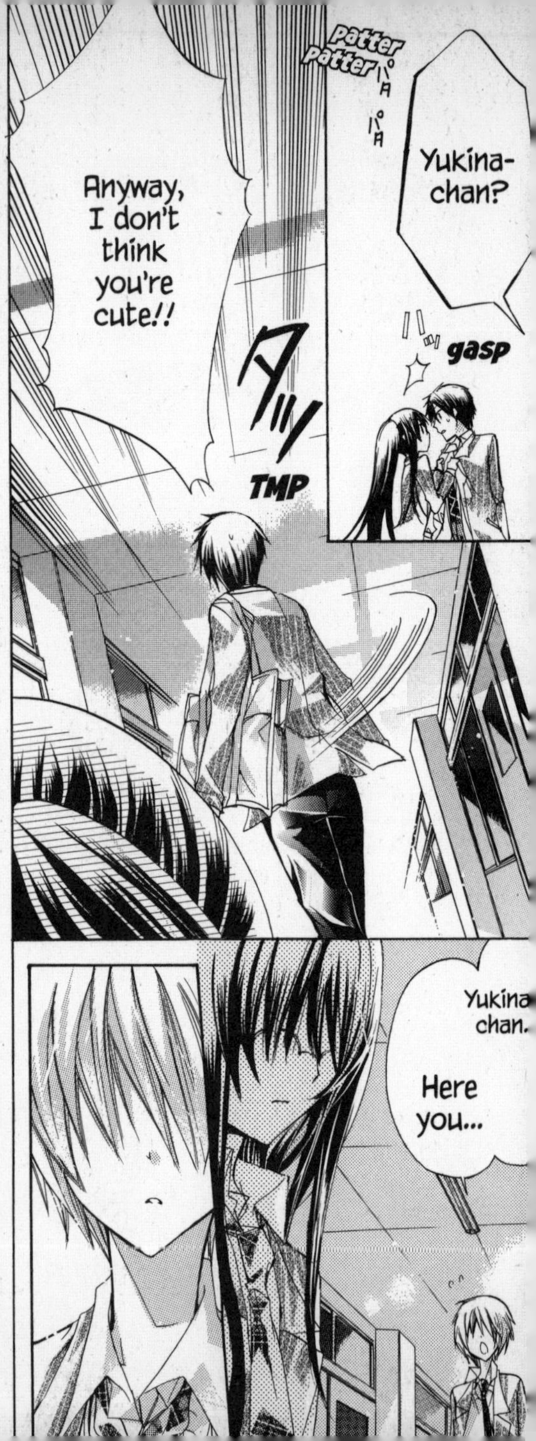
Patter Patter
Yukina-chan?
gasp
Anyway, I don't think you're cute!!
TMP
Yukina-chan.
Here you...

Snow Yukina (4)

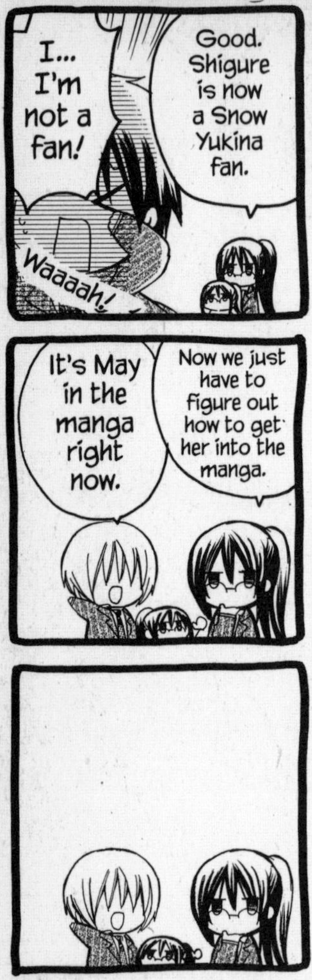
Good. Shigure is now a Snow Yukina fan.
I... I'm not a fan!
Waaaah!
Now we just have to figure out how to get her into the manga.
It's May in the manga right now.
It's not going to work.
It won't snow in May.
Nope, not going to work.

Will I ever get to put her in the manga?!

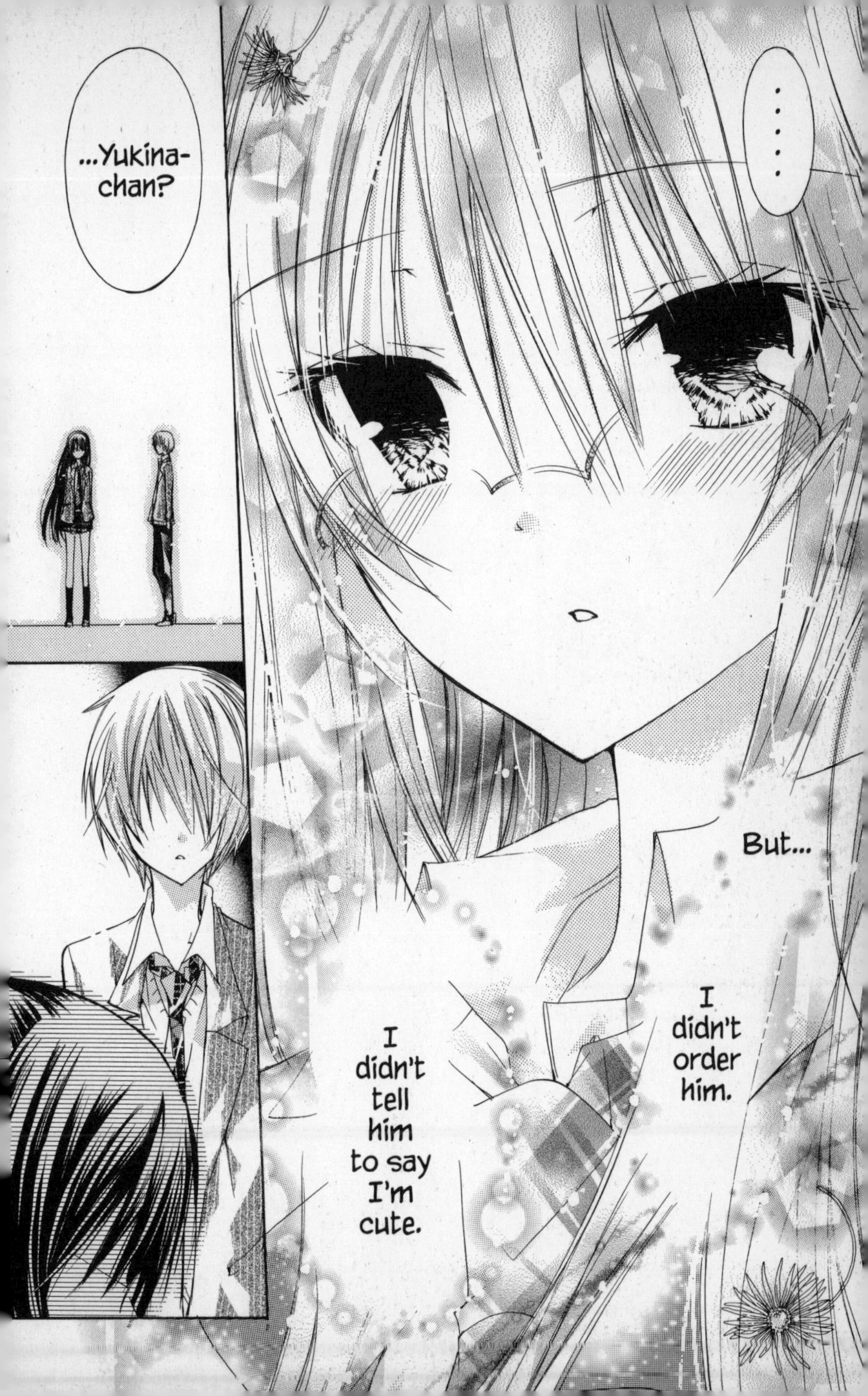
....
But...
I didn't order him.
I didn't tell him to say I'm cute.
...Yukina-chan?

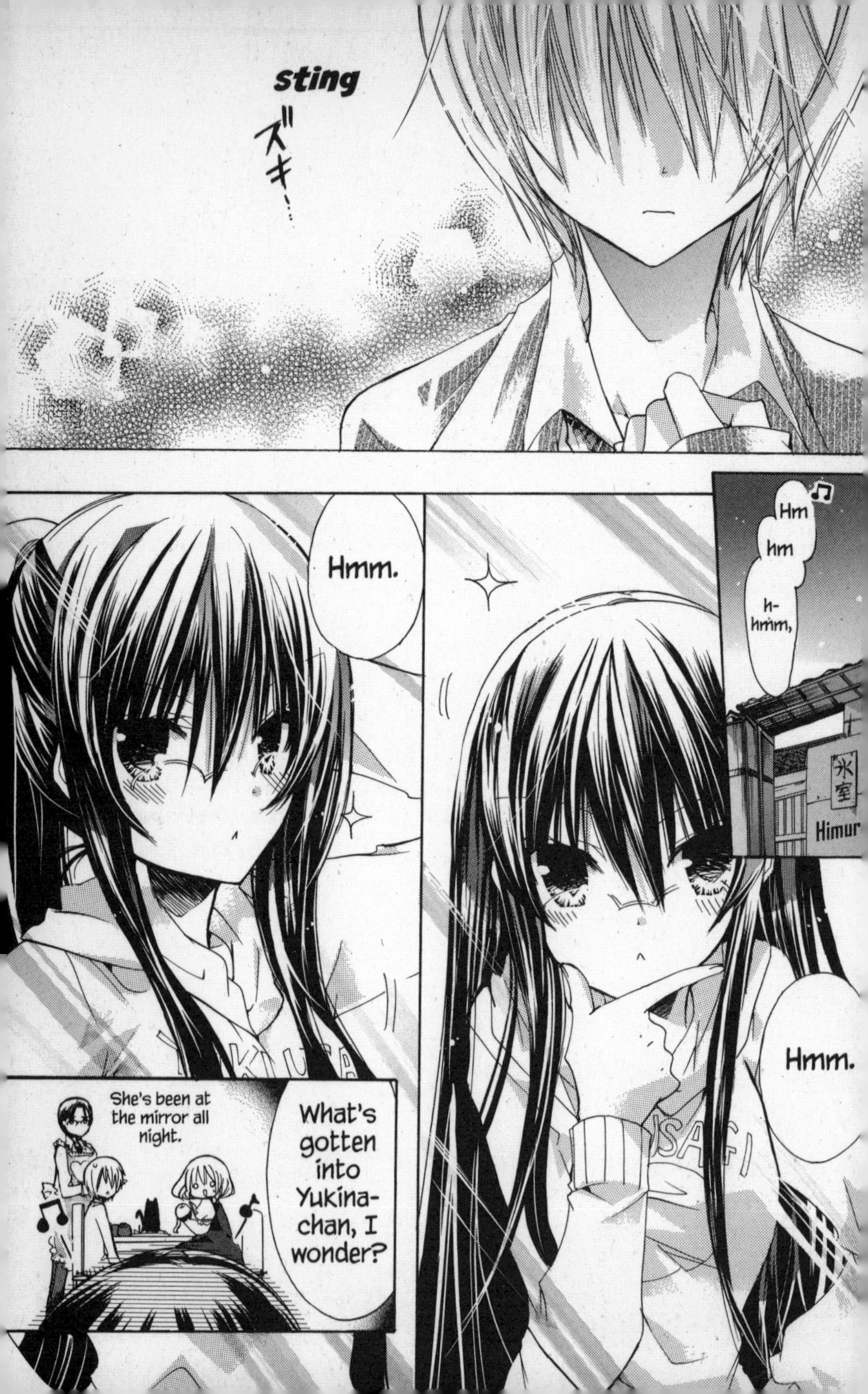
sting
ズキ…
Hm hm h-hmm,
氷室
Himur
Hmm.
Hmm.
What's gotten into Yukina-chan, I wonder?
She's been at the mirror all night.

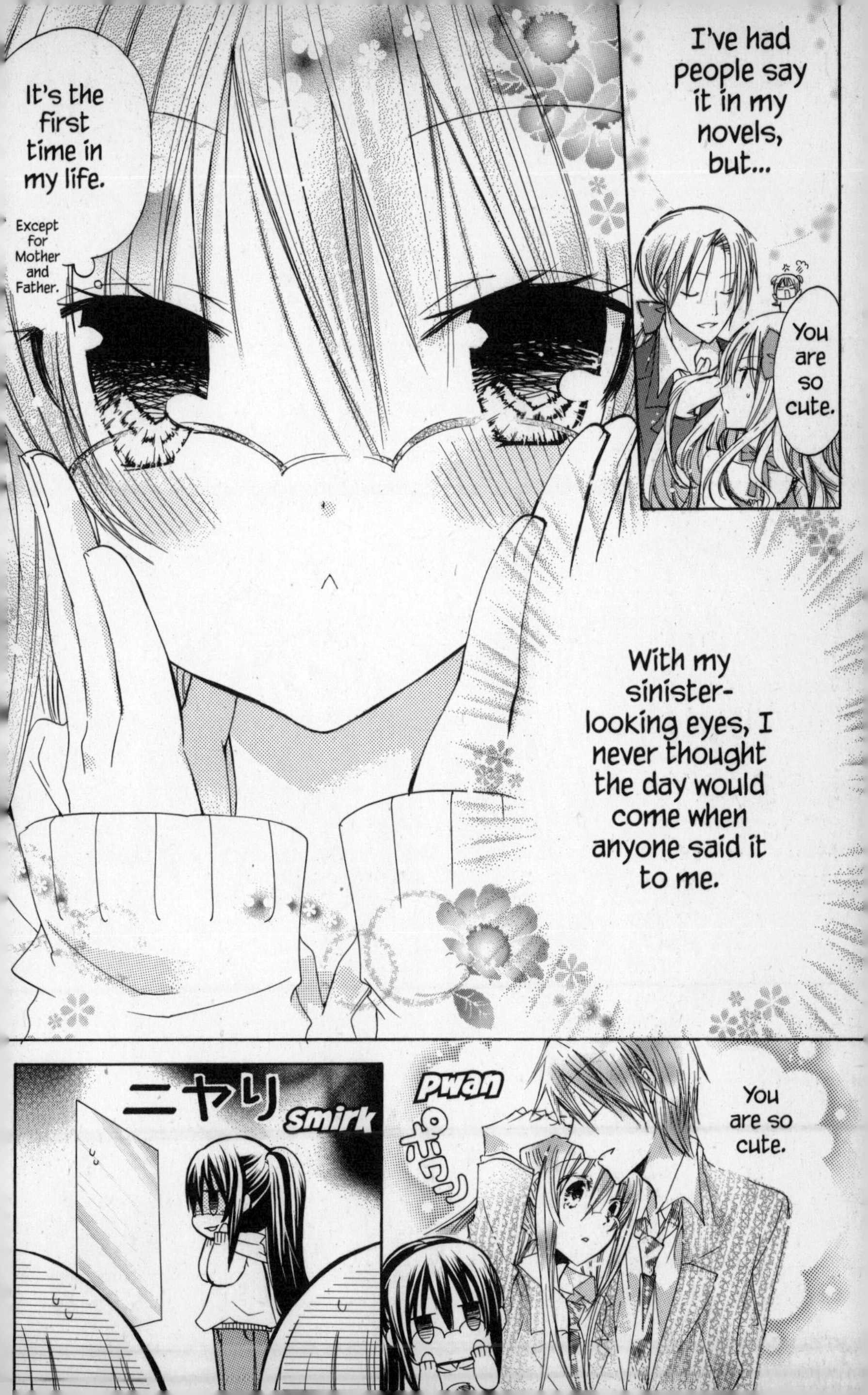
I've had people say it in my novels, but...
You are so cute.
It's the first time in my life.
Except for Mother and Father.
With my sinister-looking eyes, I never thought the day would come when anyone said it to me.
You are so cute.
Pwan
ポワン
ニヤリ
smirk

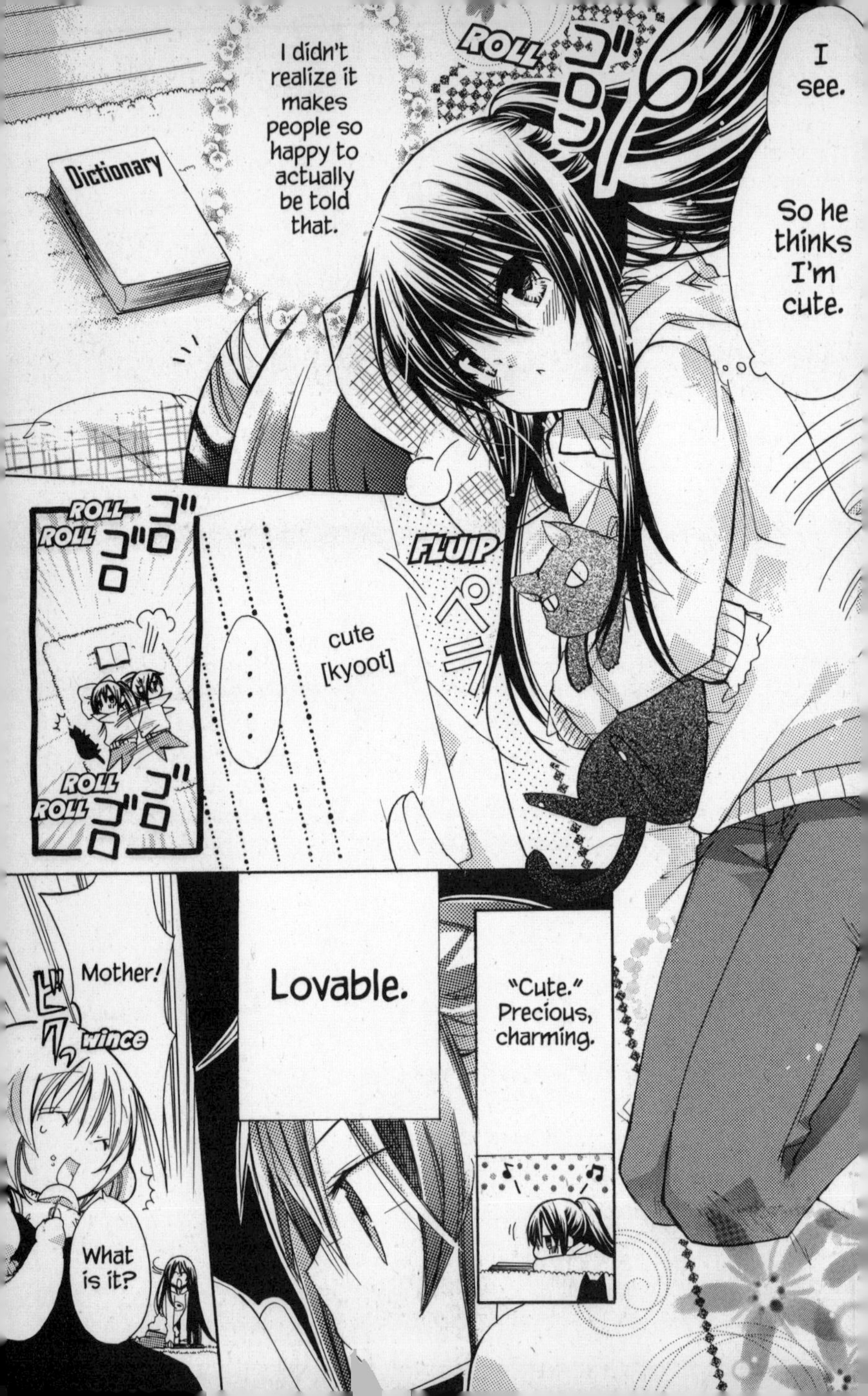

I see.
So he thinks I'm cute.
ROLL
I didn't realize it makes people so happy to actually be told that.
FLUIP
cute [kyoot]
......
ROLL ROLL
ROLL ROLL
"Cute." Precious, charming.
Lovable.
Mother!
wince
What is it?

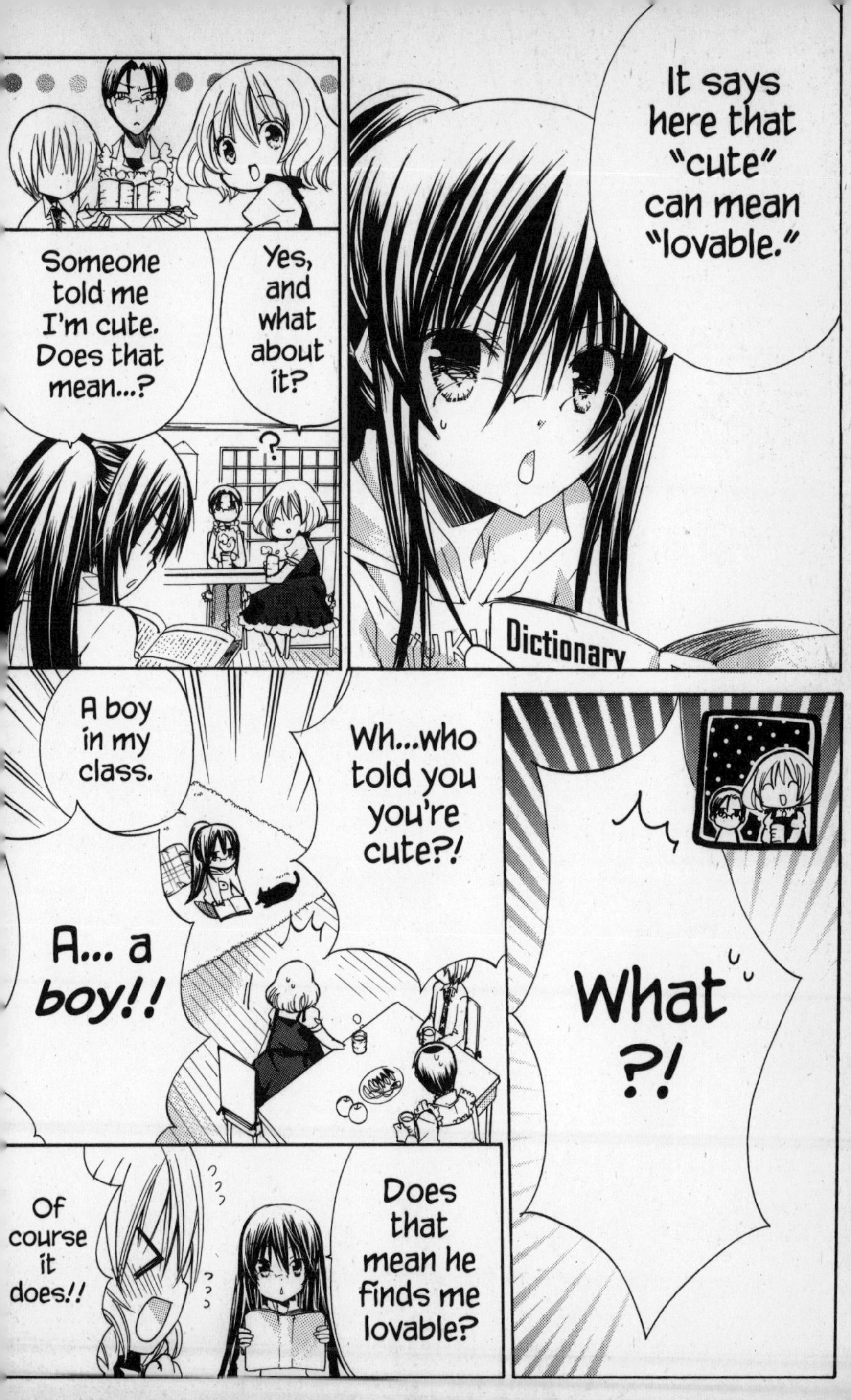
It says here that "cute" can mean "lovable."
Dictionary
Yes, and what about it?
Someone told me I'm cute. Does that mean...?
?
What ?!
Wh...who told you you're cute?!
A boy in my class.
A... a boy!!
Does that mean he finds me lovable?
Of course it does!!

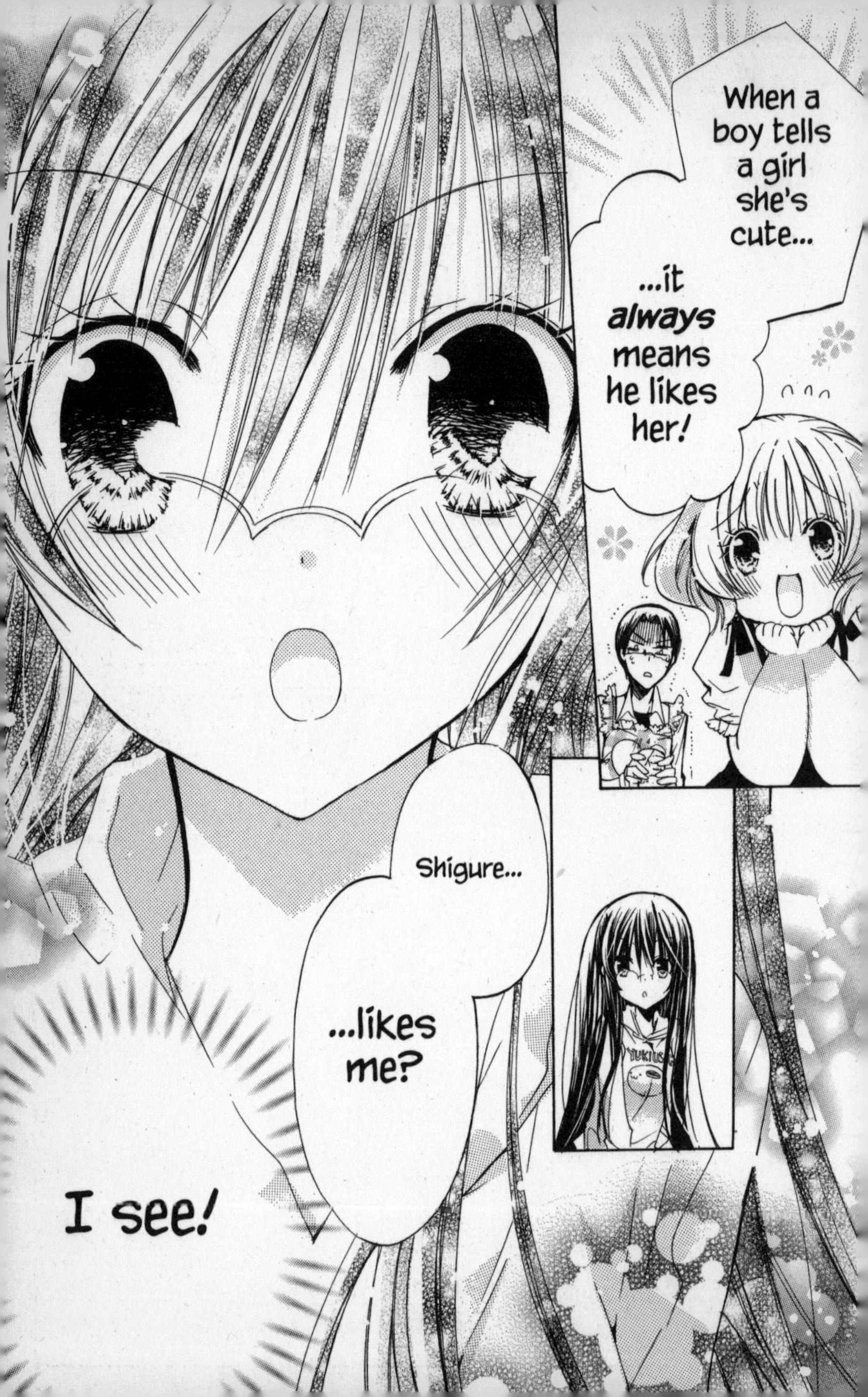
When a boy tells a girl she's cute...
...it *always* means he likes her!
Shigure...
...likes me?
I see!

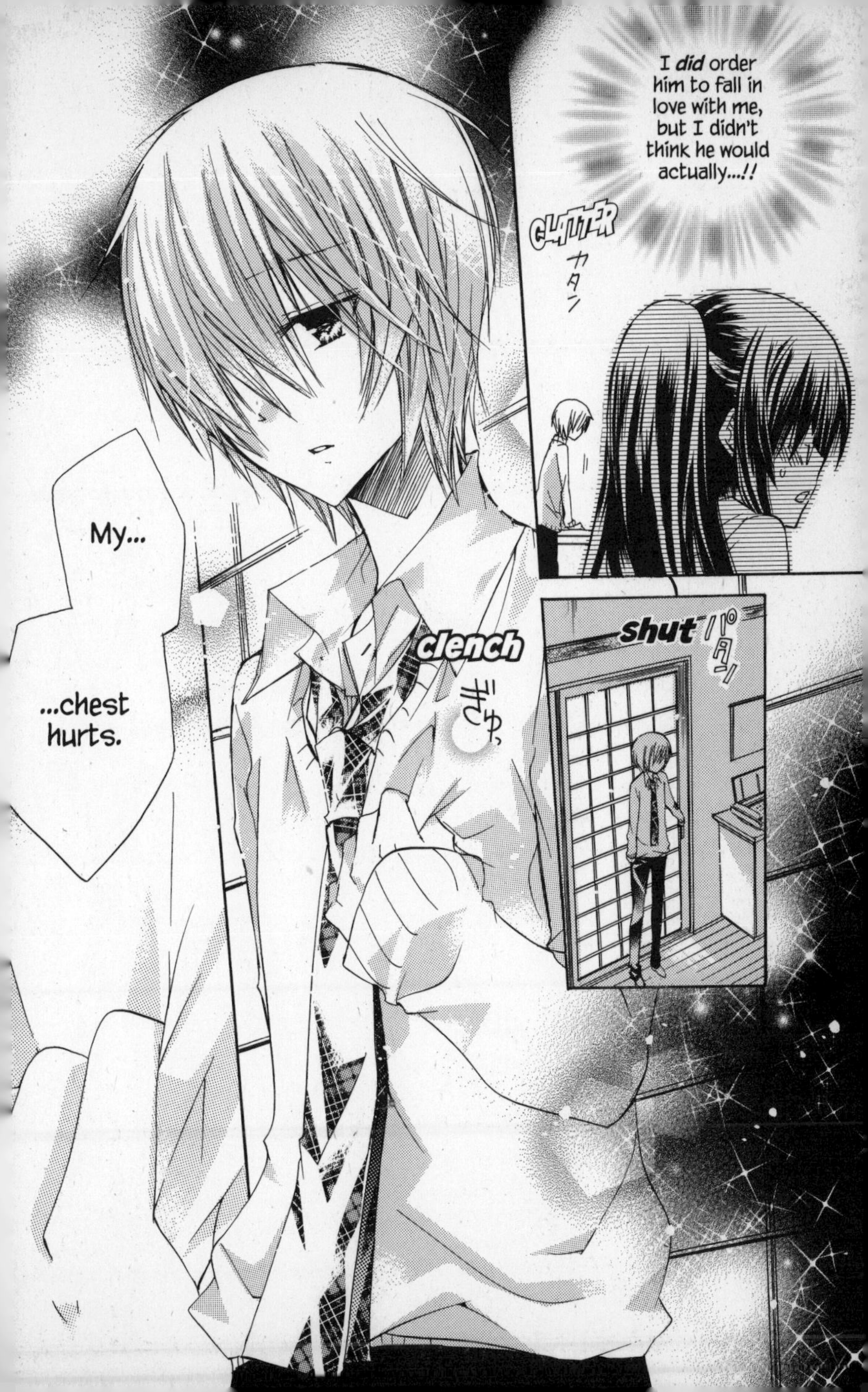
I *did* order him to fall in love with me, but I didn't think he would actually...!!
CLATTER
カタン
shut
パタン
clench
ぎゅっ
My...
...chest hurts.

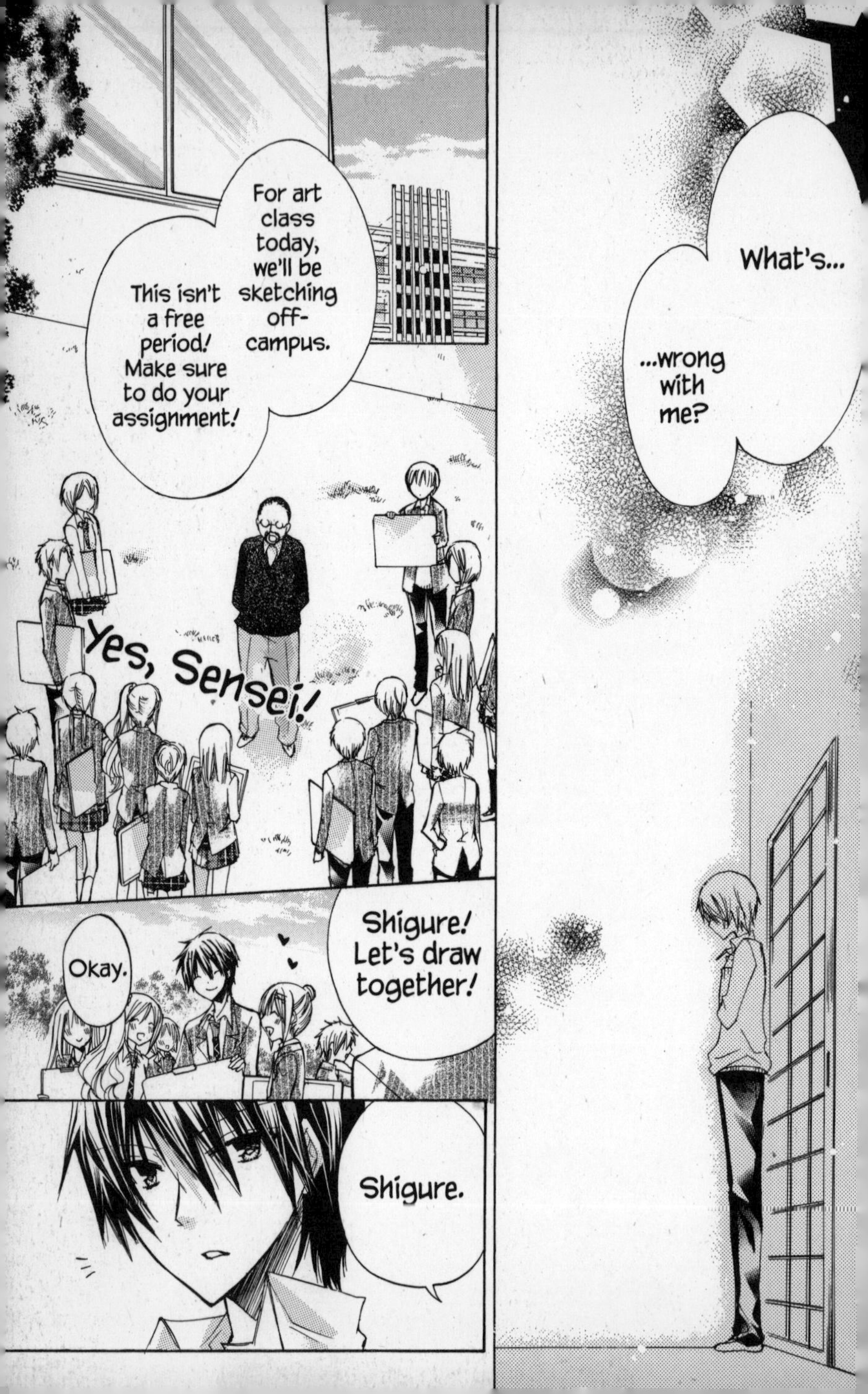
What's...
...wrong with me?
For art class today, we'll be sketching off-campus.
This isn't a free period! Make sure to do your assignment!
Yes, Sensei!
Shigure! Let's draw together!
Okay.
Shigure.

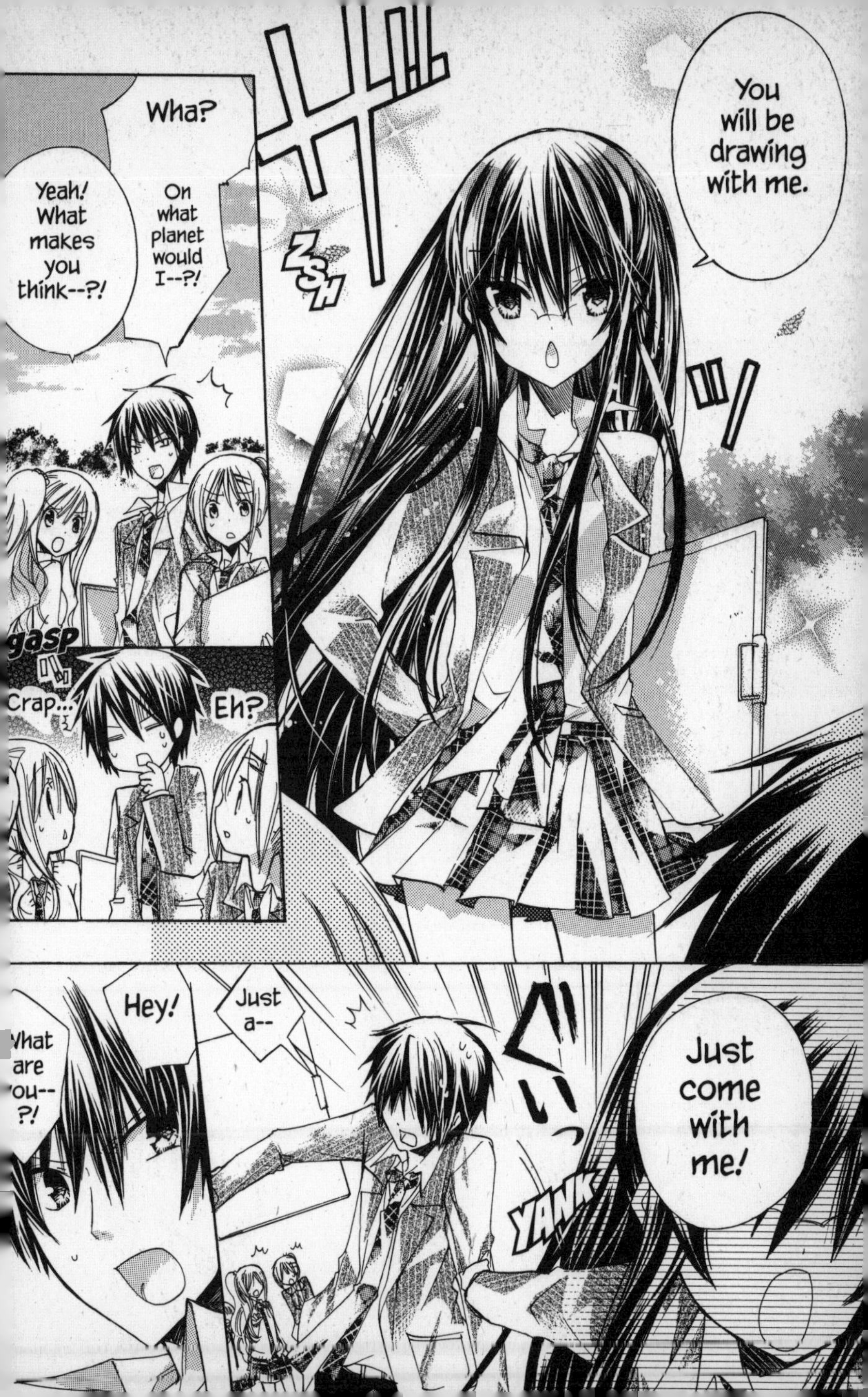

You will be drawing with me.
ZSH
Wha?
On what planet would I--?!
Yeah! What makes you think--?!
gasp
Eh?
Crap...
Just come with me!
YANK
Just a--
Hey!
What are you--?!

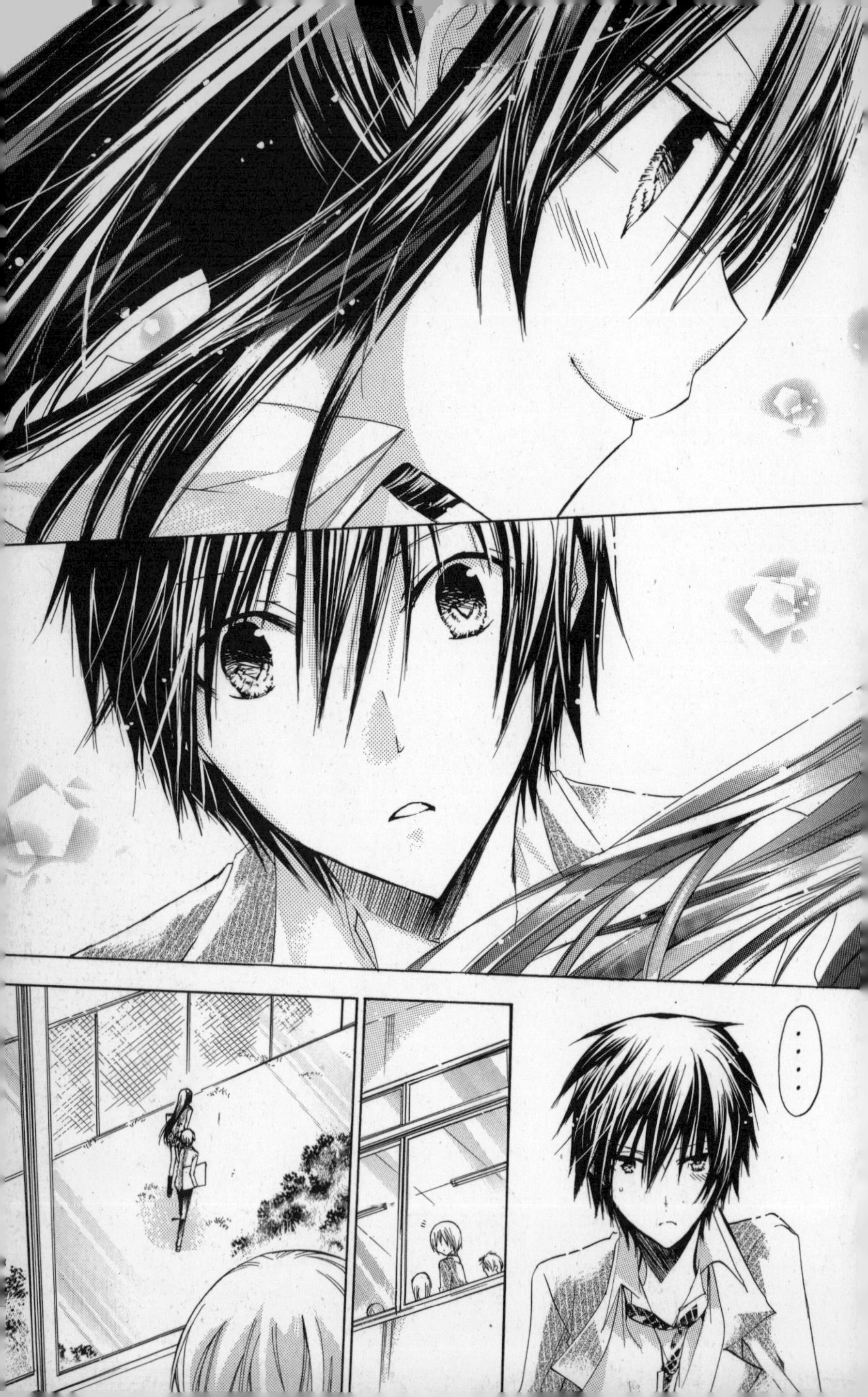
....

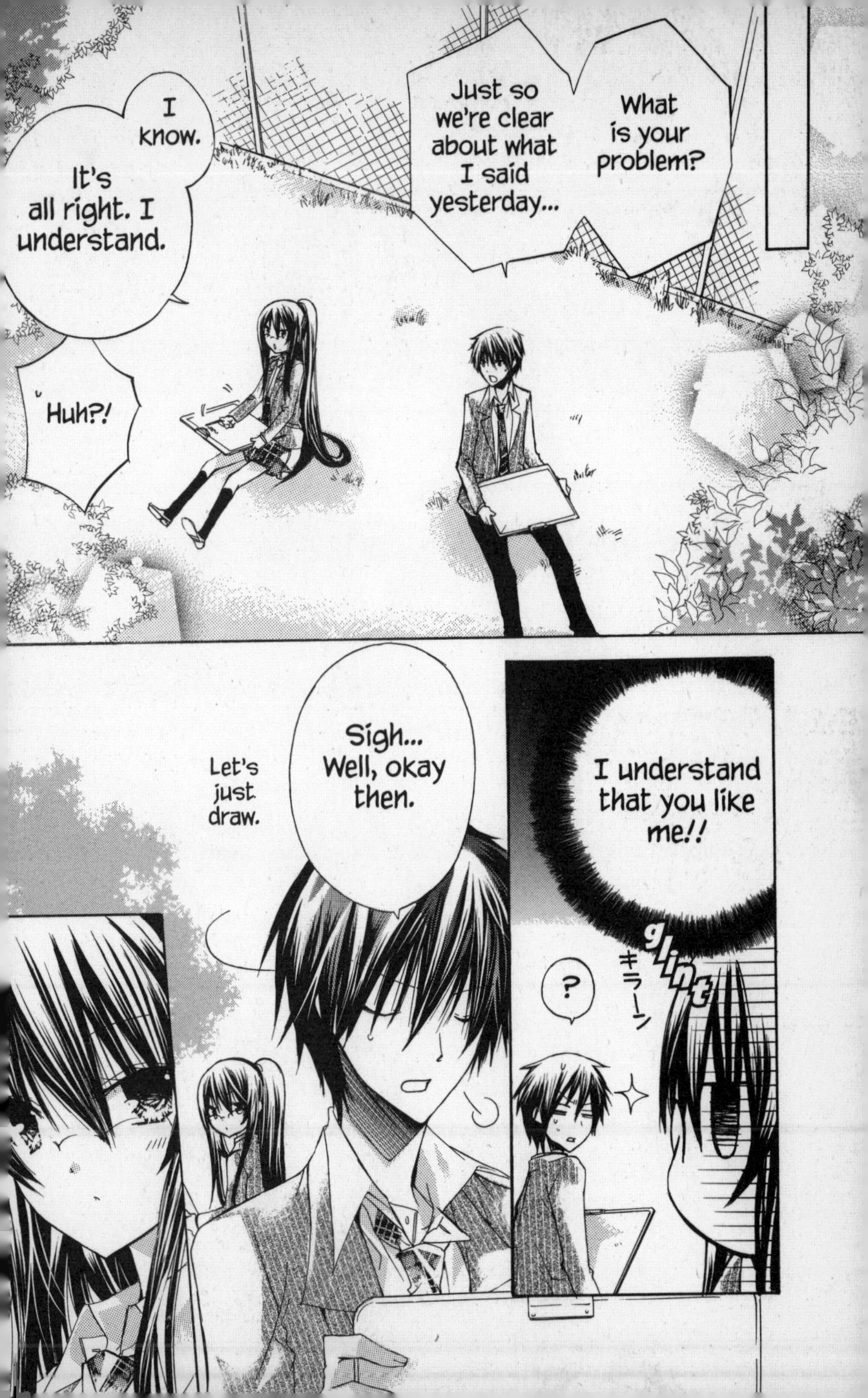
What is your problem?
Just so we're clear about what I said yesterday...
I know.
It's all right. I understand.
Huh?!
I understand that you like me!!
glint
キラーン
?
Sigh... Well, okay then.
Let's just draw.

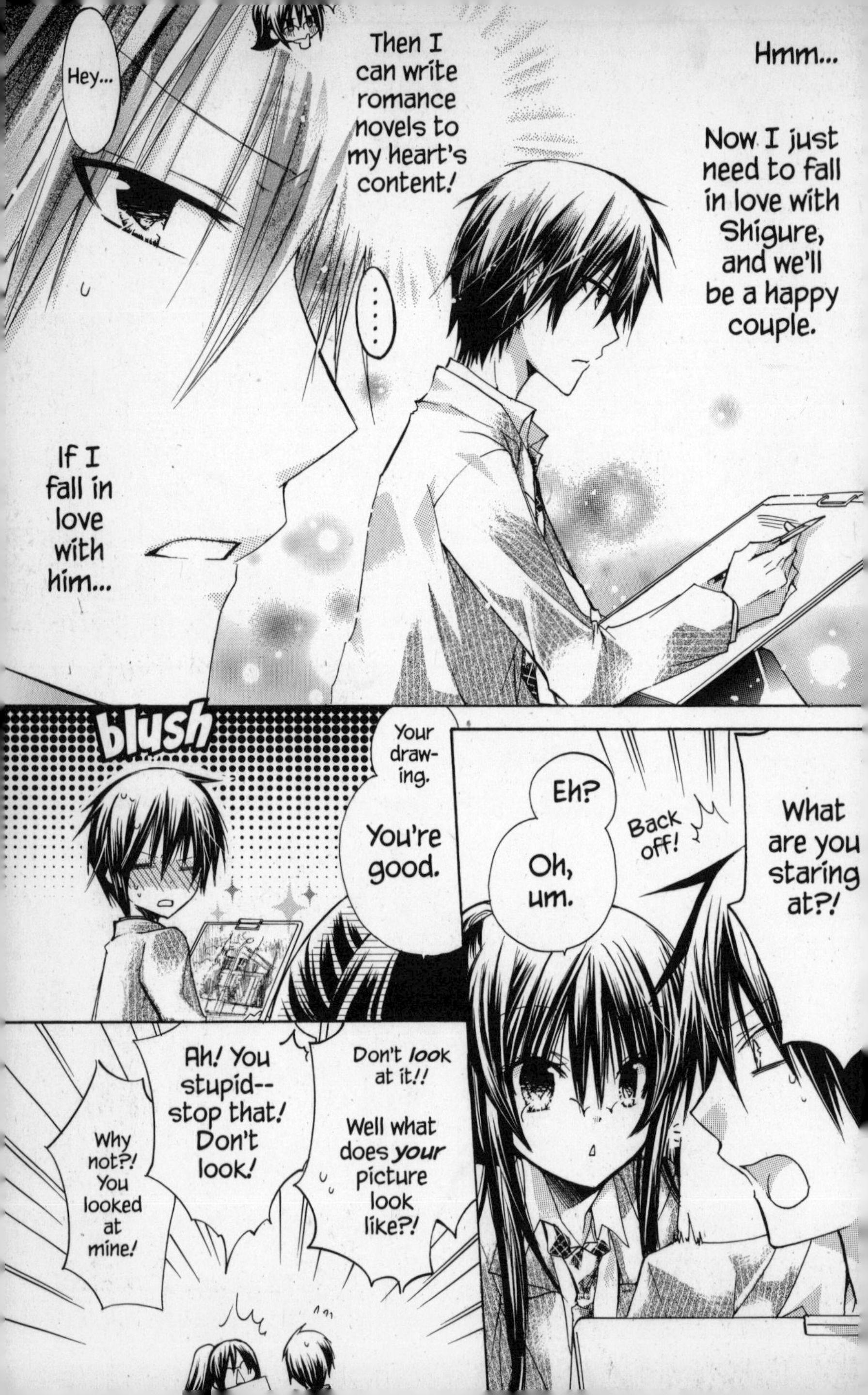
Hmm...
Now I just need to fall in love with Shigure, and we'll be a happy couple.
Then I can write romance novels to my heart's content!
Hey...
......
If I fall in love with him...
What are you staring at?!
Back off!
Eh?
Oh, um.
Your drawing.
You're good.
blush
Don't *look* at it!!
Well what does *your* picture look like?!
Ah! You stupid-- stop that! Don't look!
Why not?! You looked at mine!

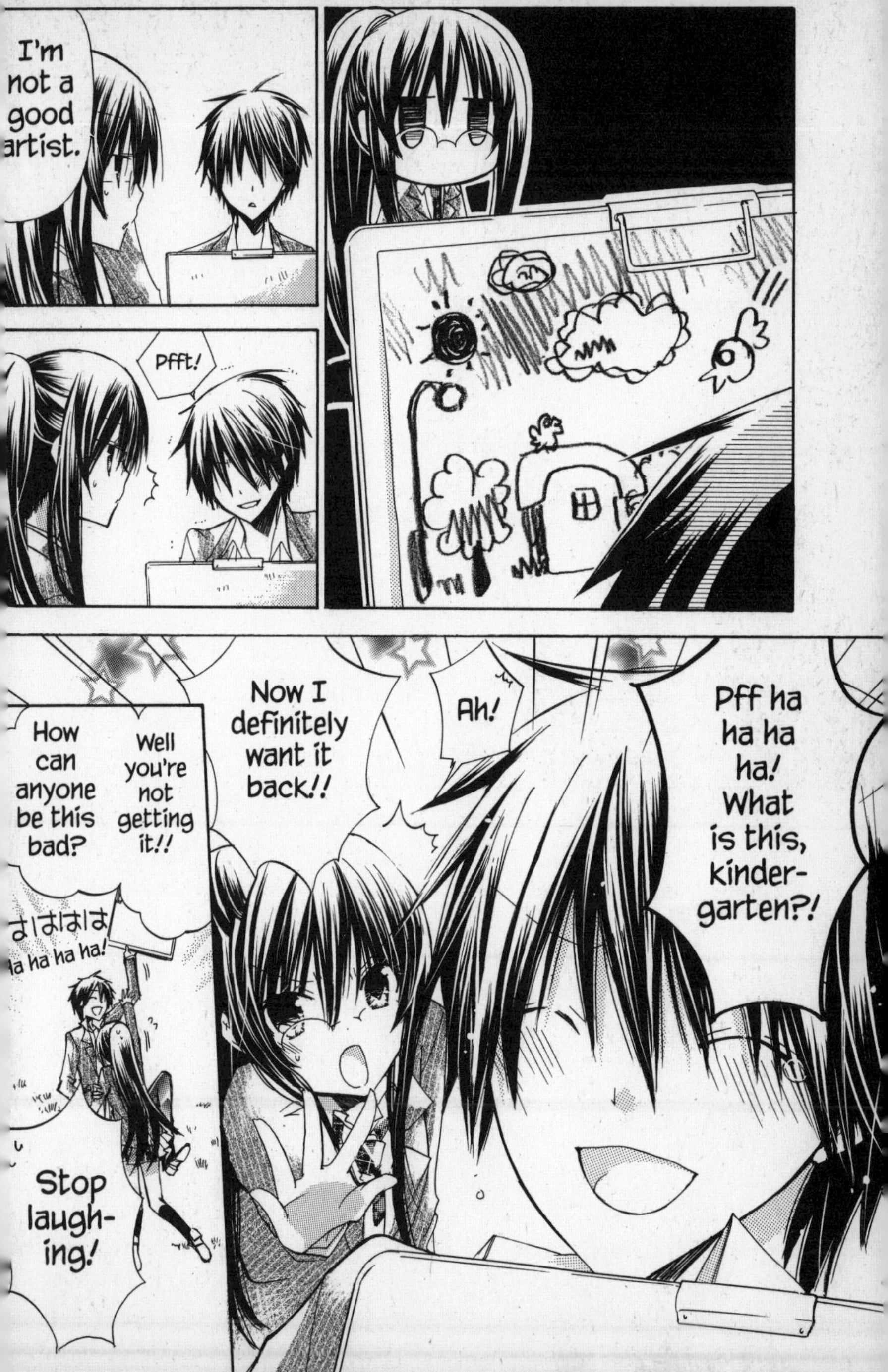
I'm not a good artist.
Pfft!
Pff ha ha ha! What is this, kinder-garten?!
Ah!
Now I definitely want it back!!
Well you're not getting it!!
How can anyone be this bad?
ははは
ha ha ha!
Stop laugh-ing!

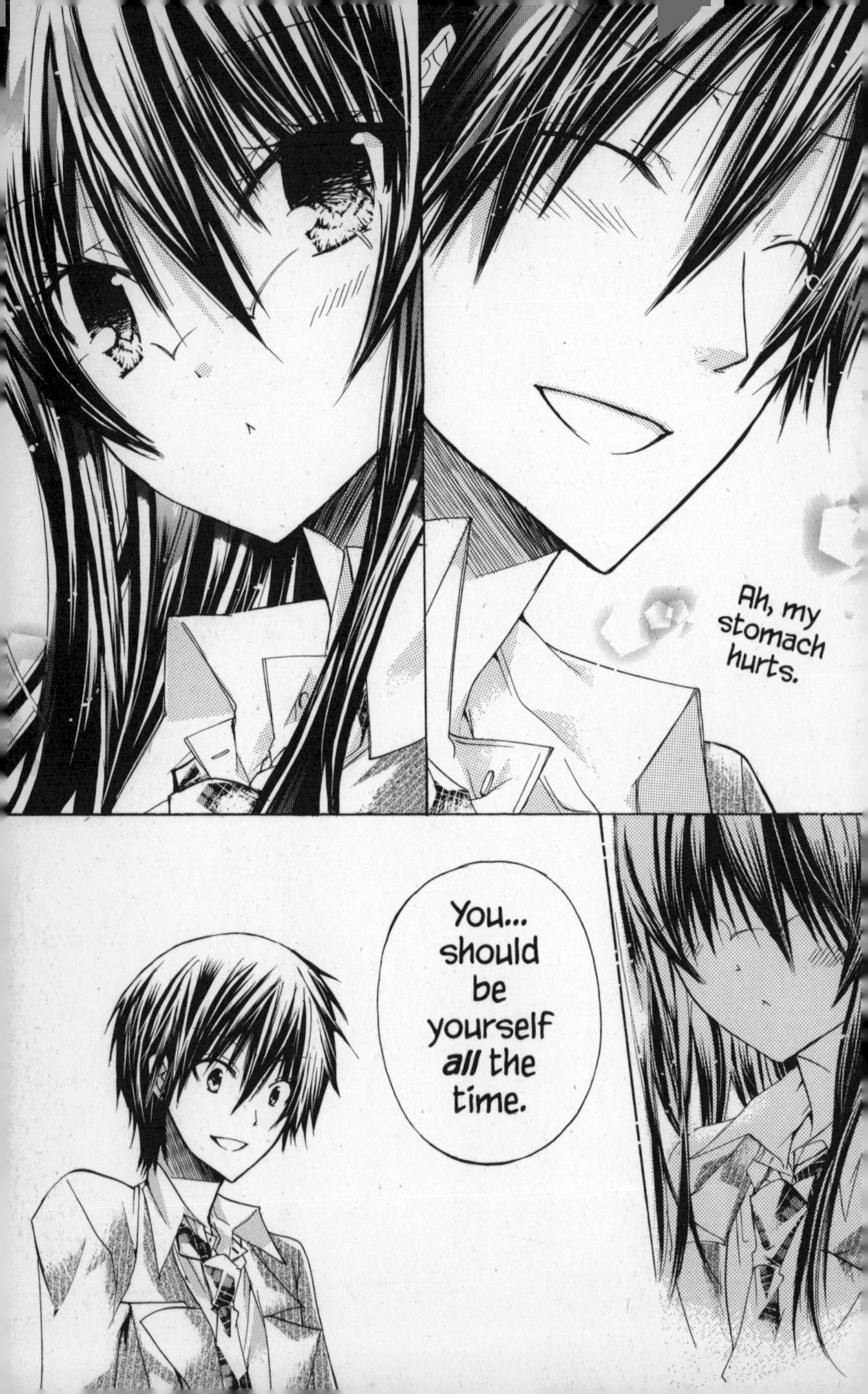
Ah, my stomach hurts.
You... should be yourself all the time.

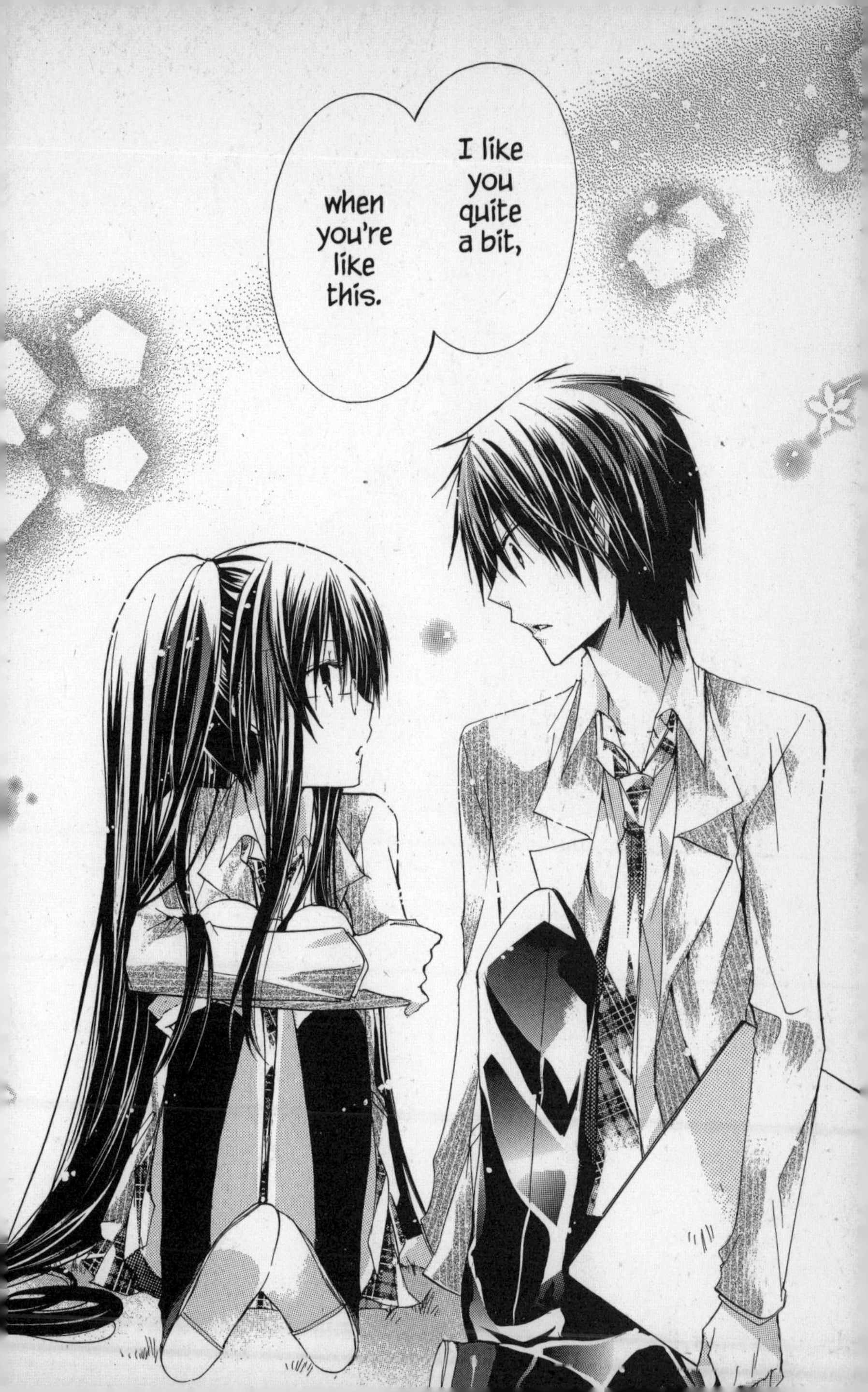
I like you quite a bit,
when you're like this.

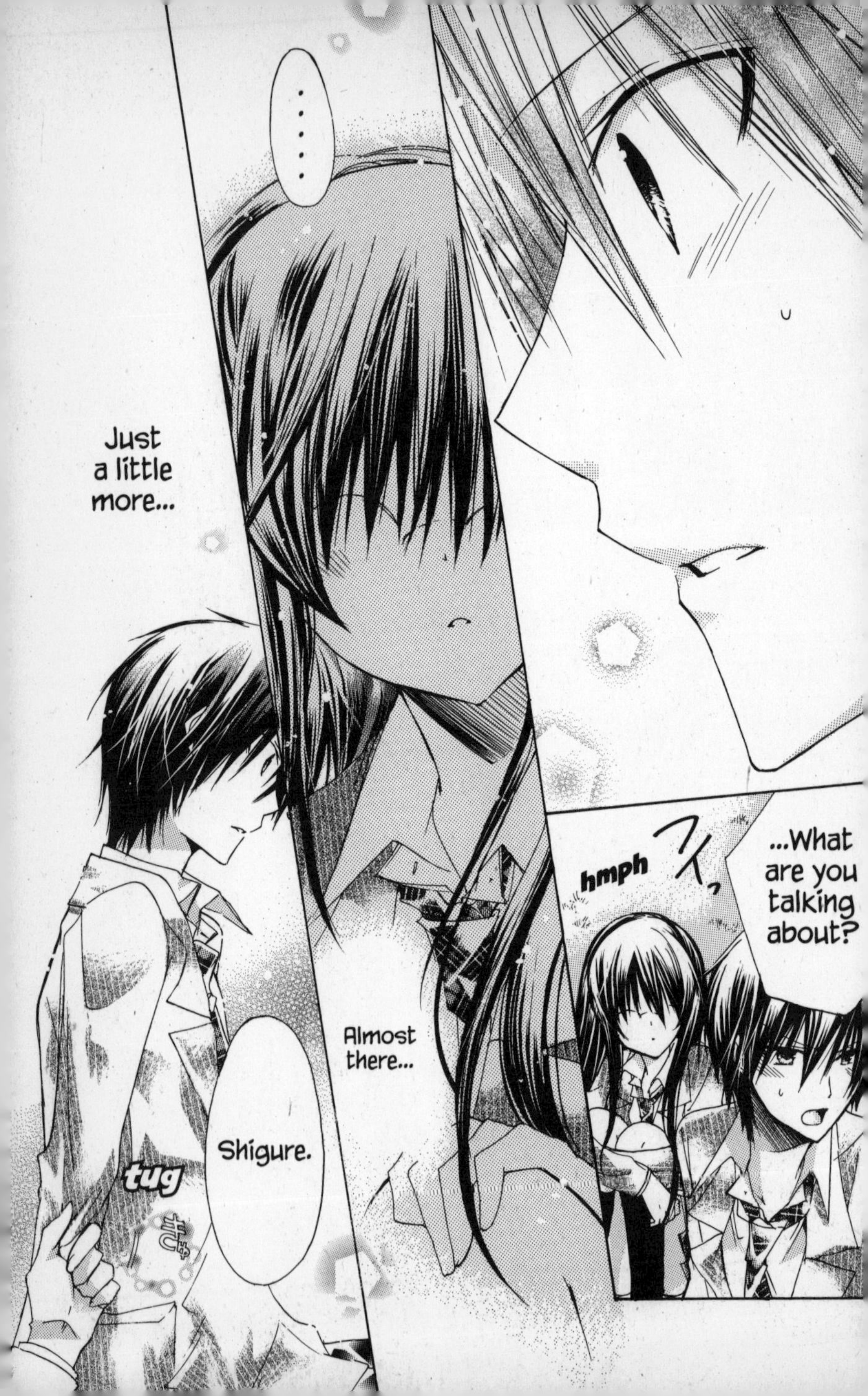
...What are you talking about?
hmph
....
Almost there...
Just a little more...
Shigure.
tug

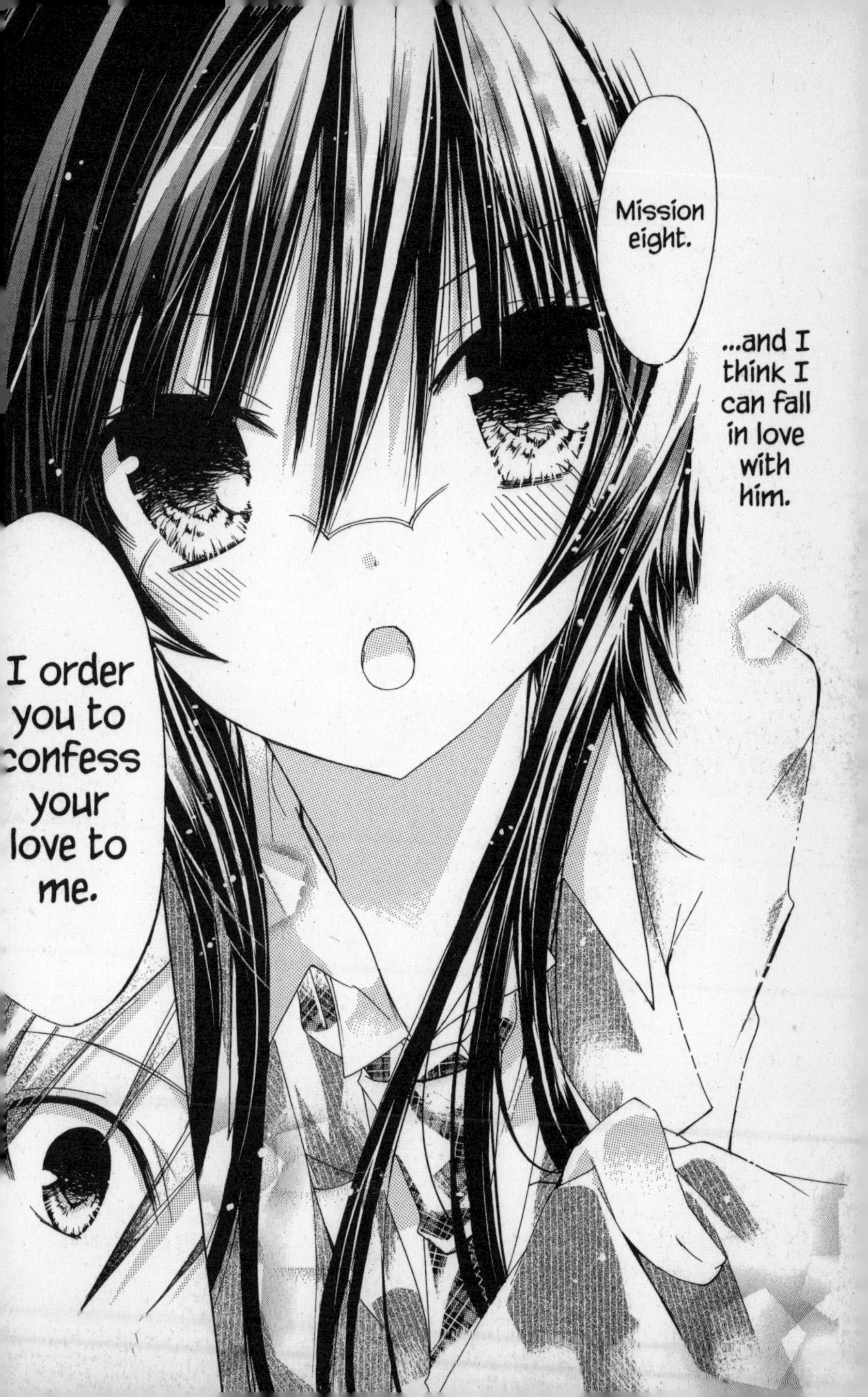
Mission eight.
...and I think I can fall in love with him.
I order you to confess your love to me.

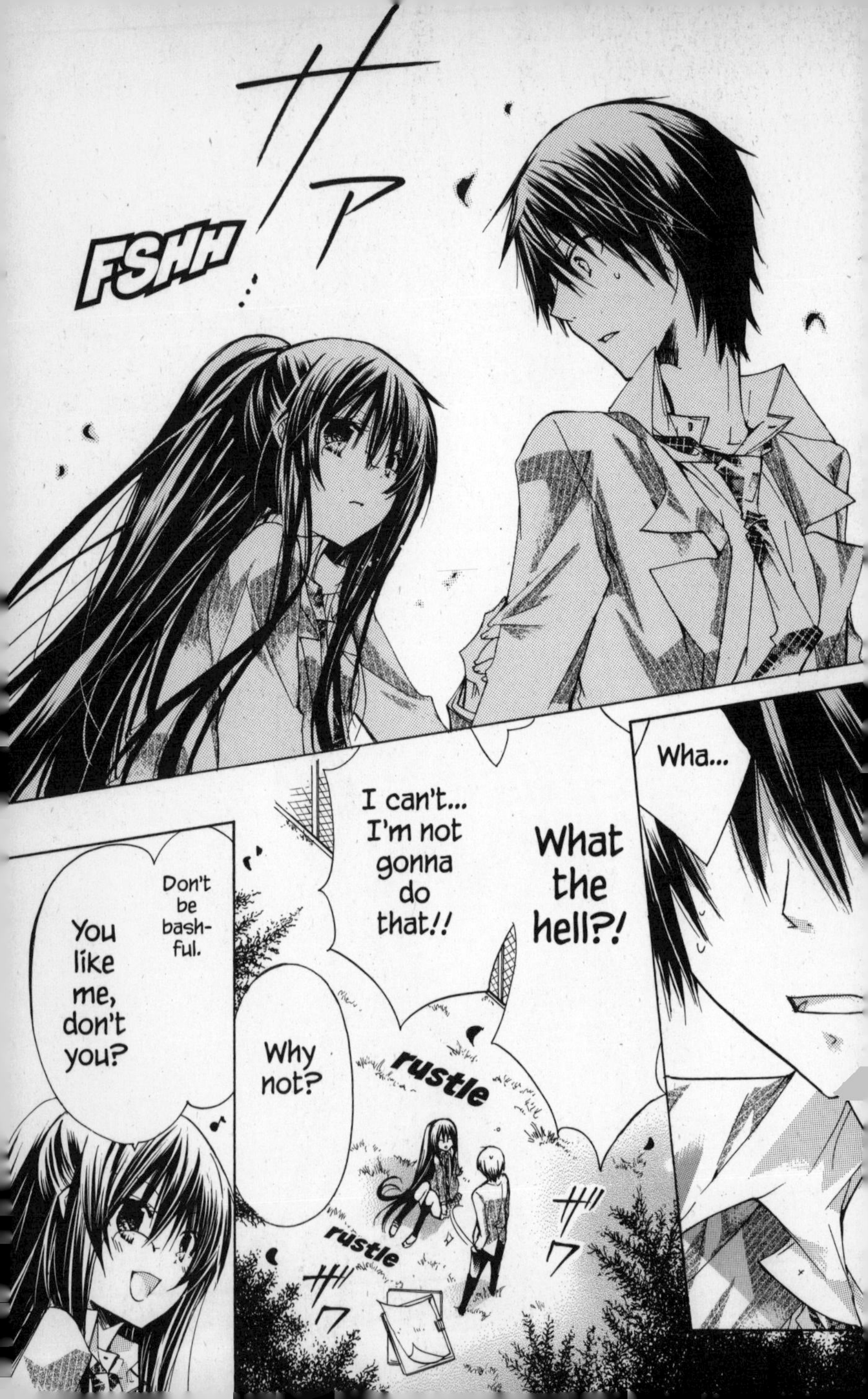
FSHH
Wha...
What the hell?!
I can't... I'm not gonna do that!!
Why not?
rustle
rustle
Don't be bash-ful.
You like me, don't you?

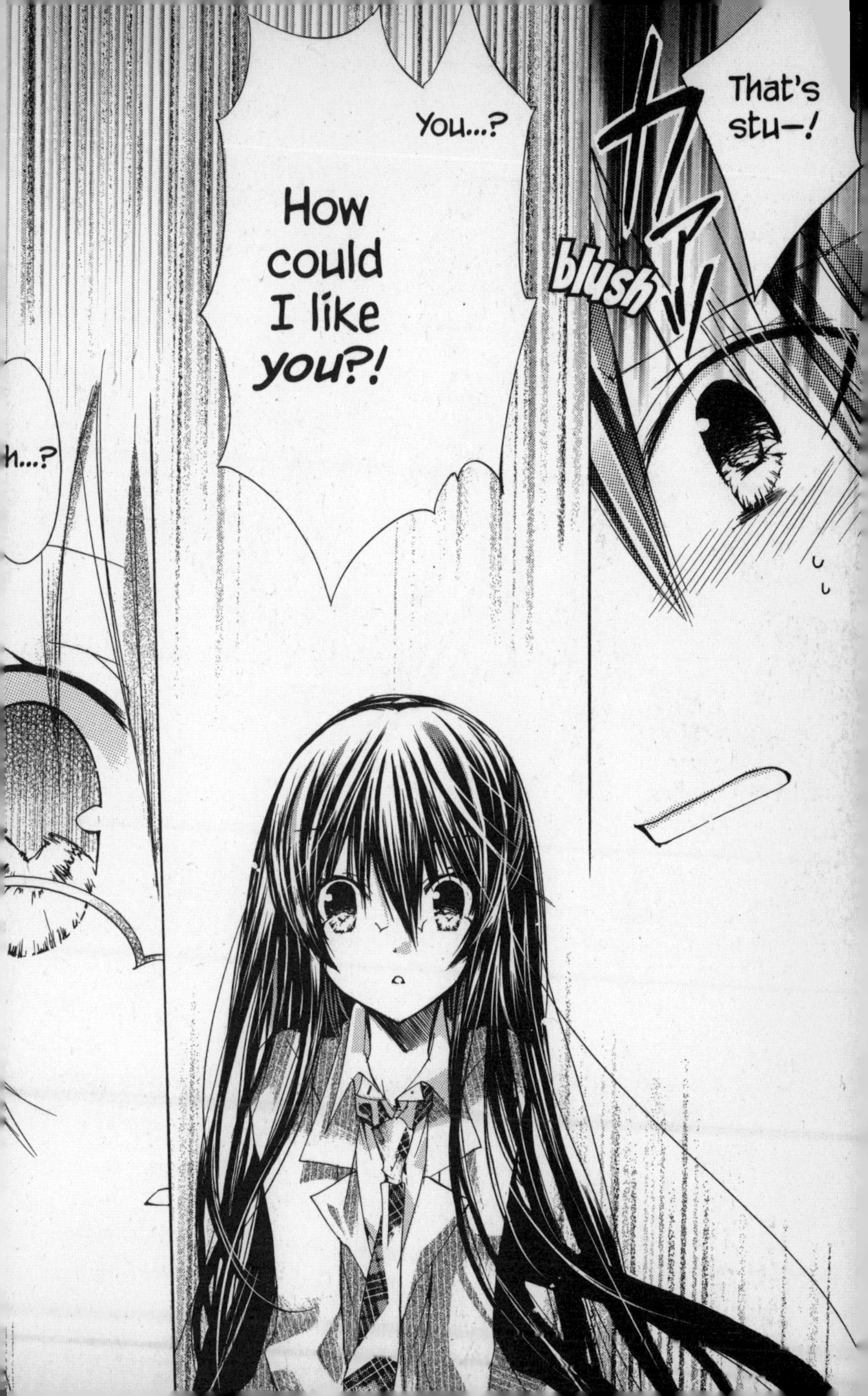
That's stu—!
blush
You...?
How could I like *you*?!
h...?

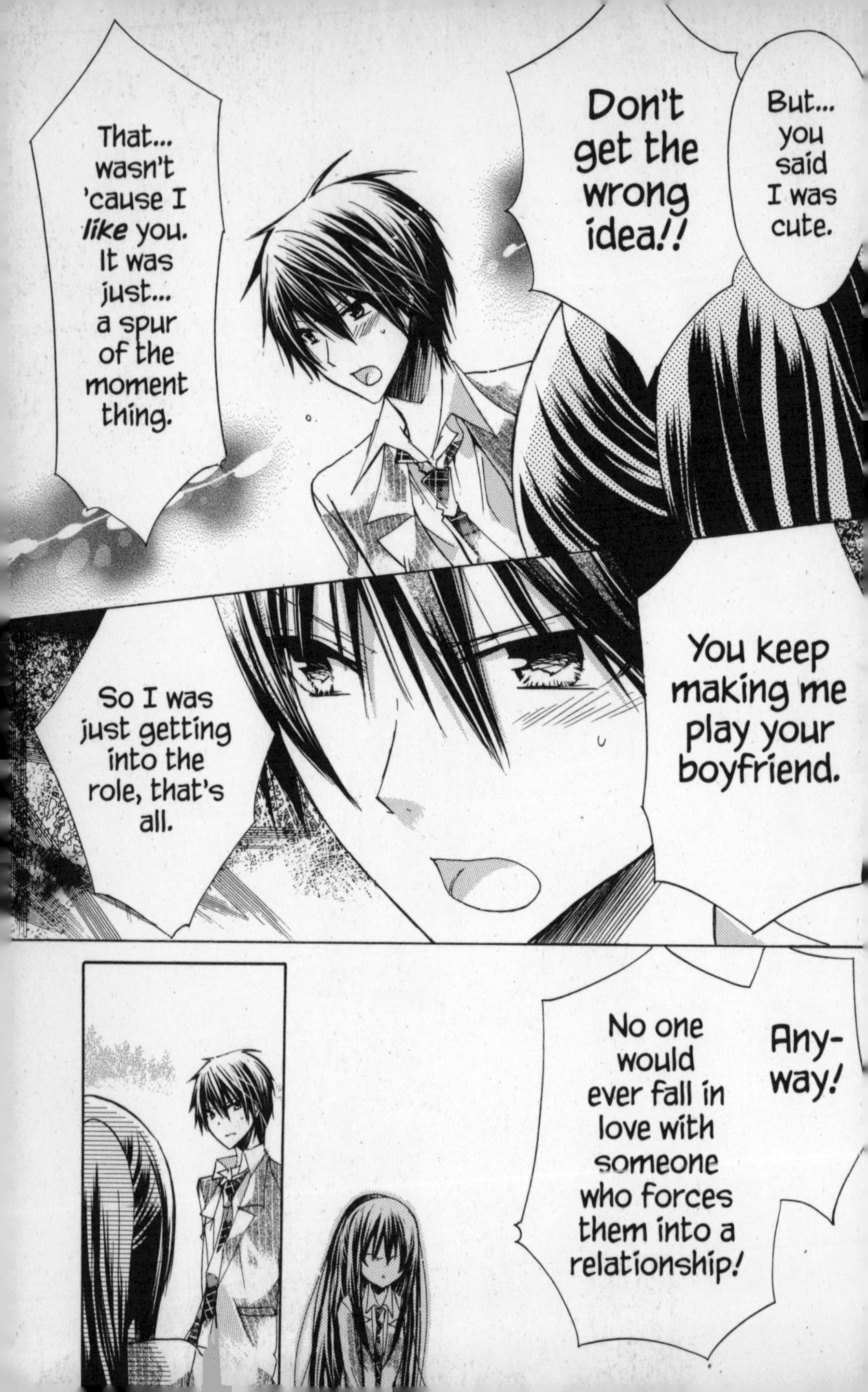
But... you said I was cute.
Don't get the wrong idea!!
That... wasn't 'cause I *like* you. It was just... a spur of the moment thing.
You keep making me play your boyfriend.
So I was just getting into the role, that's all.
Any-way!
No one would ever fall in love with someone who forces them into a relationship!

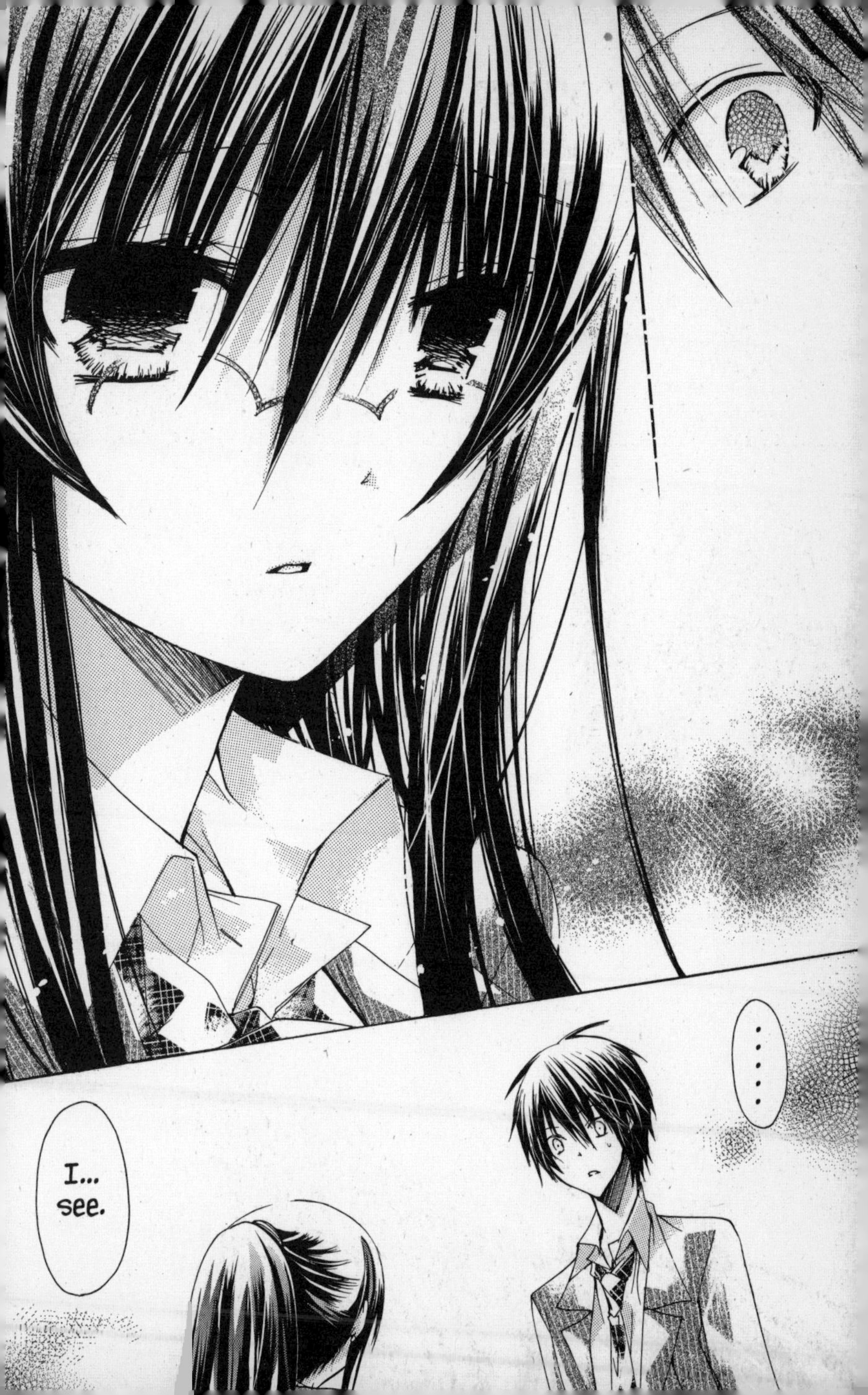
......
I... see.

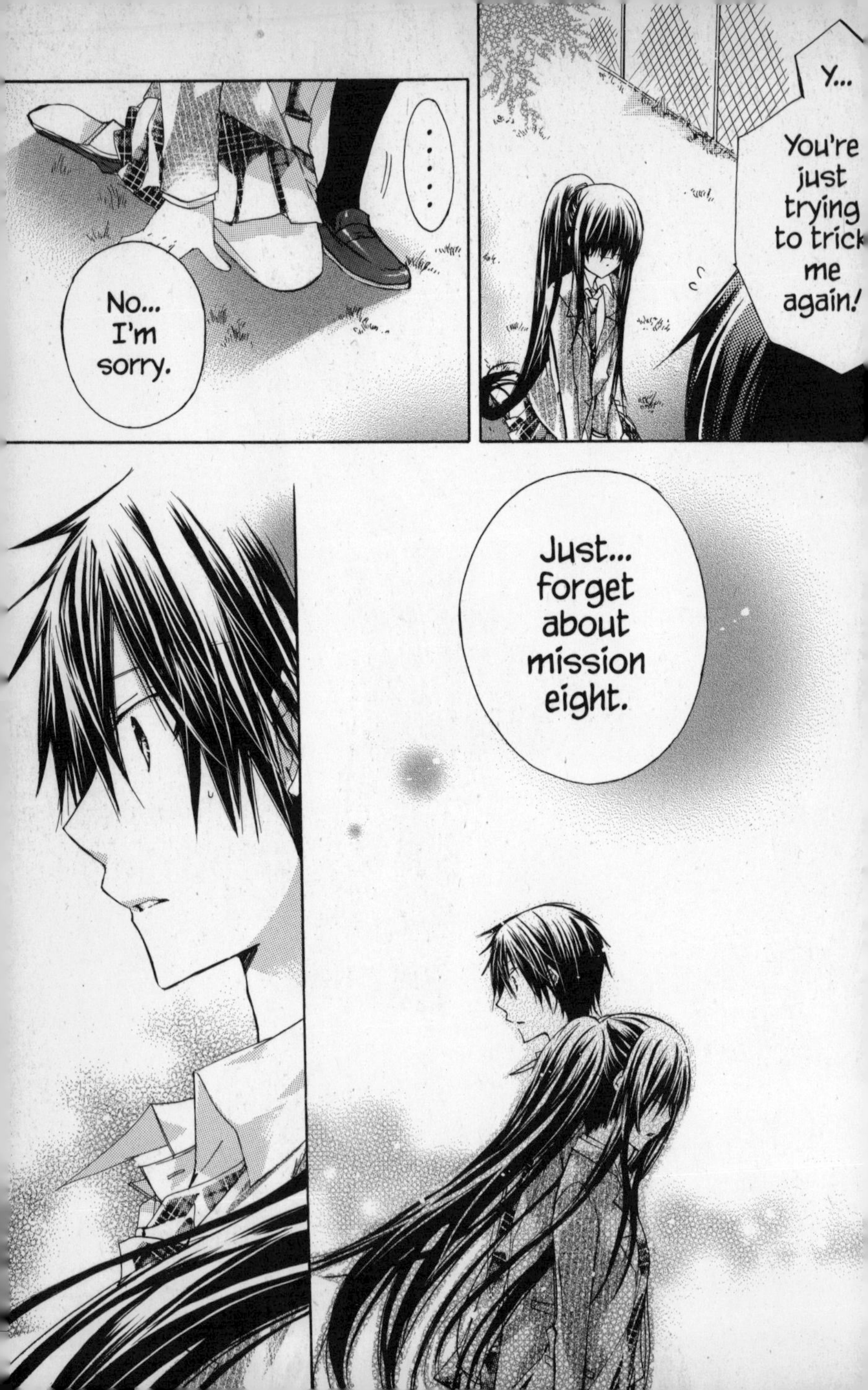
Y...
You're just trying to trick me again!
......
No... I'm sorry.
Just... forget about mission eight.

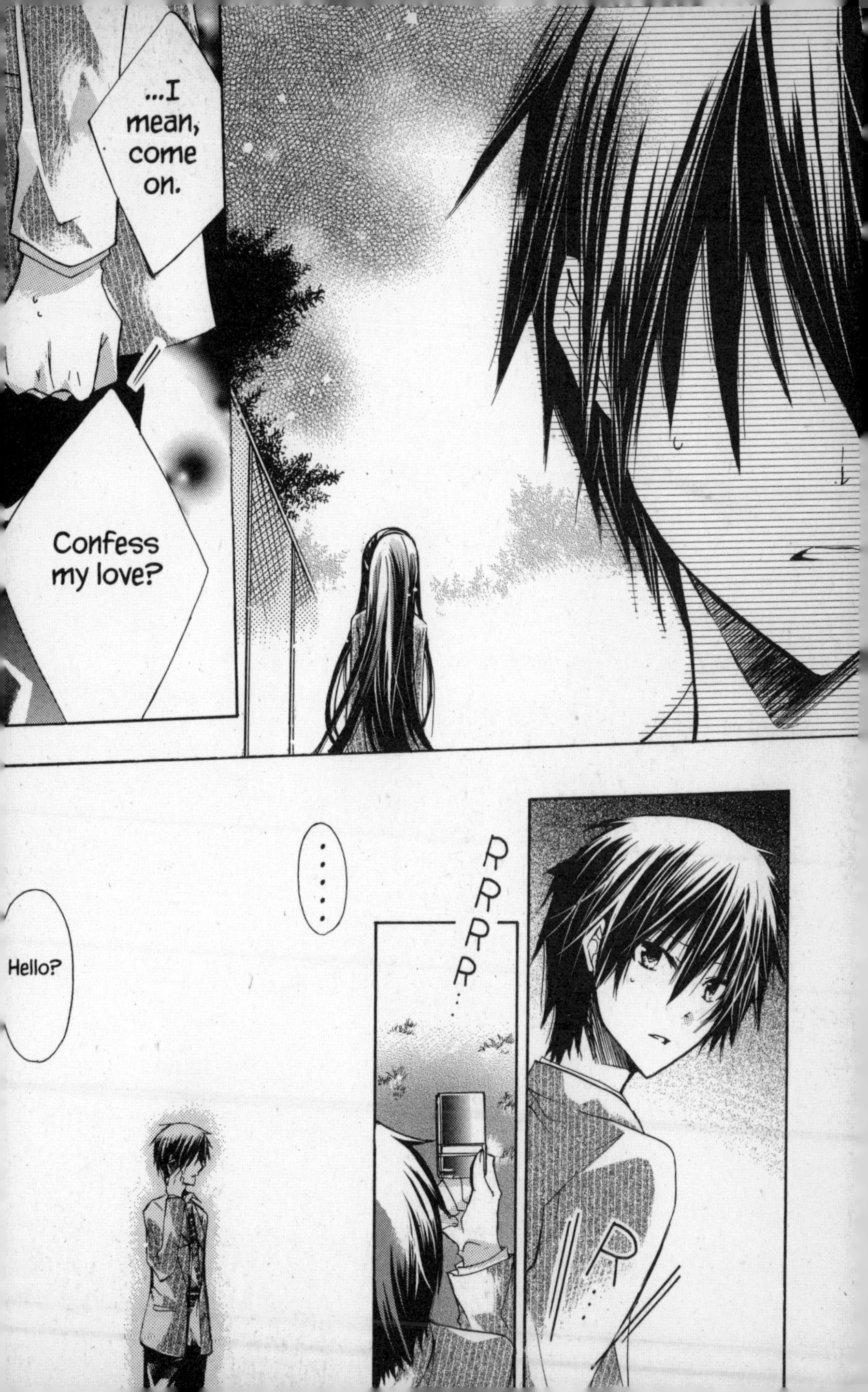
...I mean, come on.
Confess my love?
RRRR...
R...
.....
Hello?

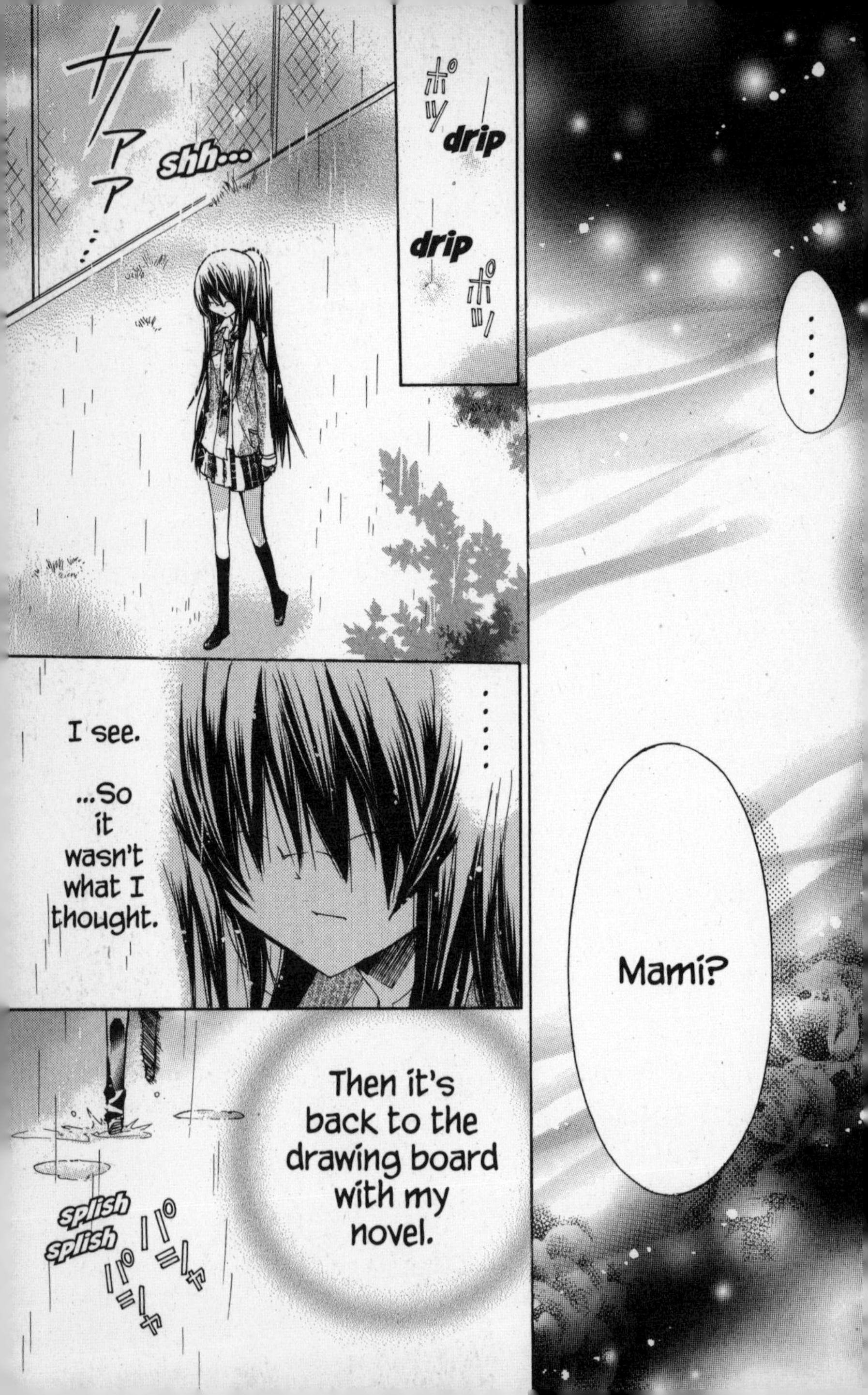
.....
Mami?
ポツ
drip
drip
ポツ
ザァア…
shh...
.....
I see.
...So it wasn't what I thought.
Then it's back to the drawing board with my novel.
splish
splish
パシャ
パシャ

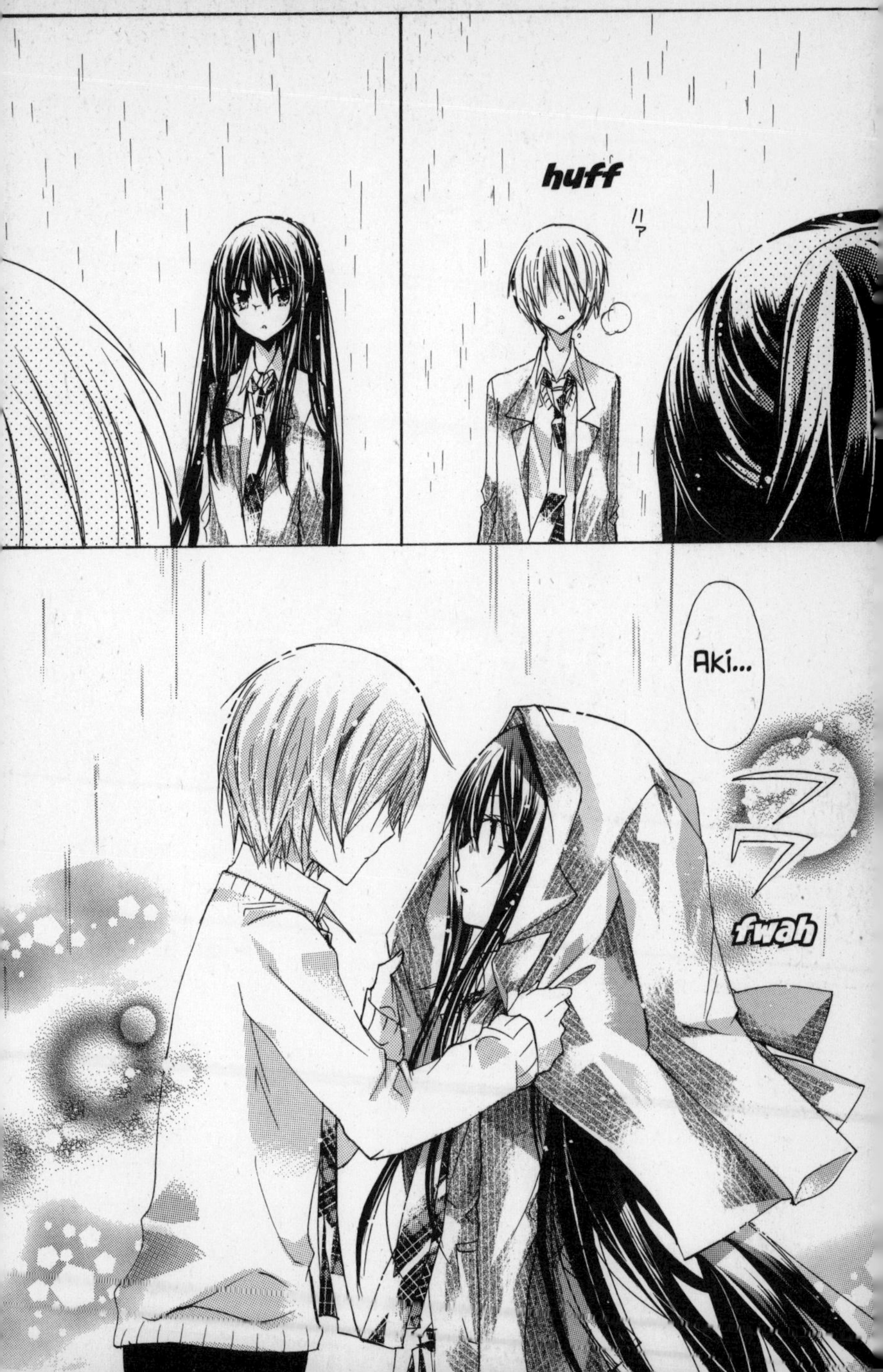
huff
ハァ
Aki...
fwah

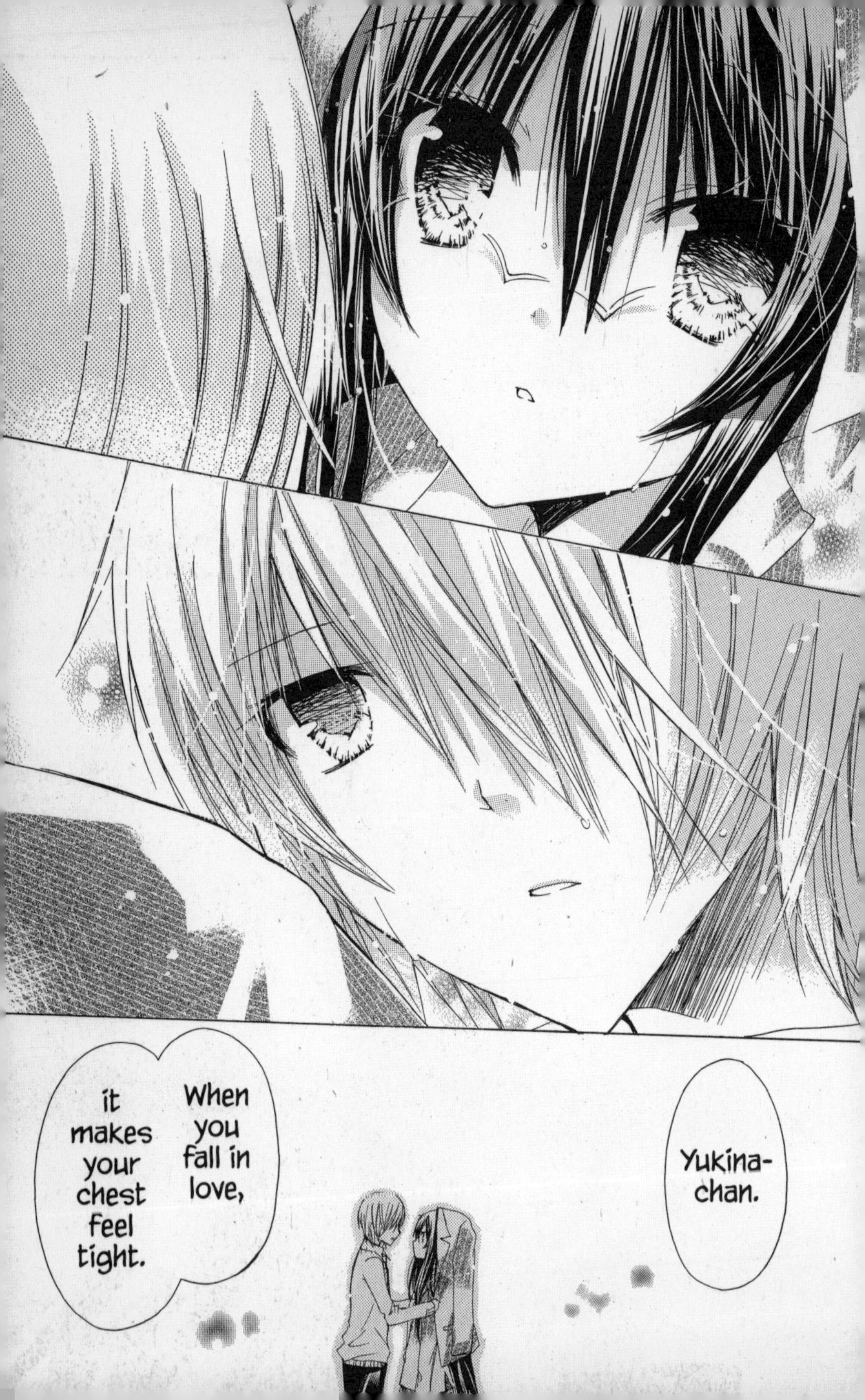
Yukina-chan.
When you fall in love, it makes your chest feel tight.

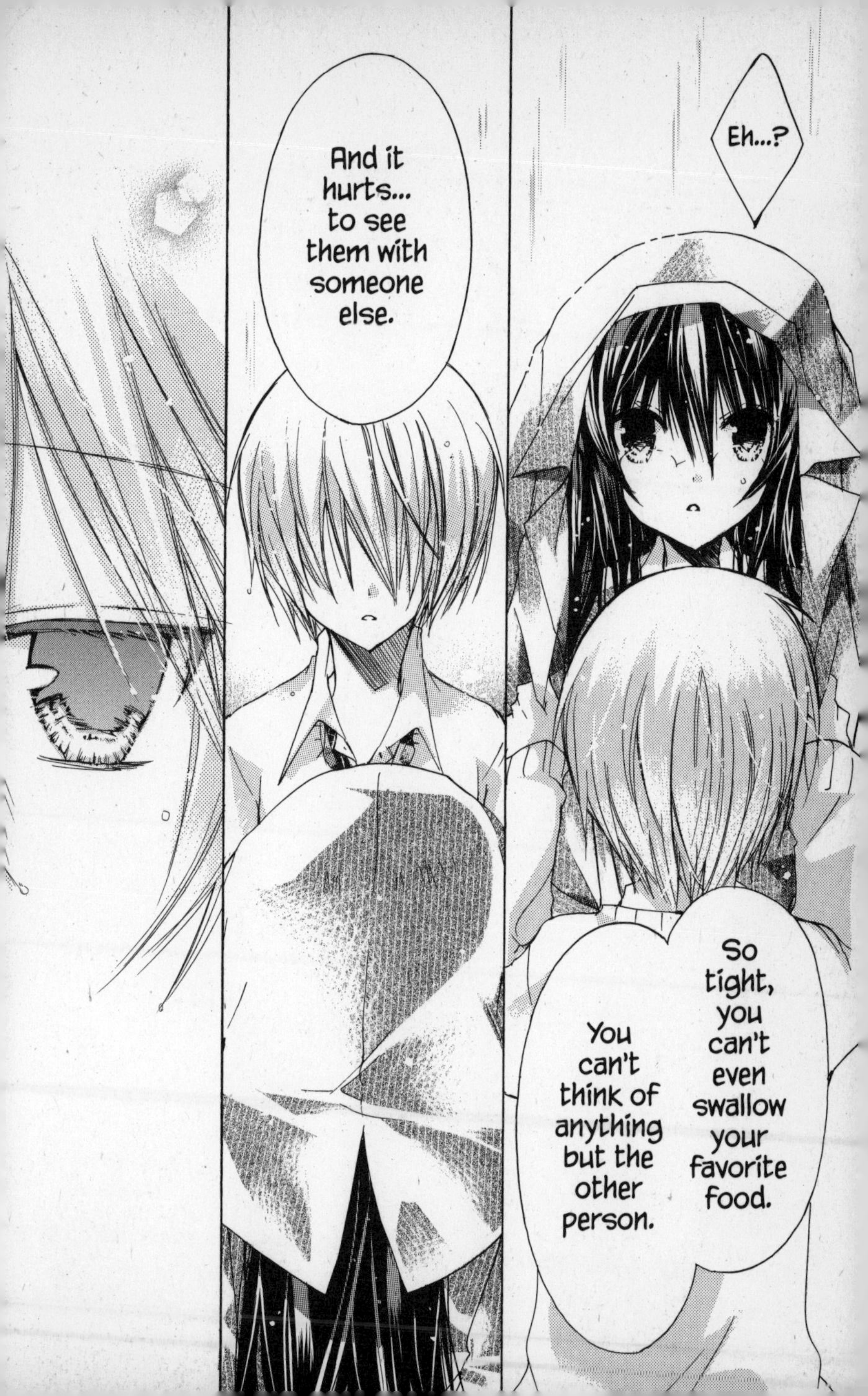
Eh...?
So tight, you can't even swallow your favorite food.
You can't think of anything but the other person.
And it hurts... to see them with someone else.

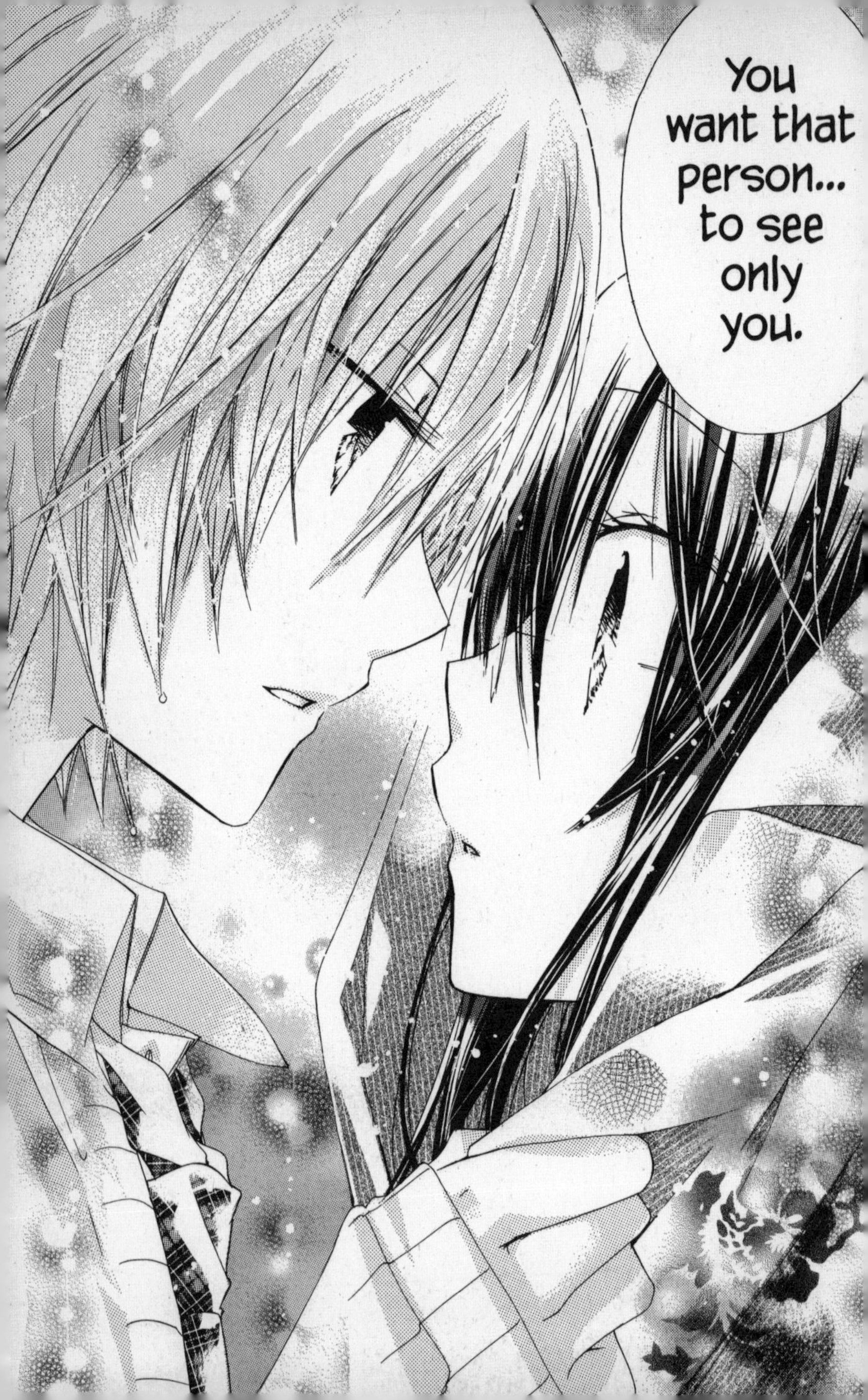
You want that person... to see only you.

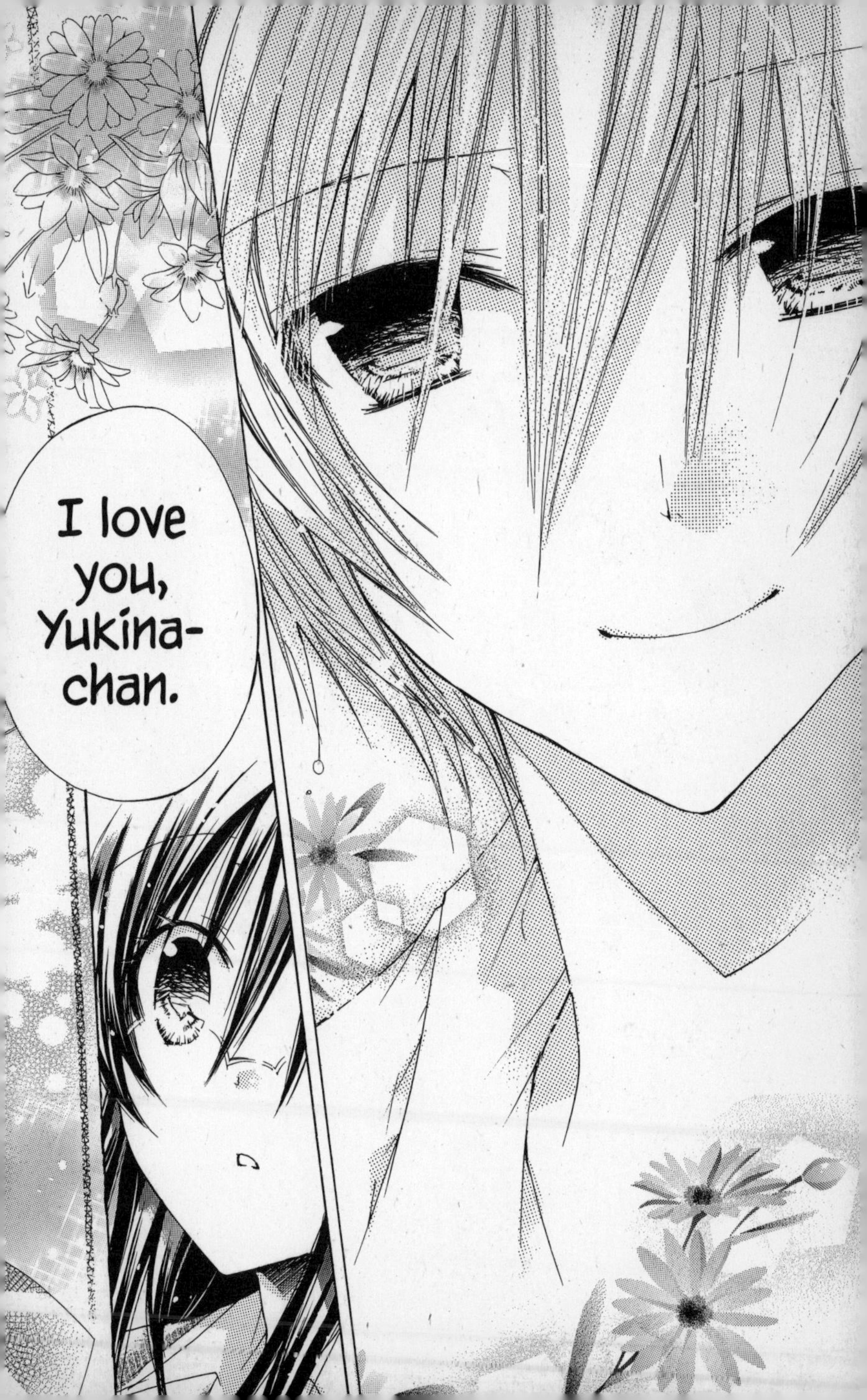
I love you, Yukina-chan.

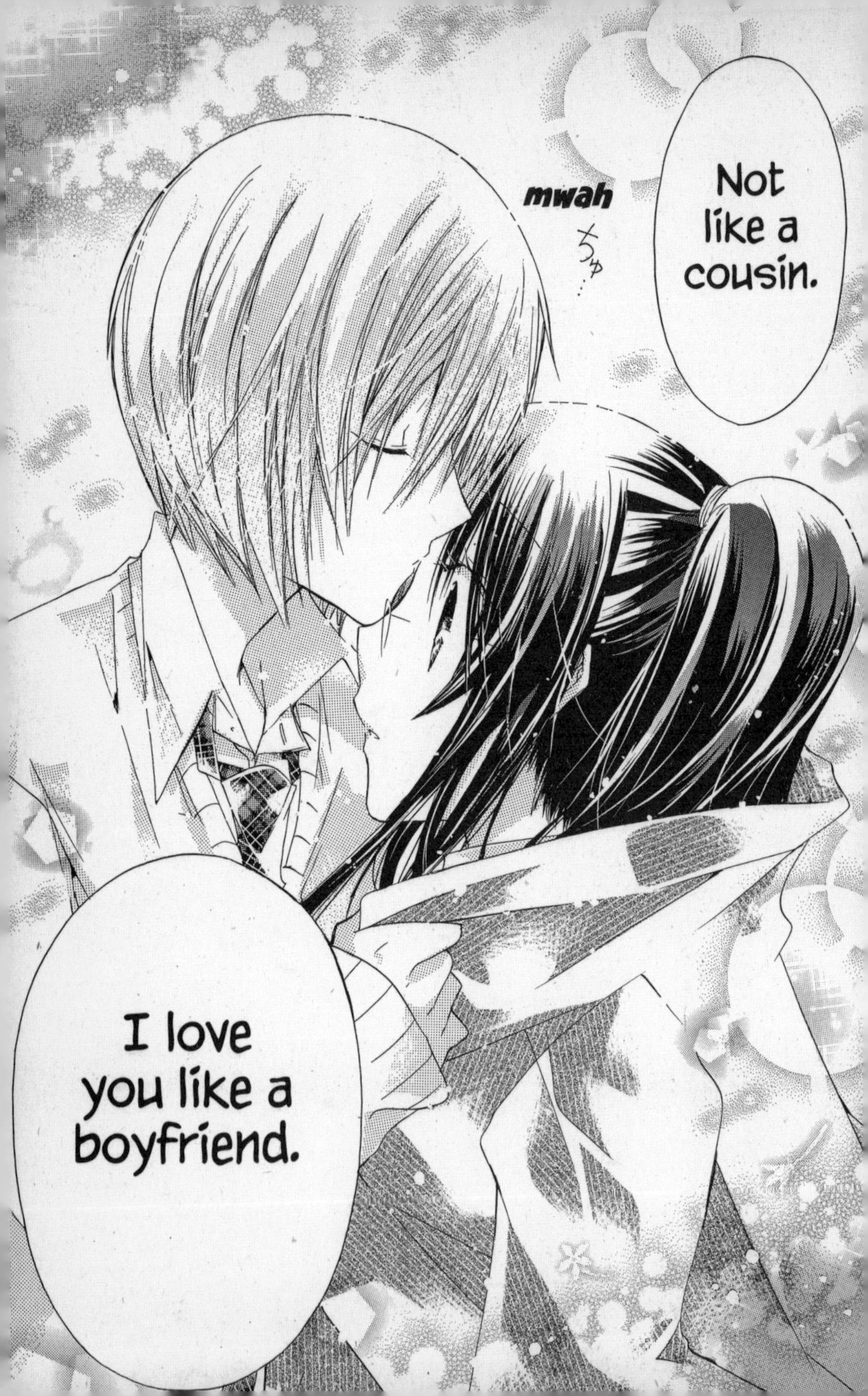
Not like a cousin.
mwah
ちゅ…
I love you like a boyfriend.

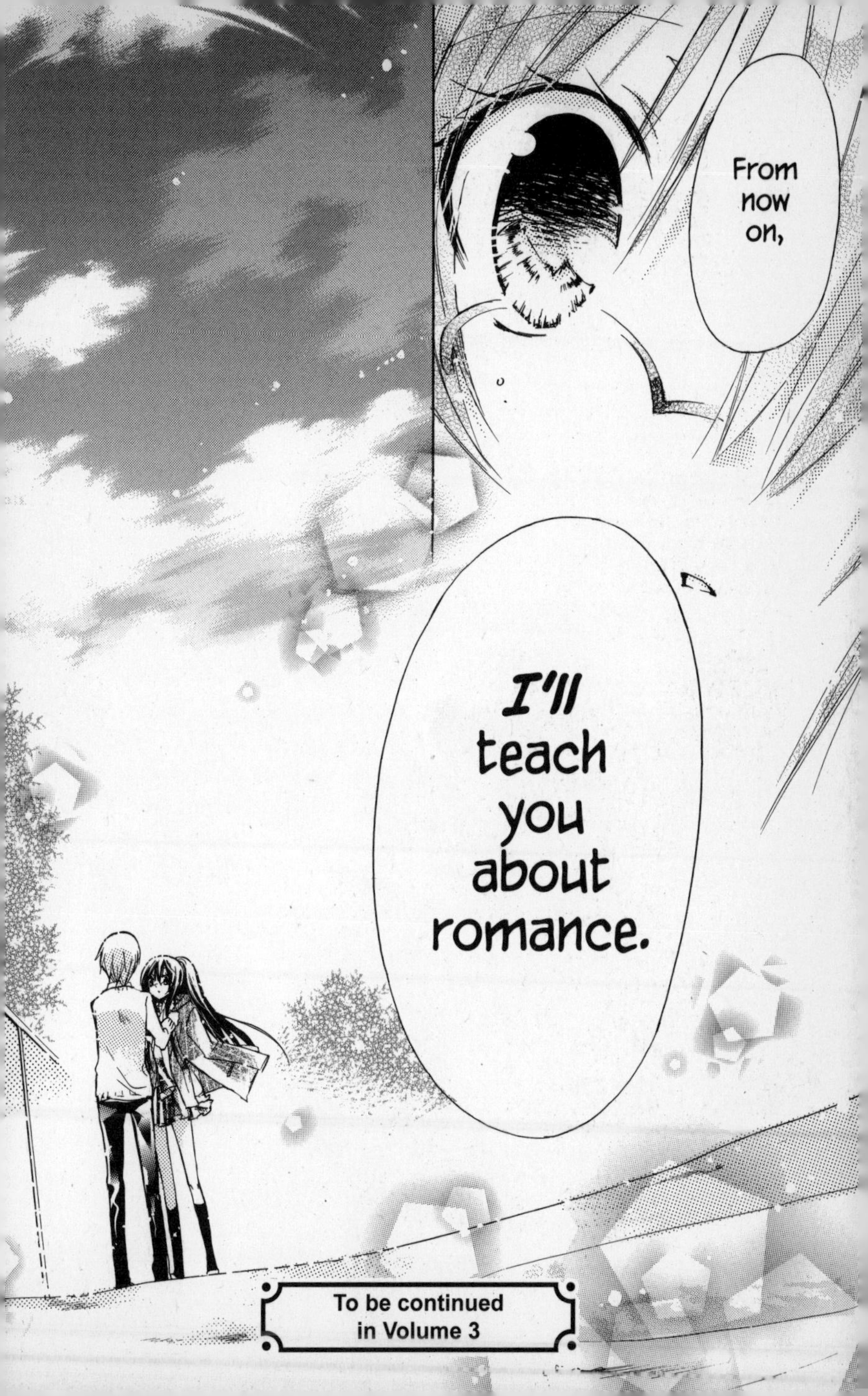
From now on,
I'll teach you about romance.
To be continued in Volume 3

It is time for love.
Secret cell phone
novelist vs. the most
popular boy in school.
A mission of love for
absolute servitude.

MISSIONS OF LOVE

**It is time for love.
Secret cell phone
novelist vs. the most
popular boy in school.
A mission of love for
absolute servitude.**

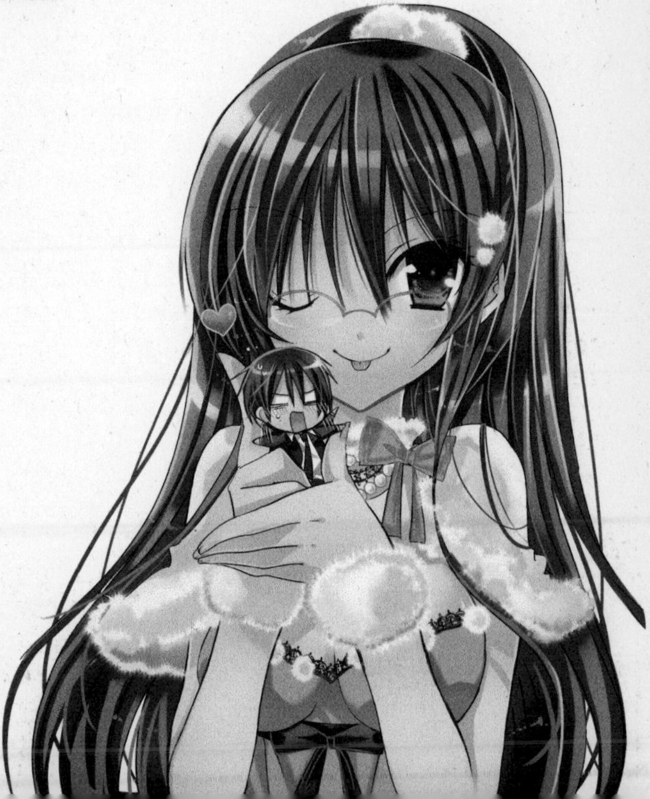

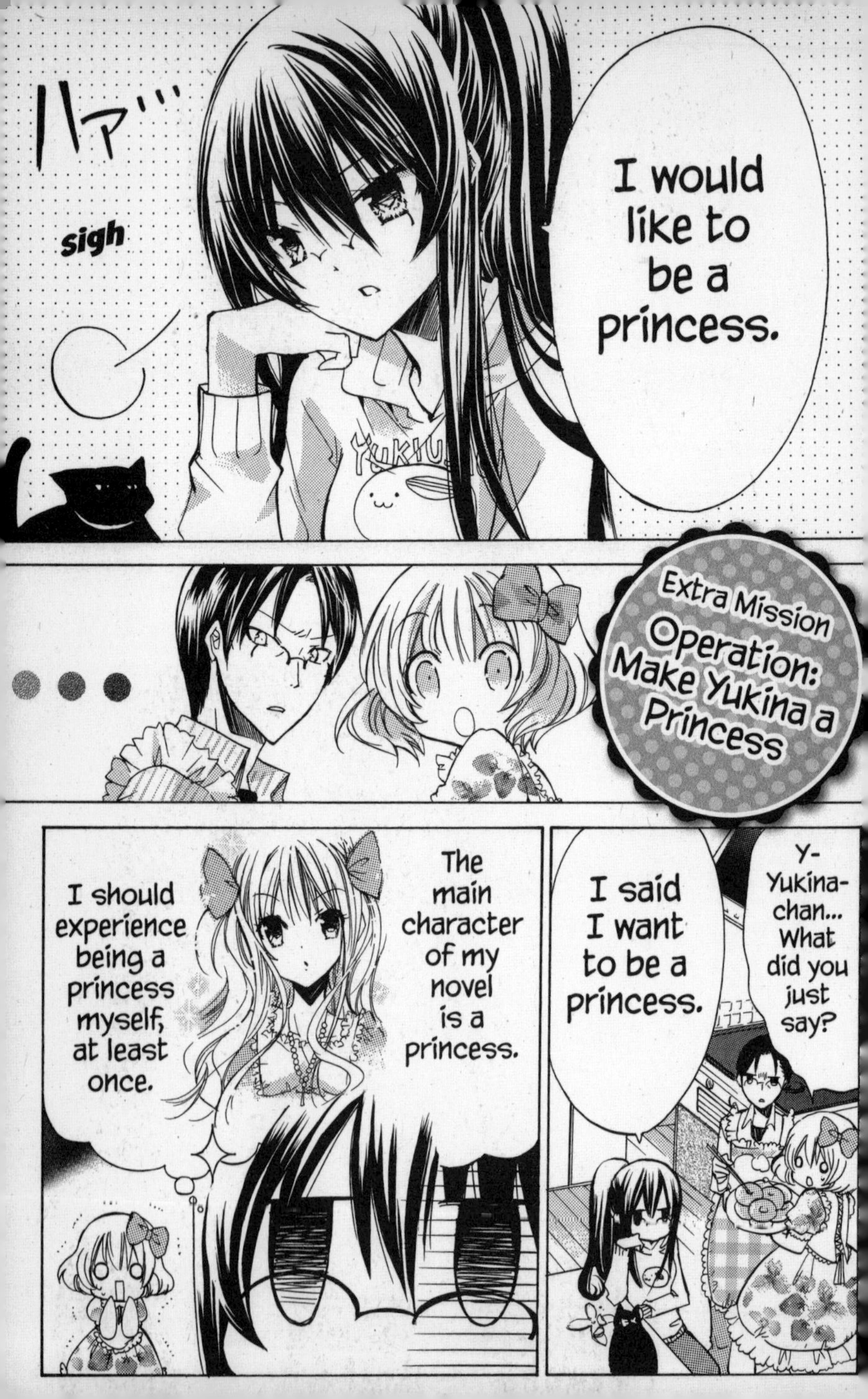
I would like to be a princess.
ハァ
sigh
Extra Mission
Operation: Make Yukina a Princess
Y- Yukina-chan... What did you just say?
I said I want to be a princess.
The main character of my novel is a princess.
I should experience being a princess myself, at least once.

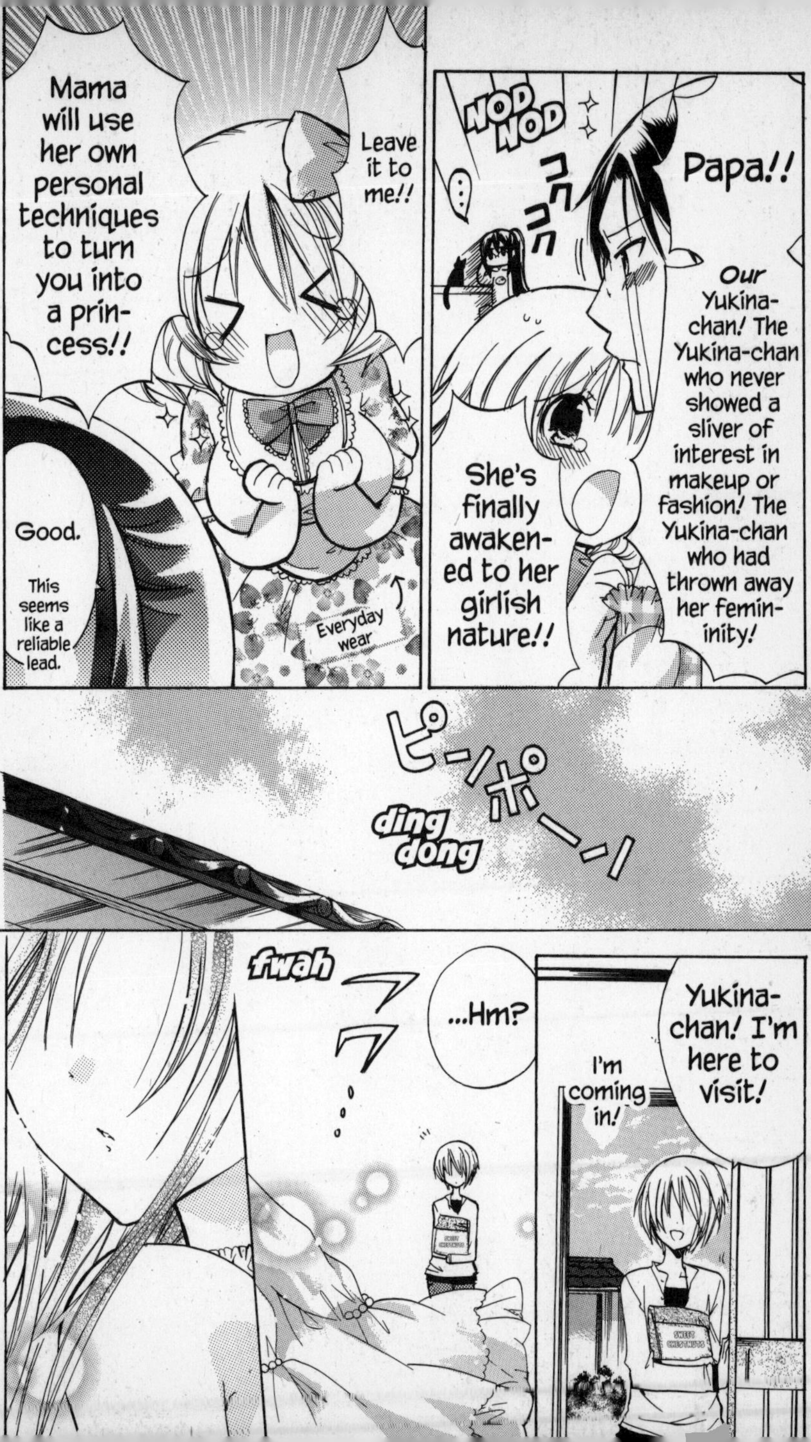
NOD NOD
Papa!!
Our Yukina-chan! The Yukina-chan who never showed a sliver of interest in makeup or fashion! The Yukina-chan who had thrown away her femininity!
She's finally awaken-ed to her girlish nature!!
Mama will use her own personal techniques to turn you into a prin-cess!!
Leave it to me!!
Everyday wear
Good.
This seems like a reliable lead.
ding dong
Yukina-chan! I'm here to visit!
I'm coming in!
SWEET CHESTNUTS
...Hm?
fwah

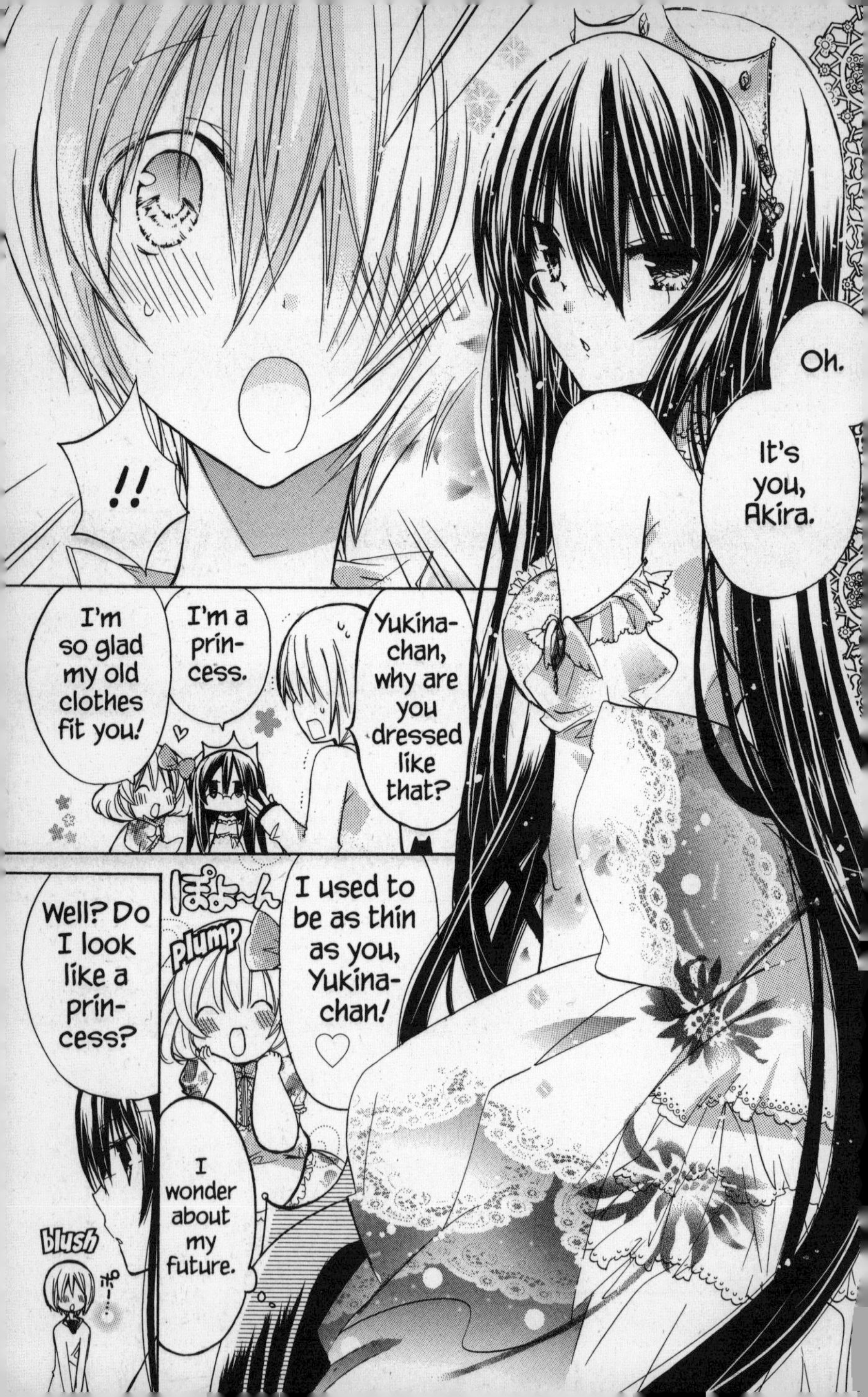
Oh.
It's you, Akira.
!!
Yukina-chan, why are you dressed like that?
I'm a princess.
I'm so glad my old clothes fit you!
ぽよ～ん
plump
I used to be as thin as you, Yukina-chan!
Well? Do I look like a princess?
I wonder about my future.
blush
ポッ

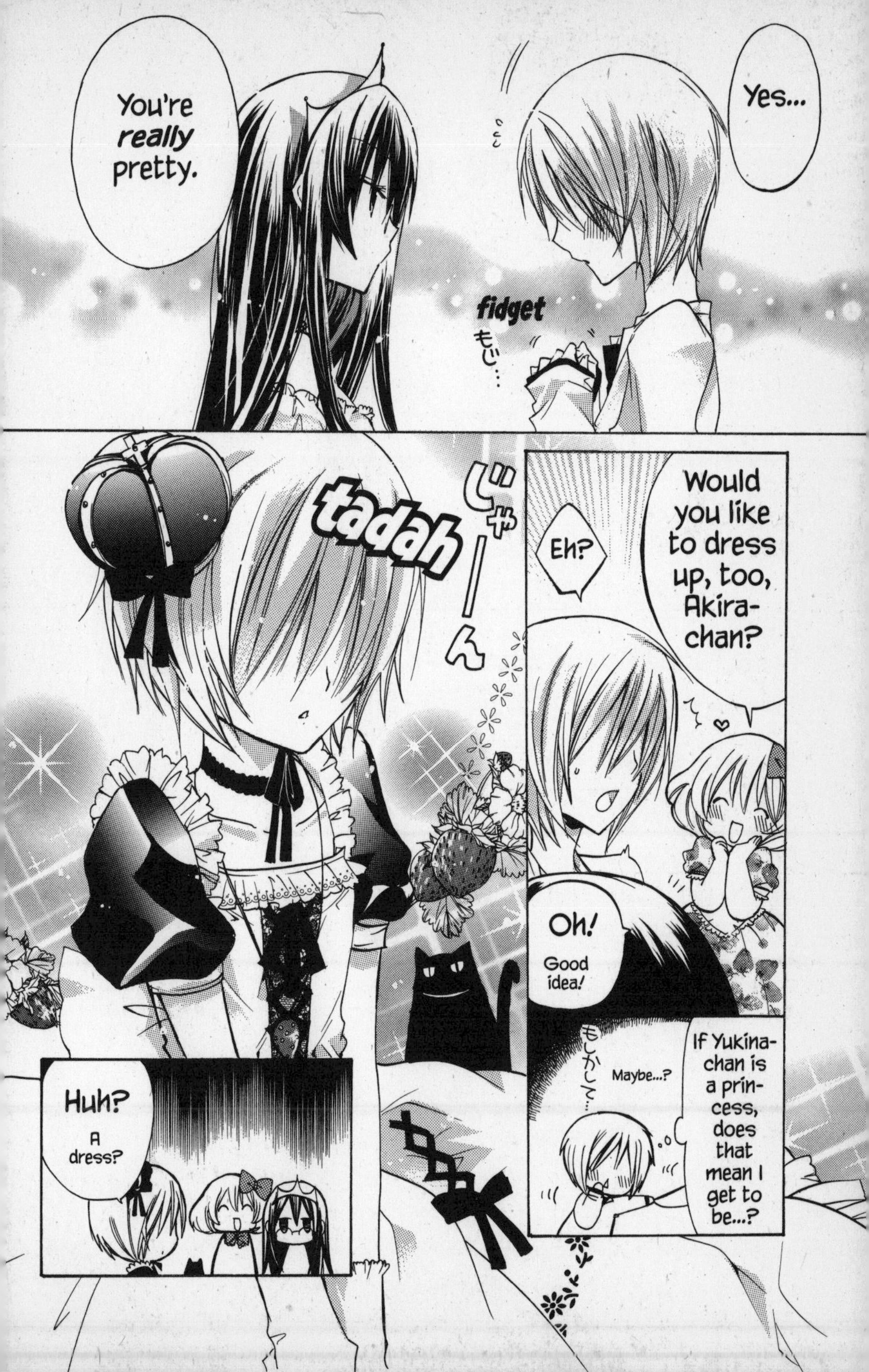

Yes...
You're *really* pretty.
fidget
もじ…
Would you like to dress up, too, Akira-chan?
Eh?
Oh!
Good idea!
If Yukina-chan is a princess, does that mean I get to be...?
Maybe...?
もしかして…
tadah
じゃーん
Huh?
A dress?

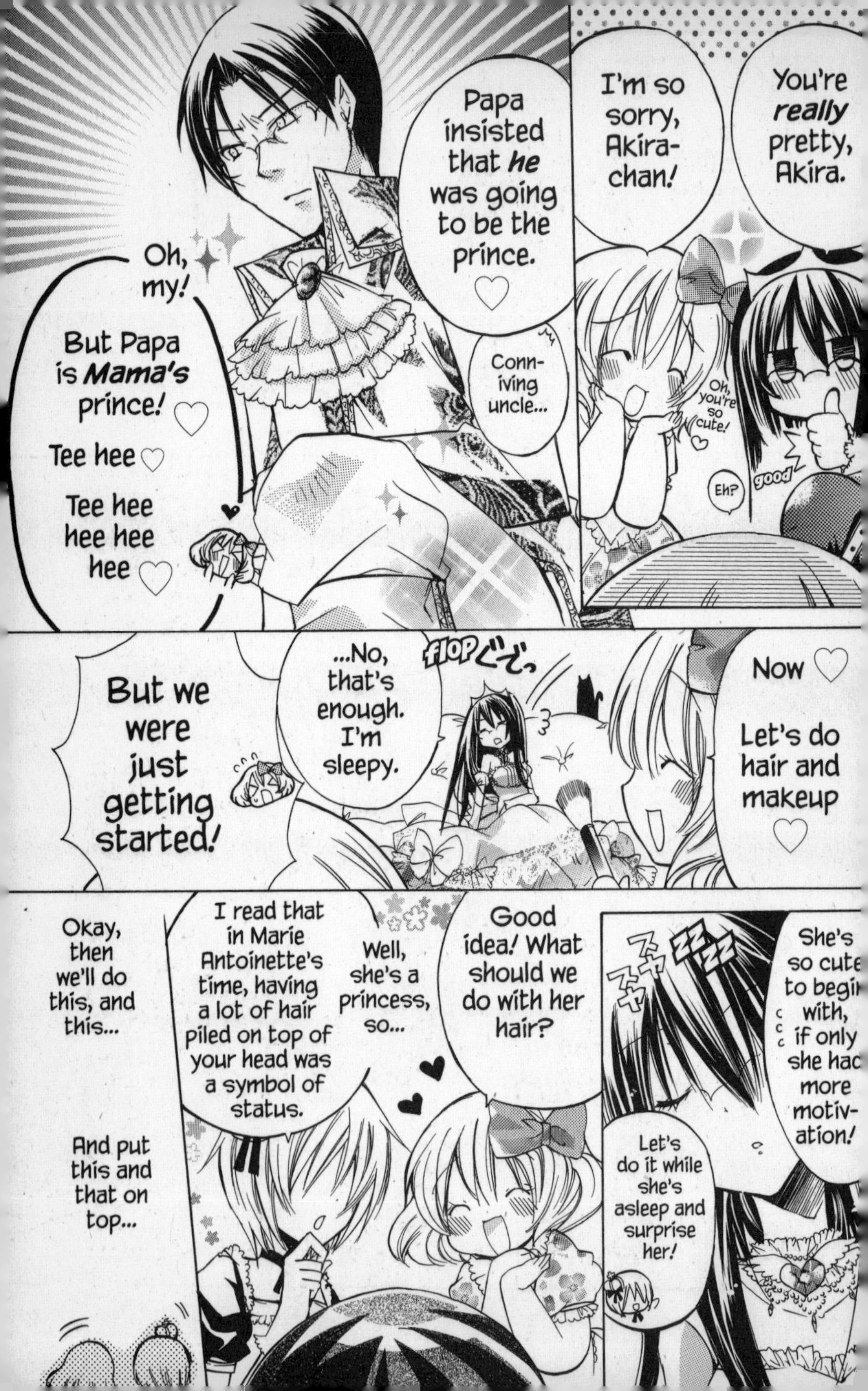
You're *really* pretty, Akira.
I'm so sorry, Akira-chan!
Oh, you're so cute!
good
Eh?
Papa insisted that *he* was going to be the prince. ♡
Conniving uncle...
Oh, my!
But Papa is *Mama's* prince! ♡
Tee hee ♡
Tee hee hee hee hee ♡
Now ♡
Let's do hair and makeup ♡
flop ぐでっ
...No, that's enough. I'm sleepy.
But we were just getting started!
She's so cute to begin with, if only she had more motivation!
ZZZ
Let's do it while she's asleep and surprise her!
Good idea! What should we do with her hair?
Well, she's a princess, so...
I read that in Marie Antoinette's time, having a lot of hair piled on top of your head was a symbol of status.
Okay, then we'll do this, and this...
And put this and that on top...

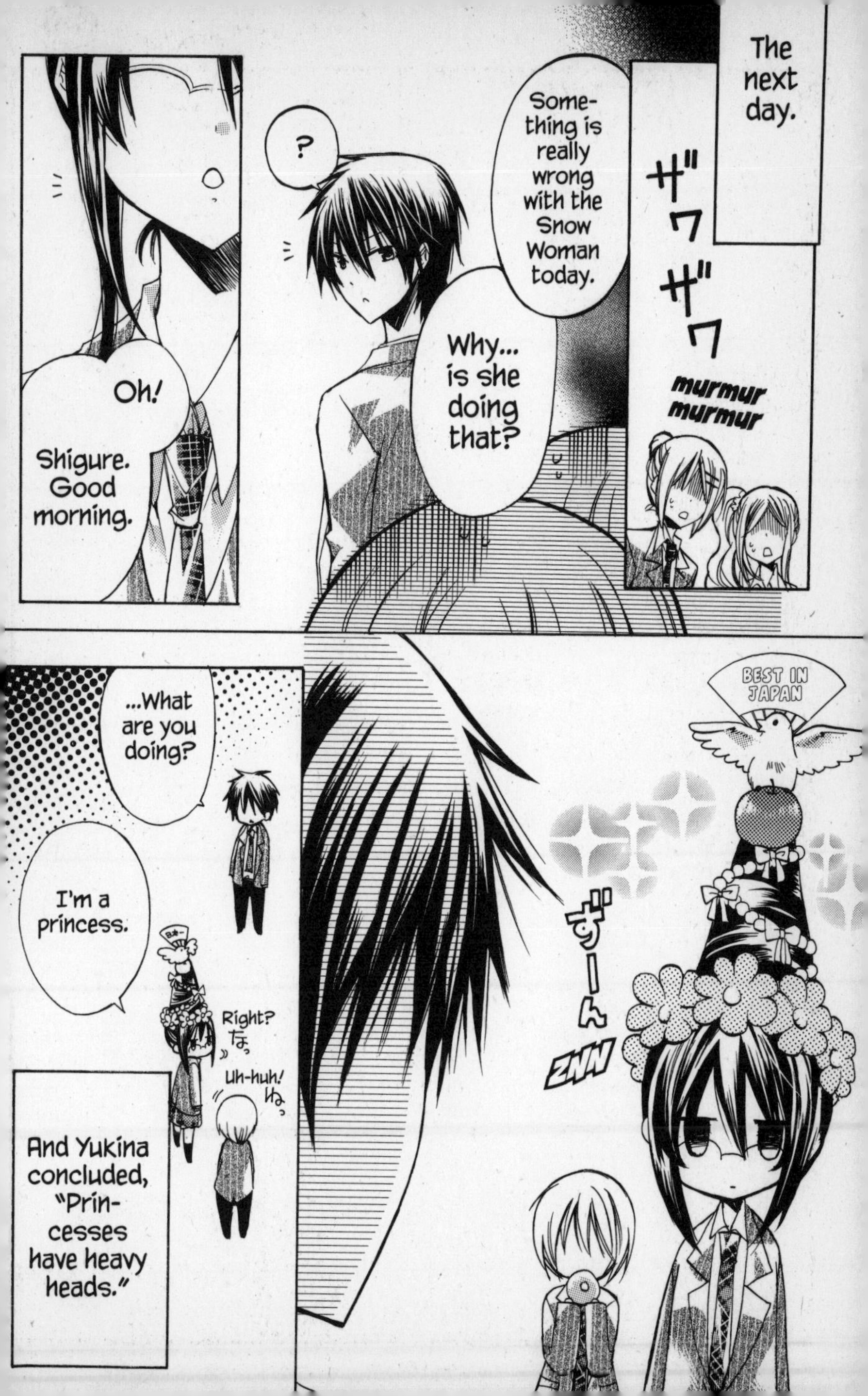

The next day.
ザワザワ
murmur murmur
Something is really wrong with the Snow Woman today.
?
Why... is she doing that?
Oh!
Shigure. Good morning.
BEST IN JAPAN
ずーん
ZNN
...What are you doing?
I'm a princess.
Right? なっ
Uh-huh! ぬっ
And Yukina concluded, "Princesses have heavy heads."

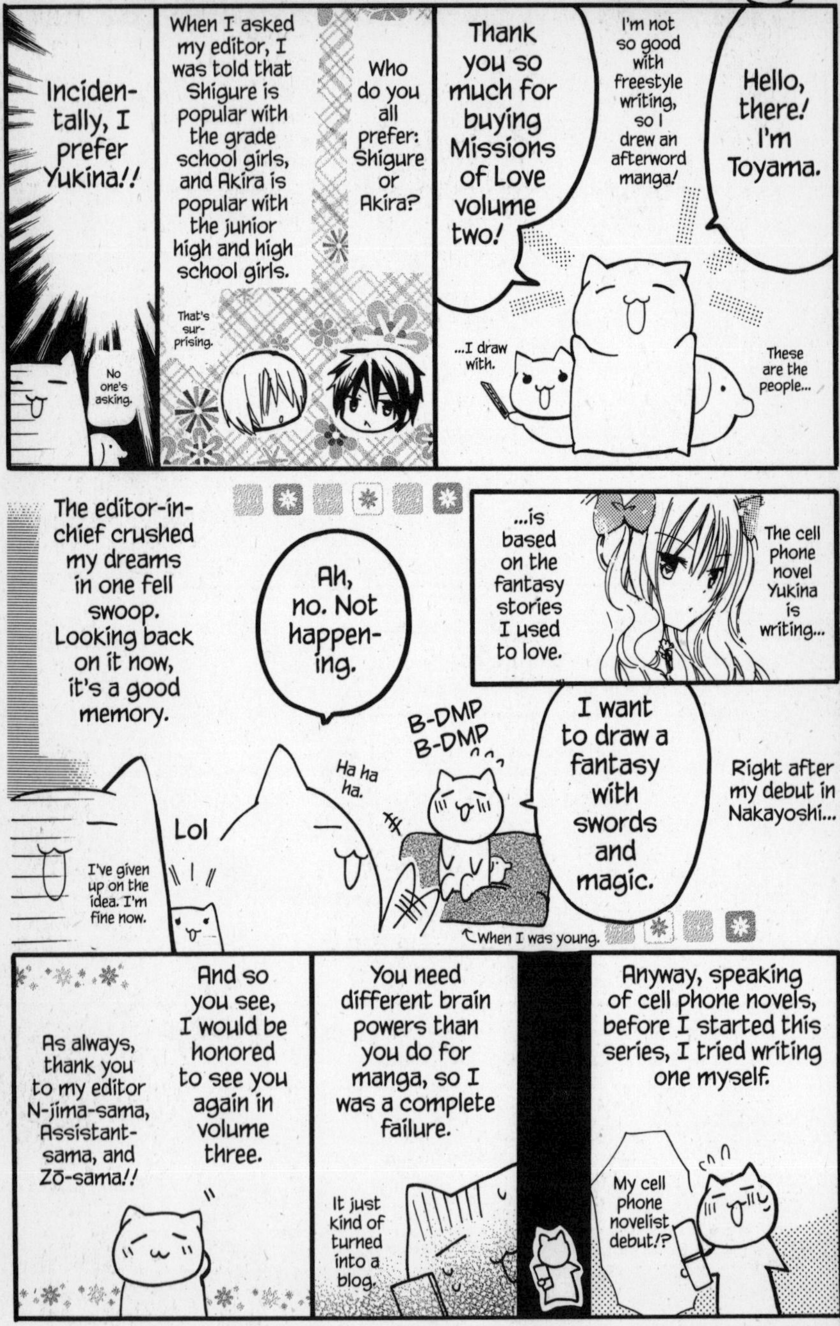
Hello, there! I'm Toyama.
I'm not so good with freestyle writing, so I drew an afterword manga!
Thank you so much for buying Missions of Love volume two!
These are the people...
...I draw with.
Who do you all prefer: Shigure or Akira?
When I asked my editor, I was told that Shigure is popular with the grade school girls, and Akira is popular with the junior high and high school girls.
That's sur-prising.
Inciden-tally, I prefer Yukina!!
No one's asking.
The cell phone novel Yukina is writing...
...is based on the fantasy stories I used to love.
Right after my debut in Nakayoshi...
I want to draw a fantasy with swords and magic.
B-DMP B-DMP
When I was young.
Ah, no. Not happen-ing.
Ha ha ha.
The editor-in-chief crushed my dreams in one fell swoop. Looking back on it now, it's a good memory.
Lol
I've given up on the idea. I'm fine now.
Anyway, speaking of cell phone novels, before I started this series, I tried writing one myself.
My cell phone novelist debut!?
You need different brain powers than you do for manga, so I was a complete failure.
It just kind of turned into a blog.
And so you see, I would be honored to see you again in volume three.
As always, thank you to my editor N-jima-sama, Assistant-sama, and Zō-sama!!

Missions of Love: Character Talk

Q&A Corner--Yukina, Shigure, and Akira will answer all of your questions!

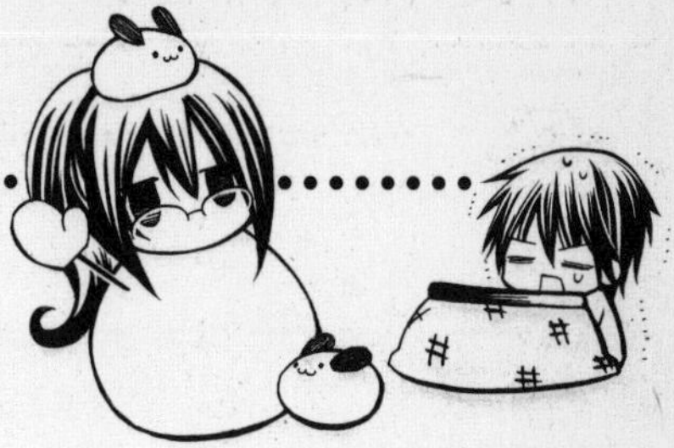

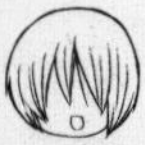

Yukina-chan, it's a Q&A corner!

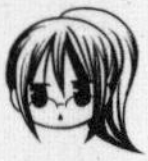

Indeed. Ask me anything!

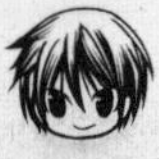

Himuro-san, why would you blackmail an upstanding citizen such as myself?

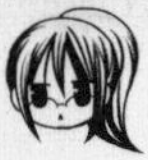

Now let's get started! (Ignore.)

This is a question for Yukina-chan. What is the name of your family's cat?

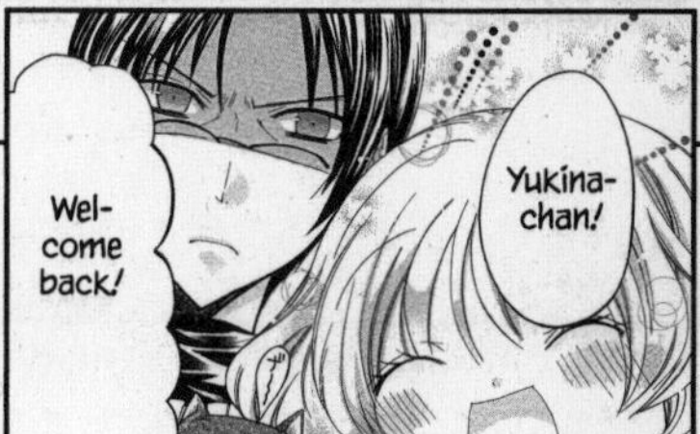
Yukina-chan!
Wel-come back!

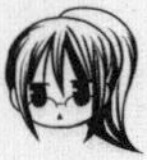

My black cat (male) is named Roman. Men do need their dreams, after all.

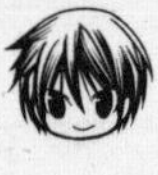

...What are you looking at me for?

I have a question for Yukina-chan. In addition to the novel about Lilia, what kind of cell phone novels has Yupina written?

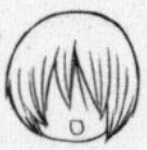

Your debut came before Lilia, right?

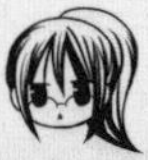

That's right. It was an epic adventure, about an honorable girl thief, who fought for world peace. I'd love for you to read it.

**This question is for Shigure.
Where did you get your name?**

I'd have to ask my parents where they got it, but it's perfect for a cool, level-headed guy like me, don't you think?

......

What? You got something to say?

**I have a question for Akira-kun.
Those girls said you were a "quarter."
What does that mean?**

A "quarter" is someone who is one-fourth a different nationality.

My grandfather is an Englishman.

Over already? That was fun, wasn't it, Yukina-chan?

Yes. Did we answer all of your questions?

You haven't answered mine yet.

Then we bid you farewell. (Ignore.)

Next Mission

Akira tries to tell Yukina exactly how he feels.

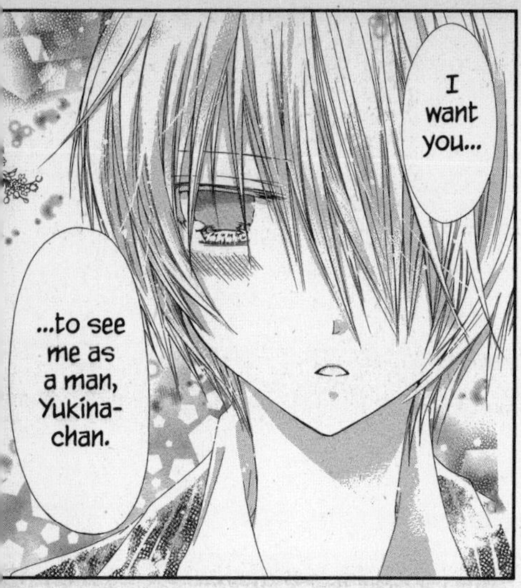
I want you...
...to see me as a man, Yukina-chan.

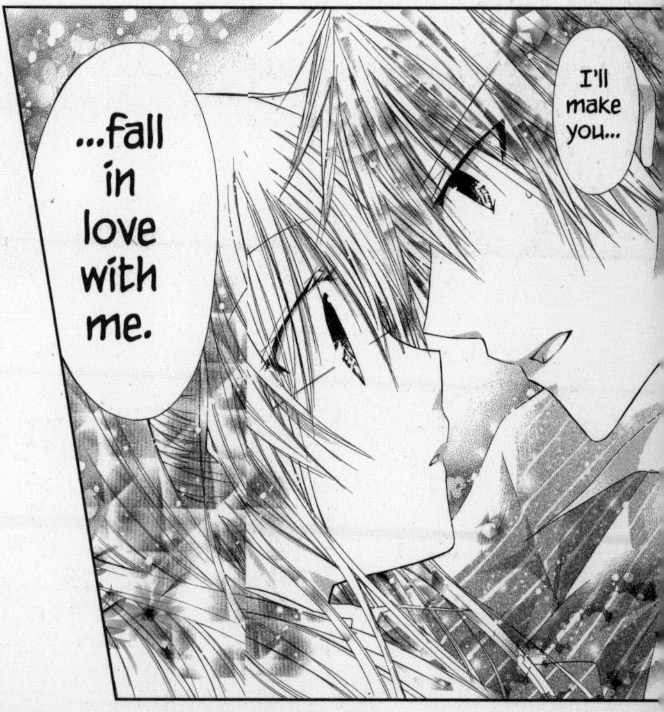
I'll make you...
...fall in love with me.

And so Shigure gets serious!

Coming Soon!!

Caught up in the first love triangle of her life, surprises abound for Yukina!

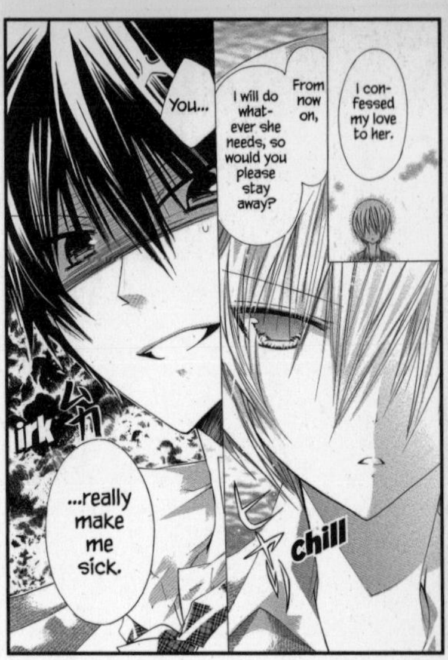
I con-
fessed my love to her.
From now on,
I will do what-ever she needs, so would you please stay away?
You...
irk
...really make me sick.
Chill

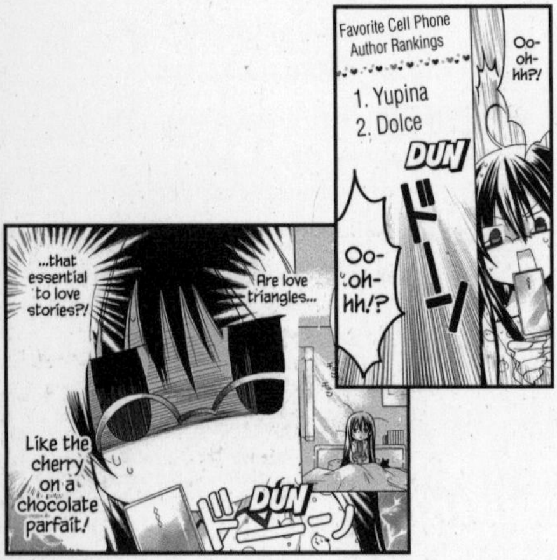
Favorite Cell Phone Author Rankings
1. Yupina
2. Dolce
Oo-oh-hh?!
DUN
Oo-oh-hh!?
Are love triangles...
...that essential to love stories?!
Like the cherry on a chocolate parfait!
DUN

But another surprise awaits Yukina and the others!!

The name "Mami" casts a shadow over Shigure's face. ...A storm approaches the romantic trio!!

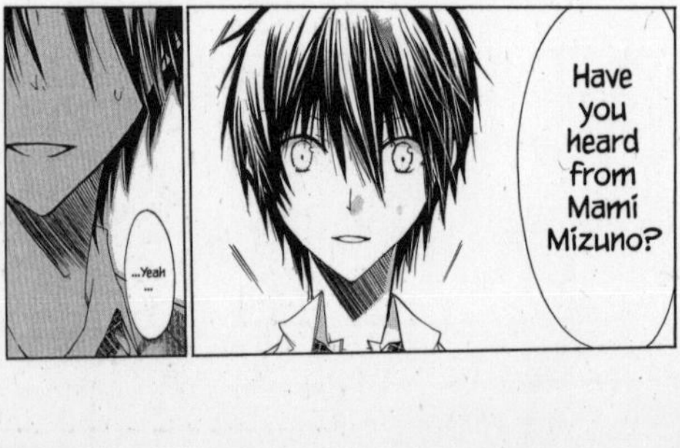
Have you heard from Mami Mizuno?
...Yeah...

Missions of Love 3

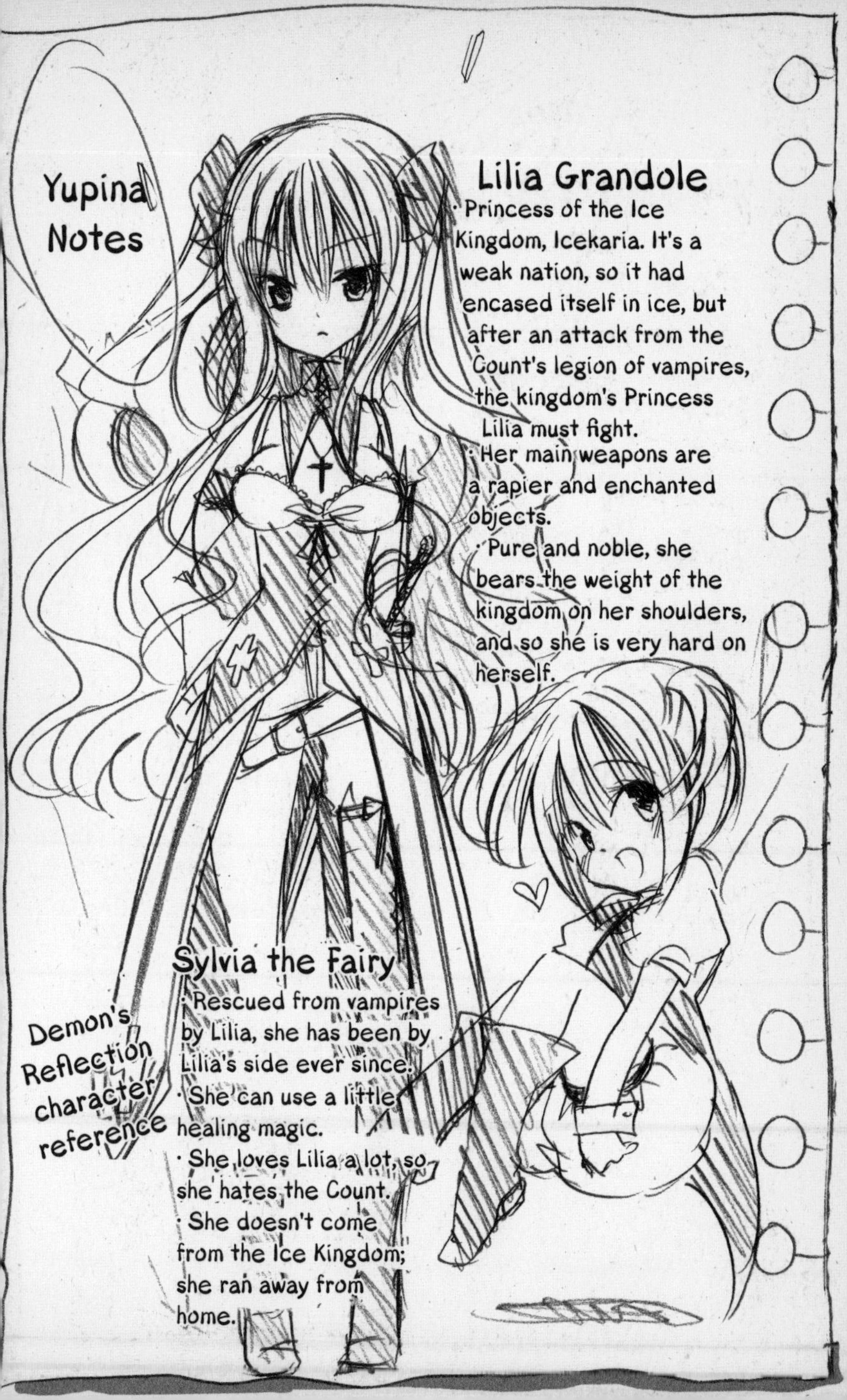
Yupina Notes
Lilia Grandole
· Princess of the Ice Kingdom, Icekaria. It's a weak nation, so it had encased itself in ice, but after an attack from the Count's legion of vampires, the kingdom's Princess Lilia must fight.
· Her main weapons are a rapier and enchanted objects.
· Pure and noble, she bears the weight of the kingdom on her shoulders, and so she is very hard on herself.
Sylvia the Fairy
· Rescued from vampires by Lilia, she has been by Lilia's side ever since.
· She can use a little healing magic.
· She loves Lilia a lot, so she hates the Count.
· She doesn't come from the Ice Kingdom; she ran away from home.
Demon's Reflection character reference

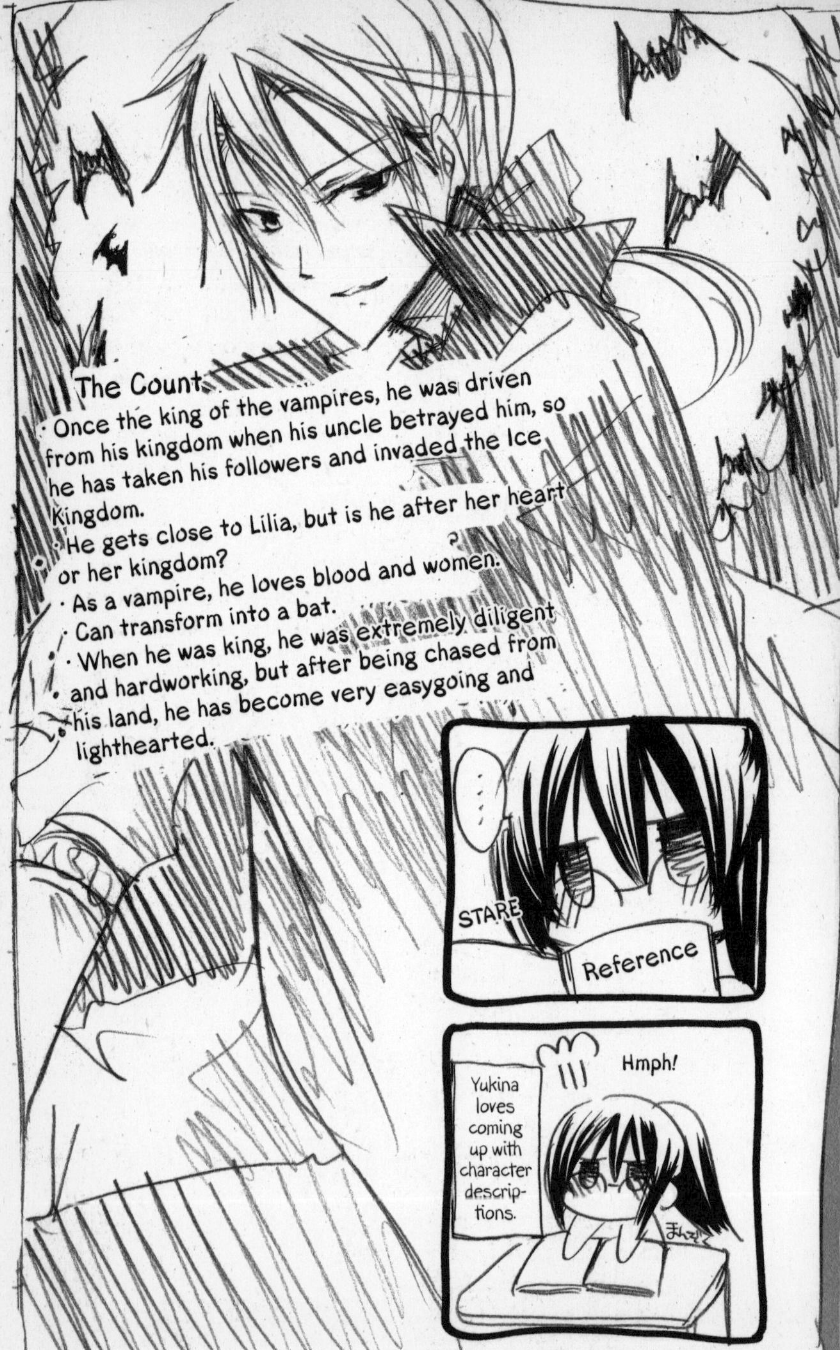
The Count
· Once the king of the vampires, he was driven from his kingdom when his uncle betrayed him, so he has taken his followers and invaded the Ice Kingdom.
· He gets close to Lilia, but is he after her heart or her kingdom?
· As a vampire, he loves blood and women.
· Can transform into a bat.
· When he was king, he was extremely diligent and hardworking, but after being chased from his land, he has become very easygoing and lighthearted.
....
STARE
Reference
Hmph!
Yukina loves coming up with character descriptions.
まんぞく

Author: Ema Toyama
Born May 23. Gemini. Blood type B
Debut work: *Tenshi no Tamago*, winner of 36th Annual Nakayoshi Newcomer Manga Award, Special Award, and published in the September 2003 issue of *Nakayoshi*.
Representative Works: *Pixie Pop: Gokkun! Pūcho*; *Mamakore*; *I Am Here!*
Toyama: This is the volume where Akira starts trying to get between Yukina and Shigure. I always worry about what I should have Akira eating. I feel like he eats an awful lot of sweets. Writing this story always gives me a renewed sense of how hard it is to get someone to fall in love with you.

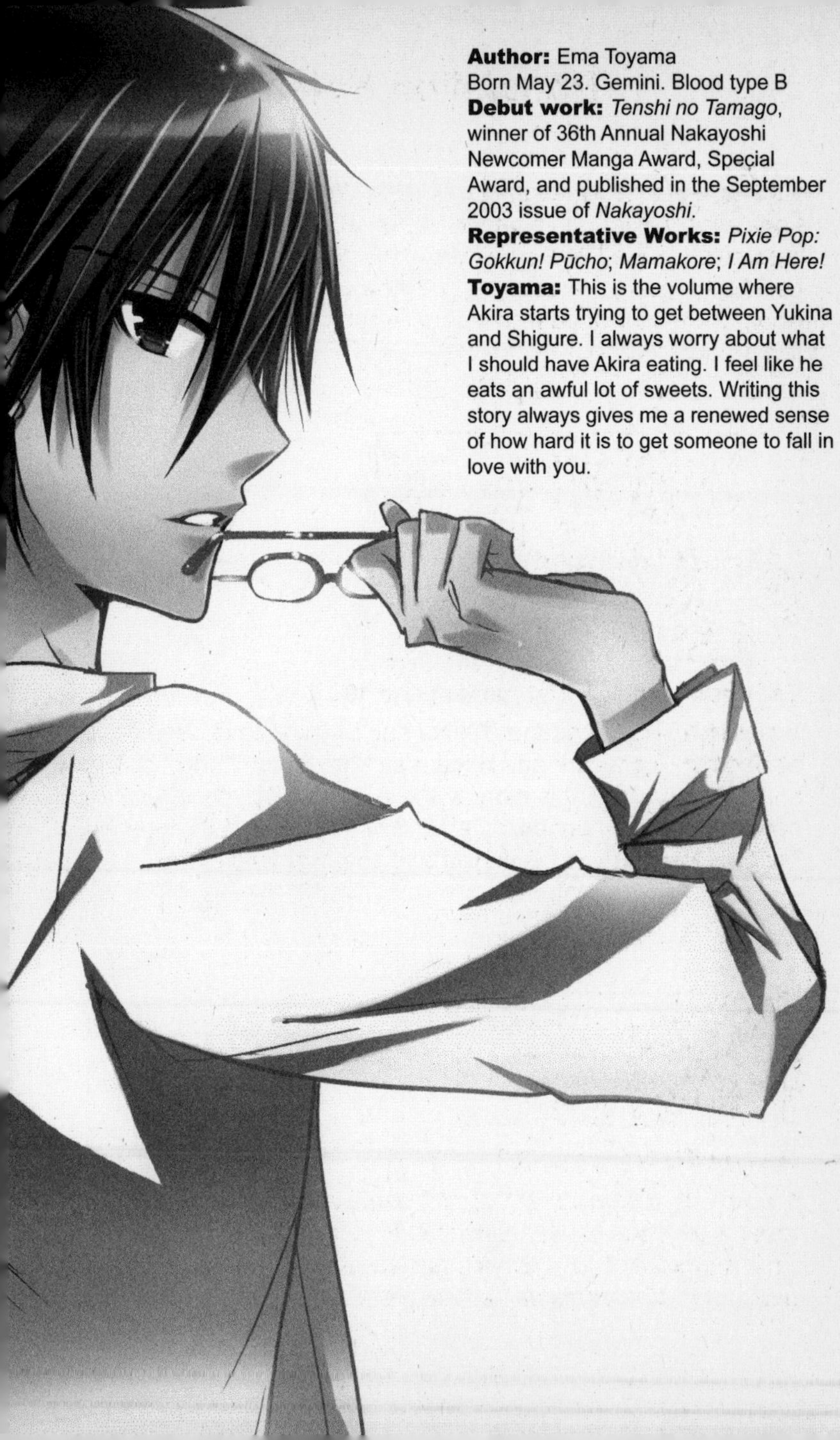

Translation Notes

Japanese is a tricky language for most Westerners, and translation is often more art than science. For your edification and reading pleasure, here are notes on some of the places where we could have gone in a different direction with our translation of the work, or where a Japanese cultural reference is used.

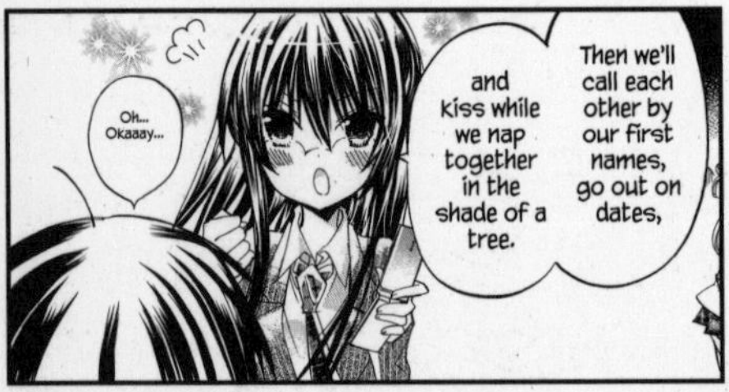
Then we'll call each other by our first names, go out on dates,
and kiss while we nap together in the shade of a tree.
Oh... Okaaay...

Call each other by first name, page 19

You may have noticed that Yukina and Shigure have been calling each other Kitami-kun and Himuro-san. In Japan, if you don't know someone very well, it is more polite to call them by their family name. Calling someone by their first name is a sign of closeness, like the closeness between girlfriend and boyfriend.

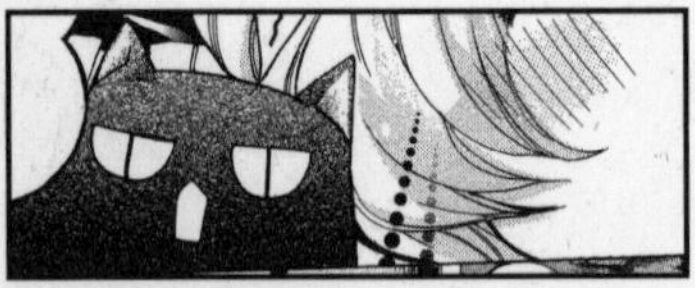

Roman the cat, page 162

Yukina's comment about the cat's name and how men need their dreams isn't quite as random as it may seem. In Japanese, the French word for novel, roman, has come to also refer to a strong attachment to dreams and adventure.

The Pretty Guardians are back!

*

Kodansha Comics is proud to present *Sailor Moon* with all new translations.

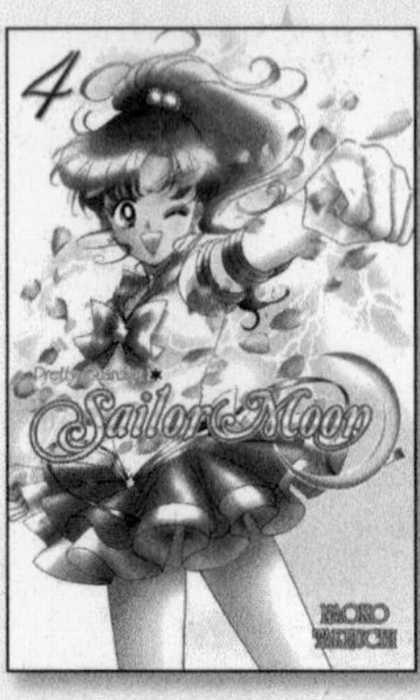
4
Pretty Guardian
Sailor Moon
NAOKO TAKEUCHI

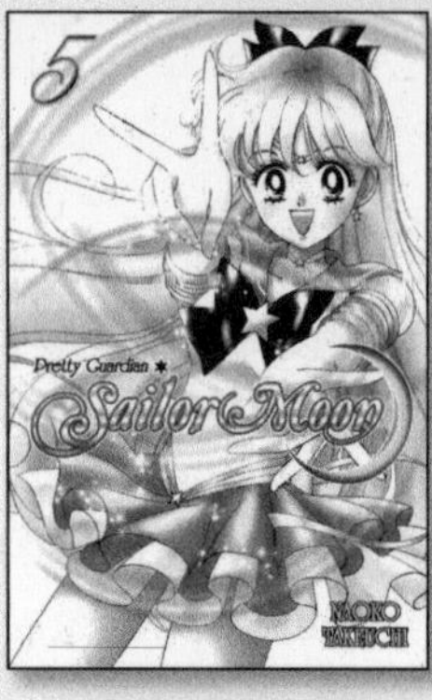
5
Pretty Guardian
Sailor Moon
NAOKO TAKEUCHI

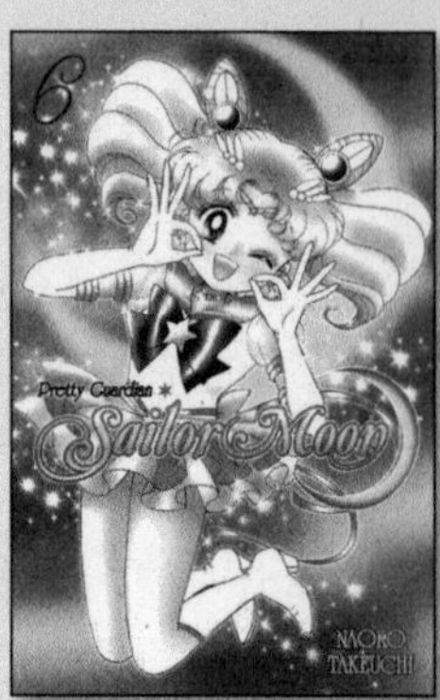
6
Pretty Guardian
Sailor Moon
NAOKO TAKEUCHI

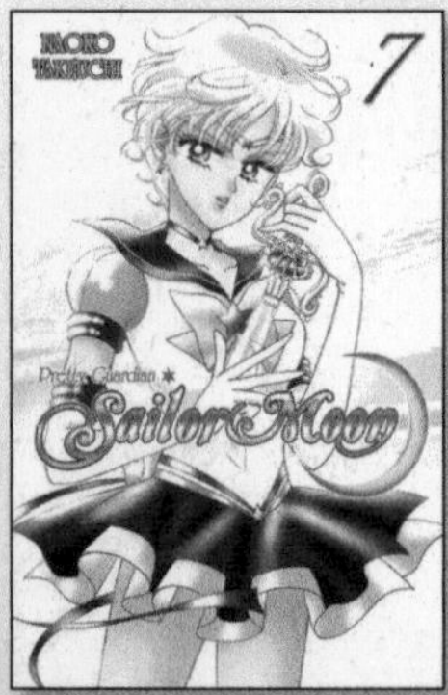
NAOKO TAKEUCHI
7
Pretty Guardian
Sailor Moon

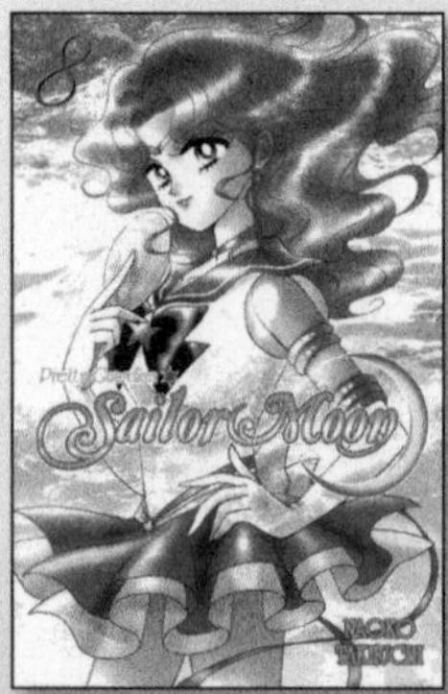
8
Sailor Moon
NAOKO TAKEUCHI

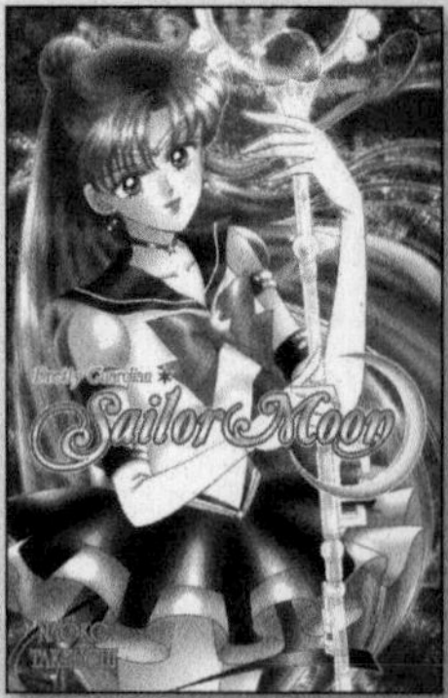
Pretty Guardian
Sailor Moon

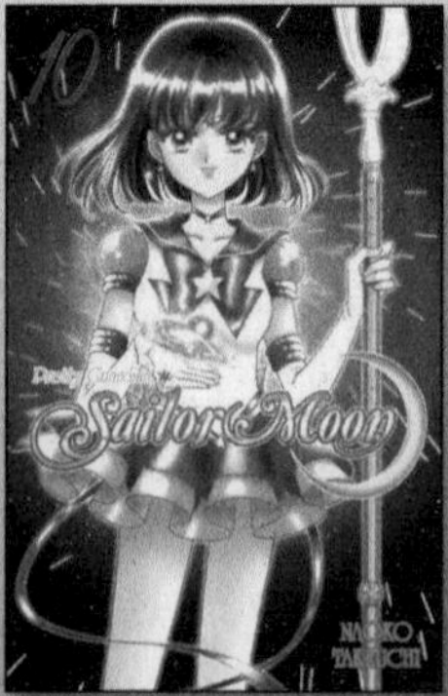
10
Sailor Moon
NAOKO TAKEUCHI

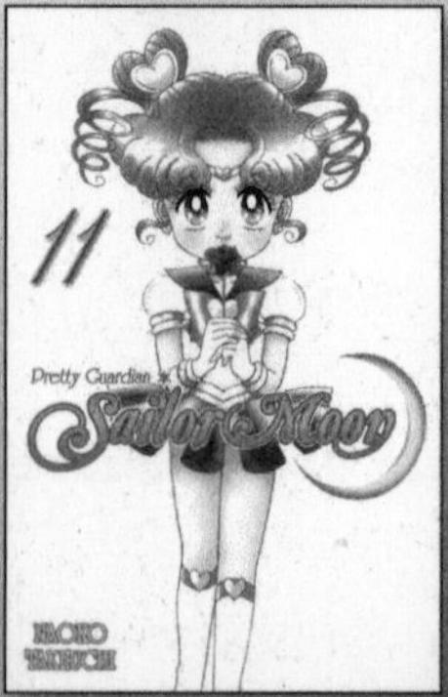
11
Pretty Guardian
Sailor Moon
NAOKO TAKEUCHI

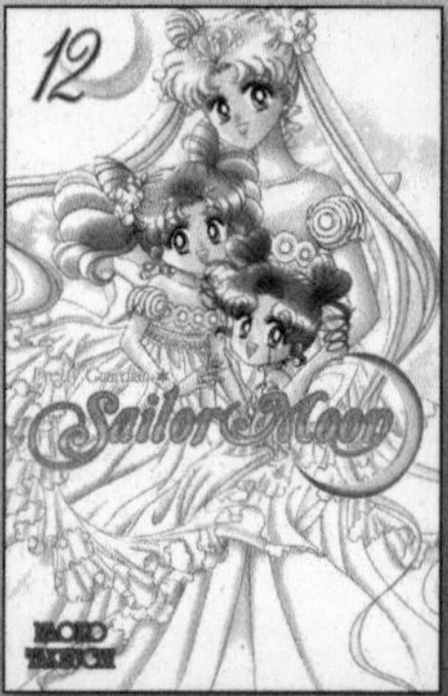
12
Pretty Guardian
Sailor Moon
NAOKO TAKEUCHI

KC
KODANSHA COMICS

THE WALLFLOWER
YAMATONADESHIKO SHICHIHENGE

BY TOMOKO HAYAKAWA

It's a beautiful, expansive mansion, and four handsome, fifteen-year-old friends are allowed to live in it for free! But there is one condition—within three years the young men must take the owner's niece and transform her into a proper lady befitting the palace in which they all live! How hard can it be?

Enter Sunako Nakahara, the horror-movie-loving, pock-faced, frizzy-haired, fashion-illiterate hermit who has a tendency to break into explosive nosebleeds whenever she sees anyone attractive. This project is going to take far more than our four heroes ever expected; it needs a miracle!

Ages: 16 +

Special extras in each volume! Read them all!

SHUGO CHARA!

PEACH-PIT
CREATORS OF *DEARS* AND *ROZEN MAIDEN*

Everybody at Seiyo Elementary thinks that stylish and supercool Amu has it all. But nobody knows the real Amu, a shy girl who wishes she had the courage to truly be herself. Changing Amu's life is going to take more than wishes and dreams—it's going to take a little magic! One morning, Amu finds a surprise in her bed: three strange little eggs. Each egg contains a Guardian Character, an angel-like being who can give her the power to be someone new. With the help of her Guardian Characters, Amu is about to discover that her true self is even more amazing than she ever dreamed.

Special extras in each volume! Read them all!

VISIT WWW.KODANSHACOMICS.COM TO:

- **View release date calendars for upcoming volumes**
- **Find out the latest about new Kodansha Comics series**

Missions of Love volume 2 is a work of fiction. Names, characters, places, and incidents are the products of the author's imagination or are used fictitiously. Any resemblance to actual events, locales, or persons, living or dead, is entirely coincidental.

A Kodansha Comics Trade Paperback Original.

Published in the United States by Kodansha Comics, an imprint of Kodansha USA Publishing, LLC, New York.

Publication rights for this English edition arranged through Kodansha Ltd., Tokyo.

First published in Japan in 2010 by Kodansha Ltd., Tokyo, as *Watashi ni xx shinasai!*, volume 2.

ISBN 978-1-61262-284-2

Printed in the United States of America.

www.kodanshacomics.com

9 8 7 6 5 4 3 2 1

Translator: Alethea Nibley & Athena Nibley
Lettering: Paige Pumphrey

Mission 0: Go Right to Left.

Japanese manga is written and drawn from right to left, which is opposite the way American graphic novels are composed. To preserve the original orientation of the art, and maintain the proper storytelling flow, this book has retained the right to left structure. Please go to what would normally be the last page and begin reading, right to left, top to bottom.

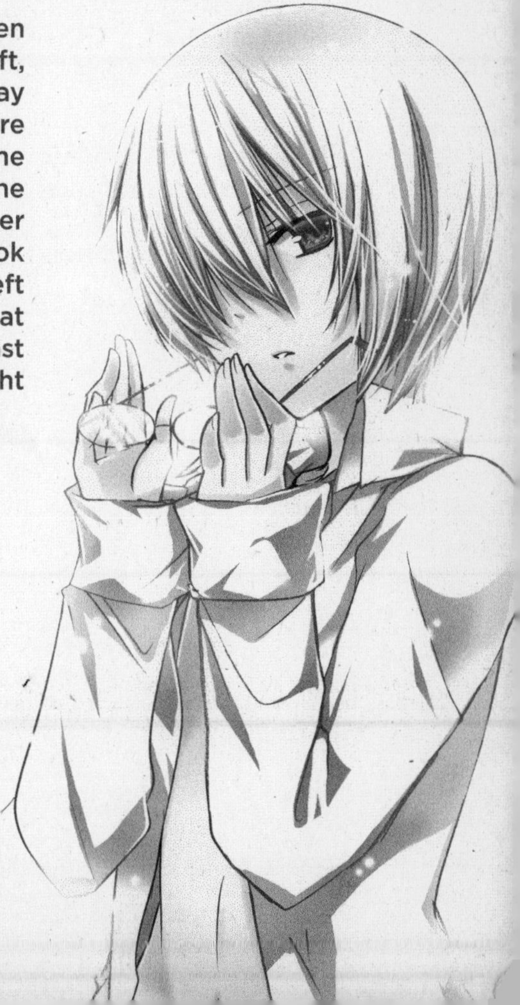